This book seeks to explain why the EU has been able to transform, even strengthen, the states in the Western Balkans. The EU does so through state building, yet it faces local resistance. Contributions by leading experts of the region explain the specifics on the ground and help to explain the difficult path these countries face from the demise of Yugoslavia to possibly joining the European Union. This volume brings to the fore the weakness in the EU external policy approach of reaching out to the political elites in the countries of the Western Balkans without giving a clear signal – a policy that clearly has had at best mixed results in the region. This path-breaking book is a must read for anyone with an interest in the developments in South Eastern Europe.

Amy Verdun is *Professor of Political Science, Jean Monnet Chair Ad Personam,* and the *Director of the Jean Monnet Centre of Excellence,* at the *University of Victoria, Victoria BC, Canada*

The EU and Member State Building

This book critically examines the process of state building by the European Union, focusing on its attempts to build Member States in the Western Balkan region.

This book analyses the EU's policies towards, and the impact they have upon the states of the Western Balkans, and assesses how these affect the nature of EU foreign policy. To this end, it focuses on the tools and mechanisms that the EU employs in its enlargement policy and examines the new instruments of direct intervention (in Bosnia, Herzegovina and Kosovo), political coercion (in the case of Croatia and Serbia in relation to the International Criminal Tribunal for the former Yugoslavia) and stricter conditionality in the Western Balkan countries.

The book discusses the key aim of this special form of state building, which is to establish functional liberal-democratic states in Albania, Bosnia and Herzegovina, Croatia, Kosovo, Macedonia, Montenegro and Serbia in order for them to join the EU and to cope with the responsibilities and pressures of membership in the future. However, the authors argue that while the EU sees itself as an international actor that promotes and protects liberal-democratic values, norms and principles, its experiences in the Western Balkans demonstrate how the EU's actions in the region have undermined the basic principles of democratic decision-making (such as the European support for impositions in Bosnia and Herzegovina) and international law (Kosovo), and have consequently contributed to new tensions (the police reform in Bosnia, and the tensions between Kosovo and Serbia) and dependencies.

This book will be of much interest to students of state building, EU politics, global governance and International Relations/Security Studies in general.

Soeren Keil is Senior Lecturer in International Relations at Canterbury Christ Church University in the UK.

Zeynep Arkan is Lecturer in International Relations at Hacettepe University in Ankara, Turkey.

Routledge Studies in Intervention and Statebuilding
Series Editor: David Chandler

Statebuilding and Intervention
Policies, practices and paradigms
Edited by David Chandler

Reintegration of Armed Groups After Conflict
Politics, violence and transition
Edited by Mats Berdal and David H. Ucko

Security, Development, and the Fragile State
Bridging the gap between theory and policy
David Carment, Stewart Prest, and Yiagadeesen Samy

Kosovo, Intervention and Statebuilding
The international community and the transition to independence
Edited by Aidan Hehir

Critical Perspectives on the Responsibility to Protect
Interrogating theory and practice
Edited by Philip Cunliffe

Statebuilding and Police Reform
The freedom of security
Barry J. Ryan

Violence in Post-Conflict Societies
Remarginalisation, remobilisers and relationships
Anders Themnér

Statebuilding in Afghanistan
Multinational contributions to reconstruction
Edited by Nik Hynek and Péter Marton

The International Community and Statebuilding
Getting its act together?
Edited by Patrice C. McMahon and Jon Western

Statebuilding and State-Formation
The political sociology of intervention
Edited by Berit Bliesemann de Guevara

Political Economy of Statebuilding
Power after peace
Edited by Mats Berdal and Dominik Zaum

New Agendas in Statebuilding
Hybridity, contingency and history
Edited by Robert Egnell and Peter Haldén

Mediation and Liberal Peacebuilding
Peace from the ashes of war?
Edited by Mikael Eriksson and Roland Kostić

Semantics of Statebuilding
Language, meanings and sovereignty
Edited by Nicolas Lemay-Hébert, Nicholas Onuf, Vojin Rakić and Petar Bojanić

Humanitarian Crises, Intervention and Security
A framework for evidence-based programming
Edited by Liesbet Heyse, Andrej Zwitter, Rafael Wittek and Joost Herman

Internal Security and Statebuilding
Aligning agencies and functions
B.K. Greener and W.J. Fish

The EU and Member State Building
European foreign policy in the Western Balkans
Edited by Soeren Keil and Zeynep Arkan

The EU and Member State Building

European foreign policy in the Western Balkans

Edited by Soeren Keil and Zeynep Arkan

LONDON AND NEW YORK

First published 2015
by Routledge
2 Park Square, Milton Park, Abingdon, Oxon OX14 4RN

and by Routledge
711 Third Avenue, New York, NY 10017

Routledge is an imprint of the Taylor & Francis Group, an informa business

© 2015 selection and editorial matter, Soeren Keil and Zeynep Arkan; individual chapters, the contributors

The right of the editors to be identified as the authors of the editorial matter, and of the authors for their individual chapters, has been asserted in accordance with sections 77 and 78 of the Copyright, Designs and Patents Act 1988.

All rights reserved. No part of this book may be reprinted or reproduced or utilized in any form or by any electronic, mechanical, or other means, now known or hereafter invented, including photocopying and recording, or in any information storage or retrieval system, without permission in writing from the publishers.

Trademark notice: Product or corporate names may be trademarks or registered trademarks, and are used only for identification and explanation without intent to infringe.

British Library Cataloguing-in-Publication Data
A catalogue record for this book is available from the British Library

Library of Congress Cataloging-in-Publication Data
The EU and member state building : European foreign policy in the Western Balkans / edited by Soeren Keil and Zeynep Arkan.
  pages cm. – (Routledge studies in intervention and statebuilding)
  Includes bibliographical references and index.
  1. European Union–Balkans. 2. Balkan Peninsula–Foreign economic relations–European Union countries.
  3. European Union countries–Foreign economic relations–Balkan Peninsula. 4. Balkan Peninsula–Politics and government–1989–
  5. Nation-building–Balkan Peninsula. I. Keil, Soeren. II. Arkan, Zeynep.
  HC240.25.B28E83 2014
  341.242'209496–dc23   2014023390

ISBN: 978-0-415-85518-1 (hbk)
ISBN: 978-0-203-72111-7 (ebk)

Typeset in Baskerville
by Wearset Ltd, Boldon, Tyne and Wear

Printed and bound in the United States of America by Publishers Graphics, LLC on sustainably sourced paper.

Contents

List of figures xi
List of tables xii
Notes on contributors xiii
Acknowledgements xvi

PART I
Enlargement and Member State building 1

1 **Introduction: European Union foreign Policy in the Western Balkans** 3
   SOEREN KEIL AND ZEYNEP ARKAN

2 **The limits of normative power?: EU Member State building in the Western Balkans** 15
   SOEREN KEIL AND ZEYNEP ARKAN

3 **Building on experience?: EU enlargement and the Western Balkans** 32
   ERHAN İÇENER AND DAVID PHINNEMORE

PART II
Case studies 55

4 **The normative power of the EU in Croatia: mixed results** 57
   SANJA BADANJAK

5 **The role of the EU in the statehood and democratization of Montenegro** 83
   JELENA DŽANKIĆ

6 The EU in Macedonia: from inter-ethnic to intra-ethnic
   political mediator in an accession deadlock   102
   SIMONIDA KACARSKA

7 Signaling right and turning left: the response to
   EU-conditionality in Serbia   122
   MLADEN MLADENOV AND BERNHARD STAHL

8 The EU's 'limited sovereignty–strong control' approach in
   the process of Member State building in Kosovo   140
   GËZIM KRASNIQI AND MEHMET MUSAJ

9 Not-so-great expectations: the EU and the constitutional
   politics of Bosnia and Herzegovina   163
   VALERY PERRY

PART III
Comparative perspectives   189

10 The European Union and the Western Balkans: time to
   move away from retributive justice?   191
   OLIVERA SIMIĆ

11 The political economy of accession: forming economically
   viable Member States   209
   WILL BARTLETT

PART IV
Conclusion   233

12 Theory and practice of EU Member State building in the
   Western Balkans   235
   SOEREN KEIL AND ZEYNEP ARKAN

   Index   240

Figures

11.1	Annual inflation rates, 2001–2012	214
11.2	Average annual general government budget deficits, 2005–2011	215
11.3	Share of banks assets in foreign ownership, 1998–2011	218
11.4	Increasing share of non-performing loans in total bank loans to the private sector, 2008 and 2012	219
11.5	Exports and imports of goods and services, 2011	223
11.6	Growth of real GDP, 2008–2012	225
11.7	Unemployment and youth unemployment rates, 2012	226

Tables

11.1	Extracts from 2013 progress reports	213
11.2	Extent of price liberalization in the Western Balkans, 2012	216
11.3	Ease of starting a business, 2013	217
11.4	Governance indicators, percentile rank, 2012	221
11.5	Aid dependency: international assistance flows and FDI, 2010–2012	227

Contributors

Zeynep Arkan, PhD, is Lecturer in International Relations at Hacettepe University in Ankara, Turkey. Her main fields of interest include EU foreign policy, International Relations Theory, identity questions, particularly in foreign policy analysis, and discourse analysis.

Sanja Badanjak is a PhD candidate in political science at the University of Wisconsin-Madison, graduating in 2015. She is working on a dissertation project on the effect of the EU on party systems in European democracies. She holds a Master's degree in political science from the Central European University in Budapest, and has previously worked for the Croatian civil service.

Will Bartlett is Senior Research Fellow in the Political Economy of South East Europe at the London School of Economics and Political Science. He has a BA in Economics from the University of Cambridge, an MSc in Development Economics from the University of London and a PhD from the University of Liverpool. He has published two monographs, *Croatia Between Europe and the Balkans*, Routledge, 2006 and *Europe's Troubled Region: Economic Development, Institutional Reform and Social Welfare in the Western Balkans*, Routledge 2008, as well as numerous articles in refereed journals and book chapters.

Jelena Džankić, PhD, is a Marie Curie Fellow at the European University Institute in Florence, Italy. Her research focuses on the interplay between citizenship, state and nation building processes and Europeanization in the post-Yugoslav states. Her other research interest includes the politics of Montenegro, and her book *Citizenship in Bosnia Herzegovina, Macedonia and Montenegro: Effects of Statehood and Identity Challenges* is forthcoming with Ashgate in June 2015.

Erhan İçener is Assistant Professor in the Department of Political Science and International Relations at Bursa Orhangazi University. He holds a BSc from Middle East Technical University and MSc and PhD degrees from Queen's University Belfast. His research and publications focus on EU enlargement, EU external relations and Romania and Turkey's integration with the EU.

Simonida Kacarska, PhD, is a research coordinator and president of the European Policy Institute in Skopje, Macedonia. Her research interests include the political transformation and European integration of the Balkans, with a focus on national minority policies. In addition to civil service and civil society experience, she was also a research fellow at the Central European University in Budapest, as well as the University of Oxford and the University of Edinburgh in the UK. Her most recent publications include chapters dealing with national minority policies in Macedonia and Croatia in edited volumes published by Ashgate and Routledge in June 2013.

Soeren Keil, PhD, is Senior Lecturer in International Relations at Canterbury Christ Church University in the United Kingdom. His research focuses on the political systems of the post-Yugoslav states, as well as territorial autonomy as a mode of conflict-resolution and the foreign policy of new states (particularly in the Balkans). His book *Multinational Federalism in Bosnia and Herzegovina* was published by Ashgate in December 2013.

Gëzim Krasniqi is a PhD candidate in Sociology and Research Assistant on the CITSEE project at the University of Edinburgh. His main research interests are politics, nationalism, nationalist movements and citizenship. He has published several articles on the politics of the Balkan region in general and Kosovo in particular.

Mladen Mladenov is a PhD candidate and lecturer in International Relations at the University of Passau in Germany. His research interests lie in the field of Serbian foreign policy as well as in an experimental approach to Europeanization research in Serbia.

Mehmet Musaj is an MA candidate of European Studies at the University of Zagreb (Croatia), Faculty of Political Science, where his research focuses on the Europeanization of Kosovo's political parties. Previously, he obtained an MA at the University of Sarajevo and University of Bologna on Democracy and Human Rights. His main area of study interests includes: political transition in post-Yugoslavia, democracy and democratization, Europeanization of Western Balkans and political ideologies.

Valery Perry has lived in Bosnia and Herzegovina since 1999, conducting research and working for organizations including the NATO Stabilization Force (SFOR), the European Center for Minority Issues (ECMI) and several NGOs. She worked at the OSCE Mission to Bosnia and Herzegovina in Sarajevo from 2004 to 2011, as Deputy Director of the Education Department, and Deputy Director of the Human Dimension Department. From 2011 to 2014 she worked as Chief of Party for the Public International Law and Policy Group (PILPG) in Sarajevo, implementing a project to increase civil society engagement in constitutional reform processes in Bosnia and Herzegovina. Valery received a PhD from George Mason University's Institute for Conflict Analysis and Resolution, has published numerous articles and book chapters, and has spoken at conferences and policy events in the United States and throughout Europe.

David Phinnemore, PhD, is Professor of European Politics at Queen's University Belfast in Northern Ireland. His main research interests include EU enlargement and EU treaty reform. He has written widely on Romania's accession to the EU as well as enlargements in comparative perspective.

Olivera Simić, PhD, is a Lecturer with the Griffith Law School, Griffith University, Australia. Her research engages with transitional justice, international peacekeeping and international human rights. Olivera has published in journals such as *International Journal of Transitional Justice, Law Text Culture, Womens' Studies International Forum* and *International Peacekeeping*, as well as in books and book chapters. Her latest collection, *The Arts of Transitional Justice: Culture, Activism, and Memory after Atrocity* (with Peter D. Rush), was published by Springer in 2014. Her forthcoming monograph, *Surviving Peace: A Political Memoir*, will be published by Spinifex in late 2014.

Bernhard Stahl is Professor of International Politics at the University of Passau, Germany. His research areas cover European foreign policy (German, French and EU foreign policy in particular) preferably vis-à-vis South East Europe, identity theory and comparative regionalism. From 2004 to 2008 he worked as Professor of European Integration on behalf of the German Ministry of Economic Co-operation in Serbia. His recent publications deal with domestic legitimation of military interventions (e.g. Germany and Libya) and identity-related problems in the accession process (e.g. the EU and Serbia).

Acknowledgements

Many people deserve recognition and thanks for their support throughout this book project, almost too many to mention. There are some, however, that we would like to highlight.

First of all, we would like to thank Andrew Humphrys, Annabelle Harris and Hannah Ferguson at Routledge for their support and help since the early days of the volume. We also would like to express our gratitude to David Chandler for his enthusiasm and encouragement for this project.

We are grateful to Charlie Povah, who brought a fresh set of eyes to the project, and completed the final spell-check and editorial proofs.

We also wish to thank our friends and colleagues for their support and critical insights, in particular David Bates, Florian Bieber, Müge Kınacıoğlu, Sarah Lieberman, Valery Perry, Altuğ Tuncel and Jens Woelk. Finally, we would like to thank our families, Claire and Malindi Parker, Alev and Sabih Arkan, Şermin Güral and Aysel Özbek for their love and support. Without the constant encouragement and academic motivation of our parents, this book project would not have been possible. We are, therefore, grateful to Peter and Regina Keil, and Alev and Sabih Arkan. This book is dedicated to them.

Soeren Keil
Zeynep Arkan
Canterbury and Ankara
2014

Part I
Enlargement and Member State building

1 Introduction

The European Union and Member State building – European Union foreign policy in the Western Balkans

Soeren Keil and Zeynep Arkan

The changing nature of the European Union's external relations

The European Union (EU) is a historically novel type of polity. As the outcome of the disastrous experiences of great wars in Europe, the EU not only offers a unique way of organizing relations between the states of Europe, but also represents their distinctive collective voice and influence in the world. The distinct contribution of the EU in international relations, which has its foundations in the narrative of a shared European history and responsibilities, is most apparent in the Union's relations with its neighbors and the wider world, and symbolized by the international identity of the EU as a global actor. This has been conceptualized in a number of ways over the years: various accounts of the nature/identity of the EU as a civilian (Duchêne 1972), normative (Manners 2002), ethical (Aggestam 2008), Kantian power – by choice or by necessity (Kagan 2003; Nikolaïdis 2004), or as a quiet superpower (Moravcsik 2002) focused on the role played by the EU in the international arena and its impact on world politics. In this respect, the term EU identity, which was often used interchangeably with European identity with its historic and cultural heritage, came to be assessed on the basis of the Union's foreign policy performance: 'the EU's role as an international actor and its international identity are considered a function of the significance of the EU and its Member States in international affairs and of the effectiveness of its policy practice' (Sedelmeier 2004: 125). The formulation and implementation of a coherent and effective foreign policy by the EU was thus seen as the chief means through which its international role and identity could be strengthened.

Over the years, a number of studies have analysed to what extent the EU succeeded in acting as an autonomous and effective actor in international politics, particularly in comparison to other key global powers such as the United States.[1] It was often argued that while the EU had the potential to become a major actor on the world stage, a number of factors hindered the achievement of its full potential, such as the lack of a strong military capacity, the limited nature of its common foreign and security policy (CFSP), and the difficulties associated with speaking and acting in unison in response to international developments and crises. Yet, it has to be kept in mind that the traditional and state-based understanding of foreign policy covers but a small part of the Union's relations with the wider world. There are a number of areas in the policy portfolio of the EU that have external impact and can be categorized under the broader framework of Union's external relations, which include policy areas such as trade, neighbourhood, enlargement and humanitarian aid.

In this broad category of external relations, it is often argued that the EU's enlargement policy has proven to be its most unique and successful policy tool. The notion that, through a process of reform and change regulated and guided by the Union, states could transform themselves into EU members and reap the benefits of membership in the European family puts the Union in a very strong position vis-à-vis potential candidates. In instances where the promise of membership is imminent, the EU exercises considerable influence over the candidate states in the difficult period of 'apprenticeship' during which 'they strive to approximate their institutions, policies and values to those of the Union' with the financial help and guidance of the EU (Bretherton and Vogler 2006: 137). The promise of EU membership has thus served as a strong driving force for domestic reform and change in many countries.

Yet, it is not only the prospective Member States that go through a process of transformation on the path to becoming part of the EU. It is also the EU's composition and nature that change along the way, as well as its policy areas. Through enlargement, the EU not only extends its zone of peace, prosperity and stability to other parts of Europe, it also becomes a stronger, more competitive and diversified actor in its region and the wider world economically and politically. Another clear example of this transformation with respect to policy change concerns the rules and standards that candidate states should adhere to as part of the enlargement process, particularly in the run up to the so-called 'big-bang enlargement' in 2004. As a policy area that initially started with the sole criterion of potential members being 'European states', Article 237 of the Treaty of Rome, the enlargement policy of the EU evolved into its current form as a response to the features of the countries that joined the Union in seven enlargement rounds, as Erhan İçener and David Phinnemore demonstrate in Chapter 3 of this volume. These enlargement rounds resulted in states with different histories, and political and economic features joining the European family. These new members of the family had distinct lineages and qualities; some were similar to the existing Member States politically and economically while a number of them had a separate history of being on the other side of the Iron Curtain and were qualitatively different compared to the existing members in terms of their political and economic standards. As a response, the EU had to develop new means and criteria through which to assess their progress and transform these countries on the path to membership. The 2004, 2007 and 2013 enlargements, which brought 11 Central and Eastern European (CEE) states into the EU,[2] were seen as quite a success both for the EU and its Member States, as well as the countries that joined the Union. In addition to the political will of both the new and the existing Member States to widen the European family, this peaceful transformation process demonstrated the success of the EU's enlargement policy and accession regime in the form of the Copenhagen Criteria, at least in the years prior to the financial crisis.

The EU's Western Balkan enlargement[3]

The 2000s were the decade that witnessed the outcomes of the EU's 'transformative power' over the post-communist countries of CEE (Grabbe 2006). While this power was not equally successful in cases such as Bulgaria and Romania, on the whole, the EU's eastern enlargement was considered to be a success in terms of creating a peaceful and harmonious union in Europe based on shared values, norms and principles. Numerous references, both on the part of the existing and potential Member States, to the theme of 'returning to Europe', coupled with the clear promise of eventual membership, implied that the policy had a teleological nature and that the candidate countries would eventually join the Union. Yet, as the financial crisis, which has been at the heart of discussions in Europe since 2009, demonstrated, economic diversity and weak economic and social structures in a number of EU Member States pointed towards the need for stricter conditions for future members, and more EU control over economic planning and government spending. Hence, it is important to keep in mind that, while the EU discourse still has a normative aspect, as a result of the recent developments, economic interests also occupy a key place in the process of European integration, and with it EU enlargement. The economic interests of the EU are currently being redefined in the wake of the financial crises in numerous Member States, and these discussions also affect the future enlargement of the Union, as Will Bartlett argues in Chapter 11 on the economic transformation of the Western Balkans.

The Western Balkan countries, on the other hand, lack a clear timeline and perspective. In fact, in the aftermath of the violent break-up of the Yugoslav Federation, the EU was caught off-guard in its foreign policy and failed to put an end to the bloodshed. It was only later that it 'stepped up its engagement in the region in the 2000s, extending the prospect of EU membership in the hope of replicating the success in Central and Eastern Europe' (Noutcheva 2012: 1). In its policy towards the Western Balkans, the EU adapted the model it originally developed for its Eastern enlargement and at the same time created a series of 'networks of bilateral and multilateral relations through a process of Stabilization and Association'

(Bretherton and Vogler 2006: 144). The Stabilisation and Association Process (SAP) was further strengthened at the Thessaloniki European Council of June 2003, which concluded that all Western Balkan countries were considered potential future members of the EU. Since then, they have been moving on the path to membership with varying levels of success: while the candidacies of the Former Yugoslav Republic of Macedonia, Serbia and Montenegro have been recognized, Albania, Bosnia and Herzegovina and Kosovo are still considered to be potential candidates. Croatia joined the Union in July 2013.

From the perspective of EU enlargement, the predominantly weaker nature of the states in the region, coupled with their conflictual pasts, implied that the relationship between the EU and the potential candidate countries was to be qualitatively different. The EU now needed to behave in a considerably different manner as the host compared to its previous enlargement rounds in preparing and assessing the Western Balkan states on the path to eventual accession. Moreover, the prior involvement of the Union in the region and its special representatives and agencies on the ground put the EU in an asymmetrically strong position regarding the local political elite. With the carrot of eventual membership, the EU often dictated its own standards, norms and rules in the region, sometimes with ambiguous success. It was claimed that, as a response to 'alleged crises' in the region, the EU intervened directly in the domestic politics of the Western Balkan states and 'on the grounds that "European values", "European identity", or "European security" are at stake' (Chandler 2008: 69). Chandler (2006) argues that the West, including the EU, has focused on institutional design and state building in non-Western societies without a deeper consideration of local practices and long-term legitimacy. The contributions in this book extend this argument. Not only is the EU an empire in denial, it is indeed a state-builder in denial. As Soeren Keil and Zeynep Arkan outline in the Chapter 2 of this volume, EU Member State building has become the most important element of the enlargement process in the Western Balkans. The EU is no longer just involved in processes of adjusting the Western Balkan states' economies, legislation and policy areas according to European standards. Instead, the EU has become an active state-builder, promoting specific institutional arrangements and adjusting political systems in Southeastern Europe.

In order to explore the centrality of Member State building in the enlargement process, the framework used in this volume treats enlargement policy as a foreign policy practice. Accordingly, in the next two parts the contributors to the volume analyse how the EU continuously promoted solutions to political questions that go well beyond the framework of the *acquis communautaire*, the EU's legal body. From police reform in Bosnia to the installation of the Union between Serbia and Montenegro, the EU has clearly been involved in state-building practices, albeit with mixed results (Bieber 2011). EU Member State building is thus seen as the extension of the EU's foreign policy to the enlargement process. It includes the traditional focus on the implementation of the *acquis*, but at the same time goes well beyond this. It is a reaction to existing and perceived state weaknesses in the Western Balkans, and an attempt by the EU to build states that fit the standardized model of a 'European state'. Yet, as most authors point out in this book, there is no such thing as a standard 'European state'. Among the EU Member States, we find unitary, federal and decentralized states, states with numerous political parties or with two or three dominant ones. We also find states with unicameral or bicameral legislatures, monarchies and republics, states where human rights are protected by strong courts and others where different institutions, including Human Rights Commissions, play a key role. In some countries, minorities are well integrated and part of governing coalitions, in others there remains a conflictual relation between the majority and the minority. The same is true for the economic models of Member States. Some, such as Germany and the Benelux countries, have strong social welfare systems, while others have weaker provisions. In the United Kingdom, the economy is dominated by the banking sector, while Germany still has a strong industrial base. Unemployment differs from well below 10 per cent in most of Western Europe to over 20–30 per cent in Eastern and Southern Europe.[4] Hence, many of the reforms and initiatives that the EU has promoted in the Western Balkans are not based on a standardized model, but on what the EU considers to be 'normal', i.e. what *should* be the standard. This normative focus links the EU's state-building activities in Southeastern Europe to its overall foreign policy, which is also driven by the assumption that there are standard models for such contested ideas as the rule of law, free market, human rights and democracy (Manners 2002).

As a response, political elites in the Western Balkan states resist the EU's push for standardized models in contested policy areas, not only because it would threaten their privileges within their own states, but also because they know that the EU's insistence on reforms is based on a norm-driven rather than practical consideration. This does not mean that all suggestions coming from the EU as part of its state-building agenda are necessarily bad or will have negative consequences. Indeed, a police reform along the lines suggested by the EU would probably have increased the efficiency and the independence of policing in Bosnia. Similarly, the EU's insistence on a dialogue between Serbia and Kosovo has resulted in a calming of the situation between the two neighbors, and the EU has been successful as an arbitrator between Macedonians and Albanians, as Simonida Kacarska demonstrates in Chapter 6. However, the elites in these countries often have their own agendas, which usually are centred on them staying in power. As Jelena Džankić demonstrates vividly in Chapter 5, in the case of Montenegro, reforms were only implemented when they did not threaten the dominance of the Democratic Party of Socialists (DPS) and Milo Đukanović. A similar argument is made by Valery Perry, who demonstrates that Bosnian elites have been particularly successful in resisting EU-induced reform efforts that focused on strengthening the state and undermining the power of nationalist party elites. The puzzle at the heart of this volume is therefore the question to what extent EU Member State building has been able to transform and strengthen the states in the Western Balkans, and why it continues to face so much local resistance. As is argued below, the majority of countries in Southeastern Europe are indeed fragile and state building is required for these societies to ensure that they can implement the *acquis communautaire* and become competitive and 'good' Member States. Yet the EU's attempts to address this issue have had mixed results, often they have failed or resulted in 'faked compliance' (Noutcheva 2012). It seems, however, that the EU lacks a Plan B. This would explain why Macedonia has been stuck in its integration process since 2005 and why there has been no progress in Bosnia since 2005/6. Having said this, there are still pockets of success in the EU's approach, such as the Serbia–Kosovo dialogue already mentioned, that is difficult for the elites from both countries, as Mladen Mladenov and Bernhard Stahl in the case of Serbia, and Gëzim Krasniqi and Mehmet Musaj in the case of Kosovo demonstrate in Chapters 7 and 8 respectively. The success of this approach lies in the unique connection between direct rewards for political reform (in this case, agreement on the dialogue) and the threat of serious sanctions in the case of non-compliance. Then why this incentive structure has not worked in other cases is a key question that many authors in this volume address. They all conclude that the EU's incentives were not clearly defined, and that the reforms demanded as part of Member State building threatened the dominant position of certain elites and thereby affected their willingness to fully comply. Finally, the authors in this volume conclude that the EU's enlargement process remains focused on political elites. There are very few attempts to involve citizens, non-governmental organizations (NGOs) and other societal actors in the enlargement process, which gives political elites a unique chance to dominate the process and hijack it for their own interests. Until the incentive structure is revised, and the EU realizes that political elites profiting from the current *status quo* might not be the main drivers of change in the fragile states of the Western Balkans, it is unlikely that the EU's current approach will be successful.

State fragility and state building in the Western Balkans

The majority of the states in the Western Balkans are 'young' states that became independent as a result of the break-up of the former Yugoslav federation.[5] While states such as Croatia and Serbia had been independent before (in the nineteenth and early twentieth century), others, such as Bosnia and Herzegovina and Macedonia had their statehood recognized for the first time in the early 1990s. Even where traditions of statehood and independence existed, these were often based on authoritarian rule and could not be seen as guiding examples once Yugoslavia dissolved.[6] Additionally, it is important to point out that state building overlapped with violent conflict in a number of countries in the Western Balkans (Croatia, Bosnia, Serbia/Kosovo, Slovenia and Albania). While this violence was more widespread in some countries (Croatia, Bosnia, Kosovo) than in others (Slovenia, Montenegro, Serbia proper), it nevertheless resulted in deeply divided societies, high levels of destruction and fatalities. These experiences matter and continue to influence the political discourse. In addition, they had a negative effect on state building and democratization in the region. Indeed, the conflict in Bosnia was the result of the contestation of the independent Bosnian state by Serbs and later Croats (Burg and Shoup 1999). The violent conflict in Kosovo and NATO's subsequent intervention were the result of a failed state and nation-building project in Serbia under the leadership of Slobodan Milošević (Daskalovski 2001). Similar reasons can be used to explain the violent conflict between Serb Nationalists and the Croat government in Croatia between 1991 and 1995 (Tanner 2010), and between Macedonian security forces and Albanian separatists in Macedonia in 2001 (Daftay 2001). Indeed, as Robert Hayden (1992) has argued, all post-Yugoslav states introduced constitutional frameworks which discriminated against minority nations and established homogenous institutions in very diverse societies. These constitutional provisions laid the foundations of alienation and conflict, which resulted in secessionist movements in Croatia, Bosnia and later in Serbia (Kosovo) and Macedonia. Thus, it can be concluded that most states in the Western Balkans are 'young' states that (re)-established their independent statehood only in the early 1990s (in the case of Kosovo only in 2008), and were created in the wake of violent inter-ethnic conflicts. These states are weak states, because they lack a tradition of strong institutionalism (at least within a democratic framework) and were (and remain) internally and externally contested.

While some states in the area established functional institutions, an efficient administration and democratic principles of governance relatively quickly (most notably Slovenia), others remained dysfunctional states (Bosnia, Albania) or had semi-authoritarian regimes (Serbia, Croatia).[7] It was only in 2000 that a 'wave' of democratization changed the political regimes in Croatia and Serbia, and led to short-term changes in Bosnia as well. The Ohrid Framework Agreement for Macedonia in 2001 also increased democratic participation in the country, and Kosovo's first constitutional framework in the same year provided for some limited form of self-governance. Yet, while Croatia has undergone some remarkable changes since 2000 and became an EU Member State in July 2013, other countries remain persistently weak.[8] Bosnia and Herzegovina has been stagnating since 2006 and there has been no major reform effort in terms of constitutional reform or economic progress. The country remains internally challenged by the Bosnian Serbs (ICG 2011a) and externally contested by nationalists in Serbia. Macedonia has been an EU candidate country since 2005 but is still waiting for a date to start accession negotiations. Its internal security situation has recently deteriorated with the rise of nationalist tendencies and new tensions between Macedonian security forces and Albanians (Marusic 2012). In Kosovo, democratic progress has stalled and relations with Serbia remain problematic. Furthermore, the situation in Northern Kosovo remains volatile for future conflicts between Serbia and Kosovo, but also for wider regional conflicts (ICG 2011b; Keil and Stahl 2013). The conflict over Kosovo's unilateral declaration of independence has also influenced developments in Serbia, where former nationalists have taken control of the government and fundamental reforms towards independence of the judiciary and towards transparency have been lacking.

Overall, Freedom House rates no country (including Croatia) as a fully consolidated democracy. While Croatia, Serbia, Macedonia and Montenegro are classified as semi-consolidated democracies, Bosnia and Albania are classified as transitional or hybrid regimes. The worst classification is given to Kosovo, which is classified as a semi-consolidated authoritarian regime.[9] The main problems for democratic consolidation in the region can be identified as (1) weak state structures, (2) internal and external contestation of the state, (3) lack of a democratic political culture, (4) weak economic structures and (5) lack of external incentives for democratization and state-consolidation. These five reasons would have to be addressed by the EU if it wants to prepare these countries for membership. This is why an analysis of the EU's enlargement policy and the frameworks to address these issues will be useful, before inferring these problems to EU enlargement practices and the process of EU Member State building.

Organization of the book

This edited volume examines the impact of the EU's enlargement policy on the fragile states of the Western Balkans. The main argument of the book is that the EU is involved in complex state-building processes as part of its enlargement policy which, however, led to the emergence of new problems in the region, such as cultures of dependencies and a lack of democratic progress in the Western Balkans. Focusing on the foreign policy dimension of this change, it is argued here that, in relation to the predominant characterization of the EU as a 'normative power' that builds on the norms, principles and values that form the foundations of the EU, the case of the Western Balkans serves as a litmus test. Through its state-building activities and tools employed in the Western Balkans (such as direct intervention in Bosnia and Kosovo, political coercion in the case of Croatia and Serbia, and stricter conditionality in all Western Balkan countries), the EU is transforming itself into an international actor with peculiar qualities that contradict its so-called normative nature. By stressing the need to look at what the EU actually *does* and *says* instead of *what it is* in the analysis of its international role, nature and identity, this volume aims to highlight the limits of the EU as a normative power by analysing its activities and involvement in the Western Balkans from the perspective of Member State building.

The first part of this book looks at some conceptual considerations, in particular on the changing nature of EU enlargement. Soeren Keil and Zeynep Arkan in Chapter 2 discuss to what extent EU enlargement policy towards the Western Balkans has diverged from previous enlargements and focus particularly on the concept of EU Member State building. This is followed by a discussion of the EU's enlargement policy context and a comparison between the frameworks used in the 2004/7 enlargement and in that of the Western Balkans by Erhan İçener and David Phinnemore. Their Chapter 3 demonstrates how the discourse on enlargement and the instruments used have changed. Yet they also highlight that the current framework has demonstrated some success stories in the Western Balkans.

Part II of this volume discusses a number of case studies. First, Sanja Badanjak in Chapter 4 demonstrates how the EU has had some mixed results in its approach to reform and preparing Croatia for membership. While reforms have been successful in areas such as minority rights and the rule of law, other areas, such as LGBT rights and the reintegration of war refugees, have been less successful. In the second case study in Chapter 5, Jelena Džankić assesses the role of the EU in state building in Montenegro. Since the country declared its independence in 2006, it has become a frontrunner in terms of EU integration. This can partially be explained by the strong focus on EU membership as a key driver for the country's independence from the Union with Serbia, and by the willingness of the Montenegrin elites to implement certain reforms. It is argued, however, that there remains a clear lack of deep-rooted reforms in the areas of rule of law, the fight against corruption and freedom of the media. The third and fourth chapters in this part look at the cases of Serbia and Kosovo. For Serbia, Mladen Mladenov and Bernhard Stahl make the point that while rhetorically all governing parties in Serbia have been pro-European since 2000, there are a number of instances that demonstrate the resistance of the ruling elite against state-building and democratization attempts from the EU. While there has been some positive change in recent times, particularly in relation to Kosovo, it remains yet to be seen to what extent the Serbian government is committed to EU integration and long-term sustainable reform. In Chapter 8 Gëzim Krasniqi and Mehmet Musaj argue that the EU has played a rather ambiguous role in Kosovo. Five Member States have still not recognized Kosovo's independence, yet the EU established its largest mission in the country, which focuses on the rule of law. The results, as so often, are mixed, with successes in some areas, but problems and new challenges in others. Valery Perry concludes this part with an assessment of the EU's impact on Bosnia and Herzegovina, focusing particularly on the debates on constitutional reform. She comes to the conclusion that, while the EU has pressed for reforms which would strengthen the state and undermine the dominance and monopoly of ethnically exclusive parties, these have been faced with strong local resistance. Due to the fact that the EU has no Plan B, there has been little progress in Bosnia and Herzegovina in recent years.

Part III looks at two policy areas in comparative perspective. First, in Chapter 10 Olivera Simić discusses the role of the EU in transitional justice. She points out that the EU has been a strong promoter of transitional justice, and cooperation with the International Tribunal for the former Yugoslavia (ICTY) became part of the EU's standard conditionality. However, this has had mixed results and other forms of transitional justice, from truth commissions to local NGO initiatives, have found less reflection and support in Brussels. In the final chapter of this part, Will Bartlett analyses the role of economic transition and the EU's focus on building economically viable Member States in the Western Balkans. He concludes that the EU's focus on free market reforms has prevented it from recognizing that the main obstacles to economic development in the region are not economic, but political. This, so he argues, has only recently been added to the EU's agenda. In his view, the need to create effective political institutions, which can control and oversee the functioning of a market economy, remains a key challenge for most Western Balkan states.

Finally, in the conclusion Soeren Keil and Zeynep Arkan reassess the concept and practices of EU Member State building in light of the contributions in this volume. They conclude that EU membership remains a key driver for change in the region; however, the EU needs to think carefully about which reforms to promote, which actors to engage with and how to deal with obstructive elites and spoilers in the process.

We hope that the contributions in this volume will stimulate the academic discussion on EU enlargement and demonstrate the need for a new approach. The authors, who are all experts in their respective fields, clearly demonstrate some of the pitfalls of the current approach. It is time for scholars and practitioners alike to rethink enlargement. This might also be a good way to revive the enlargement process towards the states in the Western Balkans.

Notes

1 For example, see Hill 1993, 1998; Toje 2008.
2 In addition, Malta and Cyprus joined in 2004.
3 This refers to Croatia, Bosnia and Herzegovina, Serbia, Kosovo, Montenegro, Macedonia and Albania.

4 For a comprehensive discussion on political and economic differences among European Member States, see Gallagher *et al.* 2011.
5 The exception to this is Albania.
6 This does not mean that they were not used as methods of legitimation. Franjo Tuđman, for example, referred extensively to the Independent State of Croatia, a fascist puppet state in the 1940s, to underline Croatia's long tradition of statehood and its right to independence and sovereignty.
7 For the connection of war, state building and authoritarian regimes, see Zakošek 2008.
8 On the concept of persistent state weakness, see Woodward 2009.
9 These data are from 2012 and are available at www.freedomhouse.org/report-types/nations-transit.

References

Aggestam, L. (2008) 'Introduction: Ethical Power Europe?', *International Affairs*, 84(1), pp. 1–11.
Bieber, F. (2011) 'Building Impossible States? State-Building Strategies and EU Membership in the Western Balkans', *Europe-Asia Studies*, 63(10), pp. 1783–1802.
Burg, S. and Shoup, P. (1999) *The War in Bosnia-Herzegovina: Ethnic Conflict and International Intervention*, London: M.E. Sharpe.
Bretherton, C. and Vogler, J. (2006) *The European Union as a Global Actor*, Abingdon: Routledge.
Chandler, D. (2006) *Empire in Denial: The Politics of Statebuilding*, London: Pluto Press.
Chandler, D. (2008) 'The EU's Promotion of Democracy in the Balkans', in Laïdi, Z. (ed.) *EU Foreign Policy in a Globalized World: Normative Power and Social Preferences*, Abingdon: Routledge, pp. 68–82.
Daftay, F. (2001) 'Conflict Resolution in FYR Macedonia: Power-Sharing or the "Civic Approach"', *Helsinki Monitor*, 12(4), pp. 291–312.
Daskalovski, Z. (2001) 'Claims to Kosovo: Nationalism and Self-Determination', in Bieber, F. and Daskalovski, Z. (eds) *Understanding the War in Kosovo*, London and Portland: Frank Cass, pp. 13–30.
Duchêne, F. (1972) 'Europe's Role in World Peace', in Mayne, R. (ed.) *Europe Tomorrow: Sixteen Europeans Look Ahead*, London: Fontana, pp. 32–47.
Edwards, G. (2011) 'The Pattern of the EU's Global Activity', in Hill, C. and Smith, S. (eds) *International Relations and the European Union*, Oxford: Oxford University Press.
European Council (2003) *EU-Western Balkans Summit-Declaration*, Document 10229/03 (Presse 163), Thessaloniki, 21 June. Available at: http://ec.europa.eu/enlargement/enlargement_process/accession_process/how_does_a_country_join_the_eu/sap/thessaloniki_summit_en.htm.
Gallagher, M., Laver, M. and Mair, P. (2011) *Representative Government in Modern Europe*, 5th edn, Maidenhead: McGraw Hill.
Grabbe, H. (2006) *The EU's Transformative Power: Europeanization through Conditionality in Central and Eastern Europe*, New York: Palgrave Macmillan.
Hayden, R. (1992) 'Constitutional Nationalism in the Formerly Yugoslav Republics', *Slavic Review*, 51(4), pp. 654–673.
Hill, C. (1993) 'The Capability–Expectations Gap, or Conceptualizing Europe's International Role', *JCMS: Journal of Common Market Studies*, 31(3), pp. 305–328.

Hill, C. (1998) 'Closing the Capability-Expectations Gap?', in Peterson, J. and Sjursen, H. (eds) *A Common Foreign Policy For Europe? Competing Visions of the CFSP*, Abingdon: Routledge, pp. 18–38.

ICG (International Crisis Group) (2011a) *Bosnia: What does Republika Srpska Want?*, Europe Report No. 214, 6 October. Available at: www.crisisgroup.org/en/regions/europe/balkans/bosnia-herzegovina/214-bosnia-what-does-republika-srpska-want.aspx.

ICG (International Crisis Group) (2011b) *North Kosovo: Dual Sovereignty in Practice*, Europe Report No. 211, 14 March. Available at: www.crisisgroup.org/en/regions/europe/balkans/kosovo/211-north-kosovo-dual-sovereignty-in-practice.aspx.

Kagan, R. (2003) *Of Paradise and Power*, New York: Knopf.

Keil, S. and Stahl, B. (2013) 'A Security Community in the Balkans? The Foreign Policies of the Post-Yugoslav States', *Südosteuropa Mitteilungen*, 53, forthcoming May.

Manners, I. (2002) 'Normative Power Europe: A Contradiction in Terms?', *JCMS: Journal of Common Market Studies*, 40(2), pp. 235–258.

Marusic, S. J. (2012) 'Ethnic Violence Simmers in Macedonia', *Balkaninsight.com*, 11 March. Available at: www.balkaninsight.com/en/article/spree-of-ethnic-violence-continues-in-macedonia.

Moravcsik, A. (2002) 'The Quiet Supowerpower', *Newsweek*, 17 June.

Nikolaïdis, K. (2004) 'The Power of the Superpowerless', in Lindberg, T. (ed.) *Beyond Paradise and Power: Europe, America and the Future of a Troubled Partnership*, New York: Routledge, pp. 93–120.

Noutcheva, G. (2012) *European Foreign Policy and the Challenges of Balkan Accession*, New York: Routledge.

Tanner, M. (2010) *Croatia: A Nation Forged in War*, 3rd edn, New Haven: Yale University Press.

Toje, A. (2008) 'The Consensus-Expectations Gap: Explaining Europe's Ineffective Foreign Policy', *Security Dialogue*, 39(1), pp. 121–141.

Sedelmeier, U. (2004) 'Collective Identity', in Carlsnaes, W., Sjursen, H. and White, B. (eds) *Contemporary European Foreign Policy*, London: SAGE, pp. 123–140.

Woodward, S. (2009) 'Measuring State Failure/Weakness: Do the Balkan Cases Fit?', in Kostovicova, D. and Bojicic-Dzelilovic, V. (eds) *Persistent State Weakness in the Global Age*, London: Ashgate.

Zakošek, Nenad (2008) 'Democratization, State-building and War: The Cases of Serbia and Croatia', *Democratization*, 15(3), pp. 588–610.

2 The limits of normative power?
EU Member State building in the Western Balkans

Soeren Keil and Zeynep Arkan

The end of the Cold War and the changing context and neighborhood of the EU had a transforming effect on its relations with the wider world. Foreign policy making, and as a vital part of it enlargement, has become an ever more complex and complicated process for the EU, particularly in the last two decades. In addition to the changing nature and qualities of the international system, this was partly because the EU itself has evolved into a complex multilayered political system, which simultaneously bore the characteristics of an international organization, a state and a supranational institution. Furthermore, the policy areas for which the EU is either directly responsible or in which it is indirectly involved have also increased. This resulted in the fact that countries aspiring to join the EU would have to prepare carefully to join such a complex institution and to be able to cope with the pressures and obligations of membership.

Having said this, it is also important to point out that the nature of EU enlargement in recent years has also changed, because the countries that aspire to become members today are principally different from those in the past. While established democracies, in the form of the United Kingdom, Ireland and Denmark, joined the Communities in 1973, the integration of younger democracies like Spain, Portugal and Greece in later years focused on stabilizing and integrating them into European frameworks to support institutional stability. The integration of ten countries in Central and Eastern Europe in 2004 and 2007 was also seen as a way of supporting young democracies and securing institutional stability. Yet, when looking at the recent developments in Hungary, Romania and Cyprus in terms of democratic consolidation and peaceful conflict resolution with neighboring countries, the effects of what has been described as the 'transformative power' of the EU (Grabbe 2006) remain uncertain.

Enlargement policy and the emergence of the EU as an active state builder

What has become clear over recent years is that the enlargement process towards candidate and potential candidate countries in the Western

Balkans has reached a new level of complexity compared to the previous enlargement rounds of the Union. The EU demands more reforms, more changes and more modifications to the existing political and economic systems of the countries in the Western Balkans than ever before. Furthermore, it is not only the quantifiable nature of the enlargement process that has changed. The EU has also become actively involved in key political reforms in the region and has actively promoted certain modes of change and transformation. In fact, it can be said that the EU has become an active state builder in the countries of the Western Balkans.

State building, which is defined as 'the creation or recovery of the authoritative, legitimate, and capable governance institutions that can provide for security and the necessary rule-of-law conditions for economic and social development' (Sisk 2013: 1) is a new field of activity for the Union. In terms of the two important dimensions of state building, i.e. building state capacity and governance capabilities, the EU is a key part of the efforts in the Western Balkans, yet has little previous experience. Despite its inexperience, the EU aims to transform the Western Balkans through its state-building efforts not only to create the necessary foundations of peace and of non-conflictual resolution of clashes, but also to reform the states in the region to prevent further conflict through efficiently functioning political institutions, and free and democratic elections.

Yet the EU is not merely interested in building efficient democratic states, but it is simultaneously supporting and indeed building future EU Member States. This has led to new forms of state building with more long-term implications, and also changed the nature of state building in the Western Balkans. The process, labelled as 'EU Member State building', involves parallel developments towards consolidating statehood and democracy in weak post-conflict societies, while at the same time preparing and reforming these countries so that they fulfill the conditions for EU membership and can join the Union as quickly as possible (Keil 2013). While the first part of the process lacks clear benchmarks, the second is summarized in the EU's own criteria for membership, which were established during the Copenhagen Summit of the European Council in 1993 and include political criteria (being a stable democracy, respect for minority rights and the rule of law), economic criteria (a functioning market economy and the ability to cope with competition and market forces) and alignment with the *acquis communautaire*, the EU's body of law.

The EU's new role as an active Member State builder has important consequences. First, it influences the process of EU enlargement and changes its nature from a policy that prepares countries for membership in the European market to a process which actively builds efficiently functioning states that can join the EU. Second, it changes the political and economic dynamics in the candidate and potential candidate countries. As the EU is now directly involved in fundamental processes of state building (such as establishing the rule of law in Kosovo or constitutional reform in Bosnia), the enlargement policy also impacts on the internal dynamics of political engagement in candidate countries. Third, the nature of the EU itself is affected, particularly regarding its international role and identity. Given that enlargement policy today is more about state building and external democratization than simpler administrative changes, 'norm transfer' and 'norm diffusion', the EU's nature, tools, role and identity as a foreign policy actor have also changed. The EU is now more focused on the establishment of stable states and democracies in its near neighborhood to ensure peace and security through direct involvement than to extend its influence and 'force for good' through civilian and indirect – mostly economic – means. Economic incentives, however, remain a key element of the current conditionality framework.

The EU's engagement in the Western Balkans and the stabilization and association process

It is important to point out that the EU does not operate as a unitary actor in the process of enlargement. Instead, all major EU institutions are involved in the process. While the enlargement process itself falls under the responsibility of the European Commission, which provides annual progress reports and strategy papers for the countries that want to join the EU, it is the European Council that decides on whether or not membership negotiations are to be launched with a particular country and the important milestones during the negotiation process such as the Stabilization and Association Agreement (SAA). The European Council also takes the final decision regarding the membership of a country, which then has to be ratified by all Member States according to their national law. In addition to this, the European Parliament regularly provides reports on the candidate countries, and also has to agree on important milestones such as the SAA and approve the membership of a country into the EU. While both the European Commission and the Parliament play a more active role in enlargement policy than in other aspects of EU foreign policy, the process itself is heavily influenced by the attitudes of the Member States. This is significant particularly in relation to the current pessimist discourse on EU enlargement in Germany and France, as well as a number of South European Member States, that demonstrates how Member States' influence can slow down and, in the case of Turkey, even halt the integration process of a previously recognized candidate on the path to membership to the Union.

The European Community that started out with six Member States has grown in 2013 to a union of 28 countries, spanning from the Atlantic Ocean to the Black Sea. It has served as a stabilizer for German–French relations, integrated the transitional democracies in Southern Europe and (re)united the European continent in 2004 and 2007, when ten countries in Eastern Europe joined the EU. The Western Balkans is very much seen as the last mosaic in the complete unification of the European continent. Unlike the discussions regarding the accession of Turkey to the EU, there is no questioning of the right of the Western Balkans to be part of the EU and indeed of Europe. The enlargement discourse is therefore not so much about whether these countries should join the EU or not, but rather about the conditions, the timing and the speed at which these countries should be integrated. Indeed, this point is underlined by the European Council (2003):

> The EU reiterates its unequivocal support to the European perspective of the Western Balkan countries. The future of the Balkans is within the European Union. The ongoing enlargement and the signing of the Treaty of Athens in April 2003 inspire and encourage the countries of the Western Balkans to follow the same successful path. Preparation for integration into European structures and ultimate membership into the European Union, through adoption of European standards, is now the big challenge ahead. [...] The speed of movement ahead lies in the hands of the countries of the region.

The enlargement process has to be understood in its historical context as a way of ensuring peace and security in the European neighborhood, widening economic prosperity by inviting new countries to join the Single Market, and also a means to offer economic and political protection to the countries in Europe. Moreover, enlargement is also the optimal way through which 'European' norms, values and principles could be spread (Sjursen 2002). More importantly, the EU can be presented as a 'power, a centre of gravity, a model, a magnet [...], or various combinations of these' in its enlargement policy (Hill and Smith 2005: 4).

Integration into European structures has been defined as the main foreign policy objective of all countries in the Western Balkans. Therefore, representations of the EU as a magnet and as a form of a 'promised land' are predominant in the policy discourse in the Western Balkans. This also means that the relations between the EU and the Western Balkans, while very much focused on the theme of 'partnership', are generally asymmetric in nature. The current EU enlargement framework, known as the Stabilization and Association Process (SAP), attempts to address weaknesses in statehood, democracy and good neighborly relations while at the same time focusing on EU integration, i.e. preparing these countries to become Member States in the future.

On the EU side, the current engagement of the Union in the Western Balkans was very much shaped by its previous experiences in the 1990s. During the conflicts in the Western Balkans in the early 1990s, the EU was perceived as weak and incapable of solving the conflicts in the region. While it played a key role in negotiations to end the violence in Croatia,

Bosnia and later in Kosovo, it was the United States (and NATO) that managed to intervene and to lead peace-making missions on the ground. The EU, however, became actively involved in the region following the resolution of the conflicts. The EU hopes to create sustainable peace, democracy and statehood in these countries through the promise of eventual membership to the Union. As Richard Caplan (2006: 8) argues,

> [T]he EU's failure to offer an effective response to the crisis in the Balkans from its early days has led the Union to seek a leadership position in the post-war rule and reconstruction of these territories, partly to strengthen its own credibility in foreign policy-making.

On the road to EU membership, the countries have to achieve different milestones including the signing of the SAA and recognition as an official EU candidate. The SAP differs from previous enlargements in two important ways. First, each country is assessed on the basis of its own progress and the successor countries of the former Yugoslavia will join the Union most likely on different dates. Second, the SAP focuses on democratization and market integration as well as addressing issues regarding state building, post-conflict management and reconciliation. Regional cooperation is one of the main themes within the process and cooperation with the International Criminal Tribunal for the former Yugoslavia (ICTY) was a key condition for all countries of the former Yugoslavia. This means that the SAP is much more detailed and specific than other enlargement processes. The conditions are more specified and, though the Copenhagen Criteria are still the main framework for eventual membership decisions, the achievement of several milestones on the way often depends on the implementation of specific and detailed conditions that heavily impact on the political, social and economic systems of the candidate and potential candidate countries. This includes the prioritization of state-building measures in the conditionality package of the EU, as well as a focus on reconciliation and cooperation with the ICTY, and on regional cooperation, first through the Stability Pact for South East Europe and now through its successor, the Regional Cooperation Council (Batt 2010). In the words of DG Enlargement (2012),

> [t]he Stabilisation and Association Process (SAP) is the European Union's policy towards the Western Balkans, established with the aim of eventual EU membership. Western Balkan countries are involved in a progressive partnership with a view of stabilising the region and establishing a free-trade area. The SAP sets out common political and economic goals although progress evaluation is based on countries' own merits.

The most important tool used in the SAP is conditionality. In this process, steps towards closer cooperation and eventual integration into the EU are connected to political and economic reforms to ensure the creation of functional states (EU Member State building) and to implement the EU's *acquis communautaire*. The advantage of conditionality lies in its clarity: if a candidate country fulfills EU obligations, the EU will offer further steps towards integration; if the candidate abstains from taking important decisions on the path to integration, the EU will not act. Yet, the case is not that simple in the Western Balkans. Due to the fact that the EU is involved in active state building as well as preparing the countries for membership, ignoring obstacles to reform in these countries can be very costly and dangerous. As most of the Western Balkans countries are not functional democracies, EU policies cannot only focus solely on the implementation of the *acquis communautaire*, but have to take elements of state building and democratization into account. This is why the EU has often favoured the status quo over some radical changes. Fundamentally, EU enlargement is about security and peace within Europe and at Europe's borders. Therefore, conditionality needs to be applied in a rather flexible, but not inconsistent manner. This naturally is a major challenge for the EU, which has been involved in democratization projects in Southern and Eastern Europe, but never in active state-building exercises.[1]

While the Copenhagen Criteria have not become part of the *acquis communautaire*, following the discussions in the Convention on the Future of Europe, what has become clear as a result of the Lisbon Treaty is that conditionality will be applied even more strictly in the future. The EU has made it very clear in the aftermath of the negative experiences in Romania and Bulgaria that it will not accept any long-term promises, but would only assess integration according to clear evidence of reforms and changes. The negotiations on different chapters of the *acquis communautaire* will only progress if evidence can be provided by the candidate country regarding the implementation of reforms.

EU enlargement policy towards the Western Balkans has three major features. First, it builds on the experiences of former enlargements of the Union and promotes the prospect of membership in the Union as a way of stabilization, democratization and state building. This policy, with the exception of state building, has already been applied when Spain and Portugal joined the European Community in 1986. Second, enlargement policy in this context is still represented as norm driven and conceptualizes the EU as an area not only of economic prosperity but also of political stability, democracy and solidarity. In recent years, the Treaty of Lisbon has further strengthened the normative dimension of EU foreign policy. Article 3.5 of the Treaty on European Union (including Lisbon changes) states that:

> In its relations with the wider world, the Union shall uphold and promote its values and interests and contribute to the protection of its citizens. It shall contribute to peace, security, the sustainable development of the

Earth, solidarity and mutual respect among peoples, free and fair trade, eradication of poverty and the protection of human rights, in particular the rights of the child, as well as to the strict observance and the development of international law, including respect for the principles of the United Nations Charter.

Hence, it is very important to point out that the Union sees itself as an active promoter of democracy, human rights and economic prosperity and that these aims are part of the foreign policy and enlargement policy discourse. Third, it has to be said that the European enlargement policy towards the Western Balkans is based on a new approach towards stabilization of new and often weak states and slow integration, both into the EU and within the region of the Western Balkans. The political engagement of the EU in the Western Balkans, which is characterized as EU Member State building, is a novel process that combines policies of traditional enlargement (such as economic integration) with classic concepts of state building (such as influencing the institutional design of candidate countries).

The question of limited and contested statehood in the Western Balkans

The problem of weak and unconsolidated states is at the heart of the current quagmire in EU–Western Balkans relations. The 'transformative power' of the EU requires functional states, because 'limited statehood seems to be the main cause of ineffective implementation of EU-induced reforms and the decoupling between formal institutional changes and rule-inconsistent behavior' in the region (Börzel 2011: 9). In short, long-term changes in the political, economic and societal systems in the former Yugoslavia, which are at the heart of the EU's integration process, fail to be implemented and reach their full potential as they did in some (but not all) countries in Central and Eastern Europe (CEE). While the SAP tackles some of the issues in the Western Balkans, such as focusing on reconciliation and regional cooperation as a key strategy to overcome some of the results of the violent conflicts in the 1990s, it does not substantially address the core problem of the majority of countries in the region: a lack of stateness. As Francis Fukuyama (2005: 84) argued, '[b]efore you can have democracy or economic development, you have to have a state'. The SAP does not fundamentally address the issue of a lack of stateness, or limited statehood, to use a term more common in governance research. Instead, the EU has developed a set of *ad hoc* policies to address signs of contested statehood, without actually addressing the root causes in each of the countries. This is also the reason why the EU's Member State building approach cannot be treated as a coherent or indeed as a long-term strategy. Instead, it consists of a number of *ad hoc* decisions. Sometimes these are connected and there is a wider medium-term strategy, such as the current EU-sponsored negotiations between Serbia and Kosovo, which aim to prepare both countries for further steps into the EU. Yet more often than not, these *ad hoc* decisions are designed to address short-term problems rather than long-term weaknesses in the political and economic systems of the region. Furthermore, the focus on short-term solutions has undermined important reform processes in a number of countries. This includes constitutional reform in Bosnia, the fight against organized crime in most Western Balkan states and the consolidation of the rule of law in many of the states in the region. Instead, the EU has focused on minor corrections to often very dysfunctional systems, always keeping the premise that the status quo is good and that security needs to be at the heart of the reform process, often in conflict with democracy and human rights promotion.

Florian Bieber (2011) argues that the EU has utilized three main strategies to address the problem of 'minimalist states' (i.e. contested states). First, it used *direct intervention* in the political systems of a number of countries. This has most obviously been the case in Bosnia and Herzegovina, where the Office of the High Representative, which has far-reaching imposition and dismissal powers, was combined with the EU Special Representative's (EUSR) position until 2011. This has resulted in a number of policies being labelled as 'EU standards' that actually focused much more on the creation of a more effective state in Bosnia, but were not directly connected to formalized EU conditionality. The most prominent example is the police reform, which had been at the centre of Bosnian politics between 2004 and 2008, which resulted in the resignation of the government in Bosnia and led the EU to lose a lot of credibility in Bosnia (Juncos 2011). The interventions of the EU's Rule of Law Mission in Kosovo (EULEX) can also be considered an example of EU Member State building through direct intervention.

The second form of EU Member State building is *coercion* and *close monitoring*. While this is not based on the direct participation of EU actors in the development and implementation of legislation as in the case of intervention, it nevertheless relies on pressure from Brussels and EU Member States' capitals to convince the local political actors to reform the existing system and to implement certain decisions. This is often connected to further advances in the EU integration process. The current EU-sponsored negotiations between Serbia and Kosovo could be seen as an example of this form of Member State building by the EU. The role that the EUSR played in Macedonia until recently can also be cited as an example, as the EUSR acted as the chief moderator and negotiator between Albanian and Macedonian parties in the country and thus pressured the different groups to arrive at joint decisions. While the EU also focused on consensual decision-making in regards to EU integration in the CEE countries, what is new in the Western Balkans is the strong focus on power-sharing, particularly in Bosnia, Kosovo and Macedonia (Bieber and Keil 2009), and the enhanced monitoring of minority integration (Kacarska 2012).

Finally, Bieber argues that *'long-distance' state building* is the third form of EU Member State building. This focuses on the use of EU conditionality to incite reforms and therefore contribute to more effective stateness and increased democratic accountability. Examples of this form of state building can be found in the EU-sponsored state union of Serbia and Montenegro, which was created to keep the two countries together and connected with a clear EU integration perspective, as well as in the strong support of the EU for constitutional reform in Bosnia in connection with the Sejdić-Finci judgment of the European Court of Human Rights.

Through these various modes of state building, the EU is aiming to further strengthen and stabilize the weak states in the Western Balkans. In doing so, it is attempting to influence the countries in its immediate neighborhood by offering the prospect of membership and providing extensive political and financial support. In this context, it is important to point out that other organizations such as NATO in Afghanistan, and countries such the United States in Iraq, have failed in their attempts to build efficient states that can protect their own citizens and borders. Thus, it can be concluded that despite the problems faced, the most obvious ones being the failure to change elite attitudes and, particularly through direct intervention, creating new structures of dependency in the region, the EU project in the Western Balkans continues, and should not be considered a failure just yet. It is important to keep in mind that the main reason for EU Member State building is not only to enhance statehood and strengthen state structures in the countries of the former Yugoslavia and Albania, but also to prepare them for membership in the EU, and by doing so, to enhance democratic governance in the region.

The problem is that the EU's attempts to intervene have more often than not resulted in political crises and new tensions. These coercive mechanisms have resulted in some short-term successes in reform efforts, yet their long-term sustainability is not at all ensured, and often these reform initiatives depend on further international pressure or fade away once the EU is satisfied with the changes made. Gergana Noutcheva (2012) refers to a process of 'fake compliance' in which the Western Balkan states would formally adopt reforms and rule changes as demanded by the EU, but local practices would not change. For example, Serbia and Kosovo have made progress in a number of areas in recent years in their EU-sponsored talks and reached agreement on a number of issues. Yet the Kosovar side has refused any further deals until the majority of these arrangements were brought into life. Similarly, Bosnian politicians have declared agreement on a number of issues in relation to constitutional reform, yet there is no intention to vote on these issues and implement them. David Chandler, one of the strongest critics of the EU's policies in the Western Balkans, argues that the EU acts in an undemocratic and inconsistent manner in the area and thereby creates new forms of dependency and undermines any form of local ownership and state sovereignty (Chandler 2010). Other critics such as Roberto Belloni (2009) have pointed out that the EU focuses too much on engaging with political elites instead of engaging with ordinary citizens and civil society organizations.

While the EU's motivation to transform the territories of the former Yugoslavia (and Albania) and to support democratization and state consolidation as well as economic reforms in the region could be seen as a positive form of engagement with its immediate neighborhood, the policies developed in this framework are often flawed and problematic. This is to some extent the fault of those that develop these policies, i.e. EU actors, because they lack a deeper understanding of the policy processes and structures in the region and believe that the carrot of eventual EU membership will cure all ills. Another reason for the problems in the EU's approach towards the Western Balkans lies in the fact that the Union is lacking a clear medium- and long-term strategy for integration. The solutions it offers to the problems it tackles, from constitutional weaknesses in Bosnia to attempting to increase the rule of law in Kosovo, are often short-term fixes that fail to address deeper structural weaknesses. The continued dominance of ethnocentric parties in Bosnia, as well as the prevalence of clan structures in Kosovo will not be altered by the EU's insistence on formal rule change. Instead, what is needed is long-term societal transformation, on which the EU can only have limited impact. The examples of Romania, Bulgaria and Cyprus demonstrate that these long-term changes will continue even after countries become EU members and that older structures often prevail and remain very resistant to any form of change. Finally, it needs to be pointed out that another reason behind the limited success of EU Member State building efforts in the region are the political elites of the countries in the Western Balkans. Many of them profit from the current status quo and remain opposed to fundamental changes in line with the EU's agenda as these threaten their privileged position not only in the political, but often also in the economic systems of these countries. Hence, there is little incentive for change as the local elites profit from the current situation. Compliance with EU conditionality would then be limited and focused on formal rule change rather than deep-rooted transformations (Noutcheva 2012). This implies that what is needed in the region is a complete change of political rule, under which current elites would not be able to protect their own interests and position in the system through formal rule change and minimal adoption to European standards. Instead, an integrative approach that is focused on strong civil society and popular involvement is required, according to which elites are properly held accountable for their actions and decisions. Ultimately, consistency plays a key role in the EU's approach towards the region. Fundamental reforms required to participate in the EU framework should not be watered down so that unwilling politicians can rely on a minimal consensual agreement. The past has proven that the EU's reform agenda can result in deep-rooted change, as can be seen by the arrest and trial of Croatia's former Prime Minister Ivo Sanader for corruption charges.

The EU's normative power: myth or reality?

The novel and unprecedented qualities of the EU as an actor in world politics rendered themes such as its international role, identity and foreign policy capabilities popular in academic research in the last two decades. Accordingly, the debates on EU foreign policy have included various characterizations of the EU's international role, identity and impact. The great scholarly interest in the EU's international role and contribution also corresponded to the search on the part of the EU for 'a new sense of collective purpose and legitimacy' following the end of the Cold War which was to be found in foreign and security policy (Aggestam 2008: 1). In this context, the gradual acquisition of military capabilities, coupled with the structural changes taking place in the international system, provided the Union with an opportunity to (re)define its position in the world and the impact it aimed to make on international relations. In this period, the EU's often ambitious norm-based and ethical discourse on foreign policy went hand in hand with characterizations of the Union as a *sui generis* foreign policy actor with a unique contribution to make, best depicted in the 'normative power Europe' label coined by Ian Manners in his 2002 article. In his attempt to go beyond the more state-centric analyses of EU's international identity, Manners founded the concept of normative power on the basis of the EU's 'ability to shape conceptions of "normal" in international relations' (Manners 2002: 239). In line with this, he argued that the EU as a foreign policy actor was not only based on a number of norms – peace, liberty, democracy, the rule of law, respect for human rights and fundamental freedoms – but it also aimed to project these to the wider world through its foreign and security policy, including its enlargement policy. According to him, the idea of the EU's normative power was based on its normative difference and basis, and derived from the unique history and evolutionary process of the EU: 'the central component of normative power Europe is that it exists as being different to pre-existing political forms and that this particular difference pre-disposes it to act in a normative way' (Manners 2002: 242). As such, he concluded, this conception of the EU's identity is based on the notion that 'the most important factor shaping the international role of the EU is *not what it does or what it says*, but *what it is*' (Manners 2002: 252, emphasis added).

From a more critical standpoint, this conception of the EU's foreign policy role and identity that engages with the ontological foundations of the Union is somewhat incomplete to the extent that it disregards or overlooks how the EU puts its normative essence into action, despite Manners' emphasis on *what the EU is* rather than what it says. To begin with, it has to be noted that, like any other international actor, the EU does not have a 'nature' or identity in the world just because of its existence or essence, or *what it is*, and that this 'nature' and identity are necessarily defined, produced and reproduced in its social practices. As Thomas Diez (2005) notes, the EU as a normative power is inherently a construct that not only denotes the EU as a specific kind of actor in international politics, but also determines the nature of the relationship the EU has with third parties – a highly asymmetrical one, in the case of the Western Balkan states – and the tools that it uses in its foreign policy. In this respect, Diez argues that discussions as to why the EU is a different kind of actor, while relevant,

> ignore the power that lies in the representation of the EU as a normative power as such. Not only is the success of this representation a precondition for other actors to agree to the norms set out by the EU; it also constructs an identity of the EU against an image of others in the 'outside world'. This has important implications for the way EU policies treat those others, and for the degree to which its adherence to its own norms is scrutinised within the EU. In that sense, the discourse of the EU as a normative power constructs a particular self of the EU (and it is indeed perhaps the only form of identity that most of the diverse set of actors within the EU can agree on), while it attempts to change others through the spread of particular norms.
> (Diez 2005: 614)

Taking into consideration the different nature of the EU's engagement with the Western Balkan states since the 1990s, it can be concluded that Diez's account of the EU's normative power is helpful in explaining the unbalanced relationship that exists between the EU and candidate states in the enlargement process. In this respect, accounts such as Manners' that rely on a clear distinction regarding the exercise of normative power through civilian (including economic) means *versus* military power is simply not enough to explain the role that the EU is currently playing in the Western Balkans. First, such an understanding of the EU as the sole or key representative of European (some might say universal) values is clearly very Eurocentric and inevitably puts the local peoples as well as their history and traditions in an inferior position regarding the Western part of the continent. Second, in the case of the Western Balkans, it has to be kept in mind that the reforms or changes that were required by the EU were not always in clear and written form and were not formalized within the *acquis*. Sometimes the EU made the rules of the game as it went along. This implied that the EU was seeking to get newly created, often seldom discussed and novel (and therefore never before applied) solutions and rules applied in the Western Balkans. In addition to this, contrary to the norms upheld and advocated by the EU, the changes and reforms required from the candidate and potential candidate states, and the prescriptions of the EU, were not discussed in great detail either in these states themselves or within EU institutions.[2] This imbalance between the two sides was also reflected in the representatives of the EU on the ground who possessed a relatively high position of authority in the political system and were not directly elected by the society in question. Overall, the developments and the responses of the local elite and peoples illustrated that the EU's policies towards these states discredited the people and their right for self-governance and put them in a disadvantaged position that almost required the leadership and guidance of their European cousins. This process is further complicated due to the EU's very structure: as a unique type of international actor, the EU is not a unitary one. Instead, particularly when it comes to foreign policy, the EU operates through a number of different institutions as well as Member State representatives. These institutions and representatives, in turn, speak on behalf of and represent different interests within the Union. Within the framework of the EU's enlargement policy towards the Western Balkan states, these actors – the most important ones being the European Council, the European Commission and the Council of the European Union, in addition to the special envoys of the EU on the ground – do not always speak with one voice, which complicates the message the Union is trying to convey. This problem of consistency within the Union with respect to its engagement in the Western Balkan states further complicates the process of transforming them into potential Member States.

In this respect, it is clear that in the case of the Western Balkan enlargement the EU did not just act on the basis of its normative basis and means based on its power of attraction. In fact, the EU, by reproducing the asymmetrical and unbalanced relationship between the candidate and potential candidate states and itself, failed to acknowledge and respond to the unique conditions and legacies of the states in the region and the needs and desires of the local people, once again based on the assumption that what is good for Europe is necessarily good for the rest of the world. In doing so, it not only reproduced a hierarchical relationship between the East and the West of Europe by creating 'a de facto "empire" to the east', but also through its experimental Member State building practices, established a 'relationship of tutelage' aimed at exporting liberal peace into the Western Balkan states (Chandler 2007: 594, 606–607). Consequently, it would not be wrong to conclude that in its relations with the Western Balkans, the EU acted contrary to the values, norms and principles upon which it was founded.

Conclusion

The study of EU Member State building and its regional consequences remains unsystematic and has only just come to the attention of leading academics interested in the developments in the Western Balkans and in

EU foreign policy. Yet, what EU Member State building actually is, how it is implemented and what its long-term effects are remain important questions for further research. As is the case with the study of state building in general (Woodward *et al.* 2013), there remains a lack of methodology and research design in the study of the EU's attempts to build effective Member States in the former Yugoslavia (and Albania).

This chapter argued that the engagement of the EU in the Western Balkans could be characterized as a form of EU Member State building, because it combines elements of the EU integration process with active state-building policies in the post-Yugoslav countries. The EU's policies towards the region focus on four main dimensions: the creation of effective states, the consolidation of democracy, the implementation of economic reforms to allow open and liberal capitalist economic systems to develop and flourish, and the preparation of these countries for membership in the EU, including legislative alignment with the *acquis communautaire*. These processes cannot be studied individually, as they are interlinked and overlapping. The more active involvement of the EU also demonstrates that these countries undergo multiple transitions, including the one from membership in the Yugoslav federation to independent statehood, from war to peace, and from an economic model characterized by workers' self-management towards one based on liberalization and free competition. The EU's initial involvement in the region is therefore seen as a way to prepare these countries for membership and to support the 'positive' elements of open markets and democracy.

Yet, as has been demonstrated, EU Member State building is not without its negative side effects. These include the creation of new dependencies and the lack of deep-rooted reform initiatives in a number of countries. From a critical perspective, it could be argued that the fact that the current EU-sponsored dialogue between Kosovo and Serbia takes place between a former KLA leader who is now the Prime Minister of Kosovo (and has been accused of war crimes many times) and the former Propaganda Minister of Slobodan Milošević, who is now the Prime Minister of Serbia, demonstrates that the EU's democratization agenda in the region has failed. Many scholars, including Bieber, Chandler and Belloni, remain sceptical of the EU's engagement in the region and point out that in recent years no state has been strengthened through the EU's state-building practices. Indeed, it could be argued that the reason why Croatia became the twenty-eighth Member State in the EU has less to do with the impact of the EU and more to do with domestic changes, both through a change of government in 2000 and through a transformation of the conservative party HDZ towards a pro-European party of the centre-right (Jović 2011). It is the lack of domestic changes in Bosnia, Kosovo, Serbia, Macedonia, Albania and Montenegro that illustrate best the key weaknesses associated with EU's Member State building approach.

When discussing EU Member State building in a regional perspective, it becomes obvious that the wider region of Western Balkans remains characterized by weak states, who have limited statehood and cannot fully provide the services that states should offer to their citizens (above all security, but also economic development, and a general good standard of living). Romania and Bulgaria remain examples of limited or even failed compliance with EU policies. Both states remain characterized by weak state structures, an increasing grey market in the economy and a strong connection between political and economic elites. Hungary demonstrates how an EU Member State can track back on some of the fundamental principles of democracy, while Cyprus was allowed to join the EU without having solved its own statehood problem. Even Greece, a longer-term EU Member State, has recently demonstrated that state structures are weak when it comes to implement certain laws on financial regulations and taxation. These all point to the fact that integration of the former Yugoslav states and Albania will be a long-term project. However, at the core of any state-building policies of the EU should be the aim to motivate deep-rooted societal changes led by local elites rather than European bureaucrats. Democracy, after all, starts at the local level.

Consequently, from the overall perspective of foreign policy, the Western Balkan enlargement represents a difficult challenge for the EU. It not only led to the questioning of the viability and validity of the solutions and recommendations of the EU with respect to the (potential) candidates but also a reconsideration of the EU's normative power and its limits. By relying on more direct, active and often interventionist responses to the situation in the Western Balkan states, the EU often contradicted its so called normative nature and identity and dictated its often ill-discussed and newly created solutions, standards and rules in the region, taking advantage of the asymmetrical power relationship that existed between itself and the Western Balkan states. In this respect, it would not be wrong to conclude that the Western Balkan enlargement of the EU served as an important litmus test for its normative identity, a test that the EU seems to have failed in recent years.

Note

1 The attempted state building in Cyprus during the enlargement process failed due to the resistance of Greek Cypriots to reunite with the Turkish Cypriots under the framework provided by the Annan Plan. For details on this, see Burgess 2007.

References

Aggestam, L. (2008) 'Introduction: Ethical Power Europe?', *International Affairs*, 84(1), pp. 1–11.

Batt, J. (2010) *The EU and the Western Balkans: Preparing for the Long-Haul*, FRIDE Policy Brief No. 62, December. Available at: www.fride.org/publication/840/the-eu-and-the-western-balkans:-preparing-for-the-long-haul.

Belloni, R. (2009) 'European Integration and the Western Balkans: Lessons, Prospects and Obstacles', *Journal of Balkan and Near Eastern Studies*, 11(3), pp. 313–331.

Bieber, F. (2011) 'Building Impossible States? State-Building Strategies and EU Membership in the Western Balkans', *Europe-Asia Studies*, 63(10), pp. 1783–1802.

Bieber, F. and Keil, S. (2009) 'Power-Sharing Revisited: Lessons Learnt in the Balkans?', *Review of Central and East European Law*, 34(4), pp. 337–360.

Burgess, M. (2007) 'What is to be Done? Bicommunalism, Federation and Confederation in Cyprus', in Burgess, M. and Pinder, J. (eds) *Multinational Federations*, London: Routledge, pp. 127–149.

Börzel, T. (2011) *When Europeanization Hits Limited Statehood*, KFG Working Paper No. 30, 30 September. Available at: http://userpage.fu-berlin.de/kfgeu/kfgwp/wpseries/WorkingPaperKFG_30.pdf.

Caplan, R. (2006) *A New Trusteeship? The International Administration of War-Torn Territories*, London: Routledge.

Chandler, D. (2007) 'EU Statebuilding: Securing the Liberal Peace through EU Enlargement', *Global Society*, 21(4), pp. 593–607.

Chandler, D. (2010) 'The EU and Southeastern Europe: the Rise of Post-Liberal Governance', *Third World Quarterly*, 31(1), pp. 69–85.

DG Enlargement (2012) *Stabilization and Association Process*. Available at: http://ec.europa.eu/enlargement/policy/glossary/terms/sap_en.htm.

Diez, T. (2005) 'Constructing the Self and Changing Others: Reconsidering "Normative Power Europe"', *Millennium: Journal of International Studies*, 33(3), pp. 613–636.

European Council (2003) *EU-Western Balkans Summit – Declaration*, Document 10229/03 (Presse 163), Thessaloniki, 21 June. Available at: http://ec.europa.eu/enlargement/enlargement_process/accession_process/how_does_a_country_join_the_eu/sap/thessaloniki_summit_en.htm.

Fukuyama, F. (2005) 'Stateness First', *Journal of Democracy*, 16(1), pp. 84–88.

Grabbe, H. (2006) *The EU's Transformative Power: Europeanization through Conditionality in Central and Eastern Europe*, New York: Palgrave Macmillan.

Hill, C. and Smith, M. (2005) 'International Relations and the European Union: Themes and Issues', in Hill, C. and Smith, M. (eds) *International Relations and the European Union*, Oxford: Oxford University Press, pp. 3–17.

Jović, D. (2011) 'Turning Nationalists into EU Supporters: The Case of Croatia', in Rupnik, J. (ed.) *The Western Balkans and the EU: 'The Hour of Europe*, Challiot Papers 126, European Union Institute for Security Studies: Paris.

Juncos, A. (2011) 'Europeanization by Decree? The Case of the Police Reform in Bosnia', *JCMS: Journal of Common Market Studies*, 49(2), pp. 367–389.

Kacarska, S. (2012) 'Minority Policies and EU Conditionality: The Case of the Republic of Macedonia', *Journal of Ethnopolitics and Minority Issues in Europe*, 11(2), pp. 60–79.

Keil, S. (2013) 'Introduction: Europeanization, State-Building and Democratization in the Western Balkans', *Nationalities Papers*, 41(3), pp. 343–353.

Manners, I. (2002) 'Normative Power Europe: A Contradiction in Terms?', *JCMS: Journal of Common Market Studies*, 40(2), pp. 235–258.

Noutcheva, G. (2012) *European Foreign Policy and the Challenges of Balkan Accession*, New York: Routledge.

Sisk, T. (2013) *Statebuilding*, Cambridge: Polity.

Sjursen, H. (2002) 'Why Expand? The Question of Legitimacy and Justification of the EU's Enlargement Policy', *JCMS: Journal of Common Market Studies*, 40(3), pp. 491–513.

Woodward, S., Kostovicova, D. and Bojicic-Dzelilovic, V. (2013) 'Introduction: Methodology and the Study of State-Building in the Western Balkans', *Südosteuropa*, 60(4), pp. 467–469.

3 Building on experience?
EU enlargement and the Western Balkans

Erhan İçener and David Phinnemore

Introduction

The last decade has witnessed an unprecedented increase in the size of the European Union (EU). With two rounds of 'eastern' enlargement in 2004 and 2007, the accessions of Cyprus and Malta in 2004 and Croatia in 2013, the EU has seen its membership grow by more than three-fifths from 15 to 28 states. Further enlargement is also envisaged, notably to admit more states from the Western Balkans: accession negotiations have been launched with Montenegro and Serbia; Macedonia applied in 2004 and has been granted candidate status; and Albania submitted its application in 2009. Moreover, the remaining Western Balkan states are expected to apply for membership in the coming years: governments in Bosnia and Herzegovina and Kosovo have both expressed a desire to see their states one day accede to the EU. With the experience it has gained over the last two decades in negotiating accession and endeavouring to assist a diverse range of applicants in making the necessary preparations and adaptations for admission, the EU has arguably never been better placed to respond constructively to the aspirations of would-be members.

However, despite the seeming consistency with which states apply for EU membership and eventually accede, there is nothing inevitable about EU enlargement. The process is ultimately political, despite the EU's portrayal of itself as a normative actor spreading its values through enlargement. So, while the experience of negotiating accession with, first, the likes of Hungary and Poland, later Bulgaria and Romania, and then Croatia may have allowed the EU to develop and refine its procedures and mechanisms for facilitating the admission of new members, the success of an application cannot be taken for granted. As the case of Turkey's membership bid demonstrates, the negotiating process can become extremely protracted and even stall; the EU's commitment to an applicant's admission can and does falter. Moreover, as the EU learns lessons from successive rounds of enlargement, it can and does adjust the requirements it makes of applicants. Adjustments are also made to address the standing of particular applicants. Hence, in the Western Balkan context, EU engagement includes measures aimed as much at consolidating fragile states and 'Member State building' as at more traditional preparations for accession.

Consequently, enlargement has to be viewed as a process involving elements of continuity and change (İçener *et al.* 2010). This applies not only to the mechanics of engagement between the EU and the applicants, but also to the context. The prospects for enlargement cannot be decoupled from the internal development of the EU; as has always been the case with the EU there are tensions between external 'widening' (enlargement) and internal 'deepening' (integration). Besides, attitudes towards enlargement are never going to be totally stable; they will shift, potentially quite dramatically, and so with significant implications for how the EU approaches enlargement. And as the EU evolves politically, patterns of decision-making influence shift too; the voices determining the EU position can and do change. Successive enlargements have though been characterized by considerable elements of continuity in how the EU has responded to applications for membership in terms of both its increasingly proactive engagement in supporting the realization of preparations and the *acquis*-focused manner in which accession has been negotiated. A rhetorical commitment to enlargement has always been present.

The various dimensions of continuity and change that have been evident in the enlargements of 2004, 2007 and 2013 provide the focus for this chapter. Its analysis of the EU's evolving approach to enlargement examines not only the formal relationships the EU has established with the states of the Western Balkans, the carrots and sticks of conditionality, and the nature of the EU's commitment to expand further into the region; it also, following İçener *et al.* (2010), explores important contextual influences on and determinants of the process. It considers, for example, continuity and change in the preferences of EU Member States, in public opinion, in the position of the European Commission. It looks too at the impact of the EU's internal 'integration capacity' debate, the contemporary equivalent of the 'widening versus deepening' debate of old.

Continuity and change in the EU's approach to enlargement

When exploring how the EU approaches enlargement, there are a range of factors that need to be considered: the level of the political commitment to admitting new member states; the conditions that the EU sets; and the resources it is willing to put in place to assist potential members realizing the goal of accession. When comparing successive rounds of enlargement, elements of continuity can be seen; and this is no less the case with regard to the process of enlargement to include the Western Balkan states. Moreover, subtle and not so subtle shifts can be detected within the process too.

Commitment

In stark contrast to eastern enlargement, the EU's engagement with the states of the Western Balkans lacks a powerful narrative that either has the potential to drive further enlargement into the region or could be seized on by champions of the process, drawing on Schimmelfennig (2001), to rhetorically entrap sceptics and feet-draggers into admitting the states. Whereas the process of eastern enlargement was profoundly influenced by a post-Cold War narrative of historic opportunity and obligation to overcome the artificial division of Europe since 1945, no such narrative exists in the case of the Western Balkans. True, the EU invokes security, stability, peace promotion and democratization as arguments in favour of Western Balkan enlargement just as it did when advocating eastern enlargement. Since eastern enlargement, and with relative stability in the Western Balkans, however, the security-based narrative, although still in use, is much less prominent and certainly lacks the sense of urgency that characterized its use in the early 2000s.

For eastern enlargement, there was, from 1993, a clear commitment about the outcome of the process. In 1992, the Commission had argued that what Europe was facing with eastern enlargement process was a 'historic opportunity' for 'unification of the whole of Europe' (European Commission 1992: point 5). A year later, the Copenhagen European Council declared that 'the associated countries of Central and Eastern Europe that so desire shall become members' of the EU, albeit provided they met certain criteria (Council of the European Union 1993: 7.A.iii). The message, however, was powerful, and unmistakable. It was reinforced four years later when the Luxembourg European Council formally launched an 'accession process' with the Central and Eastern European (CEE) states (plus Cyprus). The 11 states were declared as 'destined to join' the EU (Council of the European Union 1997: point 10). This was 'the dawn of a new era, finally putting an end to the divisions of the past' (ibid.: Introduction). Two years later, the Helsinki European Council in 1999 even declared Turkey to be 'destined to join' the EU (Council of the European Union 1999: point 12).

Although 1999 also saw the European Council issue its first direct reference to the possible accession of the Western Balkan states, the language was vaguer and the rhetoric would not be sustained. At Cologne, the European Council referred to drawing the Western Balkans 'closer to the prospect of full integration into [the EU's] structures' and indicated 'a prospect of European Union membership on the basis of the Amsterdam Treaty and fulfilment of the criteria defined at the Copenhagen European Council in June 1993'. A year later, the Feira European Council upgraded the status of the Western Balkan states to 'potential candidates for EU membership'. Although the concept of 'potential candidate' – never conferred before – lacked definition and was legally meaningless, it suggested commitment and signalled a status whose next step was 'candidate' like the CEE states. Instead, the European Council preferred a looser commitment to 'the fullest possible integration of the countries of the region into the political and economic mainstream of Europe' (Council of the European Union 2000a: point 67).

In the years since, the strength of the EU's rhetorical commitment to the Western Balkans has increased. The Zagreb Summit in November 2000 offered 'the prospect of accession' to the Western Balkan states 'on the basis of the provision of the Treaty on European Union' (Zagreb Summit 2000: point 4). The following month, the Nice European Council slightly upgraded its commitment by exceptionally stating that the EU was offering 'a *clear* prospect of accession' to the Western Balkan states and it would 'support the Western Balkans' efforts [...] which will contribute to the rapprochement of each of these countries with the Union and *form a whole*' (Council of the European Union 2000b: point 62, emphasis added).[1] The Brussels European Council in March 2003 went further, stating that '[t]he future of the Western Balkans is within the EU' (Council of the European Union 2003a: point 82). Since then, this formulation has become standard. A few months later, the Thessaloniki European Council 'reiterated its determination to fully and effectively support the European perspective of the Western Balkan countries, which will become an integral part of the EU' (Council of the European Union 2003b: point 40). The same conclusions endorsed 'the Thessaloniki Agenda for the Western Balkans' (ibid.: point 41), an annex to the Council conclusions that states that the Western Balkans' 'ultimate membership into the Union is a high priority for the EU' and '[t]he Balkans will be an integral part of a unified Europe' (Council of the European Union 2003c: Annex A). The European Council in Brussels in 2006 'reconfirmed the European perspective of the Western Balkans' and reiterated 'EU membership as [*sic*] ultimate goal' (Council of the European Union 2006a: point 56).

These statements on the Western Balkans referring to forming 'a whole', being an 'integral part of' and having a future 'within' the EU can be seen as real signs of commitment. That said, it is interesting to note how seldom EU leaders in the European Council have referred either to 'membership' for the Western Balkans states or them becoming 'members'. The language of membership as 'destiny' is conspicuously absent. Nor is there a Copenhagen-like affirmative statement that the states 'shall become members'. Moreover, it is noticeable that the conclusions from European Council meetings since 2007 hardly ever mention enlargement. Instead, the most they record is that the December European Council 'welcomes and endorses the conclusions adopted by the Council ... on Enlargement and the Stabilisation and Association Process' (e.g. European Council 2012: point 27; European Council 2013: point 43). As for the Council conclusions, they tend simply to confirm that 'Enlargement remains a key policy of the European Union' and at most refer back to previous statements. They also continue the practice of studiously avoiding the language of 'accession' and 'membership'. The language remains cautious and the intensity of the commitment has not moved.[2]

As noted, the narrative highlighting the role of integration as a provider of security, stability and peace in Europe is used for the Western Balkans. It is also reflected in the level of EU engagement (see below) and the EU's presence 'on the ground'. In terms of narrative, there is continuity here from past enlargements. However, conspicuously absent are the narratives deployed in eastern enlargement highlighting the EU's 'responsibility' and 'duty' to enlarge and the 'historic opportunity' to achieve the 'unification of Europe'.[3] The EU is clearly avoiding over-commitment. In part, this can be explained by notions of 'enlargement fatigue' and the 'renewed consensus on enlargement' announced at the European Council in December 2006, a matter of days before Bulgaria and Romania joined the EU on 1 January 2007. Here, the European Council agreed that its enlargement strategy would be based on 'consolidation, conditionality and communication' with an increased emphasis on the EU's own integration capacity being a determinant in the process. Enlargement would henceforth become a process where progress towards accession would be driven more by technical considerations than political commitment. It followed that the EU would remain cautious in the 'promises' it would make. Any sense of rhetorical entrapment was to be avoided, a point underlined by the European Council stating quite emphatically in its 'renewed consensus on enlargement' that the EU 'will refrain from setting any target dates for accession until the negotiations are close to completion' (Council of the European Union 2006b: point 7).

Conditionality

The EU's weaker rhetoric regarding its commitment to Western Balkan enlargement compared to that used in relation to eastern enlargement should not be taken as proof of a fundamental lessening of interest in the process of admitting more states. Rather, it reflects widespread caution regarding premature promises and possible rhetorical entrapment and a desire to manage expectations of would-be members more effectively. That the interest in enlargement persists is evident in the maintenance of DG Enlargement, the developing relations the EU has with potential candidates and candidates alike, and the resources that the EU continues to make available to them in support of their preparations for accession (see next section). It is evident too in the prominence given to conditionality as the formal determinant of progress towards membership. According to the 'renewed consensus', 'strict conditionality' is the basis on which negotiations on membership will be pursued (ibid.). Moreover, the range of conditions that need to be met has been extended, the thresholds for compliance have been raised, the points at which criteria need to be met have generally been brought forward, and conditionality demands have been made at more points in the accession process broadly defined. Consequently, for Western Balkan states to make progress towards accession, they need not only to demonstrate a greater level of compliance with a wider set of conditions but do so on a more frequent basis. While this is clearly designed to contribute to the 'Member State building' process and, according to the EU, will ensure candidates are better prepared for membership than at least some of their predecessors, it both lengthens the process of accession and creates more gate-keeping opportunities for the EU and its Member States to exploit.

On the range of conditions, the Western Balkan states not only have to meet the existing Copenhagen criteria, they also have to meet 'the conditionality of the Stabilisation and Association Process' (Council of the European Union 2006b: point 8). They need, therefore, to pursue regional cooperation, ensure the return of refugees and cooperate fully with the International Criminal Tribunal for the former Yugoslavia (ICTY). The second and third of these are demands reflecting the particular recent history of the region and thus should not necessarily be seen as additional to those imposed on the CEE states. The novelty of the requirement for regional cooperation is a matter of degree, it having previously been at least implicitly required of acceding states. The conditions that the Western Balkan states must meet are, however, more extensive than has ever explicitly been the case before and, through the enhanced Stabilisation and Association Process (SAP) conditionality agreed at Thessaloniki in June 2003, include 'good neighbourly relations'. This condition has gained prominence over time, supplanting regional cooperation in the EU's frameworks for accession negotiations with Croatia, Montenegro and Serbia (see, for example, Conference on Accession to the European Union – Croatia 2005: point 13). In all cases, the EU insists that candidates undertake to resolve any border disputes in conformity with the principle of peaceful settlement and, where necessary, submit to the compulsory jurisdiction of the International Court of Justice. Concerns over outstanding border disputes between Western Balkan states suggest that the attention given to this criterion is only likely to increase (ibid.).

As for increased thresholds for compliance, it is no longer the case that candidates wait until accession before having to be in a position to implement the *acquis* on accession; they need to have a proven track record of compliance before accession negotiations can be closed. Benchmarks based on 'the Commission's Opinion,... on subsequent Regular Reports and in particular on information obtained by the Commission during screening' have to be met before a chapter in the accession negotiations can be provisionally closed. Such benchmarks may also be laid down 'where appropriate', for the opening of each chapter (for example, ibid.: point 26). In all instances, decisions on whether the benchmark has been met are taken by the Council acting unanimously. With the opening of negotiations with Montenegro, there are also 'interim benchmarks' for the chapters on 'Judiciary and fundamental rights' and 'Justice, freedom and security' (Conference on Accession to the European Union – Montenegro 2012: point 41). These chapters automatically have opening benchmarks. To close these chapters, 'solid track records of reform implementation' will be required (ibid.). Securing the opening of accession negotiations, making progress in them and ultimately closing them are all tougher processes than during previous enlargements. They have also become tougher still as the process and requirements have been adapted since Croatia's accession negotiations.

Enlargement conditionality has never been static; it has evolved. So, the shifts just mentioned, whether in terms of the scope or timing or intensity of conditionality, are not surprising. Accession continues, however, to become an even more demanding process for candidates to negotiate. What has also become apparent in the EU's handling of the integration and membership aspirations of the Western Balkan states is the EU's willingness to insist on conditions being met much earlier and with increasing frequency on the road to association via the Stabilisation and Association Agreements (SAA) and then ultimately to membership. Each Western Balkan state's attempt to secure a SAA and see it enter into force has been dominated by the need to meet conditions laid down by the EU. Serbia's experience stands out. Not only were the SAA negotiations protracted due to conditionality-related issues, but the EU's insistence that Serbia fully cooperate with the ICTY delayed progress with ratification such that that SAA's entry into force did not take place until September 2013, almost four-and-a-half years after it was signed in April 2009. A second striking feature of the EU's application of conditionality in the Western Balkan context concerns the unprecedented link that is made, formally at least, between consideration of an application for membership and implementation of existing contractual obligations. Evidence of a 'satisfactory track record' in implementing SAA obligations 'including trade-related provisions' has been deemed by the European Council as 'an essential element for the EU to consider any membership application' (Council of the European Union 2006a: point 8, 2012: point 34).[4] We have therefore a criterion even for applying that has not existed before. Moreover, progress in accession negotiations once opened is, according to successive accession negotiating frameworks, conditional not only on the fulfillment of SAA obligations. In the case of Croatia, 'implementation of the European Partnership, as regularly revised' was also required (Conference on Accession to the European Union – Croatia 2005: point 13). For Montenegro and Serbia, 'addressing areas of weakness identified in the Commission's Opinion', a much lengthier document, is required (Conference on Accession to the European Union – Montenegro 2012: point 24; Conference on Accession to the European Union – Serbia 2014: point 23).

Also striking is the increasingly fragmented nature of the accession process. In the case of eastern enlargement, there were relatively few formal EU gate-keeping or veto points and so, beyond the decision to open and subsequently close accession negotiations, progress from application through Commission opinion to negotiations and ratification, and ultimately accession was relatively smooth. Indeed, the process was relatively seamless, at least in the case of the 2004 enlargement, with no state's progress being held up. By contrast, the Western Balkan states are faced with a far more bureaucratic multi-stage process. Membership applications are no longer automatically forwarded as a matter of course by the Council to the Commission for its opinion; instead Member States have forced delays. The granting of candidate status does not automatically follow a positive opinion from the Commission; instead it can be made conditional on specific actions being taken. Neither a positive opinion nor candidate status automatically leads to the opening of accession negotiations; instead Member States, most notably in the case of Greece – and to a degree Bulgaria, regarding Macedonia – have demonstrated an unabashed willingness to veto progress towards negotiations. Despite the negotiations being recommended by the Commission in 2009, they are still to be opened.[5]

Moreover, once accession negotiations commence, there is much greater formality surrounding decisions on whether or not to open and later close negotiating chapters. The adoption of new opening and now, since the opening of negotiations with Montenegro, interim benchmarks reflects not only increased monitoring,[6] but also greater technical and potentially politically inspired prescription, and provides increased opportunities to find fault in a candidate's preparations and delay or block progress. Furthermore, considerations of the benchmarks and assessments of whether candidates meet them or not have become increasingly politicized moments in negotiations, with Member States being far more vociferous in expressing their views as to whether candidates have met conditions or not. Progress in negotiations has also been made conditional on additional public assessments. In Croatia's case, the closure of negotiations was only possible after the Commission had produced in March 2011 an interim report on reforms in the field of Judiciary and Fundamental Rights (European Commission 2011a). The focus of the report was also symptomatic of the increasing attention being placed by the EU on key 'problematic' issues, i.e. the cross-cutting issues of judicial and administrative capacity and in particular anti-corruption initiatives and the maintenance of the rule of law. Their prominence has been institutionalized through the incorporation of an unprecedented equilibrium clause in the negotiating frameworks adopted by the EU for negotiations with Montenegro and Serbia. Henceforth the issues will be addressed from the outset with Chapter 23 (judiciary and fundamental rights) and Chapter 24 (justice, freedom and security) being 'tackled early in the negotiations to allow maximum time to establish the necessary legislation, institutions, and solid track records of implementation before the negotiations are closed' (Conference on Accession to the European Union – Montenegro 2012: point 42). In addition, the equilibrium clause requires the Commission to propose withholding recommendations to open and/or close other negotiating chapters should progress under Chapters 23 or 24 'significantly lag behind progress in the negotiations overall'. It is then for the Member States in the Council to decide by qualified majority and to set out the conditions to lift the measures taken (ibid.: point 25).

Engagement

The EU's comparatively weaker commitment to enlargement in the case of the Western Balkan states, coupled with its increasingly demanding conditionality requirements, have undoubtedly led to a more technocratic approach to further enlargement and one less driven by a sense of political necessity or opportunity, but nevertheless more politicized as more veto points – or 'conditionality checkpoints' (Vachudova 2014: 133) – are introduced and exploited. All the same, the EU cannot be criticized for providing less support to the Western Balkan states in meeting their integration and membership objectives than was the case with the CEE states. In fact, the opposite is the case. Whereas in handling the aspirations of the CEE states, the EU found itself dealing with relatively stable and generally uncontested states, reacting to developments, and having to develop often entirely new mechanisms, structures and processes, in engaging with the Western Balkan states, it finds itself faced with often fragile and consolidated states yet with an extensive toolkit for integration to hand. It also has experience, though this can be a double-edged sword as far as the Western Balkan states are concerned. On the one hand, it has ensured an earlier and far more proactive engagement in identifying and seeking to address reform needs, setting out the requirements for progress in relations, regular assessments and reporting, and providing financial assistance and advice. On the other hand, it has led to thresholds for compliance with conditions being raised; greater scrutiny of progress and a clear reluctance to (over-)commit or make hasty promises. It has also led the EU to focus on the states of the Western Balkans individually and so pursue a far more differentiated approach to their integration rather than develop relations with them *en bloc*. Consequently, a 'big bang' Western Balkan enlargement to match the 2004–2007 eastern enlargement of the EU has never seriously been a realistic option.

Since 1999 and the launch of the SAP, each of the Western Balkan states has been involved with the EU in a structured process involving specific conditions that have to be met, regular assessments of progress, the development of contractual relations, involvement in programmes, financial assistance and political dialogue. In effect, all the elements of the pre-accession *and* accession processes developed for the CEE states in the 1990s have been extended to the Western Balkan states (Phinnemore 2013). Progress in establishing and upgrading contractual relations has, however, not been uniform and in some cases very slow. Whereas Croatia and Macedonia were relatively quick in securing SAAs – they signed their agreements in 2001 and within almost a year of opening negotiations – others have taken much longer. The period from signature to entry into force of Serbia's SAA was almost five-and-a-half years. Bosnia and Herzegovina' SAA, which was signed two months after Serbia's, has still not entered into force. However, SAAs have been concluded (except with Kosovo); and their content has expanded in line with the EU's *acquis* such that the more recent examples are far more detailed agreements than the Europe Agreements signed with the CEE states. Each of the Western Balkan states has a European Partnership – modelled on the Accession Partnerships the EU developed for the CEE states once the accession process had been launched in 1998 – and in all cases these have been revised. These European Partnerships were first established in 2004, thus before most Western Balkan states had submitted their membership applications and certainly before any had commenced accession negotiations.[7] Most had not even concluded their SAA negotiations. Also, from an even earlier stage in the development of relations, in 2000 'Twinning' – the EU's programme for assisting states in their efforts to strengthen administrative and institutional capacities in preparation for membership – was extended to the Western Balkan states. The first Twinning projects with the CEE states had occurred only in 1998.

This earlier and more proactive engagement was also evident in the annual Stabilisation and Association Reports monitoring the progress individual Western Balkans states were making in addressing the priorities of the SAP that the Commission started issuing in April 2002. Formal monitoring of the CEE states once again only started after the accession process had been launched in 1998.[8] Annual reporting is still in place, although each state is issued with a less-SAP oriented and more integration- and accession-focused 'Progress Report'. For those currently involved in accession negotiations, and building on the experience of negotiating with Croatia, 'Action Plans' for addressing opening benchmarks are adopted based on 'substantial guidance' from the Commission (Conference on Accession to the European Union – Montenegro 2012: point 42). Additionally, there are twice-yearly Commission reports to the Council on the state of progress on Chapters 23 and 24 allowing problems to be identified and, where appropriate, updated benchmarks as well as new and amended action plans and 'other corrective measures' to be adopted (Conference on Accession to the European Union – Montenegro 2012: point 43). Finally, there is the EU's financial commitment to the Western Balkans. Since 1999, this has evolved from the OBNOVA (1996–2000) through CARDS (2000–2006) to the Instrument for Pre-Accession Assistance (2007–2013 and 2014–2020).

The changed – and changing – political context of EU enlargement

Alongside increased conditionality, the EU's more proactive engagement with the states is clearly designed to ensure that candidates are better prepared for membership than has been the case in some instances in the past and so ensure smoother enlargements. Whether the strategy will deliver remains to be seen. As Vachudova (2014: 133) notes, EU conditionality can lack both consistency and clarity. It is also often contested in the Western Balkan states (Noutcheva 2012). Moreover, when considering what drives enlargement, consideration has to be given not only to what progress candidates and potential candidates are making in meeting criteria, but also the shifting views and preferences of and in the EU's Member States. The position of the European Commission and the European Parliament also need to be considered.

The legacies of enlargements past

Clearly, as the discussion so far shows, continuities and changes in the EU's approach to enlargement demonstrate that lessons from past enlargements have been learnt regarding how the EU should enlarge. The assumed reference point tends to be the 2007 enlargement to include Bulgaria and Romania. The Croatian experience of negotiating accession bears this out. For example, the EU's evident desire to avoid having to establish another Cooperation and Verification Mechanism (CVM) to address continued shortcomings in promoting judicial reforms and addressing corruption – and in the case of Bulgaria, organized crime – ensured a much more intense set of negotiations, particularly where Croatia was having to implement reforms in the field of judiciary and regarding fundamental rights. The continued existence of the CVM seven years after Bulgaria and Romania acceded is an embarrassment to the EU, as is the fact that the Commission in early 2014 was still unable to report sufficient and sustained progress in either country.[9] Such embarrassments are ones to be avoided.

However, to focus exclusively on the Bulgarian and Romanian cases is to miss a variety of other ways in which the Western Balkan experience of integration with and accession to the EU has the shadows of past enlargements cast over it. The 'big bang' enlargement posed major challenges for and had a significant impact on the EU's institutions, its politics and policies. The national politics of existing Member States have also been affected as the merits, size and direction of eastern enlargement have been openly questioned, either directly or indirectly, as part of the increasingly critical debate on the actions, purpose and future of the EU, brought to the fore by the popular French and Dutch 'no' votes on the Constitutional Treaty in 2005 and fuelled by economic recession generally and the Eurozone crisis in particular. Announcements of the impending 'death' of enlargement (e.g. Rachman 2006) may have been premature, but the last decade has undoubtedly heralded the end of any permissive consensus on enlargement. Instead, enlargement has been presented, in some quarters at least, as a key source for many contemporary social and economic challenges facing the EU and its Member States. Such a context, with the experience of the 2007 enlargement mixed in, is far from conducive for further enlargement. 'Enlargement fatigue' – an ill-defined concept masking opposition and scepticism in the sense that the EU needs to catch its breath after eastern enlargement – appears to have enveloped the EU.

Existing commitments regarding the Western Balkans – and Turkey – have nevertheless been upheld. However, as earlier brief discussions of the EU's 'renewed consensus' on enlargement have indicated, the EU has become far more cautious in its approach to enlargement since 2004. Promoted by the Commission (e.g. Rehn 2005a), the stress is now on ensuring a far more rigorous and carefully managed process where conditionality is respected, rationales are communicated to voters, and due attention is paid to the EU's own 'absorption' – or 'integration' – capacity. Only by addressing these issues will enlargement retain – or regain – support. Furthermore, as successive Commission strategy papers have argued, there has been a need to 'improve the quality of the enlargement process' (European Commission 2006: 6; 2007: 4; 2008: 2). Consequently, there has been the introduction of the benchmarks in the negotiation frameworks adopted for Croatia, Montenegro and Serbia (as well as Turkey and Iceland); the option to suspend negotiations has been made explicit; and a much greater emphasis has been placed on candidates possessing the capacity to uphold the rule of law, practice good governance, ensure judicial reforms are implemented and corruption and organized crime are fought and rooted out prior to accession. A further departure from existing practice has been to declare the negotiations an 'open-ended process whose outcome cannot be guaranteed beforehand' even if the 'shared objective ... is accession' (e.g. Conference on Accession to the European Union – Serbia 2014: 20). While this, again, makes explicit a feature of negotiations that has always been implicit, it clearly signals that non-accession is an option that is being contemplated.

The reference to 'open-ended' negotiations is a legacy not of eastern enlargement but of the decision in 2005 to open accession negotiations with Turkey.[10] The shadow of those negotiations can also be seen in the Commission's instance that Western Balkan states solve their border disputes 'as early as possible' and do not allow bilateral issues to 'hold up the accession process' (European Commission 2011b: 24). The impact of Cyprus' accession on progress in negotiations with Turkey has proved painful for many EU members to accept.

Prioritizing the internal over the external: managing internal crises

The 'fatigue' that has ostensibly shrouded EU enlargement for the last decade contains within it the lingering concern that further enlargement runs the risk of undermining the functioning of the EU. For some, the concern is more a fear, a fear that further enlargement could lead to paralysis. Such doom-laden prognoses have been a recurrent feature of past enlargements, and if anything the experience of the eastern enlargement has done much to dispel such fears; the EU has continued to function, and no worse than before. At the macro level, the Treaty of Lisbon was concluded and the EU has managed to respond, albeit more slowly and in a too overly piecemeal manner than some would have wished, to the Eurozone crisis and seemingly saved the Euro. However, the long-established widening-deepening debate lingers on, and the EU post-2004 has been keen to ensure that its own 'integration capacity' forms an essential part of the 'renewed consensus' on enlargement.

As we have argued elsewhere, the EU's concern with its own integration capacity' is not new; rather it is an oft-forgotten element of the Copenhagen criteria: 'the EU's capacity to absorb new members while maintaining the momentum of integration' (İçener and Phinnemore 2006). For the Commission, it is imperative that the pace of enlargement is linked with the EU's absorption capacity, as '[t]he Union has to ensure it can maintain its capacity to act and decide according to a fair balance within its institutions; respect budgetary limits; and implement common policies that function well and achieve their objectives' (European Commission 2005: 3). Consequently, would-be Member States, as noted, have to be politically and institutionally prepared to assume and implement effectively the obligations of membership from the date of their accession. Moreover, and following established practice in addressing the widening-deepening issue, the clear preference is to ensure the internal development of the EU before admitting more states. This has been evident as the EU has sought to address the Eurozone crisis; enlargement, understandably given the fundamental nature of the Eurozone crisis, is a secondary concern. As Grabbe (2013: 111) has commented: 'In the crisis-ridden Union, obsessed with saving the euro, the sense of historical duty to reunite Europe and overcome the legacies of war has been overtaken by a rush to *sauve qui peut*'.[11]

A further internal consequence of the Eurozone crisis are the discussions it has triggered on increased differentiated integration, multi-level EU membership and alternatives to EU enlargement. Part of this flows from the deepening of integration within and around the Eurozone, how the interests of non-Eurozone Member States can be accommodated, and how the EU should be structured around an increasingly integrated Eurozone core. Part also flows from doubts raised by the internal UK debate on its future within – or outside – the EU. All this distracts the EU from enlargement and raises questions about the credibility of the prospect of accession for candidates and potential candidates alike. Calls have been heard for a 'pause' in enlargement after Croatia, but there have also been calls not to push the Western Balkans to 'the periphery of the periphery' (Bechev 2012) as the EU continues to focus on its own internal problems. Champions of enlargement do exist, hence Fouéré's call to 'inject momentum' into the process for the Western Balkans enlargement (Fouéré 2013). Clearly, though, there is a tension between maintaining the momentum of the EU's internal integration and maintaining the momentum of enlargement. The former, as ever, is being prioritized over the latter. Consequently, the membership prospects of the Western Balkan states will be shaped by how the EU reconciles its deepening and widening processes.

Shifts in Member States' preferences

Central to determining how the deepening process develops and how the tension between deepening and widening will be resolved are the EU's Member States. It is their preferences that will obviously play a decisive role in how and when – pessimists might add 'if' – enlargement proceeds. No Member States openly opposes further enlargement. However, in the post-eastern enlargement context, Member States enthusiasm for further enlargement has waned. Turkey has suffered the most with suggestions that it be offered some form of privileged partnership instead of membership. It has even been suggested that a similar offer might be made to the Western Balkan states (Krasniqi and Beunderman 2006). In general, however, EU Member States have stuck to the principle of *pacta sunt servanda* not to undermine the credibility of the enlargement process, as the EU's most successful foreign policy tool. Yet Member States' declining interest in further enlargement is reflected in their preference for a more gradual process with stricter conditionality and more veto points.

As already noted, conditionality is evolving and often at the behest of the Member States as they reflect on the success or otherwise of past enlargements. Indeed, Hillion (2010) makes the case for a 'creeping nationalisation' of enlargement policy with Member States becoming more assertive in directing change. The evidence can be found in: (1) the introduction of benchmarks in the accession negotiations; (2) changes in the application procedure; (3) a greater emphasis on integration capacity as an 'emergency brake' on enlargement; and (4) stricter national rules on enlargement. The first and third have already been noted. The second relates to the willingness of Member States to block a Council decision requesting the Commission prepare an opinion on an application. A first example of this was Germany insisting on consulting its parliament before supporting a Council decision referring Albania's application in 2009 to the Commission. More recently, it took the Council ten months to pass Serbia's application later in 2009 to the Commission. No longer is the forwarding of applications automatic. The issue, however, is essentially one of delay.

More serious, at least potentially, are the stricter rules that some Member States have adopted for dealing with enlargement domestically. The most prominent example is the amendment to Article 88 of the French Constitution such that henceforth '[a]ny Government Bill authorizing the ratification of a treaty pertaining to the accession of a state to the European Union shall be submitted to referendum by the President of the Republic'. So, unless there is 'a motion adopted in identical terms in each [chamber of the French Parliament] by a three-fifths majority', the ratification of all future treaties governing accessions to the EU will be put to a vote of the French people. Less dramatic have been suggestions that supermajorities might be needed in, for example, the Netherlands for the ratification of future accession treaties. In other Member States, for example Germany, the emphasis so far has been on establishing more regular consultation of the national parliament in decisions on enlargement. As *The Economist* (2013) commented: the Bundestag now 'holds a key to the future of the western Balkans'. In all three cases, the executive's control over enlargement decisions is being weakened, increasing uncertainty within the process.

In addition to such 'creeping nationalisation', the last decade has seen important shifts in Member States' preferences regarding enlargement. Leading champions of eastern enlargement have become less vocal in their support for continuing swiftly with the process. Germany stands out. Successive governments led by Angela Merkel have adopted a very cautious approach to further enlargement, most particularly towards Turkey, but also regarding the Western Balkans. It is not the case that Germany opposes further enlargement into the region, it is more that it is has no interest in driving the process. In part, this is because there are more pressing concerns, not least the Eurozone crisis. Equally, German interests in the Western Balkans simply do not compare with those it had in Poland, the Czech Republic and Hungary joining the EU. Among other champions, the United Kingdom has become far more measured in its support for enlargement, primarily because of concerns about migration. On the other hand, the EU's Nordic Member States have remained supportive of further enlargement. Even with Italy and Greece offering vocal support to the accession of the Western Balkan states, there is not a critical mass of states in support of moving with any speed.

The last decade has also seen Member States willing to block individual applicants' progress towards accession. Although the Commission has repeatedly warned that bilateral issues should not hold up the accession process, this is exactly what has happened. Slovenia blocked accession negotiations with Croatia between December 2008 and October 2009 due to a dispute over Slovenian access to the Adriatic. It also threatened to block ratification of the Treaty of Accession because of a dispute over the former Ljubljanska Bank. Greece has for more than five years been blocking the opening of accession negotiations with Macedonia due to a long-standing dispute over the latter's name. Elsewhere, the Netherlands blocked Serbia's progress with the SAA owing to concerns that the Belgrade government was not fully cooperating with the ICTY. Clearly, Member States are feeling free to express their reservations and opposition and to act accordingly. The same was not the case with eastern enlargement; arguably because the sense of historical opportunity was great, Germany was actively supporting the process, and advocates of enlargement were deploying rhetorical action to shame those less supportive into allowing the process to progress. A decade-and-a-half on, the narrative is very different, Germany no longer leads, and there is scant evidence of rhetorical action being deployed.

Shifts in public opinion

A further reason for Member States governments being less vocal in support of enlargement is that the permissive consensus on enlargement has gone and public opinion, at least in some parts of the EU, has become distinctly sceptical about, and in some cases hostile to, further enlargement. This is also reflected in government positions. More generally, Member States governments are being increasingly held to account for their positions on EU issues and so are obliged to accommodate public sentiment. This is particularly the case where national parliaments have seen their role in monitoring enlargement increase and where, as in France, a referendum may be required to ratify the treaty of accession. Turkey has suffered the most as Member States governments react to public opinion. The Western Balkan states have not been immune either. In 2013, 52 per cent of respondents across the EU expressed opposition to further enlargement (European Commission 2013: QA17.3). A decade earlier, in 2003, opposition to enlargement stood at only 36 per cent (in EU15), with support for the EU being open to further enlargement at 61 per cent (European Commission 2003: 2.1. and 2.2). When broken down, the figures for 2013 should cause alarm for advocates of enlargement given the levels of opposition in a number of Member States: Austria – 76 per cent; France – 70 per cent; Germany – 69 per cent; Finland – 65 per cent; Netherlands – 64 per cent; Italy – 59 per cent (ibid.). It is understandable with such opposition that there are few Member States willing to champion the cause. And without a significant reduction in opposition, both generally and in particular in the states highlighted, the EU is likely to remain seriously constrained in justifying any attempt to quicken the tempo of enlargement. With such opposition, emphasis will no doubt be placed on demonstrating that enlargement can only involve Western Balkan states able demonstrably to assume the obligations of membership. Given the domestic challenges that the states face and the strict and onerous conditionality the EU now applies, a lengthy process awaits.

Shifts in the Commission

A final shift to note concerns the position of the Commission. Although formally its role in enlargement is limited to issuing an opinion, in practice, it has come to play a pivotal role in managing enlargement through a combination of monitoring, strategy and negotiating roles. In the case of eastern enlargement, it proved to be an influential policy advocate and agenda-setter with its progress reports, recommendations, enlargement strategy papers and its role in the coordination of accession negotiations. The political priorities of the College of Commissioners and the Commissioner responsible for enlargement also played an important role in influencing the pace and direction of enlargement. Günter Verheugen, the first Commissioner for enlargement (1999–2004), prioritized political and strategic considerations as much as – and on some occasions over – conditionality and technical issues. The then Commission President, Romano Prodi, shared the same vision and pushed for achieving eastern enlargement.

By contrast, enlargement has not been a priority for either Commission led by José Manuel Barroso (2004–2010, 2010–2014). The focus even prior to the Eurozone crisis was economic reform. Moreover, Verheugen's successors as Commissioner for Enlargement have been far more guarded, less political and more technical in their handling of the enlargement dossier. This was certainly the case with Olli Rehn (2004–2010), who stressed careful management and so focused on the 'renewed consensus' with its consolidation of existing commitments, stricter conditionality, communications strategy and promotion of the EU's integration capacity. Within negotiations and in assessing applications, there was an evident shift in attention to the technical with an increasing focus on the administrative and technical preparedness of applicants to assume the obligations of membership prior to accession. Rehn (2005b) defined his role as being 'to ensure that any European state getting closer to the Union can not only take the benefits but also cope with obligations' and advised the Western Balkan countries 'to fulfil the conditions to the letter' to guarantee their place in the European family.

Rehn's successor, Štefan Füle, has proved to be as focused on emphasizing the 'renewed consensus'. However, he has been more alert to the need to maintain the momentum of enlargement into the Western Balkans. In 2010, he offered 'a combination of conditionality in terms of well defined technical process with the political steering' and promised 'to create appropriate political conditions and incentives if necessary' (Füle 2010). More recently, he has sought to shift attention away from the EU's own enlargement fatigue to the 'reform fatigue' in the Western Balkan states, especially with regard to the rule of law, regional cooperation and meeting the economic criteria for membership (Füle 2012; 2013). He has also pushed alternative 'carrots' for reform in the Western Balkans, notably visa-free travel. And under his watch, Croatia has acceded to the EU. The fact remains, however, that neither Füle nor Rehn compare to Verheugen in terms of their vocal advocacy of enlargement. With Barroso at the helm, the Commission has not been the champion of enlargement it was under Prodi. It appears to have been content to pull back on the throttle and put enlargement on automatic pilot.

Conclusion

The accession of Croatia to the EU on 1 July 2013 was rightly heralded as proof that EU enlargement had not come to an end with the accession of Bulgaria and Romania in 2007. The EU may have been suffering from an ill-defined 'enlargement fatigue' for the last decade, but it was not giving up on what it itself had long been proclaiming as its most successful foreign policy tool. Moreover, the pace of enlargement may have significantly slowed down, but Croatia joining the EU was proof of the European Council's 'determination' – reiterated at Thessaloniki in 2003 – 'to fully and effectively support the European perspective of the Western Balkan countries, which will become an integral part of the EU' (Council of the European Union 2003b: point 40). Enlargement into the Western Balkans might be proving to be a drawn out and lengthy process, but it is nevertheless a process.

One cannot escape the fact, however, that dynamics underpinning the process of EU enlargement into the Western Balkans do differ from those that drove eastern enlargement. Similar factors are at play; just as contentwise the processes share considerable similarities. Member State preferences remain key; commitment and conditionality play important roles; and the Commission remains an ever-present institutional actor in the process. Member State enthusiasm for enlargement has waned, fuelled by popular disaffection with the EU generally and scepticism about the merits of enlargement; the language of the EU's commitment to enlargement remains measured, cautious, unambitious; conditionality is wider in scope and more intense, with thresholds higher and more demanding; and the Commission is no longer the pioneering champion of enlargement it was in the early 2000s.

As a consequence, further enlargement into the Western Balkans is set to be driven far less by a political imperative on the part of the EU to enlarge. Instead it will be determined more by developments in the Western Balkan applicants. The focus post-2007 is on applicants proving their preparedness for membership; conditionality and demonstrating proven compliance with EU requirements have moved centre stage. The context for enlargement may change; a persuasive narrative urging the EU to admit its current applications may emerge. For the moment, however, conditionality is the central determinant of the process. When the EU next enlarges and to whom will be determined primarily by when the EU decides that an applicant state meets the criteria for admission. Even then, however, politics may intervene. Enlargement is not simply a technical process. Political decisions are needed. And here, the post-2007 experience of the EU clearly indicates that more voices want to be heard in those decisions and more opportunities have been created to accommodate them, increasing the possibilities for progress to be blocked. The EU may be investing heavily in assisting states in their preparations for accession, the process may have become more detailed and refined; but it cannot be taken for granted that enlargement will follow. The EU remains committed to enlargement. However, lessons have been learnt; for the EU, enlargement is not something that can, should or will be rushed.

Notes

1 Interestingly, the Commission's early Enlargement Strategy Papers evaluated the Western Balkans as a neighboring region alongside the Newly Independent States and the Mediterranean countries until 2003 (European Commission 2000, 2001, 2002), suggesting that the Commission did not consider the Western Balkans as part of enlargement process despite the European Council's earlier references to accession and potential candidacy.
2 In December 2013, for example, the Council conclusions declared that

> [t]en years ago at the Thessaloniki Summit of 2003, the EU reiterated its unequivocal support to the European perspective of the Western Balkan countries. These countries will become an integral part of the EU, once they meet the established criteria.
> (Council of the European Union 2013: point 2)

The previous year's statement did not even refer back to Thessaloniki. Instead it noted that

> [t]he accession of Croatia on 1 July 2013, subject to the completion of ratification procedures, as well as the start of accession negotiations with Montenegro and the granting of candidate status to Serbia are a strong testimony that, when conditions are met, the EU delivers on its commitments, and strengthen the process of reconciliation in the Western Balkans region, demonstrating the transformative and stabilising effect of the enlargement process to the benefit of both the EU and the region as a whole.
> (Council of the European Union 2012: point 2)

Note the use of 'deliver on commitments' rather than reference to membership/accession.
3 A notable exception is the speech given by the President of the Commission José Manuel Barroso in 2011. In his speech, Barroso (2011) stated that 'this reunification will not be completed without the Western Balkans as part of the Union'. It should be noted that the Commission's enlargement strategy papers and regular reports on the Western Balkan countries do not include the same argument, i.e. 'not being completed without the Western Balkans'.

4 The requirement did not stop either the Council agreeing to forward Serbia's membership application of 22 December 2009 to the Commission or the Commission issuing its opinion on 14 October 2011. However, the European Council only agreed in December 2013, following the SAA's entry into force three months previously, to launch accession negotiations with Serbia in January 2014.
5 On the name dispute, see Tziampiris (2012).
6 Interim benchmarks are designed to 'specifically target, as appropriate, the adoption of legislation and the establishment and strengthening of administrative structures and of an intermediate track record and will be closely linked to actions and milestones in the implementation of the action plans' (Conference on Accession to the European Union – Montenegro 2012: point 42).
7 Croatia and Macedonia are the exceptions. They submitted their membership applications in 2003 and 2004 respectively.
8 Of symbolic importance – and underlining a residual commitment to enlargement – the reports were included from 2005 in the Commission's annual 'Enlargement Strategy' paper.
9 See, for example, the conclusion that reform in Bulgaria was 'not yet sufficient' and remained 'fragile' (European Commission 2014a: point 3). The report on Romania was more positive, but indicated that 'concerns about judicial independence remain and there are many examples of resistance to integrity and anti-corruption measures at political and administrative level' (European Commission 2014b: point 3). On the CVM, see Vachudova and Spendzharova (2012). In concluding negotiations with Croatia, the EU was also keen to ensure that sufficient progress had been made by Croatia such that there would be no need to include in its Treaty of Accession a delay clause as had been necessary for Bulgaria and Romania. The option existed to delay the date of accession by up to one year (see Phinnemore 2009).
10 The reference to 'open-ended' negotiations first appeared in the frameworks for negotiation with Turkey and Croatia in October 2005 and very much at the insistence of states, e.g. Austria, concerned at the prospect of Turkish accession. It has been retained in all frameworks for negotiation adopted since, despite the absence of such concerns in the other cases.
11 There is also the matter of how the Eurozone crisis has affected the Western Balkans economically. Panagiotou (2013), for example, highlights the detrimental economic impact on the region of the crisis and in particular the Greek sovereign debt crisis and points to the possibility that the EU could lose its credibility as a stability anchor.

References

Barroso, J.M. (2011) 'Western Balkans: towards a more integrated Europe', *Speech at Joint Parliamentary Meeting*, Speech/11/267, 14 April.

Bechev, D. (2012) The periphery of the periphery: The Western Balkans and the euro crisis, *ECFR Policy Brief*, 60, August, London: European Council on Foreign Relations.

Conference on Accession to the European Union – Croatia (2005) *Negotiating Framework for Croatia*, 3 October, Luxembourg (http://ec.europa.eu/enlargement/pdf/st20004_05_hr_framedoc_en.pdf).

Conference on Accession to the European Union – Montenegro (2012) *Accession Document: General EU Position – Ministerial meeting opening the Intergovernmental Conference on the Accession to the European Union (Brussels, 29 June 2012)*, AD 23/12

- LIMITE – CONF-ME2, 27 June, Brussels (http://ec.europa.eu/enlargement/pdf/st20002_05_mn_framedoc_en.pdf).
Conference on Accession to the European Union – Serbia (2014) *Accession Document: General EU Position – Ministerial meeting opening the Intergovernmental Conference on the Accession to the European Union (Brussels, 21 January 2014)*, AD 1/14 – LIMITE – CONF-RS 1, 9 January, Brussels (http://register.consilium.europa.eu/doc/srv?l=EN&t=PDF&f=AD%201%202014%20INIT).
Council of the European Union (1993) *European Council in Copenhagen: Conclusions of the presidency*, 14702/02, 21–22 June, Brussels.
Council of the European Union (1997) *Presidency Conclusions – Luxembourg European Council*, SN400/97, 12–13 December.
Council of the European Union (1999) *Presidency Conclusions – Helsinki European Council*, 00300/1/99, 10–11 December.
Council of the European Union (2000a) *Presidency Conclusions – Santa Maria Da Feira European Council*, 200/1/00, 19–20 June.
Council of the European Union (2000b) *Presidency Conclusions – Nice European Council*, 400/1/00, 7–8–9 December.
Council of the European Union (2003a) *Presidency Conclusions – Brussels European Council*, 8410/03, 20–21 March.
Council of the European Union (2003b) *Presidency Conclusions – Thessaloniki European Council*, 11638/03, 19–20 June.
Council of the European Union (2003c) *General Affairs and External Relations 2518th Meeting*, 10369/03, 16 June, Luxembourg.
Council of the European Union (2006a) *Presidency Conclusions – Brussels European Council*, 10633/06, 15–16 June.
Council of the European Union (2006b) *Presidency Conclusions – Brussels European Council*, 16879/1/06 REV1, 14–15 December.
Council of the European Union (2012) *Council Conclusions on Enlargement and Stabilisation and Association Process – 3210th General Affairs Council Meeting, Brussels, 11 December*, 11 December, Brussels.
Council of the European Union (2013) *Council Conclusions on Enlargement and Stabilisation and Association Process – General Affairs Council Meeting, Brussels, 17 December*, 17 December, Brussels.
European Commission (1992) *Europe and the challenge of enlargement: Bulletin of the European Communities*, Supplement 2/92, OOPEC, 24 June, Luxembourg.
European Commission (2000) *Enlargement Strategy Paper: Report on progress towards accession by each of the candidate countries*.
European Commission (2001) *Making a success of enlargement: Strategy Paper and Report of the European Commission on the progress towards accession by each of the candidate countries*.
European Commission (2002) *Towards the Enlarged Union: Strategy Paper and Report of the European Commission on the progress towards accession by each of the candidate countries*, COM (2002) 700 final, 9 October, Brussels.
European Commission (2003) *Eurobarometer 54*, Brussels: European Commission.
European Commission (2005) *2005 Enlargement Strategy Paper*, COM(2005) 561, 9 November, Brussels.
European Commission (2006) *Enlargement Strategy and Main Challenges 2006–2007: Including annexed special report on the EU's capacity to integrate new members*, COM(2006) 649, 8 November, Brussels.

European Commission (2007) *Enlargement Strategy and Main Challenges 2007–2008*, COM(2007) 663 final, 6 November, Brussels.
European Commission (2008) *Enlargement Strategy and Main Challenges 2008–2009*, COM(2008) 674 final, 5 November, Brussels.
European Commission (2011a), *Interim report from the Commission to the Council and the European Parliament on reforms in Croatia in the field of Judiciary and Fundamental Rights (Negotiation Chapter 23)*, COM(2011) 110, 2 March.
European Commission (2011b) *Enlargement Strategy and Main Challenges 2011–2012*, COM(2011) 666, 12 October, Brussels.
European Commission (2013) *Eurobarometer 80: Tables of Results – Public Opinion in the European Union*, Brussels: European Commission.
European Commission (2014a) *On Progress in Bulgaria under the Co-operation and Verification Mechanism*, COM(2014) 36 final, 22 January, Brussels.
European Commission (2014b) *On Progress in Romania under the Co-operation and Verification Mechanism*, COM(2014) 37 final, 22 January, Brussels.
European Council (2012) *European Council – 13/14 December 2012 – Conclusions*, EUCO 205/12, 20 December, Brussels.
European Council (2013) *European Council – 19/20 December 2013 – Conclusions*, EUCO 217/13, 20 December, Brussels.
Fouéré, E. (2013) 'Thessaloniki ten years on: Injecting momentum into the enlargement process for the Western Balkans', *CEPS Commentary*, 16 May, Brussels.
Füle, Š. (2010) *Address to EU-Western Balkans High-Level Conference*, SPEECH/10/289, 2 June, Sarajevo.
Füle, Š. (2012) *Address to the 4th Western Balkan Civil Society Forum*, SPEECH/12/862, 26 November, Zagreb.
Füle, Š. (2013) *The future of enlargement on the background of the crisis: Speech given at the conference '10 Years after Thessaloniki: An appraisal of the EU perspective and challenges in the Western Balkans'*, 24 May, Dublin.
Grabbe H. (2013) 'Conclusions', in E. Prifti (ed.), *The European Future of the Western Balkans: Thessaloniki@10 (2003–2013)*, Paris: European Union Institute for Security Studies, pp. 109–113.
Hillion, C. (2010) *The Creeping Nationalisation of the EU Enlargement Policy*, SIEPS Report 6, November, Stockholm, Swedish Institute for European Policy Studies.
çener, E. and D. Phinnemore (2006) 'Enlargement and the European Union's absorption capacity: 'Oft-forgotten' condition or additional obstacle to membership?', *Insight Turkey*, 8(3), pp. 37–43.
çener, E., D. Papadimitriou and D. Phinnemore (2010) 'Continuity and change in the European Union's approach to enlargement: Central and Eastern Europe and Turkey compared', *Southeast European and Black Sea Studies*, 10(2), pp. 207–223.
Krasniqi, E. and M. Beunderman (2006) 'Merkel moots "privileged partnership" for Balkans', *EUObserver*, March 17 (http://euobserver.com/enlargement/21163).
Noutcheva, G. (2012) *European Foreign Policy and the Challenges of Balkan Accession: Conditionality, Legitimacy and Compliance*, London: Routledge.
Panagiotou, R. (2013) 'The Greek Crisis as a crisis of EU enlargement: How will the Western Balkans be affected?', *Southeast European and Black Sea Studies*, 13(1), pp. 89–104.

Phinnemore, D. (2009) 'From negotiations to accession: Lessons from the 2007 Enlargement', *Perspectives on European Politics and Society*, 10(2), pp. 240–253.

Phinnemore, D. (2013) 'The Stabilization and Association Process: A framework for European Union enlargement?', in A. Elbasani (ed.), *European Integration and Transformation in the Western Balkans: Europeanization or Business as Usual?*, Abingdon: Routledge, pp. 22–35.

Rachman, G. (2006) 'The death of enlargement', *Washington Quarterly*, 29(3), pp. 51–56.

Rehn, O. (2005a) *The Plan 'C' for enlargement: Speech given to European Parliament Foreign Affairs Committee*, SPEECH/05/369, 21 June, Brussels.

Rehn, O. (2005b) *The Balkans, Europe and Reconciliation: Speech given in the debate in Sarajevo University*, SPEECH/05/434, 11 July, Sarajevo.

Schimmelfennig, F. (2001) 'The community trap: Liberal norms, rhetorical action, and the Eastern enlargement of the European Union', *International Organization*, 55(1), pp. 47–80.

The Economist (2013) 'Eastern approaches: Germany and the Balkans: The pivot in the Balkans' EU ambitions', 26 February (www.economist.com/blogs/easternapproaches/2013/02/germany-and-balkans).

Tziampiris, A. (2012) 'The Macedonian name dispute and European Union accession', *Southeast European and Black Sea Studies*, 12(1), pp. 153–171.

Vachudova, M.A. (2014) 'EU leverage and national interests in the Balkans: The puzzles of enlargement ten years on', *JCMS: Journal of Common Market Studies*, 52(1), pp. 122–38.

Vachudova, M.A. and Spendzharova, A. (2012) 'The EU's Cooperation and Verification Mechanism: Fighting corruption in Bulgaria and Romania after EU accession', *SIEPS European Policy Analysis*, 1, March, Stockholm (www.sieps.se/sites/default/files/2012_1epa%20EN_A4.pdf).

Zagreb Summit (2000) *Final Declaration*, 24 November.

Part II
Case studies

4 The normative power of the EU in Croatia
Mixed results

Sanja Badanjak

Introduction

In July 2011, Belgium was 13 months into its government formation crisis. At that time, an event was organized in Brussels by the European Movement, with the aim of introducing Croatia as the next member of the European Union (EU). One of the speakers was the Croatian ambassador to Belgium, and during the Q&A session that followed his talk, he was asked about the state of democracy in the country he represented. His droll reply greatly amused the audience as he stated that Croatia is a democracy just like theirs, a country that does everything like Belgium, except for doing it all a bit faster.

The entertainment value of the statement notwithstanding, one cannot help but wonder whether he was right. It has been nearly 23 years since Croatia's independence, and 18 since the effective end of the war – is this enough for transition to stable democracy? More pertinently, has there been an impact of the EU on Croatia in that period? Has the EU been successful at utilizing its normative power (Bicchi 2006; Lerch and Schwellnus 2006; Manners 2002, 2006; Noutcheva 2009) in the case of Croatia? Most importantly, has the change achieved been sustainable, and would the effects continue even after EU accession? The answer to the first set of questions is in the affirmative: the EU has indeed had an effect on political and social changes in Croatia. There are at least three areas in which one can find the impact of the EU, and more specifically the impact of its normative power: the shift in Croatian foreign policy (Jović 2006, 2009), the modernization of parts of the civil service, and an overall democratic orientation. The final question, that of sustainability of the effect and its potential for self-perpetuation, does not have not a final answer – the accession only took place in July 2013, and it remains to be seen whether Croatia will provide material for the same criticisms as its neighbors, those of decline in democratic standards in the post-accession period. In Croatia, the areas where this sustainability is most in question are those of minority rights and the problem of corruption. In this chapter, the author aims to provide a detailed answer to the questions posed above, and outline some of the areas where we may find the impact of the EU's normative power. More specifically, I argue that, in Croatia, we see at least three of the mechanisms through which the EU may affect its prospective member state, as discussed by Manners (2002: 244–245): contagion, informational diffusion, and procedural diffusion.

The chapter progresses in three sections: the first deals with the Croatian path and attitudes towards the EU, and the overall change in Croatia's domestic and foreign policy orientation; the second section discusses the areas where the normative power of the EU may be observed; the last section concludes by giving an assessment of the appropriateness of the idea of normative power of the EU for explaining some of the changes we have witnessed in Croatia in the past decades.

Croatia and the EU: a bumpy ride

The literature on the effect of the EU on former Communist countries in Central and Eastern Europe (CEE) notes that the EU has not had a consistent and identical impact on all the countries concerned (Moravcsik and Vachudova 2003; Vachudova 2004, 2009). Issues of legacies, timing, and domestic political constellations made divergence a more likely scenario than convergence. Though all the countries were coming from a communist past, the challenges before them were as different as the communisms they suffered. For Croatia, the EU was not a state-building (Chandler 2010) agent, as much as it was assisting the transformation of a fairly effective state apparatus that was already in place.

The Croatian case is, in many ways, different from those of other post-communist countries in CEE, making it less likely that the same patterns of Europeanization would appear. First, the trajectory of Yugoslav communism was somewhat different, with its relative liberalism, more or less open borders, and application of workers' self-management. These factors ought to have led to a specific set of legacies that would in turn differentiate the post-Yugoslav countries from the remainder of the region. Second, Croatia has suffered and has been otherwise involved in the Balkan wars of the 1990s, which placed completely different challenges on the political agenda. Not only has the war carried a terrible human loss, but it has also acted in conjunction with the process of transition to wreak havoc on the already enfeebled economy. The issues of political and economic transition became secondary as the war dominated all political activity, public discourse, and spending for at least the first five years of the country's independence. Third, the political outcomes of transition in Croatia differ from those in the other post-Yugoslav countries: compared to Slovenia, it was a democratic and economic laggard, but it remained ahead of the remainder of the group in terms of state consolidation and economic progress.

However, like Slovakia, Croatia is one of the countries where the EU has had a real, tangible impact (Vachudova 2004). The extent of this impact is more problematic, as there is a possibility that the Croatian case might display a reversal in democratic standards in the post-accession period. It is argued here that there are areas where the impact of the EU has indeed been tangible and sustainable. A reversal of the country's general foreign policy orientation after 1999/2000 (Jović 2006, 2009), along with a decline in adversarial foreign policy, and an increased awareness of certain social problems, such as corruption, fit into this category, as does the process of modernization and the EU-ization of the civil service. An example of an area where there has been less success is that of minority protection, including ethnic and sexual minorities. Furthermore, Noutcheva and Aydin-Düzgit (2012) note that Croatia had seen a drop in rule-of-law indicators in spite of having had a clear membership perspective.

In the past two decades, Croatian attitudes towards the EU have been ambivalent. While government policy had decidedly changed at the turn of the century, the positions of citizens did not follow as vigorously. While the referendum concerning joining the EU saw an overwhelming majority of citizens voting in favour, the public opinion polls have been less favourable. In a recent Eurobarometer survey, Croatian citizens split neatly into three roughly same-sized groups: those who think that EU membership is a good thing, a bad thing, and those who do not know whether it is one or the other (European Commission 2013: 67–68).

A general European orientation is something that Croatian citizens have held for a long time, an orientation that was present even before the collapse of communism. In 1989, for example, Croatian students lamented the state that Croatia and Yugoslavia were in, worrying that it would not be adequate to allow the country back into 'Europe' (Blanuša and Šiber 2008). Opinion polls conducted on the eve of the first multi-party elections showed citizens placing European integration as the third-ranked problem that the country needs to deal with (Blanuša and Šiber 2008: 120). Those growing up in that period could not escape the constant debates about this return to Europe, along with the notion that they would only be reclaiming the spot that was unfairly lost after World War II.[1] Regardless of the Croatian situation, the dominant belief was that countries that were on the eastern side of the Iron Curtain were, in fact, historically wronged, taken off their natural course (Judt 2006). In that regard, the beliefs of Croatian citizens were similar to those of their neighbors in CEE.

The Europe to which Croatia belonged was not clearly defined, a situation that made it possible for political elites in Croatia to adopt a vague and malleable definition as the dominant one in the political discourse in the 1990s. Croatia's Europeanness was not something that was questioned, even as the EU itself was being vilified by the nationalist political elite.[2] The early 1990s were tumultuous and difficult for Croatia, as the transition to a market economy was accompanied by transition to a democratic regime, establishment of independence from Yugoslavia, and a series of violent conflicts. To a large extent, the conflicts and the issue of independence took precedence over democratic development, and the transition to a market economy took place in this chaotic state, allowing free reign for corruption, nepotism, and crime. The very first elections brought the HDZ (*Hrvatska demokratska zajednica*, Croatian Democratic Union) into power, with a large parliamentary majority partially caused by the chosen electoral system.[3] The party was promising democracy and prosperity for an independent Croatia, a platform that many supported, but with a stronger nationalist stance than any of the other opposition parties. The Communists came in second, with 26 per cent of the vote, while the remainder of the vote was scattered across a number of political options, ranging from very liberal to the extreme right. This large proportion of the vote for the party stemming from the old regime was not unexpected, as it was the Croatian Communist Party that internally deliberated the ways of transition (Čular 2001), and followed their Slovenian counterparts in participating in the revolts at the federal-level Communist party meetings. As an active party in the political changes, the Communists were not facing a certain defeat, but they certainly miscalculated and overestimated their popularity by choosing a plurality electoral system with single-member districts.

The legislature dominated by the HDZ followed Slovenia's suit and declared Croatia's independence on 25 June 1991, with a moratorium on the decision which ceased on 8 October of the same year. By that time, Croatia was already embroiled in war, and some of the worst tragedies, those of Vukovar and the siege of Dubrovnik, were to take place in November and December of the same year. International recognition followed in early 1992, with Germany and the Vatican leading the way.[4] The controversies regarding the recognition and status of Croatia, along with criticisms regarding the treatment of minorities, especially the Serb population, and democratic standards, in the realm of freedom of the press in particular, led to the political elite's change of tone regarding Europe, and European integration in particular. The regime invoked further criticism with its political and military engagement in Bosnia and Herzegovina, up until the Dayton Accords of 1995. This is the most likely locus of the ambivalent attitudes that Croatians still espouse towards the EU.

There was a possibility that Croatia would lose in 1995. Its successful participation in the Dayton Accords that finally brought peace, however fractious, to Bosnia and Herzegovina made the international climate towards it quite favourable. This could have been a chance for Croatia to shift its orientation and approach to democratization and Europeanization, along with pursuing the path of European integration that was so important to its citizens just a couple of years prior. The country was on the path to signing the Association Agreement with the EU, and first steps towards expanding the EU's Phare programme to Croatia were made. The intransigence regarding the crimes against civilians committed by Croatian forces in the aftermath of military operations Flash and Storm of 1995, along with a strong authoritarian bent in the political elite's dealing with issues of fundamental civil and political rights, made it difficult for Croatia's European trajectory to resume. The negotiations concerning the Association Agreement were halted by the EU, and Phare expansion never took place. At this moment, the dualism of the attitudes of both the citizens and the political elite towards the EU became apparent. Again, the European orientation of Croatia was not in question, but the EU and its attitude towards Croatia were seen as unjust, and potentially problematic. The only step towards European integration that Croatia successfully completed was full membership in the Council of Europe, a status achieved in 1996.

In the 1990s, the normative influence of the EU could barely be seen among the political elite. The EU was a source of criticism, and potentially a source of embarrassment for the government and the president. The then-president Franjo Tuðman rarely failed to point out the unfairness and bias of the Western European countries. In the official discourse, the EU had become an enemy, a hypocritical entity that was 'out to get' the finally independent and sovereign Croatia. Uzelac (1997) discusses the rhetoric and nationalist narrative found in Franjo Tuðman's speeches and interviews, and found a language laden with references to enemies, both internal and external, which simultaneously glorified his personal role in the process of gaining independence. European integration seemed to have been on the wrong side of the divide. For the Croatian president, there was no doubt concerning the Europeanness of Croatia, but his attitudes towards the EU were fraught with suspicion. The nation's sovereignty and independence from Yugoslavia carried a great deal of weight. Anything that had the potential of undermining them was quickly dismissed by the president. This was true with respect to various demands placed on Croatia, ranging from the conditions for joining Central European Free Trade Agreement (CEFTA), to those from the EU, and later the International Criminal Tribunal for the Former Yugoslavia (ICTY). When the European path of Croatia's neighbors became clear, the Croatian regime tried to follow, but at least to the extent that the political elites could follow. The first government ministry dealing with European integration was founded in 1998, with a small staff and relatively little influence. However, it was a move with much symbolism, as it demonstrated that there was at least a desire to produce an image of positive orientation towards the EU.

The Croatian regime of the 1990s is difficult to classify. At least in the elections up to 1997, the voters' will was indeed expressed by the policies of Franjo Tuðman and the HDZ. This was a period of national mobilization and a period of war. The nationalist positions of the president and his party reflected the position of the majority. Croatia was a democracy, but very much an illiberal one. The illiberal practices were widespread. The president himself refused to accept the popular vote in the local elections in Zagreb, the country's capital, and refused to formally appoint the mayor who had won. The critical and satirical magazine Feral Tribune was subjected to excessive taxation, as they were categorized as 'smut'. The treatment of minorities, the Serb minority in particular, was contemptuous, and the military operations in 1995 produced a wave of refugees that fled towards Bosnia and Serbia.[5] Croatia was thus an exception to the trend noted by Vachudova (2008, 402) who found that

> [d]uring the 1990s, however, we can see the demise of the categories of independence right and communist nationalist as parties transformed in response to internal and external political incentives, especially the process of joining the EU. This cleared the field and empowered the centre-right.

This type of process simply did not exist in Croatia, where the post-communists could not be nationalist, as that political field was populated by the HDZ and some of the parties further to the right, and the HDZ was not yet moving towards the centre as the incentive to do so, in the form of EU membership, was not there. The HDZ had enough support in the 1990s as a nation-forming and state-building party so that the recourse to 'ordinary' electoral topics was not necessary. As a post-war state, Croatia was not yet able to move towards ordinary politics understood as a complex of issues that define the political cleavages in European countries: economic left and right, socially liberal and conservative stances, stances on EU membership, and similar.

Though the regime could not be classified as a liberal democracy, the state apparatus was effective. Evidence of that is abundant: from the ability to organize the war efforts and activities, to the provision of various public goods, and successful efforts to stabilize the economy and recover from high levels of inflation. The execution of these policies was far from perfect, with numerous instances of persistent corruption, and abundant examples of inefficiencies. The state was present nonetheless, and the issue in Croatia was not so much that of state building, as it was a matter of a change of regime. In the case of Croatia, unlike those of more commonly cited examples of the EU building the state (e.g. Bosnia and Herzegovina),[6] the state was already present, and needed reshaping, reorienting, reforming, modernizing.

In late 1999, however, everything seemed possible. The president, Franjo Tuđman, was seriously ill, and there were constant rumours of his inability to perform official duties and of his associates' encroachments beyond the powers they officially had. The opposition was becoming more vocal, and citizens were growing tired of international isolation, economic stagnation, and unemployment. At that time, the prospect of EU membership for the CEE countries was clear, and Croatians found themselves wondering how it could be that their Polish, Slovenian, Hungarian, and other counterparts were on the verge of becoming EU citizens, while this option was nowhere in sight for them. In 1999, the economy shrunk by 1.5 per cent, and though unemployment had not reached a high (it was at 13.6 per cent, using the ILO measure),[7] the lack of liquidity in the economy meant that numerous businesses were on the verge of bankruptcy, and many were unable to pay their workers.[8] The election date was to be set for the end of the year, which was the object of much haggling and debate, and was punctuated by the death of Franjo Tuđman in December 1999.

It became obvious that Croatia was in isolation, and that the ruling party was to blame. All of the problems in the economy, problems with limits on political power, with corruption and problematic privatization made Europe and the EU something close to a battlecry for change. The EU was still associated with ineffectiveness and vacillation over a common stance on the breakup of Yugoslavia and the ensuing wars, but the economic well-being, political order, and the perceived societal fairness of established democracies were powerfully enticing. With neighbors lining up to join this club, the exclusion and differences became obvious to Croatian citizens and voters. The exclusion was accentuated by the fact that Croatia was wealthier than some of the countries with a clear perspective of joining the EU, making the political sources of this status even more conspicuous. Bunce and Wolchik (2006: 11) even noted that 'participants in second-wave postcommunist electoral revolutions consistently told [them] in interviews that they believed successful cases of transition anywhere in the postcommunist region to be highly relevant to their own respective countries'. The success of transition to democracy was affected by the region a country is in, and it is likely that the perspective of EU membership was a catalyst for much of the ongoing change. Bunce and Wolchik (2010) practically neglect the impact of the EU and the credibility of the accession perspective in their piece, but they are right to emphasize the regional effects and contagion of democratizing processes. Croatia was no exception there.

There were concerns about the direction the country would take, and the upcoming elections had many worried: would the ruling HDZ let go of power if it were to finally lose a national election? The HDZ had been in power since the first multi-party elections. As noted by Bunce and Wolchik (2010), the death of Franjo Tuđman left the HDZ in disarray, and for all its former might, it was unable to contest the looming elections with any success. Starting from the position of a broadly based national movement, the HDZ was left with the support of only the staunchest core supporters.[9] The elections on 3 January 2000 brought a left-leaning coalition to power, while the HDZ was reduced to a powerless minority and faced with a need to rebuild and reinvent itself.

Was the EU exercising its normative power towards Croatia at that time? In essence, yes. By establishing the Copenhagen Criteria for accession, the EU created a combination of normative and instrumental incentives for countries to undergo a process of political and economic change. For Croatian citizens, Europeanness was never a contested issue in terms of identity. The merits of the EU, however, had been tainted by its ineffectiveness in the early 1990s, and by the president and HDZ governments' framing of the EU as an unfair, inimical force. Geographical proximity made it impossible to hide the simple fact that EU Member States were wealthier and freer. Exclusion made the chasm between their relative well-being, and Croatia's flagging economy and society, even wider. In this instance, the normative power of the EU was felt by the citizens themselves. It was not the only issue that affected a sea of change in the attitudes of the public, but it was certainly one that invited comparisons with neighboring countries and other post-Communist peers, affirming the perception that the country was lagging under a government that was severely compromised by insufficient growth and a series of problematic cases of privatization, some of which extended back to the beginning of the decade. The case of a single country makes the assessment of causality very difficult, but posing the question as a counterfactual may be useful: had it not been for the EU and its enlargement process, would Croatia have seen the shift in power, and a change of regime? Most likely, yes. There had been enough dissatisfaction, in both economic and political terms. Would this shift have happened as quickly as it did? Most likely not. The EU and its looming enlargement certainly acted as catalysts for domestic change in Croatia. In 1999 and 2000, Croatia was all about change: change of government, a new president, constitutional changes that moved the country from a semi-presidential to a parliamentary system, change in foreign policy, both in terms of pace and direction.

A European orientation was a significant part of the campaign of the left coalition that won the 2000 elections. Even the HDZ used the aim of catching up with the EU enlargement train as part of its 1999 campaign.[10] The new government, and the new-leftist president, elected shortly after the national elections, immediately made their European ambitions clear. Their promises were as unrealistic as they were grand: a move towards the process of EU accession, a clean sweep of the corrupt bureaucracy, a review of privatization, and several hundred thousand new jobs. The response from the EU was swift and of unmistakable symbolism, as the decision was made to hold a summit of EU heads of state and government in Zagreb in November 2000. This was widely seen as a positive signal for Croatia, a signal of readmittance into the group of respectable European countries, but also as a signal for the region as a whole: positive reforms will bring a positive response from the EU.

The period after the meeting wake was characterized by significant changes for Croatia and the region. Among things agreed were the implementation of the new generation of agreements with the EU, the Stabilization and Association Agreements, and a reaffirmation of the Stability Pact for Southeastern Europe as a framework for cooperation and economic and democratic advancement. While the former had already been in place as a tool in 1999, the Zagreb summit saw a commitment on behalf of Croatia to pursue a closer relationship with the EU. This period marks a vital change in Croatia's foreign policy: from being a country on the verge of complete isolation, in fear of its neighbors and suspicious of the EU, Croatia took the course towards becoming the front-runner in the region.[11]

As noted by Jović (2006), this shift was not entirely unambiguous. The new government and president did have a long to-do list to deal with, including economic reform, constitutional reform, and several strands of matters of transitional justice. These last ones included attempts to deal with privatization offenses, which were often characterized by commentators as war profiteering, and more importantly, the prosecution of all war crimes that took place in the 1990s. At least at the rhetorical level, the Croatian government continued the policy of cooperation with the ICTY, an element that the EU insisted upon from the very beginning of the renewed and intensified contact. The true test of the policy of cooperation with the ICTY (and with it, of the European orientation) came with the first indictments of Croatian nationals, which were received with shock amongst the general public. Croatian governments and Croatian citizens were unified in their overarching view of the Homeland War, as it is known in Croatia: the war was defensive, a David vs. Goliath sort of conflict, and in this situation, the Croatian side could not have committed crimes. The truth was different, and the realities of war were indeed far from the idealized picture painted in the official narrative.

The official narrative was contradicted by the EU, by the ICTY, and by small parts of the Croatian elite. The initial response of the left-wing government to the first indictments was indecision and wavering. The pro-European orientation came to a head with political exigencies, which was a great advantage for the opposition. As the indictments and demands for the extradition of Croatian nationals were coming in, the protests began, culminating in the anti-government and anti-ICTY protest in Split in February 2001. The protest was a vehicle for various groups to protest government policy, and though they attracted a large number of citizens, it can be argued that their organizers were acting as a loose coalition of forces unified in little other than dislike for the then-governing left-wing coalition, and mutual fear of a loss of privileges. The HDZ were there to score political points and to rally the conservative and nationalist voters, some of the organizers themselves were in fear of indictments and extraditions, most were afraid of investigations into their connections with the state in the 1990s. This nationalist tide saw its high-point in the 2003 elections which saw the return to power of the HDZ.

For the leadership of the HDZ, the opposition to demands coming from the EU and the ICTY was not a matter of belief or ideology, but a simple matter of political tactics, a set of issues to be manoeuvered and directed with the aim of regaining power. In that sense, the HDZ was a chimera, a party trying simultaneously to be nationalist-conservative, modern, European, and open, trying to maintain its hard core of voters, without losing those in the centre.[12] The three electoral terms from 2000 until 2011 were dominated by this dualism, as the entire country, not just the HDZ, struggled to find its way.

The left coalition was constantly torn by these matters and fear and wavering in the face of the 2001 protests, along with disagreements within the coalition marking the first post-Tuđman government. Its tenure in power, from the historic 2000 elections to a loss in late 2003, was also marked by a decisive move towards the EU. While there were serious limitations to what the government could do domestically, as the 2001 Split protest was seen as the threat of a possible coup, accompanied by more or less serious threats to the president and the prime minister coming from the right-wing fringe, the government was successful in putting Croatia on a path towards the EU. As noted by Jović (2006), Croatia's foreign policy moved decisively towards the EU and NATO. Croatia signed the Stabilization and Association Agreement with the EU in late 2001, and became active in the Stability Pact for Southeast Europe. It joined the CEFTA and ended the period of observation by the Council of Europe, originally put in place to monitor the state of Croatian democracy. In 2003, the then-prime minister, Ivica Račan, formally submitted Croatia's application to the EU.

Thus, Croatia's foreign policy painted the picture of a role model, while domestically the struggle between closed-nationalist and open-integrationist attitudes was continuing. Paradoxically, the return of the HDZ to power in 2003 shifted the balance decisively towards the open-integrationist pole. An unlikely reformer, Ivo Sanader became Croatia's prime minister, just a couple of years after denouncing the leftist government as treacherous at the Split rally. His method of governing the country was similar to the way he ran the HDZ – with a firm hand and little tolerance for criticism. The transition to power within the party was practically a coup, with Sanader's supporters harassing opponents, and the local organizations that remained defiant being dissolved by decree. This left the party organizationally crippled, but it also allowed for its reconstitution as a textbook example of Katz and Mair's (1995) cartel party. The campaign itself was a surprise, with the HDZ placing Sanader at the forefront, along with the promises of a better European future for Croatia and its citizens. The party was abuzz with a controversial plan: detuđmanization. This abandonment of Tuđman went hand in hand with a positive, near enthusiastic pro-EU policy.

Having won the relative majority in the elections, the HDZ was in need of coalition partners, and the choices made in that particular moment would prove indicative of the direction they would take. While it was conceivable that they would choose one of the smaller right-wing parties to complete the ruling majority, they chose instead to rule with the support of ethnic minority representatives. This suggested that the HDZ was ready to move on from its past and ready to cooperate with the Croatian Serbs. Once in power, the HDZ performed a 'Nixon goes to China' type of manoeuvre by implementing the obligation to cooperate with the ICTY, and placing Croatia steadily on a path towards EU membership. Vachudova (2008: 401) states that:

> The HDZ in Croatia has transformed itself quite dramatically into a moderate right conservative party concerned with reforming the state and the economy. It has governed since the 2004 [sic] elections in Croatia and has clearly outperformed its predecessor in moving the country toward EU membership.

The overall assessment of the HDZ's time in power, from 2003 until 2011 is more ambiguous. While the path towards EU membership was clearly set, and major changes were taking place as a result of negotiations for EU entry and adoption of the *acquis communautaire*, a political storm was brewing below the surface.

In 2004, however, the HDZ was reaping the benefits of the policy shifts made by the previous government, and of its own strong move towards the centre. Much of what took place in this period was assisted by the plain fact that the HDZ government was able to make a policy U-turn, and do so without cumbersome negotiations in a coalition. Similarly, Sošić (2007) notes that at that point in the relationship between Croatia and the EU, any mutually supportive outcome was preferred by both, and he points out some of the issues that worked in favor of the HDZ government, such as the relative ease of governing with what was essentially a one-party government (as opposed to the previous left-leaning government that was initially a coalition of six rather disparate parties).

The European Commission had issued a positive opinion concerning Croatia's application to the EU, and it recommended that membership negotiations should begin. This was confirmed by the European Council, and Croatia was on schedule to begin negotiations in July 2005. The 2004 Opinion (European Commission 2004) stated that Croatia's accession was 'part of an historic process, in which the Western Balkan countries are overcoming the political crisis of their region and orienting themselves to join the area of peace, stability and prosperity created by the Union'. In the 'Thessaloniki Agenda for the Western Balkans' adopted by the European Council of June 2003, the EU stressed

> that the pace of further movement of the Western Balkans countries towards the EU lies in their own hands and will depend on each country's

performance in implementing reforms, thus respecting the criteria set by the Copenhagen European Council of 1993 and the Stabilisation and Association Process conditionality.

(European Council 2003)

Manners (2006: 186) notes that 'an EU normative commitment to sustainable peace increasingly involved combining short- and long-term conflict prevention with the building of civil capacity that facilitates reconciliation'. This was certainly true in the case of Croatia, as the rapprochement with the EU was accompanied by the EU's support for cooperation schemes in the region and by financial assistance aimed at assisting the civil society, starting with the 2003 CARDS (Community Assistance for Reconstruction, Development and Stabilisation) programme.[13]

The only remaining issue was that of cooperation with the ICTY, more specifically, the issue of general Ante Gotovina who had fled the country in 2001, shortly after an extradition request for him was issued by the ICTY to the Croatian Ministry of the Interior. There had been constant speculation that Gotovina was hiding in Croatia or in Bosnia, assisted by factions in the Croatian police and security services, and the ICTY Prosecutor's Office had, on several occasions, asserted that Croatia was not fully cooperating with them with regard to the completion of extraditions. This was the main issue that had the Commission, Council, and the Croatian Government postponing the beginning of the negotiations. It seems that Croatia provided enough evidence of its cooperation with the ICTY by October 2005, when negotiations finally started. The missing general was found shortly thereafter, and arrested in Tenerife. According to Freyburg and Richter (2010), compliance ensued as means were found to remove conflict between the deeply held national identity and national self-definition, and the idea of war crimes committed by Croatians.[14] While certainly not painless nor close to complete, this process has indeed taken place in Croatia. Initially, as noted by Samardžija and Staničić (2004):

> [p]ostponed negotiations contributed to the already existing rise of Euro-pessimism in Croatia. After the period of strong public support in Croatia for the process in early 2000 (most of the public opinion surveys carried out since 2000 on a six month basis showed that around 70% of population have positive attitude towards integration), recent surveys [had] indicated significant decrease in public opinion support. Namely, in 2004 the support for the EU fell to 51% of population while 39% of citizens were opposed.

These numbers did not change much in the wake of the arrest and as accession was approaching. The low support figures have already been noted above. However, the political tensions have subsided, and anything similar to the protests from the early 2000s became unlikely.

With this arrest and a number of ongoing trials before Croatian courts, the Croatian path towards the EU was set. In terms of the exercise of normative power, the EU certainly played a large role in facilitating Croatia's turn to democracy, and a conciliatory and pragmatic foreign policy. As Croatia became a member of the EU on 1 July 2013, these changes appeared set, and Croatia's general path clear. Did the process of EU accession bring about improvements in the quality of Croatia's democracy? There is wide agreement that Croatia has seen dramatic change in that regard after the 2000 elections. Bunce and Wolchik (2006: 7) even note Croatia's case as one of the electoral revolutions in the region, along with those of Slovakia and Serbia: 'The postcommunist region, in short, has emerged as the primary site for democratization through electoral revolutions. Why is this so? Simply put, what we find in the postcommunist region is an interaction between favorable domestic conditions and international support.' The international support was certainly provided by the EU, and by the EU's enlargement policy towards the region. This electoral revolution notwithstanding, the quality of democracy has improved in its wake, and there was assistance from the EU in this process, as there was a general sense that the path to the EU implied that Croatians would need to learn how to do some things differently.

In addition to the stabilization of democracy, the post-war issues have been at least formally resolved during the accession period.[15] The ICTY Prosecutor's Office confirmed full cooperation, but in 2005, Croatia still had a long way to go in satisfying the Copenhagen Criteria for accession. On these other issues, the record is mixed. Much of what was being done as part of the accession process was done swiftly, with the aim of implementing the form, but not always the spirit, of the criteria. However, there were aspects of the accession process that would have a lasting effect, beyond the shift in the orientation of the country as a whole. It is these topics that will be explored in the following paragraphs.

Normative power Europe: where can we see it in Croatia?

Croatia's overall shift in terms of regime and foreign policy outlook that took place in the 2000–2005 period is the most lasting and firmest legacy of the EU-ization process. However, the demands of the accession process have been different, more specific, and more encompassing. It is probably safe to say that the process has touched upon most areas of social life: the state, the economy, and the way in which the relationship between the state and the citizens functioned. Selecting areas where the EU has had or may have had the ability to exercise normative power is very difficult, as any and all topics may have been affected by the accession process. Furthermore, an additional difficulty is posed by the simple fact that the power exercised by the EU is never normative alone – it is also economic and political. The EU can lead by example and setting of norms/standards, but it can also set benchmarks and criteria that need to be satisfied. In other words, with the carrot of membership, and the stick of stalling this process, it is also really difficult to discern how normative power may be exercised.

Three areas have been selected here as possible sites of the effective exercise of normative power by the EU: civil service reform, protection of minorities, and prevention of corruption. The first of these areas was selected based on the author's personal experience, while the remaining two have been emphasized by the EU as vital to the process of joining the Union.[16]

In terms of the author's personal experience working in the Croatian civil service, it can be concluded that the negotiation and accession process had an overwhelming impact on the way in which the civil service operated. The process of accession lasted 12 years – from the signing of the Stabilization and Association Agreement in 2001, to the entry ino the EU on 1 July 2013. In the middle of that period, between 2007 and 2008, it seemed that there was no part of the Croatian civil service that was not somehow affected by the process. The modernization of the civil service was not instantaneous, but there was a marked change of emphasis, with numerous young professionals being in charge of accession-related work, from management of the EU's pre-accession funds, to the work done in the negotiating groups themselves. The negotiators in charge of the various chapters of the *acquis communautaire* were professionals in their fields,[17] and were supported by specialists from a number of different areas.[18] The effect of the accession process on the civil service was profound, not only in terms of new institutional structures being created, but also in terms of the feeling shared that the Croatian civil service needed to present its best. Changing the civil service is not an easy process, nor one which may promise fast and effective results. Nevertheless, the impact of the EU can be seen in the struggle to modernize and remain relevant in the process of accession.

Though much of what the civil service does is directed by the governing political bodies, it can be argued that the civil service has also been affected normatively by the accession process. This was supported by the EU, through continuous funding of projects concerning the reform of the civil service and the judiciary through pre-accession funds, and through the funding of various twinning projects. The latter paired Croatian civil servants and civil service divisions with their counterparts in EU Member States, with the purpose of sharing information about best practices, especially in areas that would remain relevant for the technical side of EU membership, such as disbursement and management of EU funds, internal auditing processes, and participation in preparatory and comitology committees.[19] Much of this process has been politically mandated, and many of the requirements were part of the negotiating process, but not all of the change was formal, nor was the implementation wholly conducted with reluctance. A similar process took place as a corollary of the system for contracting and disbursing the monies from the pre-accession funds: the condition of the funds being released was that proper institutional and bureaucratic structures be in place, but the process also involved institutional learning and a wider acceptance of the norms of transparency, and avoidance of practices that may be conducive to corruption. None of these processes were seamless, and none have proceeded without a degree of resistance, but they did result in a more self-conscious and professional civil service. In the typology of normative effects put forward by Manners (2002), these processes can be seen as examples of informational and procedural diffusion.

Though this may be true as a general statement, it is still unclear how the accession process affected those parts of the civil service and state apparatus that have not been directly involved with the accession process. There has been great interest on the part of regional and local governments in participation in EU-funded projects, and it may well be that Croatia is going to witness a certain level of empowerment that regional governments experienced in other EU countries (Brusis 2005; Laplant 2004). There may also be concerns about the professionalization and modernization of the civil service, as the effects of the accession process may not be trickling down to all parts of the system.

In spite of this movement towards modernization and professionalization, there is still a long way to go. In a survey conducted by the UNODC (2011), the respondents were reporting wide occurrences of corruption, with most 'small-scale' corruption taking place with the aim to speed up the process they are facing or to ensure preferential treatment. The civil service was not at the top of the list of areas in which citizens encountered requests for bribes: the people most offered bribes were doctors, nurses, and police officers. According to the survey, 18.2 per cent of Croatian citizens between the ages of 18 and 64 have had direct or indirect experiences of corruption, which is a staggering rate. Small scale corruption is widely present, though its frequency does vary regionally.

While state building was not an issue, Member State building (Keil 2013) certainly was something that the EU engaged in, in all of the acceding countries from the CEE region. As mentioned above, the process of joining the EU created incentives for the state to reshape itself in the EU's image and to transform state structures to resemble those in other EU countries. This was most obvious in the creation of structures needed to administer EU funds, such as the Central Finance and Contracting Agency, and ministry departments which have the sole aim of cooperating with the EU and other EU Member States. The demands associated with the accession criteria were simple: the country needed to be a stable democracy, a functioning market economy, and needed to be able to take on the responsibilities of membership. In that sense, the structure of funding made available to Croatia was certainly an example of the EU exercising its ability to create a member state, and did not just aim to support the development of a functioning democracy or market economy.

While it is clear that the process of accession affected state structures, did it affect the citizens as well? Did Croatians learn to do things differently? With Croatia's short tenure in the EU, providing a clear answer would be premature, especially in the light of the findings by Vachudova (2008: 387) that show that 'in new EU members, where the discipline of qualifying for EU membership is gone, conservative centre-right parties that vow to protect the country from outside influences including European integration have become more powerful'. The rise of the conservative centre-right would not be a cause of concern if it did not also carry the potential for backsliding on some important achievements of the pre-accession period.[20] This potential for a conservative reversal has already come to fruition in Croatia, as the conservative-Catholic movement 'In the name of the family' has been successful in advocating and subsequently seeing support in the referendum for a constitutionally mandated definition of marriage that excludes same-sex couples.

The protection of minorities has been a major criterion for Croatia's accession to the EU, with a particular focus on the rights of the Serb and Roma minority groups, and the members of the LGBT (lesbian, gay, bisexual, and transgender) community. After the 1995 military operation 'Storm', a large proportion of Serbs from the previously occupied areas fled the country, resulting in a drop of the Serbian population from 12.2 per cent in 1991, to 4.5 per cent in 2001, and 4.4 per cent in 2011.[21] While Croatian authorities have claimed that all refugees are welcome to return, this was much more difficult to deal with in practice, particularly due to the restrictive view of citizenship taken by the Croatian state (Ragazzi and Balalovska 2011; Štiks 2010). This has changed somewhat, as argued by Koska (2012), partly as a result of the accession process and EU pressure. At the elite level, participation of the Serb minority was evident, as their representatives took part in the governing coalition with the HDZ, but numerous problems remained in the practice of everyday life. The matter of citizenship was one, accompanied by difficulties in post-war reconstruction, and still widespread resentment and mistrust towards the Serb minority.[22]

Another minority group that the EU has taken a particular interest in during the accession process is the Roma, whose population in Croatia is nearly 17,000 officially;[23] the number is actually greater, due to problems in reaching the more remote Roma settlements, and an unwillingness of the Roma to self-identify. The problems concerning the living standards and attitudes towards the Roma are a known issue in CEE, and Croatia fits the pattern, with the problem appearing smaller simply because of a smaller Roma population. The Croatian government has been engaged in activities aimed at improving the situation of the Roma, taking part in the activities of the Roma Decade of Inclusion, and implementing the Roma

Decade Action Plan, but much work remains to be done, especially in the area of education, in which Croatia was among the countries found guilty of imposing discriminatory conditions on Roma children in primary education. There is certainly a concern that the activities aimed at improving the living standards and life chances of the Roma will slow down, if not cease, after EU accession. In general, Koska (2012: 408) notes that 'Croatia is currently witnessing a trend towards a more inclusive kind of minority relations', but this trend may be endangered by a rise in prominence of ethnic politics. The author would add that there is also a concern that any effort exerted by the Croatian state in these matters may become an area of lower priority now that the country has achieved its aim of joining the EU. Should these efforts continue without the threat of blocking negotiations on the path to EU membership, we will be able to claim that there has indeed been a normative impact of the EU on domestic politics in Croatia.

However, there is some reason for concern, as the immediate aftermath of accession saw the rise of a movement that has shown little but intolerance towards minorities. The 'In the name of the family' campaign was aimed at protecting the 'traditional' definition of marriage, and called for a referendum to be held on the issue. The group succeeded in collecting the necessary number of petition signatures, leading to a mandatory referendum concerning the constitutional definition of marriage as a union of man and woman. After a period of public debate,[24] and a request for the Constitutional Court to consider the constitutionality of the referendum question, the referendum finally took place on 1 December 2013. As expected, the largely conservative and Catholic Croatian citizens voted in favour of the above definition of marriage, by an 18 per cent margin.[25] While the result itself mirrors the will of the majority of Croatian citizens, the concern is that it indicates a worrying lack of tolerance in the population. A further concern arises from the possibility that a similar lack of tolerance was exhibited by the Constitutional Court, which proclaimed the referendum matter admissible.

The rights of the LGBT community in Croatia have been supported by the EU in the process of accession, especially with regard to the protections that ought to be guaranteed in the realm of personal rights, and in the realm of the right to engage in public advocacy and protest for equality of rights. The EU has been a vocal critic of the way in which the authorities failed to deal with the attacks by those protesting at several Gay Pride events in Croatia,[26] but has not responded with similar force to these recent events. Even though the government announced the widening of the scope of civil partnerships for same-sex couples immediately after the referendum (Government of the Republic of Croatia 2013), the concern that the legal framework and social attitudes are discriminatory towards same-sex couples and homosexuals in general remains. There is a further concern that the referendum on the ban of same-sex marriage could pave the way for other referenda that would have an impact on other minorities, such as the idea of having a referendum on banning the use of Cyrillic script in some of the areas with a substantial Serb minority.

When it comes to corruption, there is widespread agreement: there is a high level of corruption in Croatia. In a recent Eurobarometer survey, 94 per cent of Croatian respondents stated that corruption is widespread in their country (European Commission 2014a, 2014b).[27] Similar levels were reported by Transparency International (2014), and by the UN Office on Drugs and Crime (2011). Apart from being one of the most salient issues for Croatian citizens, it has also been put forward by the EU as one of the most significant areas where Croatia must make progress (European Commission 2006: 33). More recently, the European Commission has placed Croatia in the group of EU countries where corruption is most prevalent (European Commission 2014a).

Even though the citizens are unequivocal when it comes to the prevalence of corruption, there is some good news. In its 2011 Progress Report, the European Commission noted significant progress (European Commission 2011) and urged a continuation of the reforms. Even though Croatians still see a lot of corruption around them, Transparency International's CPI index for Croatia has improved in comparison with the turn of the century, and ever lower proportions of respondents in Transparency International's survey report having paid a bribe. It ought to be noted that the data are inconclusive due to problems of comparability over time and across surveys. Thus the UNODC report finds that 18.2 per cent of Croatian citizens encounter corruption on an annual basis (2011: 4), while the same measure in 2013 equals 11 per cent, according to the Eurobarometer survey (European Commission 2014b: 97). Both the Transparency International (Transparency International 2013) and the Eurobarometer (European Commission 2014b: 81) surveys note that the reported incidence of bribe-paying is much lower, at 4 per cent and 6 per cent, respectively.

Furthermore, Croatians appear to be cautiously optimistic, and have a high rate of reporting that corruption in their country is decreasing (European Commission 2014a: 37). This is comparable with the data from Transparency International (2014), which reported a steep increase in the proportion of Croatian respondents stating that corruption is decreasing. It is still too early to tell whether these results are simply products of statistical error or not, as there are insufficient data to establish a trend. It may well be that the effect of some high-profile corruption cases, such as those of the former Prime Minister, Ivo Sanader, who orchestrated the HDZ's U-turn after the 2003 elections, have influenced the survey respondents' opinions regarding the likelihood of the situation improving. If a trend of improved scores on these several corruption measures could be established in future surveys, there may be grounds for arguing that the EU's normative power has indeed been at work. This effect would be further strengthened if the suggestions of the European Commission (European

Commission 2014a) and relevant NGOs are followed and implemented, especially in the areas identified as weak (e.g. whistleblower protection).

The research on corruption in Croatia has pointed to a decisive impact of the EU:

> Although the discussions about corruption as a social problem have been part of Croatian public life since the mid-1990s, initiated primarily by the media and civil society, its political significance and, consequently, policy ramifications have been markedly strengthened since 2000, mostly due to the EU conditions and expectations expressed in negotiations over the accession process. Thus, the EU role in the anti-corruption discourse and activities in Croatia can hardly be overemphasized. Its perception, however, among the interviewed experts seemed vague and ambiguous.
>
> (Čaldarović *et al.* 2009: 18)

This quote shows the potential pitfalls of Croatia's anti-corruption policy – even the experts who were the focus of the research project cited above cannot be said to have a clear idea of the issue, something that may indicate that the transferred norms have not been properly internalized.

Conclusion

Much of the potential of the EU to influence other actors stems from its ability to offer various goods in return for compliance. This does not preclude the possibility that there are such situations in which there may exist the potential for normative power to be effective. According to Manners (2002: 244–245), 'EU norm diffusion is shaped by six factors – contagion, informational diffusion, procedural diffusion, transference, overt diffusion and the cultural filter', and any and all of these may be seen at work in any type of relationship a polity may have with the EU. In Croatia's case, as in many others, the instances of overt diffusion through accession negotiations most certainly took place. This chapter argued that the EU's influence has been seen in Croatia by means of contagion, informational diffusion, and procedural diffusion. The broad changes in the type of Croatia's regime and foreign policy orientation, as discussed by Bunce and Wolchik (2010) and Jović (2011), provide examples of norm diffusion by contagion. The changes in the civil service, though not as widespread as one would hope, have part of their source in informational and procedural diffusion of norms, through the processes of negotiation, cooperation, and coordination with the European Commission and EU Member States. There is little doubt that twinning projects in the civil service provide opportunities for a successful diffusion of norms.

The final two areas discussed above, minority protection and corruption prevention, are more difficult to define as areas where normative persuasion held the most sway in the Croatian case. These high-profile topics have been directly addressed by the EU in a way that was both normative, and accompanied by an offer of exchange. Protecting the rights of members of minority groups and stopping widespread corruption are aims that are intrinsically desirable. However, their achievement is also a condition of accession, making it difficult for analysts to see whether the observed changes and efforts are merely instrumental or possess the potential for self-sustaining themselves beyond the moment when the aims are fulfilled. Should we see a continuation of efforts to curb corruption, and a dedication to protect ethnic and other minorities in Croatia in the coming years, the normative power of the EU and its ability to influence others will have been confirmed.

In the context of Romania, Gallagher (2009) talked about pseudo-Europeanization or Euro-Balkanism, and it remains to be seen whether Croatia will be judged similarly. As Haughton (2007) noted, the EU holds the most power during negotiations for accession, but it is not clear whether this power is normative as well, especially in those policy areas that see slow change even in the face of arduous efforts. According to Epstein and Sedelmeier (2008), the ability to sway a country's actions might simply not be present in the post-accession period. At this point, there appears to be a consensus amongst the Croatian public concerning the problem of corruption, especially in the aftermath of several high-profile cases. Seeing Ivo Sanader, a former prime minister, trying to flee the country to escape corruption charges, and being subsequently imprisoned and convicted, showed that corruption was indeed present, but that it was also something that can be punished. Further cases of corruption, such as the recent one of the former head of the Croatian Chamber of Economy (essentially the employers' association) appeared particularly abhorrent,[28] adding to the urgency and concern about matters related to corruption.

In contrast, no similar momentum appears to exist when it comes to the protection of minority groups. In the light of the referendum on the definition of marriage and the calls for a referendum on the use of Cyrillic in areas with large Serb minorities, one may expect that efforts by the government would subside. With all of the improvements achieved in the past 15 years in mind, it would truly be unfortunate if entering the EU was the factor that slowed down progress in this area of affairs.

Notes

1 The nationalist elite at the time seemed to forget that post-World War II Yugoslavia was probably the only place where the transition to Communist rule happened as a result of a strong and widely supported domestic Communist Party. This forgetfulness is even more unusual given that a large part of the elite not only stemmed from Communist circles, but also actively took part in the antifascist and predominantly communist resistance in World War II.

2 In fact, Croatia was often described as truly European, Catholic, preserving real Europeanness, and again acting as the bulwark against change, as it had in the times of Ottoman conquests.
3 The first multi-party elections in Croatia saw plurality elections in single member districts, a system that allowed the HDZ to claim an absolute majority of parliamentary seats (58 per cent), with just 42 per cent of the vote. See www.izbori.hr/arhiva/pdf/1990/1990_1_1_Sabor_Rezultati_Drustveno_politicko_vijece.pdf.
4 As Gilbert (2012) notes, this was not without controversy, and many of the EU Member States resented Germany's decision to ignore its EU allies and push the recognition forward.
5 Some further examples of the practices are given by Uzelac (2002) regarding the issue of judicial independence, Padjen (1996) on the matter of presidential decrees, and Petričić (2000) on the way that privatization was conducted.
6 For Bosnia and Herzegovina, see Valery Perry's Chapter 9 in this volume.
7 These are Croatian national bank data, see www.hnb.hr/statistika/e-ekonomski_indikatori.htm.
8 The record for illiquidity and insolvency of businesses set in 1999 would be broken in the aftermath of the most recent financial crisis, which is still plaguing Croatia. See www.business.hr/ekonomija/hrvatska-dosla-na-korak-do-rekordne-nelikvidnosti-iz-1999-godine.
9 A member of the author's family, a long-serving HDZ activist, remarked at that time that he could not but feel that he should vote for the HDZ because of what they had done to protect and establish the country as an independent nation, but he knew that the HDZ losing would be the best outcome for all. This, it can be said, summarized the position of many Croatian voters who had up until then been providing unwavering electoral support to the HDZ.
10 Sporadically and unsuccessfully, it should be noted.
11 For a good example of how the Croatian government saw foreign policy in the region, see Jandroković (2008) (a speech by a former Foreign Affairs Minister) and Caratan (2008).
12 The HDZ, and Sanader in particular, were very keen to establish the party as a legitimate member of the group of Europe's mainstream right parties, going so far as to have election campaign videos in which Silvio Berlusconi, Bertie Ahern, and Edmund Stoiber praise the European credentials of the party and Sanader himself. As noted by Fink-Hafner (2008), just these contacts may contribute to a European socialization of parties. For more on the HDZ's transformation, see Haughton and Fisher (2008).
13 For some of the civil society projects funded in part by the EU, see www.uzuvrh.hr/natjecaji.aspx?pageID=20 and www.uzuvrh.hr/page.aspx?pageID=71, the website of the Croatian Government's Office for Cooperation with NGOs.
14 For a less optimistic view, see Čorkalo Biruški and Magoč (2009) and Mrakovčić (2010).
15 Only formally, as many of the consequences of war are still being felt: the war-affected areas continue to suffer economically, the process of return of refugees is becoming more and more difficult with the passage of time, and there are still feelings of hostility towards the Serb population, to name but a few of the issues that see no resolution in sight.
16 See, for example, any of the Progress Reports compiled by the European Commission: http://ec.europa.eu/enlargement/countries/strategy-and-progress-report/index_en.htm.
17 For example, Boris Vujčić, who went on to become the governor of the Croatian Central Bank, and Pero Lučin, the rector of the University of Rijeka.
18 For example, Professor Siniša Rodin, professor of European Law, who is currently serving as Croatia's first judge at the European Court of Justice.

19 For more information about twinning in Croatia, see the website of the Central Finance and Contracting Agency: www.safu.hr/en/twinning.
20 While working in the Croatian Government's Office for Ethnic Minorities, specializing in problems faced by the Roma, the author was warned by a consultant to the European Commission Delegation to find a new job, as it was likely that Croatia would disband the office after accession, as some other new Member States had done. Though the author is no longer in that position, it is encouraging to know that this Government Office is still in place.
21 According to a report by the Croatian Bureau of Statistics: www.dzs.hr/Hrv_Eng/publication/2012/SI-1469.pdf.
22 A case in point is the research done on the lifestyle and attitudes of Croatian youths, which finds a high intolerance towards Serbs, even if the youths in question have no direct memories of the conflict (Ilišin *et al.* 2013).
23 Report of the Croatian Bureau of Statistics (2012): www.dzs.hr/Hrv_Eng/publication/2012/SI-1469.pdf.
24 Unfortunately, the quality of this public debate could best be described as poor.
25 See www.izbori.hr/2013Referendum/rezult/rezultati.html.
26 The most serious of these incidents were those during the Split Gay Pride Parade in 2011.
27 For a summary of the results, see http://ec.europa.eu/dgs/home-affairs/what-we-do/policies/organized-crime-and-human-trafficking/corruption/anti-corruption-report/docs/2014_acr_croatia_factsheet_en.pdf.
28 Among the goods that were confiscated from his private home were a room full of artwork, some of it of dubious origin, along with a collection of stuffed animals, including a polar bear. This type of excessive behaviour caused general outrage and opprobrium. See, for example, *Jutarnji List* (2013) (www.jutarnji.hr/ekskluzivne-fotografije-polarni-medo-i-mosusno-govedo-cuvaju-kolekciju-slika-vrijednu-5-milijuna-eura/1139777) and *Index* (2013) (www.index.hr/vijesti/clanak/prijatelji-zivotinja-kaznite-nadana-vidosevica-zbog-prepariranih-zivotinja/711665.aspx).

References

Belloni, R. (2009) 'European Integration and the Western Balkans: Lessons, Prospects and Obstacles', *Journal of Balkan and Near Eastern Studies*, 11(3), pp. 313–331. doi:10.1080/19448950903152177.

Bicchi, F. (2006) '"Our Size Fits All". Normative Power Europe and the Mediterranean', *Journal of European Public Policy*, 13(2), pp. 286–303. doi:10.1080/13501760500451733.

Blanuša, N. and Šiber, I. (2008) 'Mladi i Europa: Strahovi i Nade', *Anali Hrvatskog politološkog društva*, 4(1), pp. 119–141.

Brusis, M. (2005) 'The Instrumental Use of European Union Conditionality: Regionalization in the Czech Republic and Slovakia', *East European Politics and Societies*, 19(2), pp. 291–316. doi:10.1177/0888325404272063.

Bunce, V. J. and Wolchik, S. L. (2006) 'Favorable Conditions and Electoral Revolutions', *Journal of Democracy*, 17(4), pp. 5–18. doi:10.1353/jod.2006.0056.

Bunce, V. J. and Wolchik, S. L. (2010) 'Defeating Dictators: Electoral Change and Stability in Competitive Authoritarian Regimes', *World Politics*, 62(1), pp. 43–86. doi:10.1017/S0043887109990207.

Čaldarović, O., Štulhofer, A., Kufrin, K., Glavašević, B., Odak, I., Gregurović, M., and Detelić, M. (2009) 'Combating Corruption in Croatia: From Expert Perceptions to Policy-Oriented Action Strategies and Back', *Revija za sociologiju*, 40[39] (1–2), pp. 3–22.

Caratan, B. (2008) 'Hrvatska u Regionalnom Kontekstu', *Anali Hrvatskog politološkog društva*, 4(1), pp. 61–72.

Chandler, D. (2010) 'The EU and Southeastern Europe: The Rise of Post-Liberal Governance', *Third World Quarterly*, 31(1), pp. 69–85. doi:10.1080/01436590903557330.

Čorkalo Biruški, D. and Magoč, A. (2009) '"We" Cannot be Guilty?! Ethnic Identity and In-group Justification as Determinants of Experiencing Collective Guilt', *Revija za sociologiju*, 40[39] (3–4), pp. 211–231.

Croatian Bureau of Statistics (2012) *Report on Census of Population, Households and Dwellings*. Available at: www.dzs.hr/Hrv_Eng/publication/2012/SI-1469.pdf (accessed 1 March 2014).

Čular, G. (2001) 'Political Development in Croatia 1990–2000: Fast Transition – Postponed Consolidation', *Politička Misao*, 37(5) pp. 30–46.

Epstein, R. A. and Sedelmeier, U. (2008) 'Beyond Conditionality: International Institutions in Postcommunist Europe after Enlargement', *Journal of European Public Policy*, 15(6) pp. 795–805. doi:10.1080/13501760802196465.

European Commission (2004) *Opinion on Croatia's Application for Membership of the European Union*. Brussels. COM/2004/0257. Available at: http://eur-lex.europa.eu/legal-content/EN/TXT/?uri=CELEX:52004DC0257.

European Commission (2006) *Enlargement Strategy and Main Challenges 2006–2007*. Brussels: European Commission. Available at: http://ec.europa.eu/enlargement/pdf/key_documents/2006/nov/com_649_strategy_paper_en.pdf.

European Commission (2011) *Croatia Progress Report for 2011*. Brussels: European Commission. Available at: http://ec.europa.eu/enlargement/pdf/key_documents/2011/package/hr_rapport_2011_en.pdf.

European Commission (2013) *Public Opinion in the European Union* (No. 79). Available at: http://ec.europa.eu/public_opinion/archives/eb/eb79/eb79_publ_en.pdf.

European Commission (2014a) *EU Anti-Corruption Report*. Brussels: European Commission. Available at: http://ec.europa.eu/dgs/home-affairs/e-library/documents/policies/organized-crime-and-human-trafficking/corruption/docs/acr_2014_en.pdf.

European Commission (2014b) *Special Eurobarometer 397 (CORRUPTION)*. Brussels: European Commission. Available at: http://ec.europa.eu/public_opinion/archives/ebs/ebs_397_en.pdf.

European Council (2003) *EU–Western Balkans Summit Thessaloniki* [Press Release], 21 June. Available at: http://europa.eu/rapid/press-release_PRES-03-163_en.htm (accessed 1 March 2014).

Fink-Hafner, D. (2008) 'Europeanization and Party System Mechanics: Comparing Croatia, Serbia and Montenegro', *Journal of Southern Europe and the Balkans*, 10(2), pp. 167–181. doi:10.1080/14613190802146216.

Freyburg, T. and Richter, S. (2010) 'National Identity Matters: The Limited Impact of EU Political Conditionality in the Western Balkans', *Journal of European Public Policy*, 17(2), pp. 263–281. doi:10.1080/13501760903561450.

Gallagher, T. (2009) *Romania and the European Union: How the Weak Vanquished the Strong*. Manchester: Manchester University Press.

Gilbert, M. (2012) *European Integration: A Concise History*. Lanham, MD: Rowman & Littlefield Publishers.

Government of the Republic of Croatia (2013) *Minister Bauk: Bill on Civil Partnership is an Attempt to Reach a Democratic Compromise between Worldviews*. Available at: www.vlada.hr/en/naslovnica/novosti_i_najave/2013/prosinac/minister_bauk_bill_on_civil_partnership_is_an_attempt_to_reach_a_democratic_compromise_between_worldviews.

Haughton, T. 'When does the EU Make a Difference? Conditionality and the Accession Process in Central and Eastern Europe', *Political Studies Review*, 5(2), pp. 233–246. doi:10.1111/j.1478-9299.2007.00130.x.

Haughton, T. and Fisher, S. (2008) 'From the Politics of State-Building to Programmatic Politics: The Post-Federal Experience and the Development of Centre-Right Party Politics in Croatia and Slovakia', *Party Politics*, 14(4), pp. 435–454. doi:10.1177/1354068808090254.

Ilišin, V., Bouillet, D., Gvozdanović, A., and Potočnik, D. (2013) *Mladi u Vremenu Krize*, Institut za Drustvena Istrazivanja. Available at: www.idi.hr/images/stories/publikacije/mladi_uvk.pdf.

Index (news portal) (2013) *Prijatelji Životinja: Kaznite Nadana Vidoševića zbog prepariranih životinja (Animal Friends: Punish Nadan Vidošević for the Taxidermied Animals)*. Available at: www.index.hr/vijesti/clanak/prijatelji-zivotinja-kaznite-nadana-vidosevica-zbog-prepariranih-zivotinja/711665.aspx (accessed 1 March 2014).

Jandroković, G. (2008) 'Hrvatska – Globalni Izazovi Vanjske Politike', *Adrias*, 15, pp. 25–40.

Jović, D. (2006) 'Croatia and the European Union: A Long Delayed Journey', *Journal of Southern Europe and the Balkans*, 8(1), pp. 85–103. doi:10.1080/14613190600595598.

Jović, D. (2009) 'Croatia after Tudjman: The ICTY and Issues of Transitional Justice', *Chaillot Paper*, 116, pp. 13–27. Available at: https://dspace.stir.ac.uk/handle/1893/1993.

Jović, D. (2011) 'Turning Nationalists into EU Supporters: The Case of Croatia', in Rupnik, J., *The Western Balkans and the EU: 'The Hour of Europe'*. Available at: https://dspace.stir.ac.uk/handle/1893/3056 (accessed 2 March 2014).

Judt, T. (2006) *Postwar: A History of Europe since 1945*. New York [etc.]: Penguin Books.

Katz, R. S. and Mair, P. (1995) 'Changing Models of Party Organization and Party Democracy', *Party Politics*, 1(1), pp. 5–28. doi:10.1177/1354068895001001001.

Keil, S. (2013) 'Europeanization, State-Building and Democratization in the Western Balkans', *Nationalities Papers*, 41(3), pp. 343–353. doi:10.1080/00905992.2013.768977.

Koska, V. (2012) 'Framing the Citizenship Regime within the Complex Triadic Nexuses: The Case Study of Croatia', *Citizenship Studies*, 16(3–4), pp. 397–411. doi:10.1080/13621025.2012.683253.

LaPlant, J. T., Baun, M., Lach, J., and Marek, D. (2004) 'Decentralization in the Czech Republic: The European Union, Political Parties, and the Creation of Regional Assemblies', *Publius*, 34(1), pp. 35–51.

Lerch, M. and Schwellnus, G. (2006) 'Normative by Nature? The Role of Coherence in Justifying the EU's External Human Rights Policy', *Journal of European Public Policy*, 13(2), pp. 304–321. doi:10.1080/13501760500452665.

Manners, I. (2002) 'Normative Power Europe: A Contradiction in Terms', *Journal of Common Market Studies*, 40(2), pp. 235–258.

Manners, I. (2006) 'Normative Power Europe Reconsidered: Beyond the Crossroads', *Journal of European Public Policy*, 13(2), pp. 182–199. doi:10.1080/13501760500451600.
Moravcsik, A. and Vachudova, M. A. (2003) 'National Interests, State Power, and EU Enlargement', *East European Politics and Societies*, 17(1), pp. 42–57. doi:10.1177/0888325402239682.
Mrakovčić, M. (2010) '(Dis)integration and Confidence in Institutions in Multiethnic Communities in Croatia', *Revija za sociologiju*, 40(2), pp. 157–184.
Nezirovic, V. (2013) 'Polarni medo čuvao kolekciju slika vrijednu 5 milijuna eura' ('Polar Bear Keeping Watch over a Collection of Art Worth 5 Million Euro'), *JutarnjiList*, 13 November. Available at: www.jutarnji.hr/ekskluzivne-fotografije-polarni-medo-i-mosusno-govedo-cuvaju-kolekciju-slika-vrijednu-5-milijuna-eura/1139777.
Noutcheva, G. (2009) 'Fake, Partial and Imposed Compliance: The Limits of the EU's Normative Power in the Western Balkans', *Journal of European Public Policy*, 16(7), pp. 1065–1084. doi:10.1080/13501760903226872.
Noutcheva, G. and Aydin-Düzgit, S. (2012) 'Lost in Europeanisation: The Western Balkans and Turkey', *West European Politics*, 35(1), pp. 59–78. doi:10.1080/01402382.2012.631313.
Padjen, I. (1996) 'Emergency Decrees of Croatian President: The Authority of French Public Law', *Politička misao*, 33(1), pp. 149–165.
Petričić, D. (2000) *Kriminal u hrvatskoj pretvorbi: tko, kako, zašto*. Zagreb: Abakus.
Ragazzi, F. R. and Balalovska, K. (2011) *Diaspora Politics and Post-Territorial Citizenship in Croatia, Serbia and Macedonia* (SSRN Scholarly Paper No. ID 2388857). Rochester, NY: Social Science Research Network. Available at: http://papers.ssrn.com/abstract=2388857.
Samardžija, V. and Staničić, M. (2004) 'Croatia on the Path towards the EU: Conditionality and Challenge of Negotiations', *Croatian International Relations Review*, 10(36/37). Available at: http://hrcak.srce.hr/index.php?show=clanak&id_clanak_jezik=10033.
Sošić, M. (2007) 'Croatian Strategy of EU Integration 2000–2007: A Comparative Study', *Croatian Political Science Review*, 44(5), pp. 91–117.
Štiks, I. (2010) 'The Citizenship Conundrum in Post-Communist Europe: The Instructive Case of Croatia', *Europe-Asia Studies*, 62(10), pp. 1621–1638. doi:10.1080/09668136.2010.522422.
Transparency International (2014) *How Corrupt is Your Country?* Available at: http://transparency.org/cpi2013/results (accessed 3 March 2014).
Transparency International (2013) *Global Corruption Barometer 2013*. Available at: www.transparency.org/gcb2013/report.
UNODC (2011) *Corruption in Croatia: Bribery as Experienced by the Population*. Vienna: United Nations Office on Drugs and Crime. Available at: www.unodc.org/documents/data-and-analysis/statistics/corruption/Croatia_corruption_report_web_version.pdf.
Uzelac, A. (2002) 'Role and Status of Judges in Croatia', in Lalić, G. (ed.), *Croatian Judiciary: Lessons and Perspectives*. Croatian Helsinki Committee.
Uzelac, G. (1997) 'Franjo Tudjman's Nationalist Ideology', *East European Quarterly*, 31(4), pp. 449–472.
Vachudova, M. A. (2004) *Europe Undivided: Democracy, Leverage and Integration after 1989*. Oxford: Oxford University Press.

Vachudova, M. A. (2008) 'Centre-Right Parties and Political Outcomes in East Central Europe', *Party Politics*, 14, pp. 387–405.

Vachudova, M. A. (2009) 'Corruption and Compliance in the EU's Post-Communist Members and Candidates', *JCMS: Journal of Common Market Studies*, 47, pp. 43–62. doi:10.1111/j.1468-5965.2009.02013.x.

5 The role of the EU in the statehood and democratization of Montenegro

Jelena Džankić

Introduction

Despite being the smallest, and one of the newest post-Yugoslav states, Montenegro has achieved significant progress in its ambition to join the European Union (EU), since its independence in 2006. In June 2012, under the Danish Presidency of the Council of European Union, Montenegro has started the EU accession negotiations. Through these developments, Montenegro has become the frontrunner among the Western Balkan states, apart from Croatia, which became the twenty-eighth EU Member State in July 2013. This progress, however, has not been endogenous to the capacity of the domestic Montenegrin actors to induce change to the governance structures or the societal actors to foster democratic values. Rather, it has been an exogenously driven process, in which the EU has been the most significant agent of domestic change.

In this context, this chapter argues that the EU has had a major role in the statehood and democratization of Montenegro through two interrelated processes: (1) the mediation of the statehood issue, which contributed to state building and (2) the forcing of consensus among domestic actors, which resulted in significant legislative changes required in the context of the EU enlargement process. By exploring these issues, the chapter also reveals a twofold dynamic related to EU's role in the Western Balkans. On the one hand, due to the asymmetry of relations between the EU and Montenegro, accession requirements have induced the political actors to improve the state's institutions for the 'top-down' absorption of legislation. On the other hand, the adaptation to EU's requirements became an elite-driven process, which had a somewhat negative spillover on civil society actors. Given the detachment of society from political transformation, inherent in the process of accession, the latter observation raises concerns about the qualities of the 'normative power' of the EU (Manners 2002) in the Western Balkans, for which Montenegro can be an illustrative example.

The two decades following the disintegration of Yugoslavia have witnessed the gradual construction of the framework for the subsequent political development of Montenegro, and paved the way for the EU to become the most significant political actor in this state. In 1992, when Yugoslavia was on its deathbed, Montenegro was the only one among its republics not to seek independence (Rancharan 1997). At the plebiscite of 1 March 1992, 95.4 per cent of the 66 per cent turnout[1] opted for Montenegro to remain in the common state with all other Yugoslav republics wishing to do so (ICG 2000: 6). With only Serbia approving a new federation, on 27 April 1992, the two established the Federal Republic of Yugoslavia (FRY). As a consequence of these developments, followed by the closeness of the ruling Montenegrin elite with the politics of Slobodan Milošević, the first years of Montenegro's transition were marked by anything but democratic development. These years witnessed the involvement of the FRY and thus of Montenegro in the wars in Croatia and Bosnia and Herzegovina, the embargo of the international community, hyperinflation, and socio-political disarray. At the same time, in these troublesome years, the involvement of the EU in the Western Balkans was minimal, as the Union's overall response to the Yugoslav disintegration was generally considered a major failure (Edwards 1997).

Thus, in the first decade of the 1990s, statehood and democratization were not major political concerns for Montenegro. The major shift in the domestic political scene, which also opened the way for greater EU involvement as an external actor (Nuttall 1993), occurred in 1997 when the ruling party of reformed communists – Democratic Party of Socialists (DPS) – split into two factions of an almost equal size. The split, which formally revolved over support for Milošević, sparked a series of political problems and resulted in a division over statehood and identity in the following decade.[2] The continued support for Milošević's policies was advocated by the DPS wing led by the then President of Montenegro, Momir Bulatović. Bulatović's party became the major opposition player and in 1998 was registered as the Socialist People's Party (SNP). The ruling DPS, under the lead of the then Prime Minister Milo Đukanović, moved away from Milošević's political course, which opened up the prospect for this party's greater cooperation with Western countries, headed by the United States (US) and followed by the EU. The political and financial assistance that Đukanović's DPS received from the US and the EU, amounting to a total of over 750 million Deutschmark (DM) in the second half of the 1990s (ESI 2001), resulted in Montenegro's greater detachment from federal institutions. This detachment, referred to in the academic literature as 'creeping independence' (Roberts 2002), entailed the establishment of Montenegro's distinct economic and political governance system mirrored in separate customs, visa regimes, currency (Montenegro unilaterally adopted the DM in 1999), and foreign policy.

Rather than being a mere description of Montenegro's transformative years in the late 1990s, the above events gradually generated a major political issue – independence – after the fall of Milošević in 2000. As the need to reinvent its political profile after the external threat (Milošević) was no longer politically salient, the ruling DPS intensified its independence agenda, making this issue the major point of political contention. By extension, the opposition – SNP – built its post-Milošević political profile on the aspiration to preserve the common state. In such a framework, the stability in the fragile Balkan region at that point became an opportunity for the EU to assert its political influence by mediating the issues between Serbia and Montenegro – the two components of the FRY. This included the transformation of the federation into a loose State Union in 2002, and the negotiation of the referendum rules, which prescribed a threshold of 55 per cent of the population voting for independence (minimum turnout of 50 per cent) in order for the country to secede (ICG 2005, 2006). In the referendum that took place in May 2006, this threshold was passed by a mere 2,046 ballots out of almost half a million votes cast (ICG 2006).

After independence, Montenegro stipulated that EU accession was its main foreign policy priority, and the country's main political goal (Ministry of Foreign Affairs of Montenegro 2012). Following the submission of its membership application in late 2008, Montenegro became an official candidate country in December 2010, and in 2012 the EU opened negotiations for accession. As a consequence, the enlargement process became the major driver of democratization, since the political and bureaucratic nature of EU conditionality fosters the establishment of exogenously driven post-liberal states (Chandler 2010).

The asymmetric relationship between the diffusion of EU rules and the democratic transformation of the countries aspiring to membership shows that even though the EU lacks the 'empirical power' it does have the 'power of ideas and norms' (Manners 2002: 238). According to Manners (2002: 243), these norms include democracy, human rights, the rule of law, social solidarity, anti-discrimination, sustainable development, and good governance. Formally, the process of EU accession does induce positive change as regards these elements. However, being an elite-driven project, it is detached from civil society and the citizens, who bear the costs of accession, while having a limited impact on the transformation of states. Equally, as will be shown in this case study, elite consensus adopted in unstable political contexts need not necessarily uphold democratic principles, such as equality or non-discrimination. Such a dynamic raises concerns over how the EU shapes 'what *can* be normal in international relations', even if indisputably it does have the ability to 'define what passes for "normal" in world politics' (Manners 2002: 253).

Therefore, this chapter explains the role of the EU in statehood and democratization of Montenegro by drawing on the idea of the EU's normative power (Manners 2002) and the practice of EU Member State building. It is divided in two empirical sections, which seek to explore the limits of the normative power of the EU (Manners 2002) in the context of Chandler's (2010) idea that in its approach to the Western Balkans, the EU is 'building' its future members. The first section provides the local historical context. It explores the role of EU state building in Montenegro, starting from the late 1990s, but with emphasis on the negotiations of the Belgrade Agreement and the referendum on independence. This section examines the modes in which changes to the formal level of state institutions were introduced and argues that such changes required elite consent, which minimized the role of civil society in the process of democratization. The second section explains the EU's effects in Montenegro in the post-independence period. It argues that while EU conditionality forges political consent, it still fails to promote a vibrant civil society, thus showing the contentious aspects of the EU's normative power. The chapter concludes with a discussion of current trends and introduces new areas of research related to the potential role of the EU in Montenegro's democratization.

EU mediation 2001 to 2006: framing the road to sovereignty

Understanding the tension between the EU as the main transformative force in the Western Balkans and the type of normative influence it exerts requires an awareness of the social, political, and economic contexts in which this influence is exercised. As noted earlier in this chapter, in the early 1990s, the EU's role in the region has largely been considered a failure (Edwards 1997). Only after the appeasement of overt conflict in the post-Yugoslav space did the EU start to have a transformative role in the region. In the case of Montenegro, the margin for the EU's involvement was created with the split in the DPS in 1997. The split was followed by the orientation of the ruling elite towards the Western countries to secure endorsement for their opposition to Milošević. The political and economic support from the Western countries, which included 334 million DM from the EU, was granted almost unconditionally to Montenegro in the years between 1997 and 2001. This aid was mostly used to cover the widening public debt, thus maintaining the social aspects of the DPS's electoral platform, and mediating the effects of the policy of 'creeping independence'.

The process of 'creeping independence' had already been launched in 1998, through the establishment of the Montenegrin security structures separate from the federal ones. As a response to the tensions between the DPS and Milošević, the latter embarked on a project of enhancing the Second Army of the Military of Yugoslavia during 1998 and 1999 along with paramilitary forces to attempt to control Montenegro (*Vijesti*, 3 April 1999). The threat of military intervention led to the establishment of a Montenegrin police force of 20,000 men aimed at counterbalancing the presence of federal and paramilitary troops in 1998 and 1999 (ICG 1999). This was the first element of detachment from the federation. Following this, during 1998 and 1999, the Montenegrin government adopted a series of policies which enabled the economic functioning of the republic independently from the federal level. The cessation of transactions between the Montenegrin and the federal budget in 1998 was followed by the decision of Đukanović's DPS-led government to pay revenues directly into the Montenegrin budget, thus avoiding interaction with the federal monetary authorities (ICG 2001). The response from the Belgrade regime was a federal law, passed in November 1998, stipulating that no goods could be collected from customs before revenues were paid into the budget of the FRY. The DPS government subsequently proceeded with establishing a separate customs control system. Simultaneously, the ban on imports of goods from Serbia, enforced by the Serbian police during 1998 and 1999, caused the Montenegrin government to establish economic links with Slovenia and Croatia, progressively loosening its ties with the federal structures (*The Economist*, 12 April 1999). The final element of economic detachment was the introduction of the DM as a parallel currency to the Yugoslav Dinar in 1998, and its full adoption in 1999. The immediate consequence of the introduction of the DM was the establishment of the Monetary Council of the National Bank of Montenegro, which was in charge of foreign currency policy in the republic. From 1997 until 2000, Montenegro, which had its own Foreign Ministry, opened representative offices in Washington D.C., New York, Brussels, Rome, London, Ljubljana, and Sarajevo. It also instituted a citizenship law and a visa regime separate from the federal ones.

The elite-driven nature of these processes, however, kept the civil society at the margins of political transition. The legislative framework for non-governmental organizations (NGOs) was created only in 1999. However, in the early years civil society was very small and not very active in socio-political processes, which had two effects. On the one hand, the lack of NGO involvement decreased the pace of democratization in the late 1990s. On the other hand, the non-interference of other societal actors helped the Montenegrin ruling elite to establish 'a state within a state'. This, in turn, opened up the prospect for the EU to resolve the outstanding issues between Montenegro and Serbia after the fall of Milošević. With the definitive shift of the Montenegrin elite towards independence, tensions between Montenegro and Serbia mounted, as did the rift between the Montenegrin government and opposition, seeking independence and the continuation of the common state respectively. These issues were resolved through the mediation of the EU, which first transformed the Yugoslav federation into a loose State Union of Serbia and Montenegro in 2002, and subsequently helped create the rules for the Montenegrin referendum on independence in 2006. This process has indeed preserved stability in the region. However, its legitimacy has often been questioned precisely due to the lack of engagement of societal actors other than the political parties.

Serbia and Montenegro in the EU designer frame

The brokering of the agreement between the authorities of Serbia and Montenegro on what the common state should look like required an external mediator. Given the increasing importance of the EU in the Western Balkans, the EU's Common Foreign and Security Policy (CFSP) representative Javier Solana was chosen as the mediator. The negotiations were concluded on 14 March 2002, and the vague *Agreement on the Principles of the Relationship between Serbia and Montenegro* (Sporazum o principima odnosa Srbije i Crne Gore u okviru državne zajednice) – usually referred to as the Belgrade Agreement – was officially confirmed at the meeting of the European Council in Barcelona held immediately after the signing of the agreement. Since the document was essentially the outcome of Solana's efforts to prevent further fragmentation and conflict in the region, it did not have the genuine consent of the parties concerned.

A further problem with the Belgrade Agreement was its temporary nature. The Belgrade Agreement had a twofold aim: to preserve the common state of Serbia and Montenegro and thwart the drive for the independence of Kosovo for at least three years. This latter aim, induced by the EU's striving to preserve stability in the region, was largely overlooked in the resulting agreement, which focused on the relationship between Serbia and Montenegro (Hasani 2005). Aside from the reference that all the documents applicable to the FRY or to Serbia and Montenegro (including UNSC resolution 1244) would be succeeded by Serbia in the case of Montenegrin secession, no mention of Kosovo was made in the Belgrade Agreement. The fact that the Agreement allowed opt-outs after three years contributed to the general unwillingness of the signatories to make long-term commitments to the common state.

Another issue was that the Belgrade Agreement was essentially elitist, as it had only six signatories: the President of the FRY (Vojislav Koštunica), the Deputy Federal Prime Minister (Miroljub Labus), the President of the Republic of Montenegro (Milo Đukanović), the Premier of the Republic of Serbia (Zoran Đinđić), and the Premier of the Republic of Montenegro (Filip Vujanović). This meant that the agreement lacked popular legitimacy, which increased people's dissatisfaction with the reformed common state.

During the negotiations between Serbia and Montenegro on the nature of the new state, Solana exerted considerable pressure on the Montenegrin government to postpone its plans for an early referendum. In an article published in the Montenegrin daily *Vijesti* (27 November 2001), Solana stated that Đukanović 'has to know that separation is not a rapid train to the EU. In a way, separation would be a slower train to the EU'. Given Đukanović's perceived image as 'Western-oriented' among the population of Montenegro, his political route was bound to follow the EU's guidelines. That, however, implied the delay of the independence project that Đukanović had embarked upon after the fall of Milošević.

Hence, the ruling DPS attempted to achieve a balance between its drive for independence and the desire not to weaken its relations with the EU. Montenegro could not afford a unilateral move, which would exclude it from foreign assistance and recognition (Bošković 2002). As a consequence of the elite driven nature of the negotiations between Montenegro and Serbia, civil society was not included in the decision-making process. The Agreement thus lacked legitimacy, although the exclusion of the underlying societal actors implied a greater contribution of the EU to state building in the region.

After the mediation of the Belgrade Agreement, the adoption of the Constitutional Charter of Serbia and Montenegro remained in a political deadlock for over a year and was ultimately resolved by another one of Solana's interventions (Teokarević 2003). The Constitutional Charter was finally adopted in December 2002, whilst the law on its implementation followed two months later. This slight delay was due to the fact that minor coalition partners of both blocs in Montenegro, as well as the minor parties of the government in Serbia, did not favour the document because they believed that it lacked substance (Šuković 2002). The Charter was negotiated with difficulty and did not have the genuine consent of the elites of Serbia and Montenegro. It also failed to provide a functional framework for the common state, whose competences were limited to foreign affairs, defence, international economic relations (including relations with the EU), internal economic relations, and the protection of minority and human rights.

The loose nature of the state proved to be a cumbersome issue during its existence from 2002 to 2006. During these four years, the State Union was sustained by a single goal – that of integration into the EU, which opened up the prospect for the European Commission to take part in the process of state building in Montenegro. The Commission asserted that its role in the functioning of the State Union 'was that of internal harmonisation aimed at furthering its EU integration' (Tocci 2004: 566). Its rationale was that the Stabilisation and Association Process (SAP) would be managed in a smoother way with a single country than with two, even though the economic and political systems of Serbia and Montenegro were separate and different (Baillot 2004: 14). In fact, the distinctiveness of economic systems of the two components of the State Union was reflected in the 'twin track' for EU accession negotiations, adopted after a stalemate in the SAP of Serbia and Montenegro (Medjak 2004). The 'twin track' was a unique approach by the Commission. It envisaged separate paths for Serbia and Montenegro to negotiate institutional arrangements with the EU, while also allowing regional cooperation and non-economic international obligations to be dealt with under the auspices of the common state (European Commission 2005).

Even though the Commission's approach was based on the need to preserve stability in the Western Balkans by providing the prospect of membership, balancing the accession process of a complex state was a rather difficult task. The Thessaloniki Summit of 2003 brought about the EU's 'promise of EU membership [as] the basis for all EU conditionality in the region, from compliance with the Hague Tribunal to institutional reforms, from trade liberalisation to the unresolved strategic issues' (ESI 2005: 6). With the Thessaloniki Agenda the EU confirmed its 'determination to fully and effectively support the European perspective of the Western Balkan countries, which will become an integral part of the EU, once they meet the established criteria' (Thessaloniki Agenda 2003). This stipulation of conditionality was in fact a *sui generis* 'Helsinki moment'[3] for EU Member State building in the Western Balkans (ESI 2005).

In this respect, the 'twin track' induced some positive change in Montenegro in terms of EU accession, while having a spillover effect on the issue of independence. On the one hand, the 'twin track' enabled the State Union to initiate the SAP, hence resulting in concrete steps towards the prospect of EU membership in future. On the other hand, given its vague nature, and the fact that it emphasized the distinct methods of organization of economic and political life in the two components of the State Union, it also gave an indirect push to the claims for independence of the ruling DPS. The latter maintained that Montenegro was 'held hostage to Serbian politics' and that the country's EU accession prospects were hampered by the lack of Serbia's cooperation with the International Criminal Tribunal for the Former Yugoslavia in the Hague (B92, 3 May 2006).

Negotiating the referendum rules

Due to the continued push of the ruling DPS for Montenegrin independence, the secession of Montenegro became a much discussed issue both within Montenegro and between Montenegro and Serbia. The key issue was to ensure that all parties concerned would respect the outcome of the popular vote, thus ensuring stability in the region. In Montenegro itself, the process was elite-driven. The pro-independence DPS and unionist opposition found it rather difficult to 'dismember the Serbian-Montenegrin node' (Đuranović 2006). The government insisted on complying with its electoral promise of a referendum on independence, while the opposition threatened a boycott. During the formulation of the referendum rules, the opposition insisted on the establishment of a transitory consensus government, and the substitution of the managers of the Agency for National Security. The proposal was rejected by the DPS on the grounds that it 'would be contradictory to the will of the people that constituted the Government of Montenegro' (*Vijesti*, 22 January 2006). As the result of the general atmosphere of utmost political mistrust, the political discourse in early 2006 revolved around finding 'a constructive and efficient dialogue, through which either an acceptable solution or the lowest common denominator would be reached' (*Vijesti*, 22 January 2006).

Due to the importance of the final outcome for both camps, establishing the rules and principles that both parties would agree on was difficult, even for an external mediator. For the government, whose agenda was the independence of Montenegro, victory in the popular vote was connected with its own political survival. In their discourse, the pro-independence politicians often associated their views with the history of Montenegrin independent statehood. They highlighted the existence of the Roman province of Docleia, or the dynastic Montenegro, in order to supplement their arguments. Each disagreement, or the attempt to criticize the government on any grounds was marked off as 'anti-referendum', 'anti-state', and 'pro-Serb' by the ruling elite (see Jovanović 2005; Malešević and Uzelac 2007). Thus, any activity of civil society not in line with the government's policies was discredited. This implied that even the negotiation of the referendum rules was an elite-driven process, which opened up the prospect for the EU to mediate between two parties.

The second party in the Montenegrin referendum debate was the opposition, whose main political programme involved the preservation of the union with Serbia and accusing the DPS of cronyism. The unionist opposition considered the failure of the referendum as vital for its political existence. The more radical member of this bloc – the Serbian People's Party (SNS) – emphasized the delicacy of this political moment in Montenegro by stating that the 'current political crisis is the greatest one that the republic has had in the past 20 to 30 years' and that 'Montenegro is on the brink of street riots and protests' (*Vijesti*, 16 January 2006). Hence, the need for mediation by the EU was considered as a victory by the opposition.

The fact that there were only two political actors, both of whom considered the EU's mediation necessary in the pursuit of their own goals, was essential in breaking the deadlock on the May 2006 referendum on independence. The referendum rules were established by the EU. According to the referendum formula, the threshold for reaching Montenegrin independence was set at 55 per cent of the turnout, with a turnout of at least 50 per cent of the electorate. The referendum formula, and in particular the 55 per cent threshold, was much debated both domestically and internationally since it disrupted the equality of votes (i.e. more than a simple majority was required). Nonetheless, by introducing guidelines for the compromise between the rival Montenegrin elites, the EU provided a framework through which the statehood issue would be resolved in a manner acceptable to both parties. By negotiating merely with the political elites while circumventing other political actors, the EU contributed to the processes of state building and democratization of Montenegro prior to the country's independence.

The process of negotiating the referendum rules, however, had two implications for the role of the EU in the country. On the one hand, the process of negotiating the referendum rules strengthened the capacity of

92 *J. Džankić*

Montenegro to absorb the 'top-down' policies and processes, which is at the heart of the EU Member State building (Chandler 2010). On the other hand, the disruption of the equality principle in the referendum rules, the focus on elites, and the marginalization of civil society give rise to legitimacy concerns, thus revealing the contentious nature of the EU's normative power (Manners 2002).

EU at the end of the tunnel: contractual relations and domestic consensus

The processes of democratic transition and consolidation in the most of post-communist Europe have been marked with the unique impact of the EU. Following the referendum on independence in 2006, Montenegro's relationship with the EU has increasingly demonstrated the Union's power in 'reforming and reinventing [of] the state in Southeastern Europe' (ESI in Chandler 2010: 72). Subsequently, the principle of 'carrot and stick', i.e. reciprocity in terms of compensation of reforms with a prospect of an eventual future in the Union was an important factor in overcoming the post-communist and post-partition heritage and opened the path for the internal consolidation of democracy in Montenegro. The export of European values, denoted in the transitional literature as 'Europeanization' (Borzel and Risse 2000; Buller and Gamble 2004; Noutcheva and Emerson 2004; Radaelli 2000), has been marked with the principle of conditionality for entry into the EU (Noutcheva 2007). The contractual nature of these processes, in particular the promise of membership following the fulfillment of the EU's criteria, inspired institutional and political transformation in Montenegro. Such political changes, therefore, have been driven both by the endogenous need for the country to reform, and by the EU as the most significant external actor. In order to understand the success of the reciprocal mechanisms the EU employed in Montenegro, it is first essential to look at the formal relationship between the two. The chapter will then explore how this contractual relationship forced political consensus among the deeply divided political actors in the small Balkan state, with minimal participation on the part of civil society.

EU and Montenegro: formal ties

The formal relations between the EU and Montenegro were conceived shortly after the country became independent in 2006. On 12 June, the EU Council officially recognized Montenegro's independent statehood, thereby allowing the new state to receive a mandate for negotiating the Stabilisation and Association Agreements (SAA) the following month. The actual negotiations for the SAA were initiated after the September 2006 parliamentary elections, and the European Partnership was launched in January 2007 (European Commission 2012). Montenegro signed the SAA on 15 October 2007 in Luxembourg, shortly before the country adopted its Constitution. This enabled the start of what Chandler (2010) referred to as 'anchoring', i.e. relating Montenegro to the development of the EU itself. According to Chandler (2010: 74), 'anchoring is seen as crucial to the encouragement of reforms in the governance sphere, relating to the rule of law and democratic and stable institutions'. This 'anchoring' sparked two interrelated processes in Montenegro, as it did in the rest of the Western Balkan states. First, the domestic political elites realized the need to commit to the requirements for EU accession. Second, the EU committed to fostering the democratic development in these countries through political as well as financial mechanisms, such as the Instrument Pre-Accession Assistance (IPA) funds. Although the entry into force of Montenegro's SAA occurred only on 1 May 2010, due to the requirement of ratification by all 27 EU Member States, the reform pace was kept on track through the Interim Agreement on Trade and Trade-related Issues between Montenegro and the EU.

The contractual relationship between Montenegro and the EU developed even further in December 2008, when the country submitted its application for EU membership. In April 2009, the Council of Ministers recommended to the European Commission to submit the *avis* (opinion) on Montenegro's application for EU membership (European Commission 2011). The Commission's opinion, which is another mechanism of the EU's conditionality, was based on a Questionnaire, which was delivered to the Montenegrin authorities in mid-2009. The main aim of the Questionnaire was to assess whether the country met the basic requirements for transposing the legislation of the EU, and the political and economic criteria for accession. The former include democracy, the rule of law, and the protection of human and minority rights, while the latter refer to the capacities of Montenegro to 'cope with the competitive pressures and market forces within the union' (European Commission 2012). The responses to the Questionnaire were compiled from July to December 2009. On grounds of the responses to the Questionnaire, the European Commission issued its Opinion, enabling Montenegro to officially become a candidate country for EU accession on 17 December 2010. While in its Opinion (European Commission 2010), the Commission recognized the progress of Montenegro, it also highlighted a number of governance related issues, which the country was required to deal with before the Commission would recommend the official start of negotiations. These issues included improving the legislative framework for elections; public administration reform; strengthening the rule of law; tackling the issue of corruption; enhancing the fight against organized crime; strengthening media freedom; and implementing the legal and policy framework on anti-discrimination in accordance with international and European standards (European Commission 2010). While the effect of these requirements is analysed in more detail in the subsequent section, it could be concluded here that they forced political actors in Montenegro to reach a series of consensual decisions that they would not have agreed upon otherwise.

In December 2011, the European Commission established that Montenegro met the necessary benchmarks for opening the accession negotiations. However, the Council did not share this belief, and it urged the country to enhance the independence of its judicial system and to tackle the long-standing issues of corruption and organized crime, which had emerged during the troublesome decade of transition in the early 1990s. Only in late June 2012 did the Council determine that Montenegro had met the necessary benchmarks to initiate the accession negotiations. Yet this decision has placed the smallest post-Yugoslav state in a position where it is largely considered a 'success story' from among the other former Yugoslav republics. This success has been induced through external pressures stemming from contractual obligations in the light of membership. However, it was also pushed forward by domestic consensus on the issue of EU membership, supported by all political players in Montenegro including both political elites and civil society.

Exogenous factors and domestic change

Chandler (2010: 83) argues that the EU accession process effectively 'prevents the building of genuine state institutions that can engage with and represent social interests'. Indeed, the asymmetry of the contractual relations between the Western Balkan states and the EU has as its effect the weakening of the sovereignty of these states. The changes in the governance structures pushed by the EU's conditionality reveal that by affecting domestic political players, the EU fosters changes that approximate these states to the Union's standards, and erode potential 'threats' that may emerge from the accession of the Western Balkans to the EU. The two most manifest examples in Montenegro were the visa liberalization process and the recommendations stipulated in the EU's Opinion for Montenegro's membership. The reason why these two exogenous processes had the greatest influence in Montenegro stems from the clarity of the requirements stipulated. On the one hand, the EU's primary interest was protecting its borders in the case of visa liberalization, and of ensuring the political stability and democratic processes in line with the Opinion recommendations. On the other hand, in both instances, the benchmarks for fulfilling the requirements were clearly stipulated, as were the benefits from their fulfillment.

In the case of visa liberalization, in the 2008 EU's Roadmap towards a Visa Free Regime with Montenegro contained specific requirements (benchmarks) related to document security, tackling illegal immigration, readmission, asylum policy, public order, judicial cooperation in criminal matters, and non-discrimination in ensuring its citizens the freedom of movement. The fulfillment of these benchmarks on behalf of Montenegro eventually resulted in a visa free regime for the citizens of Montenegro as of 19 December 2009. The Western Balkan states, including Montenegro, were considered a soft security threat for the EU, i.e. the region had almost no control over the transit of illegal immigrants and organized crime (Schelter 2006). As a consequence, the March 2001 Council Regulation 539/2001 placed the post-Yugoslav states (apart from Slovenia and Croatia) and Albania on a 'Black List' (list of countries whose citizens needed a visa to cross an external border of the EU). As the visa liberalization process directly affected the citizens who have the right to elect their representatives, it provided the motivation for the political elites to induce the institutional and administrative changes that were required in the Roadmaps. Civil society organizations, although not directly engaged in the negotiation process, were involved in the monitoring of the implementation of the benchmarks. As a consequence of the palpable benefits and the consensus of all societal actors of the necessity of visa liberalization, this process has been deemed as the strongest mechanism of the EU's conditionality (ESI 2008).

However, in the case of Montenegro, further changes at the domestic level were fostered by the Commission's Opinion of November 2010, and predominantly referred to elite-driven processes. The recommendations included the observations of the Council of Europe and the OSCE that the rule of law, democracy, and human rights in Montenegro required improvement (European Commission 2010). The major requirement was that the country needed to harmonize its election law with its Constitution. Amending the Election Code of Montenegro, however, proved to be a difficult task for the domestic political elite, because it required a two-thirds majority approval in the Montenegrin Parliament. Given the polarization of political forces in the country induced by the divide over statehood and identity, reaching this majority was complex for the domestic political elite. Yet, as political players were aware of the significance of these requirements for the country's EU accession prospect, the opposition parties conditioned their approval of the Election Code with a package of further legislative changes, which included facilitated naturalization for citizens from other republics of the former Yugoslavia, and the name of the language course in elementary schools.[4] The changes, which were contested for five years after the country's independence in 2006, came about a mere fortnight before the European Commission published its 2011 Progress Report on Montenegro, in which it recommended the opening of accession negotiations owing to the agreement on the new election legislation.

Conclusion

The process of state building in the Western Balkans over the past two decades has largely been driven by the aspiration of these countries to join the European family. Such has been the case in Montenegro, which, having recently opened its accession negotiations, has become the frontrunner in the accession process. As a consequence of its relatively smooth post-independence political course, this state has been considered a 'success story' in the context of the region's transition to democracy. Yet this chapter shows that the changes in the governance structures required from Montenegro in the context of its EU accession aspirations have not been generated through domestic consensus. Rather, they have largely been induced by the EU's rules and requirements, which affected this small state even prior to its independence. This elite-driven process had a by-product in that it kept the civil society far from political and institutional changes. Thus, the argument of the chapter supports Chandler's (2010) thesis that the effect of the EU in the region is producing post-liberal states with limited sovereignty that will be better able to integrate in the Union in due course. At the same time, the chapter raises concerns over the type of the 'normative power' (Manners 2002) that the EU diffuses in the Western Balkans. The transformation of this region corroborates the claim that the EU does have a normative effect. However, the distance of processes from civil society accompanied by the sacrifice of equality for the sake of compromise (e.g. referendum rules in Montenegro) shows that the actual policies diffused by the EU and adopted by the underlying countries do not correspond to what Manners (2002: 242) would refer to as 'the EU's normative basis'.

Indeed, the conflicts of Yugoslav disintegration and the divide over statehood and identity in Montenegro created numerous transitional problems, which obstructed both state building and democratization. In such circumstances, the conditional financial, professional, and logistical assistance of the EU aimed to build governance structures that would help to overcome the security dilemmas in the unstable Balkans. Furthermore, the fulfilment of the contractual obligations towards the EU, especially in terms of the political criterion for accession, has become a *conditio sine qua non* of democracy. Through the conditional nature of obligations for membership, the EU created a network of reciprocal obligations with governments in financial and contractual terms, which goaded the consolidation of democracy, and overcoming of transitional problems.

In the case of Montenegro much of the 'transitional traumas' have been generated during the period of conflicts in the former Yugoslavia. The political circumstances in the late 1990s, particularly following the split in the ruling party in 1997, allowed for a greater involvement of exogenous actors in the process of transition of this country. The financial and political assistance that Montenegro received during these years as a mechanism of countering Milošević were key to the start of reforms in this country. However, as ESI (ESI 2001) noted, much of the reforms during this period remained at the rhetorical level and the financial assistance was largely used to cover the public debt, thus securing the electoral victories of the ruling elite. The political support from the Western democratic states enabled the Montenegrin elite to put into practice its project of 'creeping independence', which entailed the building of state institutions separate from federal ones. The detachment from the federal level following the ouster of Milošević from power in Belgrade intensified the political divide in the smaller constituent of the FRY, which from 2001 to 2006 revolved around the questions as to whether Montenegro should be an independent state or not, and whether Montenegrins were a separate nation or a subgroup of Serbs. At the political level, the internal Montenegrin debate also entailed tension with the Serbian elite, whose aspiration was to preserve the common state. With respect to the situation in the Balkans in the early 2000s, when regional security was still a major concern owing to the unresolved status of Kosovo, the involvement in the EU played an important role at the time of the adoption of the Belgrade Agreement in 2002 and the negotiation of the referendum rules during 2005 and 2006. The desire of both camps in Montenegro to promote a pro-European agenda caused them to renegotiate their initial positions in order to meet the EU's requirements.

This had three effects. First, at the level of European foreign policy, CFSP's involvement in the events related to Serbia and Montenegro increased the 'actorness' and 'presence' of the EU in external affairs showing that the EU indeed has the power to generate norms despite its lack of empirical force. The enhanced coherence in the EU's foreign policy throughout the period studied has been paramount for the EU's redemption from its inactivity in the early 1990s, when the conflict in the former Yugoslavia erupted. Moreover, following the formalization of the conditionality of EU membership in the Thessaloniki Agenda of 2003, the EU became the major 'builder' of Europe's new states. Second, at the domestic level, the political competition has been 'Brusselized', that is, all political players in Montenegro have embraced a pro-European agenda. This generated a broad consensus over the need to meet the requirements that the EU stipulated in the context of accession. However, in a polarized society such as the Montenegrin one, the need to meet the accession requirements implied a shift in the balance of political power. By increasing the bargaining leverage of the opposition, the ruling elite was forced to make a series of concessions that have liberalized the citizenship and franchise legislation, as the amendments to the latter were a clearly stipulated requirement for opening the accession negotiations. Third, by negotiating almost exclusively with the political elites during the key moments of the country's transition, the EU has indeed helped the political parties to become aware of the institutional structures and to build their capacity for the absorption of the EU's *acquis*.

Hence, we can conclude that the EU has already had some positive effects for state building and democratization in Montenegro. Simultaneously, in negotiating almost exclusively with political elites, the EU distanced the societal transformation from its core – civil society and citizens – which reveals the limits to the EU's normative power, as argued above.

Notes

1 The 66 per cent turnout is a consequence of the boycott of the referendum by the Liberal Alliance of Montenegro (promoting the independence of the country) and ethnic minority parties.
2 The division over statehood and identity in Montenegro revolved around the question of whether Montenegrins are a separate nation or a subgroup of Serbs, and whether Montenegro should remain in the common state with Serbia or separate from it. The Montenegrin population was split on these issues into two almost equal groups.
3 The 'Helsinki moment' refers to the 1999 Helsinki European Council, when the EU leaders stipulated that all of the then accession countries were candidates for accession. This in turn accelerated institution building and economic reforms in these countries with the aim of entering the EU.
4 The language, as well as the language course in schools, was named 'Serbo-Croatian' during the existence of the former Yugoslavia. In the FRY, it was 'Serbian'. In its 2007 Constitution, Montenegro declared that the official language was 'Montenegrin', while 'Bosnian, Croatian and Serbian are languages in official use'. The opposition parties in Montenegro objected to the language name 'Montenegrin'. The consensus was reached to name the language course after all the languages used in the country 'Montenegrin – Serbian, Bosnian, Croatian language and literature'.

References

B92 (3 May 2006) 'Crna Gora kao talac'. Available at: www.b92.net/info/vesti/index.php?yyyy=2006&mm=05&dd=03&nav_category=11&nav_id=196559 (accessed 24 June 2013).
Baillot, M. (2004) 'Montenegro eyes parting from Serbia', *The Washington Times*, 21 September 2004: 14.
Bieber, F. (2003) 'Montenegrin politics since the disintegration of Yugoslavia', in Bieber, F. (ed.), *Montenegro in Transition: Problems of Identity and Statehood*, Baden-Baden: Nomos Verlagsgesellschaft, pp. 11–42.
Börzel, T. A. and Risse, T. (2000) 'When Europe Hits Home: Europeanization and Domestic Change', *European Integration Online Papers*, 4/15.
Bošković, B. (2002) 'Toward Europe with or without Serbia?', *Transitions Online*, 29 October 2002: 7.
Buller, J. and Gamble, A. (2002) 'Conceptualising Europeanisation', *Public Policy and Administration*, 17 (2). Available at: http://intranet.coleurop.be/pol (accessed 24 November 2011).
Chandler, D. (2010) 'The EU and Southeastern Europe: The Rise of Post-Liberal Governance', *Third World Quarterly*, 31 (1), pp. 69–85.
Council of the European Union (2003) *Thessaloniki European Council: Presidency Conclusions*, Thessaloniki, 19–20 June 2003. Available at: www.consilium.europa.eu/ueDocs/cms_Data/docs/pressData/en/ec/76279.pdf (accessed 3 September 2011).
Dan (25 September 2005) 'EU: Crna Gora ne može opstati sama': 3–4.

Đuranović, D. (2006) 'Crna Gora između Dejtona plus i Kosova', *Monitor*, 10 February 2006.
Đurić, D. (2005) 'Montenegro's Prospects for European Integration: On a Twin Track', *South-East Europe Review*, 79 (106), pp. 79–105.
Edwards, G. (1997) 'The Potential and Limits of the CFSP: The Yugoslav Example', in Regelsberger, E., Schoutheete de Tervant, P., and Wessels, W. (eds), *Foreign Policy of the European Union: From EPC to CFSP and Beyond*, London: Lynne Rienner, pp. 173–195.
European Commission (2005) *Communication of the Commission on the Preparedness of Serbia and Montenegro for the negotiations for SAA with the European Union*. Available at: http://ec.europa.eu/comm/enlargement/docs/pdf/sam_feasibility_report_communication_en.pdf (accessed 09 October 2011).
European Commission (2010) *Commission Opinion on Montenegro's Application for Membership of the European Union*. Available at: http://ec.europa.eu/enlargement/pdf/key_documents/2010/package/mn_opinion_2010_en.pdf (accessed 21 November 2011).
European Commission (2011) *EU Commission – Enlargement: Montenegro*. Available at: http://ec.europa.eu/enlargement/candidate-countries/montenegro/relation/index_en.htm (accessed 10 November 2011).
European Commission (2012) *Commission Staff Working Document: Montenegro 2012 Progress Report*. Available at: http://ec.europa.eu/enlargement/pdf/key_documents/2012/package/mn_rapport_2012_en.pdf (accessed 20 August 2014).
ESI (European Stability Initiative) (1999) *Montenegro: A Balancing Act*, Brussels: ESI.
ESI (European Stability Initiative) (2000) *Autonomy, Dependency, Security: The Montenegrin Dilemma*, ESI Report, Podgorica and Berlin: ESI.
ESI (European Stability Initiative) (2001) *Sovereignty, Europe and the Future of Serbia and Montenegro: A Proposal for International Mediation*, Brussels: ESI.
European Stability Initiative (2005) *The Helsinki Moment: European Member-State Building in the Balkans*, Brussels: ESI.
European Stability Initiative (2008) *The White List Project: EU Policies on Visa-Free Travel for the Western Balkans*, Background Paper, Brussels: ESI.
Grabbe, H. (2001) 'How does Europeanisation Affect CEE governance? Conditionality, Diffusion and Diversity', *Journal of European Public Policy*, 8 (4), pp. 1013–1031.
Hasani, E. (2005) 'Self-Determination under the Terms of the 2002 Union Agreement between Serbia and Montenegro: Tracing the Origins of Kosovo's Self-Determination', *Chicago-Kent Law Review*, 80 (305), pp. 305–329.
ICG (International Crisis Group) (1999) *Montenegro: Calm before the Storm*, Europe Briefing No. 10.
ICG (International Crisis Group) (2000) *Current Legal Status of the Federal Republic of Yugoslavia (FRY) and of Serbia and Montenegro*, Balkans Report No. 101, Washington and Brussels.
ICG (International Crisis Group) (2001) *Montenegro: Settling for Independence*, Balkans Report No. 107.
ICG (International Crisis Group) (2005) *Montenegro's Independence Drive*, Europe Report No. 169.
ICG (International Crisis Group) (2006) *Montenegro's Referendum*, Europe Report No. 42.

Jovanović, I. (2005) 'Ex-Ex-Yugoslavia: A Virtual Country', *Transitions Online*, 7 March 2005.

Malešević, S. and Uzelac, G. (2007) 'A Nation-State without the Nation? The Trajectories of Nation-Formation in Montenegro', *Nations and Nationalism*, 13 (4), pp. 695–716.

Manners, I. (2002) 'Normative Power Europe: A Contradiction in Terms', *JCMS: Journal of Common Market Studies*, 40 (2), pp. 235–258.

Medjak, V. (2004) *Twin-Track Approach towards Serbia-Montenegro: A Recipe for Faster EU Integration*. Available at: www.sant.ox.ac.uk/ext/seesox/OpinionPieces_files/63.pdf (accessed 22 July 2012).

Ministry of Foreign Affairs and European Integration of Montenegro (2012) Available at: www.mip.gov.me (accessed 22 July 2012).

Noutcheva, G. (2007) *Fake, Partial and Imposed Compliance: The Limits of the EU's Normative Power in the Western Balkans*, Centre for European Policy Studies Working Document No. 274. Brussels: CEPS.

Noutcheva, G. and Emerson, M. (2004) *Europeanisation as a Gravity Model of Democratisation*, Centre for European Policy Studies Working Document No. 214, Brussels: CEPS.

Nuttall, S. (1993) 'The EC and Yugoslavia: Deus ex Machina or Machina sine Deo?', in Nugent, N. (ed.), *The European Union 1993: Annual Review of Activities*, Oxford: Blackwell, for *JCMS: Journal of Common Market Studies*, pp. 11–25.

Radaelli, C. M. (2000) *Whither Europeanization? Concept Stretching and Substantive Change*, European Integration Online Papers 4.8. Available at: http://eiop.or.at/eiop/texte/2000–008.htm (accessed 24 August 2011).

Rancharan, B. G. (1997) 'Opinions of the Arbitration Commission', *The International Conference on the Former Yugoslavia: Official Papers*, The Hague: Kluwer Law International: 1258–1302.

Roberts, E. (2002) *Serbia-Montenegro: A New Federation?* Zurich: Conflict Studies Research Centre.

Schelter, K. (2006) 'Challenges for Non- (and Not Yet-) Schengen Countries', in Caparini, M. and Marenin, O. (eds), *Borders and Security Governance: Managing Borders in a Globalised World*, Geneva: DCAF.

Solana, Javier (27 November 2001) *Reuters*, re-published in *Vijesti* (27 November 2001).

'Sporazum o principima odnosa Srbije i Crne Gore u okviru državne zajednice' (2002). Available at: www.gov.me/files/1052297878.doc (accessed 17 June 2011).

Šuković, D. (2002) 'Montenegrin Reactions to the Signing of the Agreement on the Union of Serbia and Montenegro', *AIM Press*, 18 March 2002. Available at: www.aimpress.ch/dyn/trae/archive/data/200203/20323-001-trae-pod.htm (accessed 22 July 2011).

Teokarević, J. (2003) 'EU Accession and the Serbian-Montenegrin Constitutional Charter', *Romanian Journal of Political Science*, 2, pp. 39–49.

The Economist (12 April 1999) 'Independence?' 353 (8148), pp. 50–53.

The Economist (10 April 2004) 'Semi-independent', 371 (8370), p. 36.

Tocci, N. (2004) 'EU Intervention in Ethno-Political Conflicts: The Cases of Cyprus and Serbia-Montenegro', *European Foreign Affairs Review*, 9, pp. 551–573.

Van Meurs, W. (2003) 'The Belgrade Agreement: Robust Mediation between Serbia and Montenegro', in Bieber, F. (ed.), *Montenegro in Transition: Problems of Identity and Statehood*, Baden-Baden: Nomos Verlagsgesellschaft, pp. 63–82.

Vijesti (3 April 1999) 'London optužuje Miloševića da priprema puč u Crnoj Gori'.
Vijesti (9 June 2003) 'Samostalno bi i brže i lakše u EU': 1.
Vijesti (16 January 2006) 'Crnu Goru očekuju ulični nemiri i demonstracije': 3.
Vijesti (22 January 2006) 'Referendum i bez dogovora': 3–4.

6 The EU in Macedonia

From inter-ethnic to intra-ethnic political mediator in an accession deadlock

Simonida Kacarska

Introduction

In the history of EU enlargement, the involvement of the EU in the political affairs of the candidate countries of the Western Balkans has been unprecedented in terms of its scope and length. This novel form of engagement has taken place through a variety of instruments – ranging from the standard mechanisms of accession to direct partaking and mediation of the EU in resolving the remaining burning issues between and within the newly independent countries of the region. The latter have included the Kosovo–Serbia affair, internal matters of running Bosnia and Herzegovina as well as inter-ethnic and intra-ethnic political relations in Macedonia. The unique role of the EU in this region has led to arguments that the EU is more and more involved in the candidate countries, transforming the very nature of the enlargement process. At a theoretical level, this new position of the Union and its institutions challenges the conceptualization of conditionality mechanism as the primary instrument underpinning the relationship between the EU and its candidates. At a practical level, the intertwined role of the EU has resulted in embedding the EU and its institutions as domestic actors within the political landscape of the countries in question. In these conditions, the EU has obtained a bigger stake in the democratic transformation of the respective societies because 'the components of "democratic conditionality", as defined by the first Copenhagen criterion, [...are...] a litmus test of the medium- to long-term consolidation of the polities in question' (Sasse 2008: 843).

In order to examine the implications of this increased role of the EU for democratic consolidation, this chapter studies how the newly introduced EU criterion of *advancing political dialogue* between the political actors in the Republic of Macedonia materialized in the practice of EU conditionality. Since Macedonia became a candidate country for EU accession in 2005, the European Commission has included in various forms the advancement of *political dialogue* as a priority in its Partnerships and Progress Reports. In addition, the EU has formally participated in the management of the political relations in the country, increasing the scope of its involvement in domestic affairs. This chapter examines the dynamics between EU involvement through the requirements of political dialogue and the response from the national level, as well as the implications of this relationship for the democratic consolidation of the country. Illustrating the evolution of the EU's engagement from inter-ethnic to intra-ethnic relations[1] between national political actors, the chapter argues that the EU has obtained the role of a domestic actor, changing the nature of the enlargement process. The chapter is based on the process of tracing of EU and national documents, media, as well as data from interviews conducted by the author between 2010 and 2012.

The chapter consists of three major sections. This introduction is followed by a brief conceptual background on the relationship between the EU's political conditionality and democratic consolidation. This section also provides an overview of the evolution of the political conditions as part of the Copenhagen criteria since the Eastern enlargement. The chapter then studies the idiosyncrasies of the Macedonian EU accession process and the specific involvement of the EU and its institutions in the country. The empirical analysis that follows presents an examination of the EU requirements on political dialogue through a study of the conditions contained in the EU and national documents, as well as the engagement of the EU at the time of various political crises in the country. Lastly, in its conclusion, the chapter reflects on the empirical findings for the study of the role of the EU in the acceding countries of the Western Balkans.

Background: the study and practice of EU political conditionality

The study of the role of the EU in the candidate countries has conventionally been framed within the theoretical boundaries of Europeanization in the context of EU accession (see Sedelmeier 2006). This process, in turn, has been managed primarily through the instrument of conditionality defined as the 'the use of positive incentives (ultimately EU membership) as rewards for states that the EU specifies' (Sedelmeier 2006: 9). EU political conditionality emphasizes 'respect for and the furtherance of democratic rules, procedures and values' for the purposes of EU membership (Pridham 2002: 956). Whereas the literature commonly uses both the terms 'democratic conditionality' and 'political conditionality', Anastasakis (2008), in his work on the Western Balkans, supports the use of the term political conditionality instead of democratic conditionality. He also highlights that 'EU political conditionality can run counter to democratization, at least in the short term when some of the prescriptions prioritize law and order instead of elections and/or civil society development' (Anastasakis 2008: 366). Adopting the same position, this chapter operates with the term political conditionality, without the unquestionable inclusion of a democratization component.

Although a commonly used term, democratic consolidation has been understood in various ways in the academic research. Different definitions of consolidation emphasize 'various processes, levels, dimensions, locations of areas of political change' (Plasser *et al.* 1998: 11). Analysts like Schedler (1998) have pointed to the overstretching of the concept, since it has come to include elements ranging from popular legitimation to the alleviation of poverty, and economic stabilization. Alongside arguments of overstretching, Linz and Stepan's (1996) definition of democratic consolidation is one of the most widely used in research. For them, a consolidated democracy entails a multitude of conditions, the most important of which are a free and lively civil society, a relatively autonomous political society, the rule of law, a usable state bureaucracy, and an institutionalized economic society. Looking into the management of political affairs as an element of EU conditionality, this chapter focuses on the establishment of a relatively autonomous political society as an element of democratic consolidation.

In practice, the mechanism of conditionality was most extensively developed in the study of the EU's Eastern enlargement, since prior to the 1990s there was no proper monitoring of conditions for accession to the EU, especially in relation to the political criteria (Pridham 2007a). In retrospect, since their introduction in 1993, the political conditions for EU accession as an integral part of the Copenhagen criteria have gradually been extended and developed in the last two decades. In the early Progress Reports, the Commission examined solely the formal aspect of political conditions, whereas in later periods, conditionality became more precise (Pridham 2002: 957). In fact, the first Progress Reports (1997–1999) on the Eastern enlargement candidate countries lack a clear methodology regarding political conditionality for objective cross-country comparisons, which explains the general assessment that the countries fulfil the Copenhagen criteria (Pridham 2002). Hughes *et al.* (2005) argue that the priority of conditionality in this period was to secure the transposition of the *acquis* rather than to promote the consolidation of democratic society. In any case, in the 1990s, it is very difficult to point to a consistent set of political conditions and their application in the context of EU accession, leading to a common criticism of vagueness and arbitrariness (Kochenov 2004).

The post-2000 period marks the development and extension of EU political conditionality in the Eastern enlargement with a shift of focus towards the political criteria, particularly judicial reform and anti-corruption policies in the cases of Bulgaria and Romania. Assessing these developments, Pridham (2005) argues that the conditions of the EU have moved from procedural requirements of formal democracy (the rule of law, separation of institutional powers, free elections, freedom of expression) to include criteria of substantive democracy, such as the role of political parties as a vehicle of political participation, pluralism of media, importance of local government and involved civil society. Thus, Pridham (2007a: 468) concludes that 'political conditionality has become broader in its scope, [and] much tighter in its procedures'. He demonstrates this tendency in the analysis of the evolution of political conditionality with respect to Romania, arguing that criticisms of performance with respect to the political conditions had become stronger over time because of the fear of the impact of the end of the negotiations on the EU's leverage (Pridham 2007b). Overall, the Commission has gradually pursued a more interventionist attitude in comparison to previous enlargements, a tendency noted already with respect to Bulgaria and Romania (Phinnemore 2006; Pridham 2007b).

This extension of conditionality has been developing against the lack of a common set of EU requirements in relation to the political criteria (including the rule of law, judiciary, anti-corruption policy, etc.). Hence, it has been subject to criticisms concerning lack of consistency, vagueness, and increased scope for political judgments in the assessments (Sasse 2009). Pravda (2001: 13) explains this practical problem in setting democratization criteria and evaluating political performance, by highlighting that 'political targets are typically qualitative and hard to define as precisely as economic goals'. Brusis (2005: 316) also concludes that the conditions 'are likely to have a more tangible direct impact in issue areas where the EU has a more prescriptive *acquis*'. In light of these assessments, Magen and Morlino (2009: 12) criticize the tendency of the literature towards the homogenization of external influence on domestic reform processes. Hughes *et al.* (2005: 28) consider that a 'fundamental problem for the concept is that macro-level and policy-level studies are inconclusive about the causal effects of "Europeanisation" and demonstrate the persistence of deep structural divergences across national and policy contexts'. Magen and Morlino (2009) also underline that, in reality, the same factors have a varying effect on democratization outcomes, depending on the specific outcome studied.

In light of these debates, empirical research on the role of political conditionality in democratic consolidation has been inconclusive. On the one hand, the EU's conditionality has generally been considered to have a lock-in effect on the liberal forces after the overthrow of authoritarian governments (Vachudova 2005). Still, research on the previous enlargement regarding the link between conditionality and democratization has concluded that 'negative impacts could also occur notwithstanding the official commitment of Brussels to furthering democratic consolidation in Central & Eastern Europe' (Pridham 2005: 226). For example, Grabbe (2001) argues that policy choices are technocratic rather than political issues, leading to a deficit of democratic accountability in the whole process. On the latter aspect, Pridham (2006) criticizes the favouring of executive institutions over the parliament as well as the exporting of the EU's democratic deficit in these countries. Innes (2002: 101) claims that the EU accession process 'could have a debilitating effect, arresting party developments by excluding from political competition those substantive, grassroots, ideological policy conflicts around which Western Europe systems evolved'. These findings confirm the warnings of the general literature on Europeanization regarding the intended and unintended consequences of conditionality (Grabbe 2006: 49).

In the case of the Western Balkans, this risk is even higher since the EU has moved further down the path of engagement in domestic politics by assessing the national political scene and the relations between the local political actors (see Pridham 2007a). Moreover, 'the EU puts different emphasis on the way it justifies its policy of conditionality to domestic actors in the various Western Balkan countries – a differentiation closely linked to the specificity of each case' (Noutcheva 2007). The literature links this attitude with the role the EU has acquired through the brokering of peace-deals in Bosnia and Macedonia particularly (see Anastasakis and Bechev 2003). In light of the increased role of the EU, Chandler (2008: 529) argues that 'EU member state-building in the Western Balkans is a clear example of the dangers of the liberal peace approach to post-conflict situations'. In his work, he is highly critical of the role of the EU in the Western Balkans arguing that 'the externally driven nature of the policy process means that political elites seek to lobby external EU actors rather than engage in domestic constituency-building' (Chandler 2008: 529). Contrary to Chandler, O'Brennan (2008: 508) argues that that 'the policy being pursued by Brussels is consistent with the expectations of the "normative power Europe" approach to enlargement'. Similarly, Manners (2002: 252) argues that the EU is a power with normative quality, which should act to extend its norms into the international system. With these conceptual debates in mind, this chapter sheds light on the link between the processes of conditionality and democratic consolidation in Macedonia, as a country with increasing political involvement of the EU.

Why Macedonia?

Macedonia has traditionally been open to the involvement of international actors, especially the EU, though the establishment of official relations between the two in the post-independence period was complicated by the name dispute with Greece. During the early 1990s, the establishment of relations with the European Community was strained due to the objections of Greece to the constitutional name 'Republic of Macedonia'. At the Lisbon Summit in June 1992, under Greek pressure, the EU decided to withhold the recognition of Macedonia. The Council conclusions expressed 'readiness to recognise that republic within its existing borders according to their Declaration on 16 December 1991 under a name which does not include the term Macedonia' (Council 1992). A consensual (albeit temporary) solution was found with the country joining the UN in

1993 under a provisional name 'the former Yugoslav Republic of Macedonia'. Formal diplomatic relations between Macedonia and the EU were not established until December 1995, after the signing of the Interim Accord between Macedonia and Greece in September of the same year.[2] With the Interim Accord, Greece obliged itself not to veto Macedonia's entry into regional and international organizations under the provisional reference, thus creating conditions for establishing full diplomatic relations with the EU. Both countries are still engaged in UN mediated talks for finding a solution, however even these have not led to results.[3]

Since the mid 1990s, Macedonia has been a part of the various regional EU instruments and policy frameworks of the EU initiatives ranging from the Union's foreign policy to the enlargement portfolio. Generally, 'there has not been a single policy by the EU towards the region, but rather a number of different policies carried out by a host of different institutions and ad hoc bodies of the EU' (Bieber 2011: 1776). The Regional Approach launched in 1997 was the first instrument of EU conditionality in the Balkans, upgraded in 2001 through the Stabilization and Association Process and the applications for candidacy from the countries in the region since 2003. In addition, in Macedonia specifically, the EU obtained an increased political and military role during and following the signing of the 2001 Ohrid Framework Agreement (OFA). In the post-2001 period, the OFA is considered central to the EU's relationship with Macedonia.[4] Whereas the implementation of the Agreement was channelled through domestic institutions, the EU constantly provided external support and at times pressure for its implementation.[5] Javier Solana, the EU High Representative for Common Foreign and Security Policy (CFSP) at the time, was directly involved in the OFA negotiations which led to a widely accepted maxim in the national political discourse that 'the road to Brussels leads through Ohrid' (Solana 2004). As a result, the OFA implementation and inter-ethnic political relations became a core element of the conditions stipulated by the EU to Macedonia.

In addition to this form of political involvement, after the 2001 crisis, the first military peacekeeping mission in EU history, Concordia, was deployed in Macedonia and was succeeded by the EU police mission Proxima in December 2003. As a result, it has been argued that 'through the involvement on the ground, the EU gained a big stake in Macedonia's future'.[6] This role was largely accepted by local elites as well. The president of Macedonia in a speech highlighted that 'our ambition is full membership in the Union, and I would like to see this mission [...], as a step in that direction. The more of the EU we have in Macedonia, the more of Macedonia there will be in the EU' (Trajkovski 2003). The specificities of EU's involvement on the ground were also reflected in the 'double hat' representation of the EU in the country combining the position of the EU Special Representative of the Council and the Head of the Commission Delegation. 'Due to this double hat policy, the political functions of the Council have been performed by the same representative managing issues of EU enlargement, further strengthening the link between the two.'[7] As a result, EU representatives in Macedonia have become intrinsically connected with domestic politics, which is illustrated by the role they have played in forging consensus between major political actors in the country.

Parallel with this extensive involvement of the Union on the ground, Macedonia's EU accession has largely followed an idiosyncratic path. In the context of the EU accession of the Balkans, the Republic of Macedonia has regressed, in regional terms, from the position of a leader/frontrunner in 2004/2005 to that of a laggard by 2012. Despite being the first Balkan country to sign a Stabilization and Association Agreement (SAA) in early 2001 and the second after Croatia to receive 'candidate status' in 2005, Macedonia still awaits the start of its accession negotiations. The European Commission's recommendation for launching the accession negotiations of 2009 has still not been followed up by a Council decision resulting in a status quo in the country's advance towards the EU due to an ongoing dispute with Greece over the country's constitutional name.[8] At the same time, as explained above, through its various institutions the EU has been heavily involved in everyday political affairs since the 2001 inter-ethnic conflict in Macedonia. Thus, Macedonia is an illustrative, yet unique example for studying the role of the EU in stipulating political conditionality and the elites' responses to extensive EU requirements.

Political dialogue as an element of EU conditionality in the EU documents and in practice

Having elaborated on the evolution and extension of the political requirements for EU accession in general and the main features of the EU's engagement in Macedonia, this section moves on to examine how the EU's requirements on the relationship between the main political parties in the country materialized in practice since 2005. (For a background on the pre-2005 period, see Kacarska 2013). The year 2005 is endorsed as a starting point of the empirical examination in this chapter as the year that Macedonia obtained candidate status and the Commission started issuing Progress Reports for the countries of the region.[9] The analysis of the Progress Reports and other related EU and national strategic documents since 2005 illustrates the evolution of EU conditionality in relation to the political actors and the national responses to conditionality.

The years 2005–2010: gradual extension from inter-ethnic to intra-ethnic political relationships

In the first couple of years following their introduction in 2005, the EU Progress Reports focused on the relationships between political actors of the different (ethnic) communities, in light of the previously discussed role of the EU and its institutions as guarantors of the OFA. Hence, the 2005 and 2006 European Commission reports focused on general assessments of the implementation of the OFA and the conduct of elections (see European Commission 2005, 2006). The evaluation of political relationships in relation to the OFA, i.e. the inter-ethnic dimension, was a remnant of the role of the EU in the signing and implementation of the agreement as discussed above. In practice, EU officials were also informally engaged in the (inter-ethnic) government coalition building following the 2006 parliamentary elections.[10] After the elections, VMRO-DPMNE[11] made a coalition with their *traditional* coalition partner the Democratic Party of the Albanians (DPA), which came second in the Albanian block.[12] The Democratic Union for Integration (DUI), as the party with most votes in the Albanian block, interpreted this decision as a sign of disregard for the will of the Albanian community.[13] In the midst of the negotiations, the EU Head of Delegation and Special Representative of the Council Erwan Fouerre (2006) stated that 'it would be logical if the government consisted of the parties that won the most votes' [these were VMRO-DPMNE and DUI at the time]. At the national level, in Macedonia, this statement was interpreted by the media and part of the political elite as an attempt by the EU to influence the formation of the government coalition, mostly with respect to the party representing the Albanian community. A former Vice Prime Minister for EU affairs interviewed by this author singled out this event as an example of 'direct interference from the EU' and a 'disruption on the part of the EU of internal political dynamics in Macedonia'.[14] Such debates illustrate the specific embedded nature of the EU in the national politics of Macedonia since the OFA, which has been implemented with constant supervision from the Union and its institutions.

The EU engagement in the same field continued in the course of the following year as well. Namely in its 2007 report, the European Commission assessed that establishing an inclusive dialogue within the parliament remained difficult (European Commission 2007). This assessment was underpinned by the events in the course of 2007 when DUI, as the biggest Albanian opposition party, boycotted the work of the Macedonian Parliament because laws that required the support of the non-majority votes were passed without its support. This was possible since the votes of the DPA in the coalition government and the other non-majority members of Parliament were sufficient. The crisis was resolved with the signing of the so-called May Agreement, which was reached under increasing pressure from the EU, both through the ambassadors of the Member States as well as via the EU Head of Delegation and Special Representative of the Council, as was confirmed in local research (Markovic *et al.* 2011). The Agreement, among other points, contains a list of laws which are to be adopted with double majority, i.e. majority of all members of Parliament as well as majority of representatives of the non-majority communities.[15]

Markovic et al. (2011: 22) have argued that 'the May agreement case can be perceived as some sort of a turning point for EU involvement in ethnic conflict management in Macedonia as this process has been marked by the increasing persuasive role of the EU'.

In light of these forms of engagement, the position of the European Union Special Representative was also subject to debates, especially at the national level. The literature has argued that 'the more advanced the transition process, and the more stable the security situation, the more relevant the role of the Commission and the less central the position of the EU Special Representative' (Adebahr and Grevi 2007). However, in the case of Macedonia, this has not been the case. The continuous combination of the two roles resulted in a situation in which 'Macedonia was a candidate for EU membership and is being monitored from the Council. Hence, there is a dilemma whether the EU is supporting the country or is intervening with elements of a soft protectorate'.[16] Although the position of the European Union Special Representative for Macedonia was abolished in 2010, the engagement of the EU institutions through various initiatives has continued, as will be shown in the discussion that follows (Vogel 2010).

Whereas until 2007 the EU's conditions and political engagement with respect to the relationship between the political actors were mostly limited to the inter-ethnic dimension, since 2008 a shift towards stipulating broader requirements on political dialogue can be identified through the EU documents and the actions of EU officials. The 2008 Accession Partnership for Macedonia contains a *key* priority: 'Promoting a constructive and inclusive dialogue, in particular in areas which require consensus between all political parties, in the framework of the democratic institutions' (Council of the European Union 2008). The key priorities were in fact introduced by the European Commission in 2008 as the primary conditions for accession, similar to the benchmarks in the accession negotiations. Thus, the inclusion of this priority in the partnership illustrates the high significance of the specific issue for the EU. Moreover, the partnerships have legally binding effect as the only formal documents adopted by the Council of the EU and published in the Official Journal of the EU, representing the highest form of conditionality imposed by the EU upon the candidate countries. Grabbe (2006) argues that the Partnerships significantly extended EU influence to an unprecedented extent, thereby limiting the scope of negotiations with candidates. Similarly, for Smith (2003: 127), 'the Partnerships illustrate the extent to which the EU is seeking to influence the domestic and foreign affairs of membership candidates'. In this set of tasks, the Copenhagen political criteria have priority among the whole set of criteria, allowing the Union to make them instrumental at all stages of the enlargement process (Kochenov 2004).

The inclusion of this priority and the emphasis on general political dialogue, among other reasons, was primarily triggered by the decision of the

Social Democratic Union of Macedonia (SDSM)[17] to boycott the work of the Parliament due to the arrest of its vice president, at a time that the party felt was politically motivated. In the period of their absence from the Parliament, almost 172 laws were enacted, all using the emergency procedure (see European Commission 2008). Moreover, this condition also was set due to the fact that in the period between 2004 and 2007, at least one of the major parties in the country boycotted the work of the Parliament at one point or another.[18] This form of political instability between 2005 and 2008 also influenced the Commission's decision to delay the recommendation on the start of negotiations with Macedonia. In response to this priority, since 2008 the national strategic documents for EU integration have foreseen activities for the management of everyday affairs in the Parliament, and even the cohabitation of the government and the president at the time (Government of the Republic of Macedonia 2008). Although the manner of implementation of such commitments remained unclear, the inclusion of such activities denotes the acceptance of the condition by national elites. Along the same lines, the author's interviewees have confirmed that since 2008, the political dialogue between the elites became the primary condition for EU accession, which was also accepted among the political actors.[19]

Since 2008, and following the inclusion of a priority regarding the facilitation of political dialogue, this topic has become a regular component of the EU Progress Reports and conditionality. In 2009, the Commission assessed that there had been good progress on this priority recommending 'continued efforts to deepen political dialogue, including on inter–ethnic issues, [which] would consolidate the engagement of all parties' (European Commission 2009). In the report of the same year, the Commission in fact recommended opening up of the negotiations with Macedonia as a result of the fulfilment of the political criteria and hence the assessment was largely interpreted with a positive note. Moreover, during 2009 the government was directed towards fulfilling the EU requirements, among other reasons, because of the visa liberalization process at the time. The strategic documents were also prepared in light of the pending decision for the visa liberalization dialogues which took place between 2008 and 2010. In fact, other studies have shown the role of the visa liberalization process as a successful form of EU policy conditionality, especially in the area of justice and home affairs (Trauner 2009).

Post-2010: increased EU engagement as an arbitrator between the political actors

Although the expectations of scholars are that over time the role of the EU in managing everyday political affairs and crises in candidate countries would diminish, the experience of the Macedonian case illustrates opposite tendencies. Since 2011, when the opposition parties SDSM and the DPA boycotted the Parliament for around three months, EU involvement has in fact been on the rise.[20] As a result of the boycott of the Parliament, a third round of extraordinary parliamentary elections since 2006 was held in Macedonia. The decision to hold parliamentary elections by the ruling party was explained in light of the requirements for EU accession. The General Secretary of VMRO-DPMNE at the time argued that 'if there were no elections in Macedonia, the recommendation for starting the negotiations would be lost'.[21] In this respect, all major political decisions were interpreted by the main political actors in light of the requirements for EU accession, denoting an acceptance on the side of the national elites of the evolving role of the Union. In the aftermath of the elections and the return of the opposition in Parliament, in 2011, the European Commission Progress Report assesses that 'political dialogue needs to be further strengthened in order that problems can be resolved through the institutional framework. The boycott by the opposition hampered the functioning of the parliament' (European Commission 2011).

Due to the general political crisis and the post-2009 status quo in Macedonia's accession process in 2012, the Commission introduced the High Level Accession Dialogue (HLAD) as 'a new opportunity to focus on a number of priorities' (Europa Press Release 2012).[22] The dialogue lays emphasis on the freedom of expression and media, the rule of law, reform of the public administration, electoral reform, and the strengthening of the market economy, and is organized, in practice, through high-level meetings between the Commissioner for Enlargement and the Prime Minister of Macedonia. While the Commission's engagement via HLAD has been favourably assessed by the governing parties, the parties in opposition have criticized it and accused the EU of 'selective' attention and willingness to overlook any democratic backlash in the country.[23] This assessment of the opposition illustrates the largely embedded role of the EU in the Macedonian context, where the EU officials have become arbitrators between the political actors.

Since 2012, the HLAD has also progressed alongside continuous on-the-ground engagement of the EU in managing inter-party relations in Macedonia. In early 2013, the European Commissioner for Enlargement Štefan Füle was directly involved in resolving a political crisis in Macedonia following a boycott of the SDSM, in opposition, of the Parliament. This boycott was the result of a clash with the government over the adoption of the 2013 budget which resulted in the forceful removal of opposition MPs from the parliamentary hall in December 2012. The opposition MPs were removed after lengthy budget debates and having submitted more than 1,000 amendments to the draft budget as well as employing delaying tactics. The crisis escalated on 24 December when the SDSM MPs 'engaged in a strategy of blocking the session by surrounding the parliament's speaker seat and not allowing him to chair the session', after which they were forced out of the hall.[24] With the SDSM boycotting the Parliament and refusing to participate in the local elections scheduled for March 2013, an EU troika consisting of Commissioner Füle, Richard Howitt, the EP rapporteur on Macedonia, and the former EP President Jerzy Buzek, intervened to mediate the dispute between the two political parties.[25] An agreement to participate in the elections was eventually reached under extensive EU pressure in early March 2013. However, the terms of the agreement were subject to different interpretations by the opposition and government on whether it contained a promise for early parliamentary elections (Blazevska 2013).

After negotiating this contested agreement, on a visit to Macedonia in mid-April 2013, Commissioner Füle directly pointed to the relationship between the political actors as a key obstacle to Macedonia's EU accession. He noted that 'the politicians created the crisis and have the responsibility to overcome its effects by implementing the agreement, which they had still not done, at least not fully' (Mladenovska 2013). The remaining element of this agreement concerned the setting up an inquiry committee in relation to the events of 24 December. The committee was established in June 2013, half a year after the incident, due to the inability to reach consensus on its president, who later resigned, just two months after his appointment. With pressure from the EU in August 2013, the Commission tasked to investigate the events of 24 December prepared a report with recommendations focusing on improving parliamentary procedures and tightening the rules on the use of parliamentary security (Marusic 2013). After signing it, the representatives of VMRO-DPMNE still rejected the key elements of the report, noting that they had signed it just for the sake of the country's EU future. According to VMRO-DPMNE commission member Ilija Dimovski 'for us [meaning VMRO-DPMNE] the legal conclusions do not have any importance. For us they are the same as a piece of handkerchief' (Duridanski and Marusic, 2013). Brussels welcomed the signing of the report, which has since become a key element of EU conditionality, although it was evident that the recommendations did not materialize in practice. In light of this failure to meet the conditions stipulated by the EU in the last 2013 Progress Report, the Commission noted that

> the political crisis showed the degree of polarization and highlighted the need for parties to show greater political commitment to resolving problems through dialogue and in full respect of the institutional framework, with both government and opposition playing constructive roles.
>
> (European Commission 2013)

From the assessment it is clear that the notion of political dialogue is likely to remain on the EU agenda as a condition for membership, though the EU's direct involvement in the managing of political affairs also depends on the EU institutions. The EU's insistence on the notion of political dialogue has been met with differing responses in academic and practitioners' circles. Vasilev (2011: 53–54) argues that 'the EU was emphasizing the consensus principle in its rhetoric and feedback', hence the need for this condition. At the national level, nevertheless, the specific condition of 'political dialogue' was interpreted as a way of further strengthening political parties in the public sphere. The increased role of the parties has already been raised in both academic and policy literature as one of the key challenges of the transformation process of Macedonia (see Kacarska 2008). The lines of separation among the executive, legislative, and judicial bodies become blurred as one political party gains control (after elections) of both the legislature and the executive, which in turn provides an opportunity for partisan changes in the judiciary (Tsekov 2005). As a result, domestic analysts have stressed that rather than emphasizing political dialogue, the Commission should insist on 'policy dialogue' in Macedonia (Risteska 2010).

The (dis)continuation of the hands-on approach of the European institutions in managing political affairs in Macedonia has been subject to discussions both within the EU institutions and at the national level. For example, a debate is ongoing within the European Commission concerning how long this involvement should last. On the one hand, it has been pointed out that due to the OFA, the EU holds a responsibility in the Macedonian case, making 'Macedonia important to the EU'.[26] On the other hand, a high-ranking Commission official pointed out that 'the view of the Commission in general is that we should not perpetuate this policy. In relation to political criteria, a state must be sovereign. We have no business in deciding on directions.'[27] Contrary to these expectations, the experience of 2012 and 2013 denotes a shift towards increased involvement of the EU Commissioner personally on the ground level, a role previously played by the local Head of the EU Delegation and EU Special Representative.[28] A similar dilemma regarding the role of the Commission is increasingly present also at the national level. A former Vice Prime Minister for EU affairs in the country stressed that 'Macedonia has reached a point where the EU needs to take its hand off the saddle. The elites need to reach an agreement by themselves, instead of trying to communicate through an external actor.'[29] This view is commonly contrasted with the position of political representatives in Macedonia who have continuously called for EU involvement in various political affairs.[30]

This evolution of the EU's role in the case of Macedonia has taken place against the background of a deadlock in the country's accession due to the dispute with Greece since 2009, when the Commission proposed that the country start accession negotiations. For the past four years, however, this recommendation was not followed up by a Council decision. The preparedness to commence negotiations has been confirmed in every Progress Report since 2009 without a positive response from the Council.

Commission representatives consider the issue as exogenous to the accession process, but recognize that it impedes upon the regular functioning of conditionality.[31] At the national level, in Macedonia, the name issue is considered as an interference with the expected course of conditionality, and this situation has been weakening the credibility of the membership perspective in the eyes of the elites and broader population.[32] These background conditions have contributed to diminishing trust in the EU and could potentially also endanger the traditionally high support for EU membership among the population in Macedonia if the status quo continues in the future.[33]

Conclusions

This chapter examined EU conditionality with respect to political dialogue and the relations between the political actors in the case of Macedonia since 2005. Starting with the extension of EU political conditionality in the Western Balkans and the novel role of the EU, the chapter sought to examine the implications of the hands-on approach of the EU for democratic consolidation. By looking into the EU requirements for political dialogue and the national responses to these novel conditions, the chapter has demonstrated the evolution of the role of the EU as an inter-ethnic to an intra-ethnic arbitrator between the Macedonian political elites. Whereas increased EU engagement originated in the inter-ethnic negotiations in relation to the OFA, since then the EU has been involved both in intra- and inter-ethnic negotiations, and has managed various political crises in the country. On an institutional level, the chapter has also demonstrated that whereas prior to 2010 the EU's involvement on the ground in Macedonia was foremost through the activities of the local Head of the Delegation and Special Representative of the Council, since 2011 the EU Commissioner for Enlargement directly partook in resolving political crises in the country. These intensive on-the-ground involvements have taken place in the midst of a status quo in terms of Macedonia's advancement to the EU due to the name dispute with Greece, which weakens the credibility of the EU and its membership perspective.

The chapter has illustrated that the involvement of the EU institutions on the ground has persisted in various forms since 2005, despite Macedonia's gaining the status of a candidate country, arguably upon its fulfilling the political criteria. These developments question the relationship between conditionality and democratic consolidation on several levels. First, the involvement of the EU, especially over the last two years, points to the development of a culture of dependence on the external actors (in this case the EU) among national political elites. Second, the experience of negotiating a report on the events of 24 December also has indicated that the elites have only formally managed to act for the purposes of ticking the box of the EU requirement. In this vein, the Macedonian experience illustrates the dangers of placing the political relationships between the national elites in the bureaucratic mechanisms of enlargement, especially under the conditions of a stagnating accession process. Both the focus on political affairs and the name issue have altered the nature of the accession process from an exercise of adapting to standards to resolving solely political issues and dealing with thorny bilateral issues.

Hence, the analysis has shown that the extensive EU requirements in terms of the relations between political actors in the country have not brought about substantial shifts in the political transformation of Macedonia. In addition to confirming the continued fake compliance in the Balkans (Noutcheva 2007), the chapter also shed light on the dangers of increased involvement of the EU and its institutions in everyday political affairs. These have included persistent political crises in which the domestic elites have relied extensively on the EU's involvement for the resolution of disputes. As the EU institutions have obtained an embedded role at the national level, the domestic elites have predominantly grounded their actions in light of the requirements of the EU officials, instead of their respective constituencies. In turn, these developments raise concerns about the prospects of creating an autonomous political society as an integral element of a democratically consolidated polity.

From a broader perspective, studying the EU's increasing involvement in the political affairs in Macedonia also illustrated the changing nature of EU enlargement in the Western Balkans. With the novel roles of the Union and its institutions, the accession process has gradually been transformed from an exercise of predominantly accommodating to the EU legislation to exclusively fulfilling political requirements. As mentioned in the introduction, this tendency was already noticeable in the Romanian and Bulgarian accession, yet has been further extended in the present case study. The focus on the political arena and relationships between the domestic political actors, as well as bilateral issues, have largely marginalized the rest of the accession requirements. Such developments raise both immediate and long-term concerns for the nature of the ongoing accession of the region to the EU. Whereas in the short term, the focus on the political issues facilitates the role of the EU as an actor on the domestic political scene, in the long term this changed role of the EU will have implications for these countries as future members of the Union.

Notes

1 That is, relations between and within the various communities in the country.
2 Ministry of Foreign Affairs of Republic of Macedonia, 'Relations between Republic of Macedonia and EU', www.mfa.gov.mk, last accessed on 16 June 2010.
3 For a factual background, see Karajkov 2008.
4 Author's interview with European Commission official, Brussels, 11 October 2010.

5 Author's interview with former Vice Prime Minister for EU Affairs, Skopje, 23 December 2010.
6 Author's interview with think tank analyst, Brussels, 11 October 2010.
7 Author's interview with think tank analyst, Brussels, 11 October 2010.
8 For a background on the name dispute, see Karajkov 2008.
9 Between 2002 and 2004 the Commission issued the SAA reports which were significantly less detailed than the regular progress reports.
10 Although not a legal requirement, all governments in Macedonia since independence have consisted of both an ethnic Macedonian and ethnic Albanian political party.
11 Internal Democratic Revolutionary Organisation – Democratic Party for Macedonian National Unity [original: Внатрешно Македонска Револуционерна Организација – Демократска Партија за Македонско Национално Единство] declares itself as a party of Christian-Democrat orientation, 'founded by a group of like-minded individuals in opposition to the communist regime'. See official website of the party, available at: www.vmro-dpmne.org.mk/english/who-we-are.htm, last accessed on 30 July 2010.
12 The VMRO-DPMNE and DPA previously formed a coalition government in 1998.
13 Nikolovski, Zoran, 'Macedonia got a new government: DUI started to use militant rhetoric [Македонија доби нова влада, ДУИ почна да користи милитантна реторика]', *Southeast European Times*, 28 August 2006, available at: www.setimes.com/cocoon/setimes/xhtml/mk/features/setimes/features/2006/08/28/feature-02, last accessed on 5 March 2013.
14 Author's interview with former Vice Prime Minister for EU Affairs, Skopje, 25 December 2010.
15 The Agreement is not publicly available, but its main points are summarized by a newspaper article at the time, 'VMRO-DPMNE and DUI hide the Agreement [ВМРО-ДПМНЕ и ДУИ го заскриваат договорот]', *Dnevnik*, 30 May 2007, available at: www.dnevnik.com.mk/?itemID=C13A64D422158841A5A52709A2C06E08&arc=1, last accessed on 5 March 2013.
16 Author's interview with former Ambassador to the EU, Tetovo, 22 December 2010.
17 The Social Democratic Union of Macedonia [Социјалдемократски сојуз на Македонија] (SDSM) is the successor to the former Communist Party.
18 In the period between 2005–2007, one of the two major parties of the Albanian community with representatives in Parliament (that is, the Democratic Party of the Albanians and Democratic Union for Integration) was not participating in the work of this body.
19 Author's interview with high-level civil servant from the Secretariat for European Affairs, 22 December 2010.
20 See 'Four months of Parliamentary boycott by the opposition lead Nikola Gruevski to convene early general elections in Macedonia', Foundation Robert Schuman, www.robert-schuman.eu/en/eem/1225-four-months-of-parliamentary-boycott-by-the-opposition-lead-nikola-gruevski-to-convene-early-general-elections-in-macedonia.
21 'Протоѓер: Ако нема избори ќе нема ни препорака за ЕУ [Protoger: Without elections there will be no EU recommendation]', 5 March 2011; see more at http://star.press24.mk/story/makedonija/protogjer-ako-nema-izbori-kje-nema-ni-preporaka-za-eu#sthash.HwHGdEGA.dpuf.
22 Similar initiatives were launched in Bosnia and Serbia at the time.
23 'Macedonian opposition: EU ignores democratic backslide', *EurActiv*, 4 January 2013, available at www.euractiv.com/enlargement/macedonia-opposition-eu-turns-bl-news-516863, last accessed on 5 March 2013.

24 The exact events are still subject to different interpretation. For a summary, see Karajkov, Risto, 'Macedonian political crisis: opposition to run in local elections', 14 March 2013, available at www.balcanicaucaso.org/eng/Regions-and-countries/Macedonia/Macedonian-political-crisis-opposition-to-run-in-local-elections-132074, last accessed on 10 June 2013.
25 'An Agreement for solving the crisis has been reached – the opposition is coming back to the Parliament [Постигнат договор за излез од кризата – опозицијата се враќа во Собрание]', *Dnevnik*, 1 March 2013, available at http://dnevnik.com.mk/?itemID=845599F9009C8B408019A7204FE59CED&arc=1, last accessed on 5 March 2013.
26 Author's interview with think tank analyst, Brussels, 11 October 2010.
27 Author's interview with European Commission official, Brussels, 15 November 2010.
28 During my interviews, this development was linked to the personal engagement of the Head of the Delegation and the EU enlargement commissioner.
29 Author's interview with former Vice Prime Minister for EU Affairs, Skopje, 25 December 2010.
30 Author's interview with former Vice Prime Minister for EU affairs, Skopje, 23 December 2010.
31 Author's interview with European Commission official, Brussels, 15 November 2010.
32 While public support for membership is still steady, trust in the EU has been declining. In the Autumn 2011 Eurobarometer for the first time a majority of the population polled expressed distrust of the EU. See 'Public Opinion in the European Union', Standard Eurobarometer 76, Autumn 2011, available at http://.europa.eu/public_opinion/archives/eb/eb76/eb76_agreport_en.pdf, last accessed on 5 March 2013.
33 Macedonia has traditionally had high support for EU membership (around 80 per cent) among the population. For an overview of polls, see Secretariat for European Affairs, 'Public opinion polls', www.sep.gov.mk/portal/mak/default.asp?id=10.

References

Adebahr, C. and Grevi, G. (2007) 'The EU Special Representatives: What lessons for the EEAS?', *European Policy Centre Working Paper No. 28: The EU Foreign Service: How to build a more effective common policy*. Available at: http://epc.eu/documents/uploads/555858396_EPC%20Working%20Paper%2028%20The%20EU%20Foreign%20Service.pdf.

Anastasakis, O. (2008) 'The EU's political conditionality in the Western Balkans: Towards a more pragmatic approach', *Southeast European and Black Sea Studies*, 8(4), pp. 365–377.

Anastasakis, O. and Bechev, D. (2003) 'EU conditionality in South East Europe: Bringing commitment to the process', South East European Studies Programme at Oxford Policy Paper.

Bieber, F. (2011) 'Introduction', *Europe-Asia Studies*, 63(10), pp. 1775–1781.

Blazevska, K. (2013) 'The election compromise lost in translation!? [Изборниот компромис изгубен во преводот!?]', *Deutsche Welle*, 2 March.

Brusis, M. (2005) 'The instrumental use of European Union conditionality: Regionalization in the Czech Republic and Slovakia', *East European Politics and Societies*, 19(2), pp. 291–316.

Chandler, D. (2008) 'Normative power and the liberal peace: A rejoinder to John O'Brennan', *Global Society*, 22(4), pp. 519–529.
Council of the European Union (2008) *Council Decision of 18 February 2008 on the principles, priorities and conditions contained in the Accession Partnership with the former Yugoslav Republic of Macedonia and repealing Decision 2006/57/EC*, 2008/212/EC.
Duridanski, D. and Marusic, S.J. (2013) 'Macedonia agrees crisis report as political row continues', *Balkan Insight*, 26 August.
European Commission (2005) *Analytical report for the Opinion on the application from the former Yugoslav Republic of Macedonia for EU membership, Commission Staff Working Paper*. Brussels: Commission of the European Communities.
European Commission (2006) *The Former Yugoslav Republic of Macedonia 2006 Progress Report, Commission Staff Working Paper*, Brussels.
European Commission (2007) *The Former Yugoslav Republic of Macedonia 2007 Progress Report, Commission Staff Working Paper*, Brussels.
European Commission (2008) *The Former Yugoslav Republic of Macedonia 2008 Progress Report, Commission Staff Working Paper*, Brussels.
European Commission (2009) *The Former Yugoslav Republic of Macedonia 2009 Progress Report, Commission Staff Working Paper*, Brussels.
European Commission (2011) *The Former Yugoslav Republic of Macedonia 2011 Progress Report, Commission Staff Working Paper*, Brussels.
European Commission (2013) *The Former Yugoslav Republic of Macedonia 2013 Progress Report, Commission Staff Working Paper*, Brussels.
European Commission (2012) *Start of the High Level Accession Dialogue with the government of the Former Yugoslav Republic of Macedonia*. Press Release. 15 March. Available at: http://europa.eu/rapid/press-release_MEMO-12-187_en.htm?locale=en.
European Council (1992) *Annex to the Council's conclusions on the development of the Common Foreign and Security Policy (CFSP)*, Lisbon.
Government of the Republic of Macedonia (2008) *Blueprint on the realisation of the recommendations in the European Commission Progress Report on the Republic of Macedonia 2008*.
Grabbe, H. (2001) 'How does Europeanization affect CEE governance? Conditionality, diffusion and diversity', *Journal of European Public Policy*, 8(6), pp. 1013–1031.
Grabbe, H. (2006) *The EU's transformative power: Europeanization through conditionality in Central and Eastern Europe*. London: Palgrave Macmillan.
Hughes, J., Sasse, G., and Gordon, C. (2005) *Europeanization and regionalization in the EU's enlargement: The myth of conditionality (One Europe or several?)*. London: Palgrave MacMillan.
Innes, A. (2002) 'Party competition in postcommunist Europe: The great electoral lottery', *Comparative Politics*, 35(1) (October), pp. 85–104.
Kacarska, S. (2008) 'Political parties and the state in the Republic of Macedonia: Implications for democratic consolidation', *CEU Political Science Journal*, 3(1), p. 49.
Kacarska, S. (2013) 'The EU in the Republic of Macedonia: An active player, a framework for integration or both?', in Radeljic, B. (ed.) *Europe and the post-Yugoslav space*. Farnham: Ashgate, pp. 87–108.
Karajkov, R. (2008) 'Facts on the Macedonian–Greek name dispute', *Osservatorio Balcani e Caucaso*. Available at: www.balcanicaucaso.org/eng/Materials/Facts-on-the-Macedonian-Greek-Name-Dispute-39899.

Kochenov, D. (2004) *Behind the Copenhagen façade: The meaning and structure of the Copenhagen political criterion of democracy and the rule of law*, European Integration Online Papers, Vol. 8, No. 10. Available at: www.eiop.or.at/eiop/pdf/2004-010.pdf.

Linz, J. and Stepan, A. (1996) *Problems of democratic transition and consolidation: Southern Europe, South America, and post-communist Europe*. London: Johns Hopkins University Press.

Magen, A. and Morlino, L. (2009) 'Hybrid regimes, the rule of law, and external influence', in Magen, A. and Morlino, L. (eds) *International Actors, Democratization and the Rule of Law: Anchoring Democracy?* London: Routledge, pp. 1–25.

Manners, I. (2002) 'Normative power Europe: A contradiction in terms?' *JCMS: Journal of Common Market Studies*, 40(2), pp. 235–258.

Markovic, N., Ilievski, Z., Damjanovski, I., and Bozinovski, V. (2011) *The role of the European Union in the democratic consolidation and ethnic conflict management in the Republic of Macedonia*, Regional Research Promotion Programme Western Balkans.

Marusic, S.J. (2013) 'Brussels welcomes Macedonian Crisis Report', *Balkan Insight*, 27 August.

Mladenovska, P. (2013) 'Füle – The Eurointegration should not be a hostage to the political battle [Филе – Евроинтеграциите да не бидат заложник на политичката борба]', *Radio Free Europe*, 11 April.

Noutcheva, G. (2007) *Fake, partial and imposed compliance: The limits of the EU's normative power in the Western Balkans*, CEPS Working Document.

O'Brennan, J. (2008) 'The EU in the Western Balkans: Enlargement as empire? A response to David Chandler', *Global Society*, 22(4), pp. 507–518.

Phinnemore, D. (2006) 'Beyond 25—the changing face of EU enlargement: Commitment, conditionality and the Constitutional Treaty', *Journal of Southern Europe and the Balkans Online*, 8(1), pp. 7–26.

Plasser, F., Ulram, P.A., and Waldrauch, H. (1998) *Democratic consolidation in East-Central Europe*, London: Palgrave Macmillan.

Pravda, A. (2001) 'Introduction', in Zielonka, J. and Pravda, A. (eds) *Democratic consolidation in Eastern Europe: International and transnational factors*. Oxford: Oxford University Press, pp. 1–27.

Pridham, G. (2002) 'EU enlargement and consolidating democracy in post-Communist states: Formality and reality', *JCMS: Journal of Common Market Studies*, 40(5), pp. 953–973.

Pridham, G. (2005) *Designing democracy: EU enlargement and regime change in post-Communist Europe*. London: Palgrave Macmillan.

Pridham, G. (2006) 'European Union accession dynamics and democratization in Central and Eastern Europe: Past and future perspectives', *Government and Opposition*, 41(3) (June), pp. 373–400.

Pridham, G. (2007a) 'Change and continuity in the European Union's political conditionality: Aims, approach, and priorities', *Democratization*, 14(3), pp. 446–471.

Pridham, G. (2007b) 'The effects of the European Union's democratic conditionality: The case of Romania during accession', *The Journal of Communist Studies and Transition Politics*, 23(2), pp. 233–258.

Risteska, M. (2010) 'Политички дијалог или дијалог на политики? [Political dialogue or policy dialogue?]', *Dnevnik*.

Sasse, G. (2008) 'The politics of EU conditionality: The norm of minority protection during and beyond EU accession', *Journal of European Public Policy*, 15(6), pp. 842–860.

Sasse, G. (2009) 'Tracing the construction and effects of EU conditionality', in Rechel, B. (ed.) *Minority rights in Central and Eastern Europe*. London: Taylor & Francis.

Schedler, A. (1998) 'What is democratic consolidation?', *Journal of Democracy*, 9, pp. 91–107.

Sedelmeier, U. (2006) 'Europeanisation in new member and candidate states', *Living Reviews in European Governance 1*.

Smith, K.E. (2003) 'EU membership conditionality', in Cremona, M. (ed.) *The enlargement of the European Union*. Oxford: Oxford University Press.

Solana, J. (2004) 'A European Era'. *Dnevnik*.

Trajkovski, B. (2003) *Speech by Boris Trajkovski, at the ceremony marking the ending of NATO's Operation Allied Harmony and transfer of authority to EU*, 31 March. Available at: www.nato.int/docu/speech/2003/s030331d.htm.

Trauner, F. (2009) 'From membership conditionality to policy conditionality: EU external governance in South Eastern Europe', *Journal of European Public Policy*, 16(5), pp. 774–790.

Tsekov, G. (2005) 'Freedom House "Nations in transit" report on Macedonia'. Available at: www.freedomhouse.org/report/nations-transit/2005/macedonia#.U3to7O1OWP8.

Vachudova, M.A. (2005) *Europe undivided: Democracy, leverage, and integration after communism*. Oxford: Oxford University Press.

Vasilev, G. (2011) 'EU conditionality and ethnic coexistence in the Balkans: Macedonia and Bosnia in a comparative perspective', *Ethnopolitics*, 10(1), pp. 51–76.

Vogel, T. (2010) 'Ministers agree to scrap four EUSR posts'. *European Voice*.

7 Signaling right and turning left
The response to EU-conditionality in Serbia

Mladen Mladenov and Bernhard Stahl

Introduction

In its approach to Europeanization, which we define for the purpose of this chapter as the alignment with formal and informal EU norms and values on the part of membership aspirants (Radaelli 2000: 2–4), and democratization in Serbia, the EU has been eager to cover almost every possible aspect. Thus, the European Commission in its 2002 Stabilisation and Association Report on the Federal Republic of Yugoslavia (FRY) demands reforms of the constitution, public administration and the police forces, a more efficient parliament, electoral integrity, judicial independence, the elimination of corruption, improvements with regard to antidiscrimination, media freedom, freedom of association, religious freedoms, workers' rights, and rights of minorities and refugees and access to courts (European Commission 2002).

In the academic literature, Europeanization in the Western Balkans has already attracted much attention, but it is rather seen from different perspectives prompting very different judgements about its effects and ultimately its success. One part of the literature concentrates on the technical, rationalist character of the Europeanization process (Kelley 2010; Schimmelfennig 2005; Vachudova 2005). It implies that a cost-benefit analysis determines whether Europeanization will go ahead, i.e. if the benefits are big and certain enough to outweigh the costs, demands will be fulfilled. A second part (see Freyburg and Richter 2010; Subotić 2010, 2011) makes the case for the relevance of identity. Subotić (2011: 309) argues that 'in states where European identity is a widely shared social value, the inevitable short-term costs of Europeanization – economic, social, and political – will still be worth the price of admission because becoming "European" trumps other domestic political concerns'. In contrast, 'in cases where national identity is incompatible with external actors' demands, domestic actors will not or will only partially comply with externally set political conditions' (Pawelec and Grimm 2014: 1). Here, particular costs and benefits are still part of the equation, but are weighted in accordance with their significance from an identity perspective. Thus, they are not the same for the different EU membership aspirants, which provides for a sensible explanation of the different pace of EU integration across the Western Balkans. Comparing the trajectories of Serbia and Croatia, Subotić (2011: 323) comes to the conclusion that in Serbia 'identity divergence' has been a central feature in delaying Serbia's EU candidacy. In a nutshell, she argues, 'Europe is a state of mind' and thereby offers a representative view of this body of literature.

This chapter will take into consideration the identity dimension of Europeanization while at the same time emphasizing the impact of the original cost-benefit aspects. Thereby, the authors aim to offer a comprehensive account of Serbia's progress towards European integration thus far. Within the framework of their analysis, the authors come to the conclusion that both identity and the traditional provision/withholding of incentives do play a role, but they also have an influence on one another leading to perhaps unexpected outcomes. The chapter starts with an overview of the formal relations between the EU and Serbia since 1995. This sets the stage for a subsequent analysis of the EU's engagement with Serbian political elites and its influence on them to date, followed by two case studies – Serbia's cooperation with the International Criminal Tribunal for the Former Yugoslavia (ICTY) and Serbia's positioning regarding Kosovo – which represent the two most visible tests for the country's Europeanization progress. The chapter concludes by summarizing the results and providing an assessment of Europeanization's future in Serbia.

Overview of EU–Serbia relations since 1995

EU-membership has been the major goal for all Western Balkan countries for more than a decade. They have enjoyed very different degrees of success on their journey, including the model for a new Member State par excellence (Slovenia), scepticism on both sides (Croatia), the young and ambitious (Montenegro), the would-be candidate (Macedonia), the missing partners (Bosnia and Kosovo), and finally the special case of Serbia where the process of European integration has been more troubled than elsewhere in the Balkans as a result of the wars in the 1990s. Hence, relations between the EU and Serbia have been marked by mistrust during the 1990s. The only significant step towards developing bilateral relations was the fact that Serbia was included among the five countries in South-Eastern Europe for which a new Stabilisation and Association Process (SAP) was proposed in 1999. This came after the EU had already settled for a regional approach since 1997 when the EU Council of Ministers established political and economic conditionality for the development of bilateral relations.

Naturally, the EU became much more involved as soon as the regime was overthrown. Already three days into the tenure of Vojslav Koštunica as the new president of the Federal Republic of Yugoslavia (FRY), he was invited to the European Union summit in Biarritz and on the same date the FRY officially joined the SAP. At the Thessaloniki European Council summit in June 2003, the SAP was confirmed as EU policy for the Western Balkans and a year later the process for a Stabilisation and Association Agreement (SAA) was set up with negotiations beginning in October 2005. In May 2006, however, those negotiations were brought to a halt as Serbia's cooperation with the ICTY was deemed insufficient. Only a pledge by the Serbian government to fully cooperate with the ICTY ensured negotiations started again in June 2007. The SAA, together with an Interim agreement on trade and trade-related issues, was signed in April 2008. The upward trend in the relations between Serbia and the EU, at least formally, continued in 2009 when in December the visa requirements for Serbs travelling to Schengen countries was lifted and the country officially applied for EU membership (Grabbe *et al.* 2010: 7). Soon after, in June 2010, the EU started the process of ratifying the SAA. Serbia faced a major struggle to be confirmed by the EU as a candidate country. It finally gained this status in March 2012, shortly before the national elections for electing the parliament and the president. After a breakthrough in negotiations on the normalization of relations with Kosovo, the European Council decided in June 2013 to endorse the Commission's recommendation to open negotiations with Serbia. Following that, the Council adopted the negotiating framework with Serbia in December 2013. Meanwhile the SAA finally entered into force in September 2013.

The EU's engagement with Serbian elites and its effects on Serbia's political system

The criteria set out at the Copenhagen European Council in 1993 were designed to minimize the risk of new Member States becoming politically unstable and economically burdensome to the EU (Grabbe 2006: 10). EU conditionality with regard to the Western Balkans was based on the 1993 Copenhagen criteria but additional conditions were added to reflect the special need to stabilize the region. Particularly Serbia faced these new conditions, as it is one of the main countries in the Western Balkans facing unresolved status conflicts (Grabbe *et al.* 2010: 2). These new conditions include regional cooperation, good neighborly relations with enlargement countries and Member States and respect for international obligations, and they have drawn most of the attention and to date represent a 'stumbling block on the road to Brussels' (Subotić 2010: 600). That in itself demonstrates the ambition of the EU to take an active role in shaping the accession aspirants' political systems and thus their conceptions of 'normal' as Manners (2002: 240) argues in relation to the normative power of the EU. The following section will therefore engage in examining this influence on the political system of Serbia.

On 6 October 2000 Slobodan Milošević recognized the victory of Vojislav Koštunica, the leader of the Democratic Party of Serbia (DSS), in the presidential elections by 51.71 per cent to Milošević's 38.24 per cent and on the next day Koštunica was sworn into office (Birch 2002: 507). The West immediately welcomed the change in Yugoslavia and acted swiftly to reward it. The country was readmitted into the United Nations and the OSCE in early November and into the IMF on 20 December. Trade sanctions were also lifted and diplomatic relations were restored with most Western states in November and December. Additionally, the EU and the US showed more support for Koštunica by swiftly sending aid packages (Birch 2002: 507). Soon after, the democratic transition gained further pace as the Democratic Opposition of Serbia (DOS) won the parliamentary elections in December 2000 and another main figure of the opposition and leader of the Democratic Party (DS), Zoran Djindjić, was appointed prime minister. The political scene, however, was bound to split into two.[1] On the one hand, Prime Minister Djindjić was determined to advance Serbia's integration in the West, pledging to fulfill most demands put in front of him. This was met with fierce opposition by Koštunica who strongly opposed any radical break with the past, including the dismissal of members of Milošević's regime from state institutions and security services (Natalya Clark 2008).

Immediately after the overturn of the Milošević regime, the EU put its faith in the designated president of the FRY Vojislav Koštunica. This led to a very swift establishment of relations with the EU and personal recognition for the new president as he almost secured *Time* magazine's 'person of the year' title. Even with his nationalist views being no secret, Koštunica was a trusted partner and, despite a large number of disappointments, he continued to maintain for a long time that the only future Serbia has was in the European Union. In hindsight, such rhetoric has proven to be true for the EU's aid and assistance which Koštunica was keen on. Using evidence provided by the Helsinki Committee for Human Rights, which claims that a great number of violations of human and minority rights have been observed in the period from 2004 to 2006, Adam Fagan (2010: 119) believes that all the government was prepared to do was to make some 'legal, institutional and procedural changes [...] without even attempting the necessary fundamental shift in political values, practices and norms', while it was also 'guilty of perpetuating public denial of atrocities committed in the name of the Serbian nation and reinforcing the political culture of ethno-nationalism'.

Koštunica's nationalist views and increasing anti-EU rhetoric became evident during his time as prime minister and led to serious doubts about the European prospects of Serbia. He subordinated Serbia's accession to the EU to the same nationalist project of the Milošević era, which included never relinquishing the former province of Kosovo. Ensuring a smooth dissolution of the state union of Serbia and Montenegro in 2006 remained one of the few successes of the EU's engagement with Serbian elites during this time. Even the January election of 2007, in which Boris Tadić[2] gained 10 per cent (up to 22.7 per cent, partly at the expense of G17+) and the Liberal Democrats entered the Parliament (5.3 per cent), forcing Koštunica to form a new government including the DS (Bochsler 2008a), did not have any significant effect on Serbia's membership aspirations. Yet, in 2008, the pro-Europeans in Serbia received a considerable boost. After having been misled for several years by Koštunica, the EU decided to play a one-two with pro-European political forces in the country. President Boris Tadić's DS was the one with most potential among these pro-European forces and consequently the biggest beneficiary of the events that were to unfold. The EU was not willing to make its support public or official for any one political party or coalition which meant that any endorsement had to be implicit. At the same time the EU was also forced to make its support very clear because of the strong positions of Koštunica's DSS, the Socialists and above all the most anti-European Serbian Radical Party (SRS). Thus, after Tadić had won the presidential election in early 2008 by a very small margin (Bochsler 2008b), the EU made a 'timely' decision to sign the SAA as was recommended by Javier Solana. In addition, the EU publicly endorsed the 'Pro-Europeans' even though no concrete party was prioritized. In April, only a few weeks before the elections, the Serbian president and Finance Minister Djelić travelled to Luxembourg and signed the SAA with EU officials. Meanwhile at home in Belgrade, the Serbian prime minister declared the President's signature as void and denounced the signing of the SAA as 'Solana's agreement' (B92 10 April 2008), but any attempts made to link EU accession with Kosovo's independence by Koštunica were unsuccessful. After a long stalemate, an unequivocal signal was sent to the Serbian public that the country's integration in the EU is 'a serious prospect and that the Commission took Serbia's membership seriously' (Fagan 2010: 116). Another incentive was provided as some Schengen countries decided to lift visa fees for Serbian citizens shortly before the polls (Petritsch 2008).

At least to some extent the strategy worked: in the Serbian elections of May 2008, Tadić's coalition 'Serbia for Europe' (including DS, G17+, SPO) won 39 per cent of the votes and declared itself the winner of the elections (Konitzer 2009). The pro-European parties gained 6 per cent vis-à-vis the centre parties around Koštunica, who had been boosted by Kosovo's declaration of independence (Grabbe *et al.* 2010: 1). This result was praised in the Western press as a huge victory for Europe. But still, the pro-European parties did not hold the majority in parliament. So President Tadić formed a government with the Socialists – the party of the former dictator Milošević – as a junior partner, assuring the EU that Serbia would stay on an integration track. The May elections made the pro-EU shift complete – after the preceding re-election of Tadić – and the new government in Belgrade responded in style by arresting one of the main fugitives, Radovan Karadžić, only a couple of months later in July 2008. While conditionality worked its magic in this case, the normative power of Europe did not. The government complied with a condition but it did so reluctantly and with the great majority of the public against it, suggesting that a diffusion of norms had not taken place.

The EU's conditionality curtailed another political effect which proved to be sustainable and consequential: when parts of the SAA were discussed in the Serbian parliament, the Serbian Radical Party split over the issue and Tomislav Nikolić left the party to launch the Serbian Progressive Party (SPS). As a consequence, the EU-sceptics were severely weakened and from that time onwards, pro-Europeans have been dominating Serbian politics.

In 2012, Tadić attempted a repeat of the trick. Determined to seize the chance of utilizing the positive reaction to another small step towards EU accession, he called early presidential elections to be held together with the parliamentary elections in May 2012. The granting of candidate status, however, did not suffice to keep him in place. Surprisingly, his challenger Tomislav Nikolić from the Serbian Progressive Party won the elections, while his party succeeded in luring Dačić's (SPS) into a coalition government in which the SPS leader was awarded the post of prime minister for turning his back on the DS (Konitzer 2013). Neither the personal defeat of Tadić, nor that of his party has proved to have adverse consequences on the eagerness of the Serbian government to join the EU. Indeed, it could be argued that the SNS and the SPS have achieved more with regard to advancing their country's chances of joining the EU in less than two years than the DS and Tadić have in a whole legislative term. The Brussels agreement, despite some fears in relation to its implementation, triggered the start of membership negotiations which is but one example for this trend.

Overall, it became evident that the EU has the means to influence the political system and the political elites operating in it. The EU's efforts in influencing Serbia's elites, for all their deficiencies, have borne some fruit even if that may have happened accidentally rather than intentionally. After decades of supporting democratic forces, it was the former extremists and proponents of the idea of Greater Serbia that have transformed themselves into supporters of EU integration to put an end to any significant opposition to EU integration (FAZ 2014). No political party in parliament bar the DSS is against EU membership today and this is likely to remain the case after the early elections in March 2014. However, the Copenhagen criteria aim at Europeanizing candidate countries, i.e. not just influencing the political system, but doing that in a certain way. Hence, the chapter now turns its attention to the question of whether the EU's influence has achieved its goals and the effect it has had on democratization.

EU conditionality and democratization in Serbia

EU conditionality has been aimed at enforcing a process of Europeanization and democratization in Serbia. This has become all the more important since the EU is not willing anymore to buy into the argument that deep-rooted democratization will necessarily follow European integration. In particular, two issues have been used by the EU as a litmus test in order to determine whether its efforts have been successful: ICTY cooperation and the handling of the Kosovo issue by Serbia. The following paragraphs will focus on these two specific topics to provide an analysis of the impact of conditionality.

ICTY cooperation

Established in May 1993 by a decision of the UN Security Council, during the first seven years of its existence the ICTY faced Slobodan Milošević as the president of the FRY. He portrayed the tribunal as yet another anti-Serb measure by a world that had taken the side of Serbia's enemies and firmly refused to cooperate with it. This uncompromising attitude, coupled with daily propaganda aimed against the ICTY, ensured a lasting influence on the country's relationship with the tribunal. As Orentlicher (2008: 34) argues, this period left a strong impact on public perception with regard to Serbia's accountability for committed atrocities.

By the end of the war in Kosovo, Serbia's international image had been extremely diminished and the country was seen as 'a modern-day version of Nazi Germany' (Subotić and Zarakol 2013: 925). The issue of cooperation with the ICTY has therefore been very high on the EU's agenda ever since the Union started to engage more closely with Serbian elites. For Serbia, cooperation with the ICTY meant that it had to arrest and extradite war crime indictees to The Hague. As Serbia continued to perceive itself as a victim rather than perpetrator, a notion that had a long tradition in the country and was successfully nurtured further during Milošević's reign (Judah 2002: xi), compliance with this condition was to prove very difficult. The elite and the public alike viewed the tribunal with great distrust and therefore showed resistance to working with it.[3]

Nevertheless, the beginning of this process did bear some promise. For all the obstacles the Serbian government faced in the wake of regime change in October 2000, Serbia did manage to 'rapidly gain credibility in the eyes of the international institutions once Slobodan Milošević was on trial in The Hague' (Grabbe 2006: 100). This came as a result of a struggle between President Koštunica and Prime Minister Djindjić, which the latter won in the end (Pörzgen 2003: 30). Paradoxically, it was this victory that proved fatal for Djindjić himself as he was assassinated in March 2003, with evidence pointing to a motive closely related to the determination of the old elites to prevent future extraditions (Subotić 2010: 601).

After Djindjić's assassination, Koštunica took over as prime minister in early 2004. It soon became evident that the Koštunica-led government was reluctant to extradite fugitives. It insisted from the outset that cooperation with the ICTY should involve and take into consideration Serbia's own necessities, including the legalization of cooperation in domestic law (BETA News 18 July 2006), a procedure which took a considerable amount of time and which has been heavily criticized as it has practically resulted in postponing cooperation, with political reasons being the obvious motive (Kostovicova 2006: 29). Moreover, in March 2004 the Serbian parliament voted in favour of providing financial aid to Milošević and Šeselj, who had voluntarily surrendered in 2003.[4] Washington reacted immediately by suspending the US$25 million tranche of aid to Belgrade (Institute for War and Peace Reporting 9 November 2005). Under serious pressure from the EU, Koštunica began to encourage the surrender of suspected war criminals in an attempt to avoid the perception of the government's actions as betraying Serbs. Consequently, it officially hailed the decision by General Vladimir Lazarević to surrender as a 'highly patriotic act' (SRNA News Agency 28 January 2005). Another four generals surrendered and were extradited in April 2005. In line with the prime minister's open disdain for the tribunal, the media discourse concentrated on praising the heroic sacrifice of the indictees without losing too much time mentioning the reasons for which their arrests were demanded by the prosecutors in The Hague (Stahl 2013: 456). President Boris Tadić took a similar approach by claiming that the extraditions were part of the bargaining on Kosovo (BETA News Agency, cf. Deutsche Welle 11 October 2004).[5] The Koštunica government, however, was yet to demonstrate the degree of its intransigence regarding the issue. It paid a very high price for the lack of co-operation as negotiations on the SAA with the EU were suspended in the spring of 2006 (Helsinki Committee for Human Rights in Serbia 2007). The EU claimed that only if full cooperation with the ICTY was provided, would the SAA talks be opened. In the years to come, the EU linked cooperation with the ICTY and on Kosovo to the SAA negotiations (Stahl 2011).

The described attitude by the government, the president and the media once again had a particularly negative effect on Serbs coming to terms with the past. Yet the suspension of the SAA negotiations proved to be a step too far and change seemed possible when the modernist G17+ party was no longer prepared to tolerate Prime Minister Koštunica's non-cooperative policy vis-à-vis Brussels and the ICTY, bringing the government down.[6] Koštunica, in turn, lamented that '(t)he policy of a permanent setting of conditions, that has been conducted for a while towards Serbia, is deeply wrong and so far produced exclusively negative effects' (EUobserver 19 June 2006).

With the change produced by the 2008 parliamentary elections and the re-election of Tadić, there was reason to believe that cooperation would improve at last. This did happen as Radovan Karadžić was arrested and sent to The Hague. Nevertheless, while the European Union signed the SAA, its implementation was put on hold until the chief prosecutor confirmed Serbia's full cooperation with the Tribunal, a condition that was seen to imply the arrest and transfer of all remaining suspects, particularly Ratko Mladić (Spoerri and Freyberg-Inan 2008: 366). It took three long years for that to happen in which the EU, and in particular Belgium and the Netherlands, continued to veto any progress for Serbia. In 2010, the Council could not agree on accepting Serbia's application for candidate status as some Member States were seeking assurances that demands for cooperation were met (Grabbe *et al.* 2010: 3). Thus, it was only when Mladić and Goran Hadžić were finally delivered to the prosecution in The Hague in the summer of 2011 that receiving candidate status became a realistic prospect. Once again this did not imply any change in the attitude of the governing elites who continued to perceive cooperation as an act aimed at satisfying functional needs. Accordingly, regular polls in Serbia have shown that the public view of the ICTY has consistently been negative and, if anything, has deteriorated over the years (Klarin 2009: 92).

It is obvious that cooperation with the ICTY on the part of Serbia has been very inconsistent. But why has that been the case? After all Serbia has delivered all fugitives to The Hague in the end. Thus, one might ask why compliance has not happened earlier. One particularly convincing line of argumentation is offered by Fagan (2010: 123) who maintains that cooperation with the ICTY constitutes an intrinsic component of EU conditionality. It is therefore civil society in which change has to begin. However, the EU has concentrated instead on pressuring governments to cooperate and has barely invested any efforts in supporting NGOs dealing with the issue of war crimes. All the evidence presented above points to the conclusion that the EU approach to Member State building in Serbia has been experiencing grave limitations as the underlying central issue of reconciliation after the violent conflicts of the 1990s has remained largely untouched to date. However, this explanation falls short of clarifying why Serbia still complied. It seems that engaging solely with the elites has probably not been a very efficient way of enforcing compliance and should have been complemented. As it stands it seems that the EU has become less interested in implementing deep-rooted changes and a shift in norms towards democratic governance, the protection of human rights and the rule of law, and concentrates its efforts instead on enforcing functional progress which will ensure the application of the pre-set membership criteria.

The issue of Kosovo's status and Serbia (1999–2013)

When Milošević was purged in October 2000, Serbia's peaceful transition to democracy gave additional credibility to the argument of not raising the

Kosovo issue. Remaining silent on the status question seemed all the more plausible considering that the lost war had not substantially altered Serbia's position on Kosovo. For instance, the new Prime Minister Djindjić – though pro-Western minded in general – took a tough stance on the issue (Cohen 2002: 31). The Kosovo Liberation Army (KLA)-initiated violence against Serbian policemen and state-institutions in the Albanian populated Preševo Valley in Serbia and the subsequent riots in Macedonia contributed to the worsening of the KLA's image but did not help to gather more support for the Serbian position. When the Serbian government proposed to divide up Kosovo in May 2001, the international community harshly rejected the initiative (Cohen 2002: 32). In order to address the Kosovo-Albanian concerns while at the same time holding onto the EU's ambivalence on the status question, UNMIK chief Michael Steiner in November 2002 invented a new doctrine – the so-called 'standards before status' principle: only if certain standards of good governance were met would the status question be addressed.

In March 2004, thousands of people in the province looted some 800 Serbian houses and 30 churches, expelling Kosovo Serbs from their former homeland enclaves in central and eastern Kosovo. Nineteen people died in the turmoil, including several members of UNMIK. KFOR's military forces could neither prevent nor stop the violence. The 2004 pogrom activated the Serbian government, which reiterated its plans for a 'cantonization' of the province (Judah 2004: 20–22). But UN Special Representative Eide rejected the idea by excluding further territorial changes – be they the unification with Albania or the division of the province. In fact, the KLA-triggered violent pogroms have transformed the Western position in favour of Kosovo-Albanian aims. The international community now launched status talks in order to solve the issue. Serbia's position hardened immediately. In June 2004, the Serbian Parliament, with the votes of the Radicals, the Socialists and the majority of the government parties, decided to grant financial aid to Milošević's and Šešelj's relatives.[7] In addition, the Serbs in Kosovo, supported by Belgrade, turned their back on the UNMIK and the EU, subsequently boycotting all common institutions and their programmes in Kosovo (Koeth 2010: 232). When the EU suspended the SAA in May 2006, the centre-conservative minority government in Belgrade broke apart. What followed was a domestic power struggle between Prime Minister Koštunica and President Tadić. The former made the Kosovo question the central theme in the election campaigns of 2006, 2007 and 2008 and prompted Tadić thereby to actively engage in the debate on Kosovo as well (Stahl 2013: 13). Since the EU had rejected the cantonization plan, Tadić called for a 'national consensus on Kosovo' and closed ranks with Koštunica's DSS, the Socialists and the Radicals. The president agreed to a new Serbian constitution which hailed Kosovo as an integral part of Serbia. Since the fall of Milošević in 2000, the work on the constitution had been pending. In a sudden coup, it was rushed through parliament once the commitment to Kosovo was added. Remarkably, for securing a majority in the referendum on the constitution, the government erased Kosovo-Albanians from the election register (Deutsche Welle 26 October 2006). By doing so, the Kosovo-Albanians were deprived of a core right of citizenship. This clearly indicates that the government's later slogan 'Kosovo is Serbia' only alludes to the territory but not to 90 per cent of its inhabitants. The unity on the domestic front was complemented by a foreign policy reorientation: Tadić and Koštunica sought support for the Serbian position in Moscow.

Despite a more pro-European government coming to power after the January 2007 elections with a stronger DS in it, Koštunica still rejected any deal with the EU linking the SAA to Serbia's goodwill on the Kosovo question: 'Belgrade will not bargain on Kosovo' (EUobserver 20 September 2007). He also insisted that the EULEX mission – an EU initiative initially meant to succeed UNMIK – would prejudice statehood. In his view, the EULEX mission would help to establish a 'puppet state' on Serbian soil, 'the most dangerous precedent after WWII' (BBC 14 December 2007). By contrast, President Tadić argued that EULEX would be 'status-neutral' so that Serbia's position on Kosovo would by no means jeopardize its EU integration. In order to support Tadić, the EU's special envoy to Kosovo, Pieter Feith, announced that EULEX deployment in Northern Kosovo would be postponed until after the Serbian elections (B92 13 March 2008).

The UN's Special Envoy (UNOSEK) Martti Ahtisaari chaired a total of 15 rounds of direct talks between the conflicting parties with an agenda imposed by UNOSEK. In March 2007, after the respective positions hardened over the course of 2006, Ahtisaari declared that a compromise was not in reach and called off further negotiations, 'Belgrade would agree to almost anything but independence, whereas Pristina would accept nothing but full independence' (UNOSEK 2007). Following his mandate, UNOSEK provided a draft proposal to the Security Council, foreseeing a 'conditional independence' for Kosovo (UNSC 2007). Against the backdrop of growing discontent in Kosovo[8] and Russia threatening to veto any declaration in the Security Council, a new round of direct talks ensued under the guidance of a Contact Group troika (the EU, the United States, Russia). None too soon, Serbia's president launched a substantial proposal offering far-reaching autonomy for Kosovo including access to international financial institutions, a flag and a national anthem. But Tadić's efforts were undermined by Prime Minister Koštunica's uninspired pleas and came too late to induce the Kosovars to move (Weller 2008, 65). Indeed, the international community had already given up all hopes that a final compromise was still in reach. After five different resolutions drafted by the United States, France and the United Kingdom, all mediation efforts reached a final deadlock in December 2007. Meanwhile, the Kosovo negotiations resonated badly with the Serbian public. A Serbian daily newspaper, the *Kurier*, even compared the UN chief negotiator Ahtisaari to Hitler (Ramet 2007: 52). When the UN chief negotiator launched his plan for the province, Prime Minister Koštunica called his plan 'an act of legal aggression' and refused to meet him when he came to Belgrade to present his plan (EUobserver 27 March 2007). In the end, the Kosovo problem in Serbia turned into a Serbian problem in Kosovo, thereby adding to the EU's credibility problem as well as Serbia's accession obstacles.

The unilateral Kosovar declaration of independence on 17 February 2008 triggered protests in Belgrade and Northern Kosovo. In the Serbian capital, demonstrators looted western bank subsidiaries and supermarkets, attacked the Turkish, British, Croatian, German and US embassies and a border check-point in Kosovo. A furious prime minister commented on the declaration of independence: 'It has to be legally annulled the moment it was legally proclaimed by a leadership of convicted terrorists' (cf. BBC 12 February 2008). Accordingly, Serbia's government did not protect Western embassies. Prime Minister Koštunica even praised the Serbian youth for their commitment and wisdom (B92 27 February 2008). Some sources also suggest that the government in Belgrade orchestrated attacks on a UN border check-point in Northern Kosovo (BBC 18 March 2008). After having condemned the violence initially, the EU's High Representative Javier Solana made a U-turn and recommended an early signing of the SAA just before the approaching Serbian elections in May (DW 17 April 2008; NYT 23 February 2008) resulting in the formation of a pro-European government and a considerable weakening of EU-sceptics.

This did not, however, imply any change concerning the Kosovo consensus. Even after Kosovo's declaration of independence in February 2008, all Serbian parties further agreed on a 'united state policy' on Kosovo (B92 12 February 2008). Instead of accepting EU incentives, Serbia launched a diplomatic lobbying campaign against Kosovo's independence. In October 2008, Serbia won the UN Assembly's approval for bringing the Kosovo issue to the International Court of Justice (ICJ). Hence, the EU countries were pressed to legally justify their position on Kosovo's independence.

The ICJ opinion,[9] released in July 2010, gave a boost to the majority of EU Member States' view that Kosovo's independence should be treated as a *fait accompli*.[10] Yet the five non-recognizing Member States (Cyprus, Greece, Romania, Slovakia and Spain) did not make use of the opportunity to change their mind. Serbia, by contrast, intended to launch a proposal to the UN General Assembly criticizing the ICJ's opinion. The British and German foreign ministers warned Belgrade not to continue with this policy and the EU put great pressure on Belgrade to change the proposal (EUbusiness.com 27 August 2010). After the Serbian government had diluted the text, High Representative Catherine Ashton and most Member States reiterated their willingness to grant Serbia a 'fast-track' to membership (EUobserver 10 June 2010).

In mid-2011, the EU succeeded in bringing about a first agreement on Kosovo regarding freedom of travel, exchange of residence registries, as well as the mutual recognition of identity cards, school and university diplomas and car licenses. When the Serbian government promised to cease violence in Northern Kosovo and agreed to open talks on further technical matters, the three reluctant EU Member States gave in: in March 2012 Serbia received the candidate status. On 19 April 2013 Kosovo and Serbia struck a deal to abolish the parallel political structures in Northern Kosovo. While Serbs continue to select the local police officers, judges and civil servants, their decisions must now be approved by Prishtina. In addition, they receive their salary from the state of Kosovo. Furthermore, both sides affirm not to hinder each other's EU accession efforts. Whether the Serbian government of former Radicals and Communists will stick to its promises remains to be seen. The fact that the agreement was a verbal one highlights the likely problems the government might face at home.[11] Meanwhile, Germany and the United Kingdom drafted a working paper which entails guidelines and caveats for dealing with Kosovo diplomatically (Tanjug 20 September 2013).

In Kosovo, the situation remains tense.[12] The international community has been solving the problem of the Kosovo-Albanians in Serbia by creating a problem for the Serbs in Kosovo. The latter have organized themselves as a parallel society which has become a ground of lawlessness (Tansai and Zaum 2009). The EU – *nolens volens* – plays a double game, being properly inconsistent: For Prishtina, it exercises state building with the help of the EULEX, but for Belgrade it pretends to be 'status-neutral', serving as a follow-up of UNMIK and UN Security Council Resolution 1244 (Vogel 2009). This double-game inevitably leads to frustrations on both sides. Violence against EULEX and a substantial loss of credibility with both the Kosovo people and their government carry the day. Smuggling and organized crime led to violent clashes with border guards forcing KFOR to take over border posts. In September 2013, one EULEX policeman was shot in an ambush (FAZ 20 September 2013).

Conclusion

The results of this analysis provide for a peculiar finding. The reaction to Europeanization in Serbia has been particularly erratic since 2000. Demands by the EU have neither been fulfilled on a regular basis nor have they been consistently rejected. What is more puzzling is the fact that this has been true in any constellation of political elites governing the country for more than a decade. As this is also observed elsewhere in the Western Balkans,[13] it can be concluded that it reflects a deep rooted legacy of the history of a nation reinforced by the conflicts of the 1990s in 'a delicate region' (Swoboda 2009: 33). Serbia thus faces a conundrum in which a choice between potential benefits of belonging in Europe and preserving the basic idea of the nation is ever too present. Moreover, in every instance in which the EU has expected Serbia to finally turn the corner on its journey towards Brussels, it has been bitterly disappointed. This happened shortly after Milošević's overturn in 2000 and then again after pro-EU forces took hold of all executive power in 2008. On both occasions, serious Europeanization efforts were short-lived and the whole process stalled for years to come. Likewise, when the Union has feared the worst about Serbia's future in Europe, nothing as dramatic has occurred.

Focusing on the EU's role during the Kosovo negotiations and the events that followed Kosovo's independence, as well as compliance with obligations relating to the ICTY, illustrate that the EU faces severe limitations in its Member State building efforts when candidate countries are not consolidated and key questions about state formation, nation building and reconciliation remain unanswered. Our analysis demonstrates that Serbia does not lack the capacity to introduce changes. Progress was rather hindered by the unwillingness to cooperate. This stems from the fact that protection of minority rights and regional cooperation with neighbors, both of which range high on the EU's agenda, incurs a particularly high cost in countries with contested borders and still clashing ethnic identities (Börzel 2011). From the perspective of a normative enlargement policy, the challenge for the EU has been to shape views of 'normal' in Serbia with the desired outcome of exporting democracy (Chandler 2008: 81). With its approach focused on technical progress rather than paying attention to the aforementioned underlying issues, the EU has shown that it is hardly aware of their significance. Yet it has persisted with Serbia's European destiny despite all setbacks. One way of accounting for this is that the EU considers Serbia to be the key country in the Western Balkans. Thus, as Judah (2009: 30) argues, not only Serbia itself is influenced by the EU, but a whole Serbian sphere including large parts of the neighboring countries that 'consume the same media, academics, students, doctors … and the area is … a single cultural sphere'. One could argue that the EU has bought into this and declared Serbia as 'too big to fail'. This persistence has been inefficient, but at the same time it has not been unsuccessful. Today Serbia is not governed by those in whom the EU had once put its trust. However, the fact that former nationalists have turned into genuine supporters of European integration and readily conceded that Serbs have committed atrocities and that they themselves have made errors in the past (FAZ 2014) implies the possibility of real change. It also tells us something about the transformative power of the EU, in particular if its conditionality is applied consistently and strongly, as had been the case in Serbia in relation to cooperation with the ICTY. At long last, after many decades marked by failure, the West seems to have led Serbia to stumble into Europeanization. The balance, however, is very fragile and whether it can be maintained remains to be seen, as the manner it has been reached resembles more an accident than a strategy.

Notes

1 Koštunica had been one of the founders of the Democratic Party in 1989. It was precisely after disagreements with Djindjić that he and his supporters left the party in 1992 and formed the Democratic Party of Serbia.
2 Boris Tadić became the leader of the Democratic Party (DS) after Djindjić was shot dead in March 2003.
3 For a detailed picture of public opinion with regard to the ICTY, see Gallup's *Balkan Monitor* (2012) or the OSCE sponsored survey by the Belgrade Centre for Human Rights (2009).
4 According to Saxon (2005, 566) the emerging uncompromising attitude of Koštunica can be attributed to a certain extent to the overwhelming electoral victory of the nationalist Radicals on 28 December 2004 and the particularly strong anti-ICTY sentiment at the core of it.
5 This sort of *pragmatic* approach has been broadly shared by the citizens of Serbia (Klarin 2009, 93).
6 See the interview with the resigned vice-chancellor Miroljub Labus: 'The Prime Minister broke his promise' (B92, 3 May 2006).
7 Šešelj, who continues as the leader of the Serbian Radical Party, was the leading politician of Serbia's 'nationalist turn' in the late 1980s and 1990s. He voluntarily went to the ICTY in The Hague to face numerous accusations. The verdict on his case is expected soon.
8 Faik Fazliu, the leader of the KLA veterans, was outspoken: 'If there is no independence for Kosovo, we will be forced to act as KLA soldiers' (Reuters 8 July 2007).
9 The ICJ ruled, in essence, that the Security Council Resolution 1244 had not ruled out Kosovo's declaration of independence. In this regard, the unilateral declaration of independence was not in breach of international law as Serbia was claiming.
10 For instance, the German Foreign Minister Westerwelle, when visiting Belgrade, claimed that 'Kosovo's borders are fixed' (*Die Welt*, 27 August 2010).
11 There exists only a photograph of the agreement, taken by a mobile phone, which does not carry any signatures. A copy has been published by the Kosovar newspaper *Gazeta Express*; the Kosovar parliament accepted the agreement in a vote in June 2013 (Deda and Qosaj-Mustafa 2013, 9–10).
12 See Gëzim Kransiqi's and Mehmet Musaj's Chapter 8 on Kosovo in this volume on the role of the EU in building an independent Kosovo and its consequences.
13 See, for example, Chapter 5 on Montenegro by Jelena Džankić and Chapter 6 on Macedonia by Simonida Kacarska in this volume.

References

Balkan Monitor (2012). Available at: www.balkan-monitor.eu/index.php/dashboard (accessed 10 July 2013).
Belgrade Centre for Human Rights (2009) *Public Awareness Raising Project of the OSCE Mission to Serbia*. Available at: http://wcjp.unicri.it/proceedings/docs/OSCESrb_ICTY_Perception_in_Serbia.pdf (accessed 10 March 2014).
Birch, S. (2002) 'The 2000 Elections in Yugoslavia: The "Bulldozer Revolution"', *Electoral Studies*, 21(3), pp. 499–511.
Bochsler, D. (2008a) 'The Parliamentary Election in Serbia, 21 January 2007', *Electoral Studies*, 27(1), pp. 160–165.

Bochsler, D. (2008b) 'The Presidential Election in Serbia, January–February 2008', *Electoral Studies*, 27(4), pp. 745–748.
Börzel, T. (2011) *When Europeanization Hits Limited Statehood.* KFG Working Paper 30 (September 2011). Available at: http://userpage.fu-berlin.de/kfgeu/kfgwp/wpseries/WorkingPaperKFG_30.pdf (accessed 20 February 2014).
Chandler, D. (2008) 'The EU's Promotion of Democracy in the Balkans', in Laïdi, Z. (ed.) *EU Foreign Policy in a Globalized World.* Abingdon, UK and New York: Routledge, pp. 68–82.
Cohen, L. (2002) *Serpent in the Bosom: The Rise and Fall of Slobodan Milošević.* Boulder: Westview Press.
Deda, I. and Qosaj-Mustafa, A. (2013) *The Implementation of Agreements of Kosovo-Serbia Political Dialogue.* Kosovar Institute for Policy Research and Development Policy Paper, 4(13). Available at: www.kipred.org/advCms/documents/22356_The_Implementation_of_Agreements_of_Political_Dialogue.pdf (accesssed 1 September 2013).
European Commission (2002) *Federal Republic of Yugoslavia Stabilisation and Association Report. SEC(2002) 343.* Available at: http://ec.europa.eu/enlargement/archives/pdf/serbia_and_montenegro/com02_343_en.pdf (accessed 5 March 2014).
Fagan, A. (2010) *Europe's Balkan Dilemma: Paths to Civil Society or State-Building?* London: I.B. Tauris.
FAZ (2014) 'Ich fürchte mich vor unserer Mentalität', Interview with Aleksandar Vučić. Available at: www.faz.net/aktuell/politik/ausland/europa/serbien-ich-fuerchte-mich-vor-unserer-mentalitaet-12761129.html?printPagedArticle=true (accessed 20 January 2014).
Freyburg, T. and Richter, S. (2010) 'National Identity Matters: The Limited Impact of EU Political Conditionality in the Western Balkans', *Journal of European Public Policy*, 17(2), pp. 263–281.
Grabbe, H. (2006) *The EU's Transformative Power: Europeanization through Conditionality in Central and Eastern Europe.* Basingstoke: Palgrave Macmillan.
Grabbe, H., Knaus, G. and Korski, D. (2010) *Beyond Wait-and-See: The Way Forward for EU Balkan Policy, European Council on Foreign Relations Policy Brief.* Available at: http://ecfr.eu/page/-/ECFR21_BALKAN_BRIEF.pdf (accessed 4 March 2014).
Helsinki Committee for Human Rights in Serbia (2007) *Annual Report: Serbia 2006, Human Rights: Hostage to the State's Regression.* Available at: www.helsinki.org.rs/doc/Report2006.pdf (accessed 2 March 2014).
Judah, T. (2002) *Kosovo: War and Revenge.* New Haven, Connecticut: Yale University Press.
Judah, T. (2004) 'Serbia's Kosovo Policy'. *European and US Policies in the Balkans, Different Views and Perceptions, Common Interests and Platforms*, 24.
Judah, T. (2009) 'Serbia: Is the Good News Old News?', in Petritsch, W. and Svilanović, G. (eds) *Serbia Matters: Domestic Reforms and European Integration.* Baden-Baden: Nomos, pp. 25–31.
Kelley, J. G. (2010) *Ethnic Politics in Europe: The Power of Norms and Incentives.* Princeton: Princeton University Press.
Klarin, M. (2009) 'The Impact of the ICTY Trials on Public Opinion in the Former Yugoslavia', *Journal of International Criminal Justice*, 7(1), pp. 89–96.
Koeth, W. (2010) 'State Building without a State: The EU's Dilemma in Defining its Relations with Kosovo', *European Foreign Affairs Review*, 15(2), pp. 227–247.

Konitzer, A. (2009) 'The Parliamentary Election in Serbia, May 2008', *Electoral Studies*, 28(1), pp. 141–145.
Konitzer, A. (2013) 'The Parliamentary Elections in Serbia, May 2012', *Electoral Studies*, 32(2), pp. 380–385.
Kostovicova, D. (2006) 'Civil Society and Post-Communist Democratization: Facing a Double Challenge in Post-Milošević Serbia', *Journal of Civil Society*, 2(1), pp. 21–37.
Manners, I. (2002) 'Normative Power Europe: A Contradiction in Terms?', *JCMS: Journal of Common Market Studies*, 40(2), pp. 235–258.
Natalya Clark, J. (2008) 'Vojislav Koštunica: Some Reflections on His Time as Serbian Premier', *Journal of Southern Europe and the Balkans Online*, 10(1), pp. 31–46.
Orentlicher, D. (2008) *Shrinking the Space of Denial: The Impact of the ICTY in Serbia.* New York: Open Society Institute.
Pawelec, M. and Grimm, S. (2014) 'Does National Identity Matter? Political Conditionality and the Crucial Case of Serbia's (Non-)Co-operation with the ICTY', *JCMS: Journal of Common Market Studies*, online first, DOI: 10.1111/jcms.12140.
Petritsch, W. (2008) *Der Balkan als europäische Herausforderung*, Speech at the University of Zürich on 14 May 2008. Available at: www.wolfgangpetritsch.com/books/doc/2009/2009_zurich.pdf (accessed 7 March 2014).
Pörzgen, G. (2003) 'Nach dem Mord an Zoran Djindjić: Serbien entdeckt die Größe seines führenden Reformpolitikers', *Südosteuropa Mitteilungen*, 2003(2), pp. 28–33.
Radaelli, C. (2000) 'Whither Europeanization? Concept Stretching and Substantive Change', *European Integration Online Papers*, 4(8). Available at: www.eiop.or.at/eiop/pdf/2000-008.pdf (accessed 21 March 2014).
Ramet, S. P. (2007) 'The Denial Syndrome and its Consequences: Serbian Political Culture Since 2000', *Communist and Post-Communist Studies*, 40(1), pp. 41–58.
Saxon, D. (2005) 'Exporting Justice: Perceptions of the ICTY among the Serbian, Croatian, and Muslim Communities in the Former Yugoslavia', *Journal of Human Rights*, 4(4), pp. 559–572.
Schimmelfennig, F. (2005) 'Strategic Calculation and International Socialization: Membership Incentives, Party Constellations, and Sustained Compliance in Central and Eastern Europe', *International Organization*, 59(4), pp. 827–860.
Spoerri, M. and Freyberg-Inan, A. (2008) 'From Prosecution to Persecution: Perceptions of the International Criminal Tribunal for the Former Yugoslavia (ICTY) in Serbian Domestic Politics', *Journal of International Relations and Development*, 11(4), pp. 350–384.
Stahl, B. (2011) '"Perverted Conditionality": The Stabilization and Association Agreement between the European Union and Serbia', *European Foreign Affairs Review*, 16(4), pp. 465–487.
Stahl, B. (2013) 'Another "Strategic Accession"? The EU and Serbia (2000–2010)', *Nationalities Papers*, 41(3), pp. 447–468.
Subotić, J. (2010) 'Explaining Difficult States: The Problems of Europeanization in Serbia'. *East European Politics and Societies*, 24(4), pp. 595–616.
Subotić, J. (2011) 'Europe is a State of Mind: Identity and Europeanization in the Balkans', *International Studies Quarterly*, 55(2), pp. 309–330.
Subotić, J. and Zarakol, A. (2013) 'Cultural Intimacy in International Relations', *European Journal of International Relations*, 19(4), pp. 915–938.

Swoboda, H. (2009) 'Serbia and European Integration', in Petritsch, W., Svilanović. G. and Solioz, C. (eds) *Serbia Matters: Domestic Reforms and European Integration.* Baden-Baden: Nomos, pp. 33–40.

Tansai, O. and Zaum, D. (2009) 'Muddling through in Kosovo', *Survival*, 51(1), pp. 13–20.

UN Security Council (2007) 'Report of the Special Envoy of the Secretary-General on Kosovo's future status'. 26 March. Available at: http://daccessdds.un.org/doc/UNDOC/GEN/N07/272/23/PDF/N0727223.pdf?OpenElement (accessed 3 February 2008).

UNOSEK (2007) *Vienna High-level Meeting Concludes 14 Months of Talks on the Future Status Process for Kosovo* (Press Release). 10 March. Available at: www.unosek.org/pressrelease/UNOSEK-PR-19-Vienna_High-level_meeting_concludes_14_months_of_talks_on_the_future_status_¬process_for_¬Kosovo.doc (accessed 10 June 2010).

Vachudova, M. A. (2005) *Europe Undivided: Democracy, Leverage, and Integration after Communism.* Oxford: Oxford University Press.

Vogel, H. (2009) 'Die EU und die Staatswerdung des Kosovo (1999–2008): Gespaltene Actorness und die nicht intendierten Folgen', in Stahl, B. and Harnisch, S. (eds) *Vergleichende Außenpolitikforschung und nationale Identitäten: Die Europäische Union im Kosovo-Konflikt (1996–2008).* Baden-Baden: Nomos, pp. 233–274.

Weller, M. (2008) *Negotiating the Final Status of Kosovo.* Chaillot Paper Institute for Security Studies, 114.

8 The EU's 'limited sovereignty–strong control' approach in the process of Member State building in Kosovo

Gëzim Krasniqi and Mehmet Musaj

Introduction

Today, the European Union (EU) is the main international actor in Kosovo. The EU's influence in Kosovo has been expanding gradually and stretches into the political, judicial, economic and security spheres. The EU's omnipresence in Kosovo is a result of more than a decade-long period of direct involvement in stabilization and reconstruction as well as in Member State building. Throughout these years, various EU institutions have been involved in the establishment of political, judicial and economic institutions and a system that mirrored the predominant liberal-democratic model of a polity. The EU's involvement in Kosovo has been characterized by the lack of a clear and shared vision for state building and it has been susceptible to its internal disagreements and predominance of particular state interests over the wider European ones, as well as to Kosovo's peculiar legal and political conundrum.

This chapter examines the EU's involvement in the process of Member State building in Kosovo. The main argument of the chapter is twofold. First, it argues that the EU's approach in Kosovo is dominated by its direct involvement in the process of Member State building. In other words, the EU is engaged in Kosovo to build a member state from scratch. As a potential member, Kosovo, unlike any other EU Member State that pooled its sovereignty with that of others as part of the integration process, is a state with minimal sovereignty. Second, as a result of EU strategy, the process of state building in Kosovo has been inherently linked to the EU integration process and the 'normalization' of relations with Serbia. Consequently, Kosovo risks developing a form of double dependency on the EU on the one hand and Serbia on the other. This would certainly allow for EU institutions to exercise strong control in Kosovo and also force it to share its limited sovereignty with Serbia, thus leading to a form of 'tripartite sovereignty partnership' over the territory of Kosovo.

As regards the structure, this chapter is divided into three main sections. The first section looks at the issue of democratization and state building in Kosovo in the context of internal and external contestation.

The second section traces the origins of the international and European involvement in Kosovo, with a particular focus on the current EU presence. The third section of the chapter assesses the EU's strategy of 'limited sovereignty–strong control' and the issue of Kosovo's double dependency.

The democratization–stateness nexus in Kosovo

More than a decade after the end of the war in Kosovo and five years since the declaration of independence, Kosovo still faces issues of sovereignty and statehood. The current situation in which a considerable number of people within the new state, in addition to a considerable number of states, challenge Kosovo's statehood has made the case of Kosovo unique in the international context. Kosovo still does not possess attributes of a state, including external and internal sovereignty, thus making it a contested polity which takes its toll on the process of democratization and state building. Therefore, Kosovo faces what Linz and Stepan (1996: 16) refer to as the 'stateness' problem, which refers to the existence of a significant proportion of the population that does not accept the boundaries of the territorial state and that question its legitimacy.

One of the biggest problems in relation to Kosovo is its contested statehood, both internally and externally. As regards the international aspect, Kosovo's declared independence in February 2008 has been fiercely opposed by Serbia, but also other states such as Russia and Spain. This opposition and the very unilateral character of its declaration of independence [without approval from either Serbia or the Security Council of the UN (UNSC)] have resulted in a limited number (110 countries as of 2014) of recognitions of Kosovo's sovereignty and independence thus far. Internally, Kosovo's Serbs, backed by the Serbian state, have opposed the new state. Consequently, Kosovo's sovereignty is limited in some areas of the country, especially in northern Kosovo, which is *de facto* under the control of Serbia.

This certainly has a major bearing on the process of democratization. In this respect, recent attempts to define the process of democratization were largely informed by the sudden and traumatic fall of the communist regimes in Eastern Europe. For Hague and Harrop (2001), the process of democratization can be divided into three phases: liberalization, transition and consolidation. Other authors (Kaldor and Vejvoda 2002) distinguish between formal, substantial and consolidated democracies. In short, with consolidation, democracy becomes routinized and deeply internalized in social, institutional and even psychological life, as well as in calculations for achieving success (Linz and Stepan 1996: 4–5).

On the other hand, O'Donnell (cited in Tansey 2007: 131) identified three elements of a polity that are absolute requirements for a functional democracy: a legal system that supports the rights and freedoms entailed by a democratic regime, a state apparatus that can enforce such rights throughout the territory and, finally, official ideological discourses and practices that increase state capacities to reinforce democratic values. In the case of Kosovo, all these elements are either weak or non-existent, and Kosovo's obscure legal status and its highly complex relation with international organizations and institutions such as the UN and the EU play a great part in this uncertainty. In a situation when neither the UN nor the EU recognises Kosovo as a sovereign state, the challenges of achieving democracy cannot be overcome unless Kosovo is recognized and functions as a sovereign state. Linz and Stepan clearly argue that the sovereign state is a "prerequisite to democracy" (1996: 17).

In fact, the present stateness problem and contestation stem from the troubled record of international administration in Kosovo and the failure to build an integrated, cohesive society with capable and functional local institutions.

Institution and state building under international administration

At the end of the Kosovo war, different international organizations had established their presence in Kosovo following the adoption of Resolution 1244 by the UNSC that placed the territory of Kosovo under UN administration. UN Resolution 1244 vested all legislative and executive powers, including administration of the judiciary, in the hands of the Special Representative of the Secretary General (SRSG). The SRSG and the United Nations Interim Administration Mission in Kosovo (UNMIK) initiated the process of creating separate Kosovar institutions in all three fields of governance: legislative, executive and judicial. In time, UNMIK transferred these responsibilities to local institutions.

These international actors present in Kosovo initiated the process of democratic change and the creation of local institutions, thus engaging in a situation of 'democratisation without statehood' (Tansey 2007). Thus, 'despite the lack of international recognition of statehood, domestic democratic structures have developed over time, and have evolved into an unconventional hybrid political system, part domestic democratic regime, part international authority' (Tansey 2007: 145). As regards international institutions, UNMIK was a 'coalition' between the UN (responsible for civil administration, police and justice), the OSCE (institution building) and the EU (economic reconstruction) (Papadimitriou and Petrov 2012, p. 753). Following the approval of the Constitutional Framework in 2001, Kosovo started to establish its own institutions, known as Kosovo's Provisional Institutions of Self-Government (PISG), yet despite this, UNMIK was still entitled to the highest level of competencies in the legislative, judiciary and executive branches, including the right to veto the Special Representative of the Secretary General (SRSG). Therefore, though various UN officials repeatedly upheld the mantra of 'building local capacities', they granted the locals voting rights, but no rights to self-rule (Ignatieff 2003: 133). This had two main consequences. First, as Lemay-Hébert (2013: 99–100) argues,

> The setup of an international administration with executive, legislative and judicial powers put the international officials in an intractable conundrum, resulting in a 'legitimacy dilemma': what the interveners do to reinforce their legitimacy perpetuates their weakness.

Second, by creating a political climate of unaccountability and dependence of local politicians on international missions rather than local people, the international mission in Kosovo contributed to the creation of weak local institutions. Therefore, as a result, the state building agenda was seen as progressively more exogenous, further reinforcing the delegitimization process (ibid). This model, which was also applied in Bosnia, that aimed at fostering institutional development in post-conflict countries 'by creating international structures that assume extensive, undemocratic, and generally unaccountable powers within the domestic constitutional sphere' has been described by Gerald Knaus and Marcus Cox as 'authoritarian state-building' (2005: 40).

The main aim of international actors involved in Kosovo was ' "conflict resolution" through liberal peacebuilding and neoliberal state-building' (Lidén et al. 2009: 593). The external state builders' mantra of 'state-building from scratch' (Boege et al. 2008: 11), based on a pre-established single model that contains a general 'diagnosis' and appropriate 'cures', invokes a pre-defined process with clear-cut criteria and a supposedly attainable 'happy end'. The predominant logic of 'measuring countries against a single universal standard based on a normative model of the modern European state that ignores the different histories of state formations in other parts of the world and alternative ways of governing' (Woodward 2011: 316) often generated political instability and economic crises. As Boege et al.'s (2008: 12) study on East Timor shows,

> Efforts to rapidly introduce liberal governance norms and structures without paying attention to how they interact with local customary values have contributed to the erosion of institutions and cultural values underpinning order, and have led to the adoption of often very poorly understood liberal norms (particularly in urban areas). As a consequence, the notion of 'democracy' has become widely identified with 'conflict between competing factions of the political elite' and with 'top-down imposition of values'.

Similarly, in the case of Kosovo, the international community's prevailing assumption that democratic and multicultural institutional frameworks would automatically give rise to liberal democracy in the former Yugoslavia, irrespective of the establishment of the rule of law, has harmed efforts to create well-functioning democracies and stable societies (Krasniqi 2010). UNMIK also failed to create a unified political structure governing the entire territory, as Serbian-sponsored 'parallel structures' were allowed to operate in Serb-inhabited areas of Kosovo.

By the time Kosovo was negotiating its political status, the 'state-in-waiting' still faced the crucial challenges of limited domestic capacity and lack of political cohesion (Tansey 2007: 147). This way, once Kosovo declared its independence in 2008 without Serbia's consent and without the UNSC approval, it entered a new stage of international legal obscurity, thus facing a prolonged statehood conundrum.

The EU's role in economic recovery and institution building

The EU's original mandate to assist in the rebuilding of the war-ravaged country and in laying the foundations for viable economic development derived directly from Security Council Resolution 1244 (Džihić and Kramer 2009: 14). Yet under the UN umbrella, the EU had become closely involved in almost all aspects of governance in Kosovo. The EU formed an integral part of UNMIK – Pillar IV responsible for economic reconstruction, it was and still is Kosovo's largest aid donor and coordinated (and financed) the most comprehensive network of training programmes for the PISG. It was also in charge of the country's custom services and privatization programme, had extensive regulatory powers over the economy and supervises the Banking and Payment Authority (Kosovo's embryonic Central Bank) (Papadimitriou *et al.* 2007: 220). In addition to its role under the UN umbrella, the EU was present in Kosovo through an extensive web of institutions and policy instruments such as the European Agency of Reconstruction (EAR), the European Union Monitoring Mission (EUMM), the Common Foreign and Security Policy (CFSP) office and the EU Commission Liaison Office.

Between 1999 and 2008 while UNMIK was engaged in building Kosovo's political institutions from scratch, the EU engaged in shaping Kosovo's economic system and structures, both part of the 'neoliberal state-building' agenda. However, the EU's record, similar to that of the UN, is mixed and contested. It was generally characterized by a number of strategic defects – political instability in the case of the UN, and macroeconomic instability in the case of the EU. As regards the role of the EU in the economic recovery, Džihić and Kramer (2009: 14) argue that 'given the EU's enormous financial outlay – 2.3 billion Euros between 1999 and 2008 – the reward, in terms of the real effects on the Kosovan economy and its modernisation, has been meagre indeed'. In particular, the privatization process, which virtually became a symbol of the misguided policies of UNMIK and the EU (Džihić and Kramer

2009: 14; Papadimitriou *et al.* 2007: 233–234), failed to kick-start Kosovo's economic recovery.

With respect to the issue of European integration, due to its status issue, the EU did not include Kosovo in the EU integration process immediately after the end of the war. When the EU created the Stabilization and Association Process (SAP) in 1999 as its primary contribution to the Stability Pact for Southeast Europe, other countries in the region were offered access to SAP, whereas Kosovo became part of the SAP through a special mechanism, the Stabilization and Association Process Tracking Mechanism (SATM). This mechanism was devised in 2005 with the aim of securing Kosovo's access to the SAP content without prejudicing its future status (Palokaj 2013: 9). Kosovo's EU integration perspective was further reiterated in the Thessaloniki agenda for the Western Balkans, in 2003. Nonetheless, being a non-state entity, it was impossible for Kosovo to enter into any form of contractual relations with the EU.

In short, the record of the international administration in Kosovo, including the political, security and economic pillars, is mixed and highly contested. In large part this was due to the predominance of the paradigm of (precarious) stability that has come at the expense of democratization, state building and economic recovery. Nonetheless, as Kosovo prepared to declare its independence, the EU was preparing for an enhanced role in the political and security field in Kosovo under 'supervised' or 'conditional' independence, which as Tansey predicted in 2007, 'would still leave Kosovo as a non-state entity, with final international recognition, and genuine independent government, still pending further developments' (145). As it will be argued below, this projected direct intervention continued to nourish the culture of dependency and even compromised the issue of 'ownership' in Kosovo's EU integration path. This certainly undermines the fundamental EU values such as democratic accountability and the very idea of a norm-driven enlargement and foreign policy. For as Woelk put it, '[w]hile the "democratic deficit" has become a commonplace when referring to the EU, the dynamics of direct intervention and dependency create a "democratic deficit" within the (future) candidate States, too' (2013: 473).

As regards the role of the EU as part of the UN-led endeavour to build a state from scratch in Kosovo, its strategy and effectiveness have clearly been undermined by institutional fragmentation, poor coordination and the absence of a clear vision of how Kosovo fits into the wider EU policy in the Balkans (Papadimitriou *et al.* 2007: 238). Equally, 'the limitations of EU actorness in the area have also undermined its ability to utilize effectively enlargement-led conditionalities as a means of accelerating Kosovo's Europeanization' (ibid). Nevertheless, this did not prevent the EU from assuming an increased and double-hatted role in post-status Kosovo, both as part of the local government structure and as the external assessor of Kosovo's membership criteria. By assuming a central role in post-status

Kosovo, the EU would at the same time amend the international strategy of 'state-building from scratch' by adding to it a membership component. Hence the new task of 'Member State building from scratch'.

The challenge of building a state and a potential member state simultaneously: the EU's presence in Kosovo and its 'status-neutral' approach

The EU's active involvement in Kosovo since 1999 and the decision of the majority of EU states to recognise Kosovo's statehood has been considered as a vital move in redressing the situation in its favour, or as a 'first step towards the "Europeanisation" of the Kosovo issue' (Ker-Lindsay 2009: 124). The Ahtisaari Plan, which formed the basis for Kosovo to declare its independence in February 2008, foresaw a smooth transfer of power from the UN to the EU. This meant the termination of UNMIK's mandate and an increased role for the EULEX mission and International Civilian Office (ICO) to strengthen its institutions and to monitor their performance, and the implementation of the Ahtisaari Plan. After the declaration of independence, Kosovo invited the EU to deploy a rule of law mission in Kosovo, but because of the lack of consensus at the UN and the EU (Spain, Greece, Cyprus, Romania and Slovakia refused to recognise Kosovo's independence), EULEX was deployed in Kosovo – 'under the general framework of United Nations Security Resolution 1244' – which conditions it to adopt a 'status neutral' approach. Having accepted temporary limits to their sovereignty in return for recognition from the EU, Kosovar leaders felt cheated by the EU's failure to deliver its side of the bargain, which complicated the relationship between the Kosovar government and EULEX at the very outset (ICG 2010: 3). This slowed down the process of transition from the UN to the EU and created confusion amongst the EU and EULEX officials.

As the 'European Union's success in Kosovo is inextricably linked to its ability to speak "with one voice"', (Papadimitrou *et al.* 2007: 221), present disagreements among the EU Member States on Kosovo's status diminish its position and reflect negatively on the internal developments in Kosovo and the EU's role as a state builder. Despite the fact that Kosovo hosts the biggest ever EU Mission abroad, its relations with the EU are highly complicated. The EU's 'status neutral' approach prevents Kosovo from establishing the types of contractual relations with the EU akin to other states in the Western Balkans. Likewise, though one of the main aims of the EU presence in Kosovo is to 'support Kosovo's European integration', Kosovo lags far behind other countries of the region in terms of the level of integration achieved.

Although the general observation that the EU through EULEX and other financial assistance programmes is essentially engaged in the twin processes of Europeanization and state building in Kosovo (Ker-Lindsay and Economides 2012: 83) holds some truth, both these processes are undermined for the following reasons. The first one is related to the mandate of EULEX: 'The placement of EULEX under the legal basis of UNSC Resolution 1244 (which guaranteed Serbia's territorial integrity), [...] necessitated a major departure from the mission's earlier inception as "feeding into" the Ahtisaari proposals for Kosovo's "supervised independence"' (Papadimitriou and Petrov 2012: 758). In practice, this meant that EULEX's mandate would be rendered technical since it cannot openly engage in state building without recognizing the state itself. Second, as regards the process of Europeanization as a means of EU integration, despite encouraging institutional and political reforms in Kosovo, the EU was unable to offer Kosovo a clear tangible European integration perspective. Rather, it initiated a spiral of improvisations that were embodied in the appealing but unbinding mantra of 'Kosovo has a clear European perspective'. Thus, as Papadimitriou and Petrov (2012: 758) argue, these shaped an EU presence in post-2008 Kosovo that was underpinned by 'constructive ambiguity'.

Irrespective of the fact that originally the EULEX mandate was to engage in the process of state building in Kosovo, due to its (self-imposed) 'neutrality', the mission was rendered technical, thus retaining only supervisory and executive powers without the obligation to recognize the mandate and legitimacy of the newly created independent Kosovan institutions. Having been entangled in Resolution 1244, the EU mission in Kosovo put itself in a similar position to that of its *de facto* predecessor (UNMIK), thus raising issues of efficacy and legitimacy.

The EU rule of law mission on the ground in Kosovo

According to the initial plan, the EULEX Mission was supposed to be operational soon after the declaration of the independence of Kosovo. Nonetheless, its deployment and achievement of operational capacities was delayed for almost a year due to the controversies regarding its mandate. Only by the end of 2008 was an agreement between the UN, Serbia and the EU achieved, known as the 'Six points plan', thereby paving the way for EULEX to deploy all over Kosovo (Dijkstra 2011: 203–205). However, while the agreement in the UNSC in November 2008 formally paved the way for the deployment of EULEX across the entire territory of Kosovo (in exchange for the mission being fully anchored to the UNSC Resolution 1244), in reality, such a prerogative was never exercised (Papadimitriou and Petrov 2012: 759). In this way, EULEX followed the path of UNMIK when it came to its approach of tolerating Serb-funded and controlled political and security structures in northern Kosovo.

The deployment of EULEX under the UN mandate deriving from Resolution 1244 added to the overlapping jurisdictions of the international bodies involved in Kosovo (above all the EU, NATO and UN), as well as the local ones (Serbia and Kosovo), the result being a proliferation of parallel lines of authority and competing dynamics that operate to the detriment of a functioning state (Montanaro 2009: 16–17). The end result is that at least four different sets of institutions operate in Kosovo (Kosovo's, UNMIK's, EULEX's and Serbia's) creating a highly complex net of institutions, legal norms and jurisdictions that often overlap, with Kosovo residents being tied to at least two polities (Kosovo and Serbia) and even more political authorities that determine their legal rights (Krasniqi 2012: 362).

As regards EULEX's competencies and tasks, the mandate of EULEX included non-executive and executive tasks. While the non-executive competencies concerned the monitoring, mentoring and advising of Kosovo's local police, judiciary and custom services, the executive competencies included functions carried out by EULEX staff themselves, such as the fight against high-level organized crime or court rulings by EULEX judges (Dijkstra 2011: 205). Having achieved operational strength only in April 2009, EULEX enjoyed only modest success during its first six months of operation (Džihić and Kramer 2009: 18). Over the years, the debate on and criticism of EULEX activities have grown more vocal. In October 2012, the European Court of Auditors published a very critical report regarding the results obtained by EULEX. The report stated that:

> Although the EU helped to build capacity, notably in the area of customs, assistance to the police and the judiciary has had only modest success. Levels of organised crime and corruption in Kosovo remain high. The judiciary continues to suffer from political interference, inefficiency and a lack of transparency and enforcement. Kosovo's limited capacity to protect key witnesses and the difficulties relocating witnesses abroad are important shortcomings. There has been almost no progress in establishing the rule of law in the north of Kosovo.
> (ECA 2012)

Similarly, a local think-tank in Kosovo found out that five years after its deployment, EULEX's staff presence in all the necessary institutions and cases has been weak and the strengthening of the rule of law has moved forward only incrementally despite of a budget of 613.8 million Euros (KIPRED 2013a). The lack of results in establishing the rule of law in northern Kosovo as well as in the fight against organized crime and 'high profile' cases generated criticism from EU Member States as well. A case in point is the German Defence Minister Thomas de Maizière, who broke a diplomatic taboo, saying that the mission in Kosovo needed 'a new start, a new name, a new structure, and new people' (cited in Smolar 2013).

From the time of its deployment in 2008 up to the end of 2012, EULEX has treated a fair number of criminal cases, with its prosecutors being involved in more than 2,078 cases, and 380 verdicts have already been handed down, including 51 verdicts in high level organized crime and corruption cases (KIPRED 2013a: 12). Yet 'the number and quality of cases that have to do with "high profile" organized crime and corruption remain at disappointing levels' (ibid). One of the reasons for this is the predominance of the paradigm of 'stability', which in fact undermines the rule of law – the very reason for the existence of the EULEX. Since the end of the war in Kosovo in 1999, the various international missions in Kosovo have put their emphasis on security and stability, i.e. prevention of open conflict. Such an approach created a sense of impunity among war-time perpetuators as well as post-war criminals and corrupt ethnic leaders. Therefore, by subscribing to this approach, the EU Mission is undermining fundamental EU values such as the rule of law, democracy and fundamental human rights.

Despite high expectations, during its first four years of the mandate, the EULEX Mission did not produce any significant results in the field of rule of law and fight against corruption and organized crime. Although EULEX has taken over the rule-of law prerogatives, it failed to establish Kosovo as one single legal and customs zone (Surroi 2011: 113). However, as part of the initiative to end Kosovo's supervision in September 2012, when the International Steering Group decided to end the period of Kosovo's supervised independence and the mandate of the ICO (BBC 2012), EULEX's mandate was put into question again. Following the process of constitutional changes by the Kosovan Parliament that would reflect the departure of the ICO and transfer of the International Civilian Representative's (ICR) responsibilities over to local authorities, the EU demanded that Kosovo make the EULEX Mission an integral part of its constitution, a proposal refused by Prishtina. Instead, Kosovo agreed that the Mission's legal basis was established with an exchange of letters between Kosovo's President and the High Representative of Foreign Affairs and Security Policy, which in September 2012 was voted in the Kosovo parliament as an 'international agreement between the Republic of Kosovo and the European Union on the European Union Rule of Law Mission in Kosovo' in order to create a 'sufficient' domestic legal basis for the Mission to continue to operate (KIPRED 2013a: 9). However, whereas the Kosovo side provided 'sufficient' domestic basis for EULEX, the latter still continues to operate on the basis of the European Council Joint Action (Council Joint Action 2008/124/CFSP) from 2008, which does not establish any links to Kosovo's legal instruments. Moreover, this gives EULEX the power, in coordination with other international actors in Kosovo, to reverse and annul operational decisions taken by Kosovan authorities, something that is not in the spirit of the end of supervised independence (KIPRED 2013a: 10).

In short, by maintaining a 'status neutral' position, thus denying the existence of a Kosovan state on the one hand, and showing little success in fulfilling its mandate and tasks set on the other, in many respects, EULEX remains 'a carbon copy' of UNMIK.

The EU's strategy of 'limited sovereignty–strong control'

The EU policy of conditionality in the case of the Balkans has been 'enhanced' (Kostovicova and Bojicic-Dzelilovic 2006: 225) gradually thus changing the limits of conditionality towards a more pragmatic approach (Anastasakis 2008). However, EU engagement in Kosovo goes beyond mere supervision or conditionality; the EU is 'controlling' and 'maintaining' the new state, making it dependent on the EU (Ker-Lindsay and Economides 2012: 83). As an external power, the EU's approach to Member State building in Kosovo is similar to Brezhnev's concept of 'limited sovereignty'. And the result is a particular form of state that Florian Bieber (2011) calls a 'minimalist state'. A 'minimalist state' is 'a state with limited legitimacy and a weak scope and strength of the state' (Bieber 2011: 1786). In this case, the weakness of the state does not necessary precede EU intervention; rather it is a consequence of it. Bieber argued that 'the minimalist states of Serbia and Montenegro, Kosovo and BiH [Bosnia and Herzegovina] have either been created with the substantial input of the European Union, or at least the EU has evolved into the role of the prime international backer' (2011, p. 1789). It suffices to look at the limited scope and capacities of Kosovo's political, security (lack of an army) and economic (lack of currency and monetary autonomy) institutions to grasp the scale of limitation imposed on Kosovo by international state builders, above all the EU.

The EU's model of 'minimalist state' has a direct bearing on Kosovo's sovereignty and statehood. As a result, Kosovo's sovereignty is limited in two different yet interconnected ways. First, the EU's presence in Kosovo through EULEX and its executive powers is a serious challenge to the internal sovereignty of Kosovo. Second, the process of negotiation between Kosovo and Serbia (with EU mediation) has created a 'triple sovereignty partnership'.

At the domestic level, Kosovo's domestic sovereignty is challenged both by the EU through EULEX and by Serbia through its 'parallel structures' in Serb-inhabited areas, most notably in northern Kosovo. We have already analyzed the role of EULEX and its failure to establish the rule of law in Kosovo. In a nutshell, EULEX failed in both its mission to establish the rule of law, and to nurture local institutions that would be capable of doing it instead. Widespread corruption in the Kosovan political system and the persistence of lawlessness in northern Kosovo even five years after the deployment of the EULEX mission bear the mark of this failure. EULEX is seeing itself more as a replacement of the local institutions rather than an adviser or monitor, and thus had little incentive to build a sovereign state (Dijkstra 2011: 208). This is manifested in particular in the relationship between EULEX and Kosovo police. Instead of a partnership or monitoring relationship, the EULEX police, through its dismissive attitude and arbitrary take-over of cases originally handled by the Kosovan police has discredited the latter in the eyes of the local people in general and non-dominant communities in particular. Thus, even after its eventual departure, EULEX will leave behind a Kosovo struggling to establish the rule of law and an incapable police service suffering from lack of capacity and legitimacy.

In sum, the predominant logic is that of a 'minimalist state' that creates institutions with limited functions and capacities, which nevertheless endure precisely due to these limitations (Bieber 2011: 1784). In the case of Kosovo, it turns out that basic functionality and stability justify state weakness and a lack of sovereignty. As a Kosovan publicist and former politician put it, 'the joint product of both Kosovo's and the internationals' incompetence is the establishment of a very low standard for the functioning of the state: Success of a state's performance is called its basic stability or the lack of violence' (Surroi 2011: 8). Therefore it is clear that the predominance of the mantra of stability has kept Kosovo devoid of its domestic sovereignty. Clearly, the EU Mission in Kosovo has been measuring its performance and that of the local institutions based on its ability to be in control and maintain the status quo in Kosovo, rather than on the basis of core EU values such as democratic governance. This way, through its approach of 'strong control' and direct involvement in potential member states, the EU undermines some of its fundamental normative values.

EU brokered agreements between Kosovo and Serbia: heading towards a 'triple sovereignty partnership'

According to the Ahtisaari Plan, both the EU and Serbia had to play a role in the implementation of the Plan in post-status Kosovo in coordination with Kosovo's institutions, all part of the plan of 'supervised independence'. Nonetheless, since neither Serbia nor the EU approved the plan, Kosovo was the only party to take its obligations deriving from the proposal. Given the fact that the Ahtisaari Plan was a 'proposal' that was not endorsed by the UNSC, the source of obligation 'is the self-limitation of sovereignty offered by Kosovo in its Declaration of Independence' (Weller 2009: 245). Nonetheless, even after the declaration of independence, both the EU and Serbia were present in Kosovo through their sets of institutions and instruments creating a highly complex net of overlapping institutions, legal norms and jurisdictions. Certainly, this had a detrimental effect by undermining the new country's efforts to establish internal sovereignty.

After years of stalemate and a status quo in the north that was cementing the division of Kosovo and increasing pressures from Kosovo's

Albanian population and leaders, the EU used the International Court of Justice's (ICJ) opinion on the legality of the declaration of independence of Kosovo to bring both parties together. Following the adoption of an EU-Serbia resolution at the General Assembly of the UN (A/RES/64/298), a 'technical dialogue' between Kosovo and Serbia began in March 2011, which has produced several agreements on the return of civil registries and cadastre records, and on the freedom of movement of persons (Bajrami 2013: 6). Regardless of the initial progress, tensions rose in the summer of 2011 following the decision of the Kosovo government to send the special police to border crossings with Serbia in the north in order to enforce a trade boycott of Serbian goods. This triggered a violent reaction by local Serbs which left a Kosovan policeman dead and other international soldiers and policemen wounded. In addition, it led to a series of incidents and the establishment of a system of roadblocks to prevent free movement between the north and the rest of Kosovo.

However, the EU eventually succeeded in relaunching dialogue, and through the use of strong leverage on both sides, the EU negotiators obtained agreements on customs stamps and on the integrated management of border crossings and the representation of Kosovo in regional cooperation (Lehne 2012: 2). As regards the agreement on Kosovo's regional representation, it will allow for Kosovo to sign new regional agreements for itself and participate in various regional organizations and meetings provided that the word 'Kosovo' is accompanied by an asterisk and the footnote: 'This designation is without prejudice to status, and is in line with UNSC 1244 Resolution and the ICJ Opinion on the Kosovo Declaration of Independence.' This is a clear indication that yet again, the logic of 'creative obscurity' dominates the EU's approach in the case of Kosovo. In addition, it puts Kosovo on an unequal footing with other states. As Lehne (2012: 3) put it, 'by consenting to a rather peculiar nameplate, Pristina for its part acknowledged that it was not quite yet a normal state'.

Thus, despite the talk on an 'EU-facilitated technical dialogue', the tripartite dialogue was neither technical nor facilitated. As Lehne (2012: 8) argues, it had a highly political character, as each of the issues discussed had its status-sensitive aspects, with the EU engaged in rather heavy-duty mediation, including setting the agenda and elaborating solutions while using massive carrots and sticks. Nonetheless, the dialogue became even formally political in October 2012, when Kosovo Prime Minister Hashim Thaçi and Serbia Prime Minister Ivica Dačić met in Brussels. Although the parties were discussing various issues from the previous rounds of the dialogue such as the exchange of liaison officers and energy and telecommunication, it soon became clear the issue of 'the north' became the critical theme in the EU-facilitated dialogue between Prishtina and Belgrade. After ten rounds of often gruelling talks in the EU-facilitated dialogue, Kosovo and Serbia reached a landmark agreement on 19 April

2013, as the respective prime ministers initialled a text agreement[1] aimed at normalizing relations between Serbia and Kosovo.

This agreement entitled 'First Agreement of Principles Governing the Normalization of Relations' is a 15-point document that establishes the parameters for the inclusion of northern Kosovo within Prishtina's legal framework, while increasing the level of autonomy for the four Serb-dominated municipalities in northern Kosovo. It creates the Association/Community of Serb majority municipalities in Kosovo, initially comprising of four Serb northern municipalities of Kosovo, while leaving the door open for other Serb-dominated municipalities. The Association/Community will have governing authority over five key areas: economic development, health, education, urban and rural planning (KIPRED 2013b: 9). The agreement foresees the dismemberment of the Serbian security structures through their absorption into Kosovo's equivalent structures and the creation of new local institutions emerging from free and fair elections organized by Kosovo with the help of the OSCE. The last point of the agreement contains a commitment by Kosovo and Serbia not to block each other on their EU integration path. The agreement does not deal with the issue of the Serb education and health systems in Kosovo, which continue to be run by Serbia.

While the agreement will eventually enable Kosovan institutions to establish nominal control in the northern part of the country (through the integration of the existing judicial and security structures into the Kosovan system), certain elements of the agreement will enhance the position of northern Kosovo as a special territory within the country. This is evident in two fields: judiciary and policing. According to point 9 of the agreement, there shall be a Police Regional Command for the four northern Serb majority municipalities (Northern Mitrovica, Zvecan, Zubin Potok and Leposavic). This will impose changes in the present organization of the police in Kosovo, thus elevating northern Kosovo to a status of a separate region. Likewise, regarding the organization of the judiciary, the agreement foresees the establishment of a panel composed of a majority of Kosovo Serb judges by the Appellate Court in Prishtina to deal with all Kosovo Serb majority municipalities. A division of this Appellate Court composed of both administrative staff and judges will sit permanently in northern Mitrovica (Mitrovica District Court). In an another attempt to single out northern Kosovo from the rest of the country and Serb-dominated municipalities, the Serbian government demanded NATO provide written guarantees that the Security Force of Kosovo (KSF), or a future Kosovan army, will not be present in northern Kosovo. In many ways, this agreement has legitimized Serbia's 'territorial approach' to the Kosovo Serb problem, i.e. keeping north Kosovo as separate as possible from the rest of Kosovo, which could later be useful in a potential territorial reconfiguration or land swap.

This landmark agreement was followed by other agreements on the implementation of the April Agreement, especially on the issue of elections, as well as on energy and telecommunications. However, a key momentum in the implementation of the agreement was the municipal elections of 3 November 2013.

This vote, considered a landmark due to the fact that it was organized throughout the territory of Kosovo for the first time, was characterized by a higher turnout on the part of the local Serbs and the interruption of voting in three polling stations in North Mitrovica as masked men stormed the stations (*The Economist* 2013). Despite this, the November election was considered 'a Positive Step Forward for Democracy in Kosovo' by the EU Election Observation Mission (EU EOM 2013). Nonetheless, the repeated election in North Mitrovica on the 19 November, and the run-off on 1 December 2013, resulted in the election of new Serbian mayors and local councils in ten Serb-dominated municipalities in Kosovo, thus paving the way for the creation of the Association of the Serb Municipalities in Kosovo (Peci 2013a).

Although these elections represent a landmark in the implementation of the Brussels Agreement and the inclusion of local Serbs into the Kosovan political system and society, it is too early to predict the real effects of the Kosovo-Serbia agreement. As regards the impact of the agreement on Kosovo's sovereignty and state building, it raises six crucial issues. First, although the agreement presupposes that Kosovo's legal system is supreme in the territory of Kosovo, Serbia's insistence on the 'status neutral' character of the agreement can easily become an insurmountable barrier to the implementation of its provisions. For instance, the Serb municipalities in Kosovo or the Association of the Serb Municipalities could easily choose to respect only those provisions deriving from the Brussels Agreement or Kosovan legislation that suit them (cooperation with and funding from Serbia) and ignore their obligations and legal ties with the Kosovan institutions that they might consider not to be 'status neutral'. A precedent has been set already with the refusal of Serbs and Serbia to use Kosovan IDs to vote or the Kosovo institutions logo on ballot papers because, according to them, it amounts to a claim that Kosovo is a sovereign state, which Serbia continues to reject (Zulfaj 2013). Certainly this leaves an open door to the Kosovan Serbs to oppose various Kosovan legal provisions and institutional decisions, thus leading to a political stalemate that hinders Kosovo's internal functionality and could potentially undermine the negotiating process. A case in point is the recent disagreement between the Government in Prishtina and the four northern municipalities over the content of the new municipality statutes. Moreover, Serbia has already demonstrated that in its relations with Kosovo it will stick to the agreed conclusions while refusing to respect/recognise other legal provisions in Kosovo that were not part of the Brussels' talks. Thus, for Serbia, Kosovo's legality is confined exclusively within the Brussels agreements.

Second, most of the agreements achieved in Brussels are very abstract and legally ambiguous, leaving room for different interpretations by the two parties. As a result, experts of both parties have been engaged in endless discussions about the terms of implementation of these agreements up to the point of *de facto* renegotiation. For instance, the implementation of the Integrated Border/Boundary Management Agreement had to be renegotiated by the Prime Ministers of Kosovo and Serbia, thus resulting in a protracted process of negotiation that postponed the implementation (Bajrami 2013: 8). Judging from this, one can foresee a new round of extensive and long negotiations on the statute and functioning of the Association/Community of Serb majority municipalities. For starters, as Marko Prelec (2013) points out:

> the dual name is another sign of trouble ahead: for Serbia, it is a Zajednica (union or community) of municipalities, a governing entity newly established by the agreement, while for Kosovo, it is merely an inter-municipal association like one that already exists to help local governments coordinate and share expertise.

Third, irrespective of the fact that as a result of the Brussels Agreement Kosovo will be able to establish nominal control over the entire territory of Kosovo, the April 2013 Agreement has *de facto* created a self-governing sub-state political unit within Kosovo, which despite its legal ties to Kosovo, does not recognise it as an independent polity. In addition, the April agreement reinforces the already asymmetrical nature of rights between the Kosovo Serbs from the north and those Serbs living in other parts of the country, thus creating two separate categories of ethnic Serbs in Kosovo (Krasniqi 2013: 15–16).

Fourth, the process of negotiations in Brussels has often had a negative effect on the democratic consolidation of Kosovo. First, the need to achieve results in the negotiations pushed the EU to rely exclusively on strong political leadership both in Serbia and Kosovo, ignoring wider institutional and societal participation. Second, before the start of the dialogue Kosovo had just elected a central government through a process characterized by massive fraud and irregularities (EU EEM 2011). Nevertheless, the EU largely ignored this fact due to the imminent need to engage Prishtina and Belgrade in a dialogue. Third, in a similar vein, in summer 2013 the EU urged and even pressured the Kosovo parliament to adopt the Law on Amnesty, derived from the Brussels Agreement, amid opposition from civil society organizations which expressed concerns that the proposed version of the law provided room even for the amnesty of persons/entities engaged in criminal activities and who were not subjects of the Agreement (Peci 2013b).[2] Fourth, more recently, Serbia was heavily involved in the Kosovo elections by creating and supporting a single Serb list (the 'Serbian Civic Initiative'), thus undermining democratic competition and pluralism amongst local Serbs in Kosovo. Moreover, fearing a low turnout in the November 2013 elections, Serbian institutions coerced local Serbs in Northern Mitrovica to go and vote (Robinson and Krstic 2013). In short, the format, content and the overall handling of the dialogue have certainly hindered the democratic functioning and consolidation of Kosovo, at least in the short run.

Fifth, the Brussels Agreement has provided an opportunity for the state of Serbia to have a say in the internal affairs and constitutional order of Kosovo without the obligation to recognise its independence. Moreover, Kosovo was required to approve the April Agreement in the Assembly and amend relevant legislation, whereas the Serbian parliament refused to vote on the Agreement itself, claiming that to do so would constitute the recognition of Kosovo (KIPRED 2013b: 10–11; Prelec 2013). On the other hand, Serbia is looking for legal ways to maintain ties with the new Association/Community, most probably through the enactment of a 'Law on substantial autonomy for Kosovo and Metohija', including provisions for the Community of Serb Municipalities (ibid.). This would certainly imply that the new Association/Community is tied to both Kosovo and Serbia, thus resulting in a condominium-like situation of overlapping Serbian and Kosovan jurisdictions in the Serb-majority municipalities, above all in the north (Krasniqi 2012: 354).

Sixth, all these agreements foresee a crucial role for the EU to play in the implementation of these agreements. Although the EU and its mission in Kosovo should assist both parties in the implementation of the Agreement and help overcome disagreements, having in mind its 'status neutral' position, its crucial role could easily work to the detriment of the affirmation of Kosovo's statehood prerogatives in the process of implementation. On the other hand, the very nature of the agreements and the ongoing Kosovo-Serbia status impasse oblige the EU to be involved in Kosovo's internal affairs and politics even after the eventual departure of the EULEX Mission. Its role certainly goes beyond a mere 'neutral arbiter' thereby allowing the EU to 'maintain' Kosovo's limited sovereignty.

The last two points are particularly significant for Kosovo for two reasons. First, the crucial role of the EU and Serbia in the implementation of the Brussels Agreement provides both the EU and Serbia with a major political stake in Kosovo thus leading to a situation of a *de facto* triple 'Kosovo-Serbia-EU' 'sovereignty partnership'. Undoubtedly, this hinders Kosovo's efforts to assume domestic sovereignty. Second, as a result of this 'triple sovereignty partnership', Kosovo has developed a double dependency on the EU and Serbia on its path to state building. Likewise, following the EU's tying of the EU integration process to the normalization of relations with Serbia, Kosovo's integration into the Union will depend both on the EU and Serbia.

Kosovo's EU path

A major impasse in Kosovo's path towards the EU is the lack of formal contractual relations. This stems from the fact that not all EU members recognise Kosovo as a sovereign state. This certainly undermines Kosovo's international sovereignty, weakens its position in the tripartite negotiations with the EU and Serbia and hinders its European integration process. Therefore, despite the heavy presence of the EU in Kosovo for many years and the formal reaffirmation of Kosovo's 'European perspective' by EU officials, Kosovo remains at the end of the queue of countries aspiring to join the Union. This has not only prevented Kosovo's EU integration progress, but also rendered conditionality entirely irrelevant as an EU state building tool in the case of Kosovo (Bieber 2011: 1793). Having failed to clarify the fundamental issue – whether Kosovo is a state[3] or not – the EU has been muddling through and improvising for many years regarding its relations with Kosovo. This discouraged reforms and at the same time increased the gap between Kosovo and the other countries in the region.

Thus, lacking leverage to reward compliance, in 2011 the EU made the dialogue with Serbia a key condition in Kosovo's relations with the EU. As a result, things started to progress by the end of 2011, when the EU upgraded its presence in Kosovo through the creation of the EU Office, which was created by unifying the existing European Commission Liaison Office and the Office of the EU Special Representative (EUSR), each of which had a different representative (Brajshori and Jovanovic 2011). Later on, following the agreement between Serbia and Kosovo on regional representation, the EU managed to build up consensus among its members in allowing Kosovo to progress towards the establishment of contractual relations with the EU. In this light, the Commission proposed to launch a feasibility study for a Stabilisation and Association Agreement between Kosovo and the EU, a proposal endorsed by the Council of the European Union on 28 February 2012. The EU formally launched the 'Feasibility Study' during a visit of the Enlargement Commissioner Štefan Füle to Kosovo at the end of March 2012, which corresponded with the launching of Kosovo's National Council for European Integration (Aliu 2012). In October 2012, the European Commission confirmed that, based on the findings in the study, there is no legal obstacle to conclude a Stabilisation and Association Agreement between the EU and Kosovo and that Kosovo is largely ready to open negotiations for a Stabilisation and Association Agreement (European Commission 2012a).

Following the landmark agreement in April 2013, the European Commission asked the Council to authorise the opening of negotiations on a Stabilisation and Association Agreement between the EU and Kosovo, a recommendation endorsed by the European Council (2013) in June. Negotiations started in October 2013 and were concluded in May 2014. Although this is an important milestone on Kosovo's EU integration path, the way forward remains uncertain due to the statehood issue. As a result, according to the European Commission (2013), the negotiations would be led by the Commission and the provisions on the political dialogue and the Common Foreign and Security Policy (CFSP) would be negotiated by the High Representative of the Union for Foreign Affairs and Security Policy, and, following the Lisbon Treaty, which conferred legal personality to the European Union, the Agreement would be concluded in the form of an EU-only agreement.

As regards the issue of visas, too, Kosovo moved closer to an eventual visa liberalization with the EU following, first, the launch of the Structured Dialogue on the Rule of Law with the EU on 30 May 2012 in Brussels, and the handing over to the Kosovo Government of the roadmap for visa liberalization by the European Commissioner for Home Affairs in June 2012 (European Commission 2012b). Although there is no set date as to when Kosovars can travel to the Schengen area visa-free, the roadmap to visa liberalization is a major step forward as it sets out reforms that the Kosovo government will need to implement to create a secure environment for visa-free travel.

Conclusion

The EU's involvement in the Balkans has increased gradually to the point of making it the main actor in the area in large part due to its dual capacity of engaging in state building and European integration simultaneously. This has led to the emergence of state building conditionality, which according to Bieber is problematic for two reasons: first, the EU lacks rules in the sphere of state building, and also struggles to impose them and, second, it remains divided between different Union institutions and Member States when it comes to state building (Bieber 2011: 1793). This is nowhere more obvious than in the case of Kosovo. Although the EU has emerged as the main political actor in the post-2008 Kosovo, its dual strategy of 'state building' and 'EU integration' has yielded symbolic results mainly because of its inability to overcome the statehood impasse in Kosovo.

The EU's approach of 'limited sovereignty–strong control' has resulted in a quasi-state with minimal sovereignty, characterized by institutions with limited capacity and scope on the one hand, and multiple external mechanisms of control and supervision on the other. Therefore, Kosovo remains a highly 'penetrated society' due to extensive external influences and interferences as well as the strong EU presence, above all through its EULEX Mission, thus having a 'forced-course development' (Ágh 1999: 264). Moreover, as Fagan (2010: 162) put it, 'the EU's relationship with Kosovo is thus somewhat hegemonic insofar as it combines corrective powers a reformulation of the role of the international community – with the rigidities of conditionality'. Nonetheless, the mere presence of the EU in the country is not sufficient and does not bring about automatic Europeanization and democratization of the Kosovar society and state.

Lacking a solid legal basis on which to build relations with Kosovo, including the functioning of the EULEX Mission, the EU, just like the UN before, has entangled itself in a vicious circle of 'creative obscurity' which in essence prevents Kosovo from assuming both domestic and international sovereignty. Indeed, as Chandler (2006: 33) points out, external actors engaged in state building have redefined sovereignty as a variable capacity rather than an indivisible right in order to legitimate external mechanisms of regulation. Thus, similar to UNMIK's not-that-successful endeavour of 'state building from scratch' in Kosovo in conditions of the absence of statehood between 1999 and 2008, the EU has engaged in the process of 'Member State building from scratch' in a polity and territory devoid of many essential statehood prerogatives. However, many policy makers in the EU seem to have forgotten that 'the paradox of European integration is that in order to transfer and share parts of substantial sovereignty, it is necessary to first become a sovereign State (traditional style)' (Woelk 2013: 472).

Nonetheless, by refusing to deal with the issue of sovereignty and, worse, undermining it through its 'status neutral' position, the EU's strategy of 'Member State building' in the case of Kosovo is reduced to mere 'neutral' institution building. Likewise, the process of negotiations between Kosovo and Serbia under the auspices of the EU has created a 'tripartite sovereignty partnership' in Kosovo that makes Kosovo dependent both on Serbia and the EU regarding both its state building and European integration. As a result of the decision to link Kosovo's EU integration process to the process of negotiations with Serbia, instead of focusing on the compliance of Kosovo with the *acquis communautaire*, the EU will be judging Kosovo above all based on the results (compromises) in the dialogue with Serbia. This certainly undermines the process of reforms in Kosovo, thus damaging the process of democratization and Europeanization. Thus, to paraphrase Bieber (2011: 1800), the main challenge of the EU in Kosovo is how to build institutions that give the new country the capacity to achieve membership without losing the state along the way.

Notes

1 No official text of the agreement has been circulated. Various local and international media have published unofficial versions of the text.
2 This law is problematic for two main reasons. By insisting on amnestying almost all crimes not only in the north, but in other parts of Kosovo as well, the EU clearly was utilizing the Kosovo-Serbia dialogue to absolve itself of all responsibility regarding EULEX's failure to fight corruption and criminality in the North, and also in the rest of Kosovo. In other words, through this law, EULEX amnestied crimes/criminals that it failed to punish. Second, it demonstrated yet again that the EU compromises its fundamental value of the rule of law in the face of short-term political gains.
3 Article 49 of the Consolidated Treaty of the European Union clearly states that 'Any European State which respects the principles set out in Article 6(1) may apply to become a member of the Union.'

References

Ágh, A. (1999) 'Process of Democratisation in the East Central European and Balkan States: Sovereignty-Related Conflicts in the Context of Europeanization', *Communist and Post-Communist Studies*, 32, pp. 263–279.

Aliu, F. (2012) 'EU Launches Kosovo Feasibility Study', *Balkan Insight*, 27 March. Available at: www.balkaninsight.com/en/page/all-balkans-home.

Anastasakis, O. (2008) 'The EU's Political Conditionality in the Western Balkans: Towards a More Pragmatic Approach', *Southeast European and Black Sea Studies*, 8 (4), pp. 365–377.

Bajrami, A. (2013) *Kosovo–Serbia Dialogue: Windows of Opportunity or a House of Cards?* Policy Analysis No. 03/2013. Prishtina: Group for Legal and Political Studies. Available at: http://legalpoliticalstudies.org/download/Policy%20Analysis%2003%202013.pdf (accessed 28 November 2013).

BBC (2012) 'Kosovo Declared "Fully Independent"', *BBC*, 10 September. Available at: www.bbc.co.uk.

Bieber, F. (2011) 'Building Impossible States? State-Building Strategies and EU Membership in the Western Balkans', *Europe-Asia Studies*, 63 (10), pp. 1783–1802.

Boege, V., Brown, A., Clements, K. and Nolan, A. (2008) *States Emerging from Hybrid Political Orders: Pacific Experiences*. Occasional Paper No 11. Brisbane: Australian Centre for Peace and Conflict Studies, University of Queensland.

Börzel, T. A. (2011) *When Europeanization Hits Limited Statehood. The Western Balkans as a Test Case for the Transformative Power of Europe*. KFG Working Paper Series, No. 30. Berlin: Freie Universität Berlin.

Brajshori, M. and Jovanovic, I. (2011) 'EU Upgrades Presence in Kosovo, Appoints New Representative', *SETimes*, 23 December. Available at: www.setimes.com.

Chandler, D. (2006) *Empire in Denial: The Politics of State-Building*. London: Pluto Press.

Dijkstra, H. (2011) 'The Planning and Implementation of the Rule of Law Mission of the European Union in Kosovo', *Journal of Intervention and Statebuilding*, 5 (2), pp. 192–210.

Džihić, V. and Kramer, H. (2009) *Kosovo after Independence: Is the EU's EULEX Mission Delivering on its Promises?* Berlin: Friedrich-Ebert-Stiftung.

ECA (European Court of Auditors) (2012) *ECA/12/41*, Press Release. Luxembourg, 30 October. Available at: http://europa.eu/rapid/press-release_ECA-12-41_en.htm (accessed 28 November 2013).

EU EEM (European Union Election Expert Mission to Kosovo) (2011) *Final Report*. 25 January. Available at: http://eeas.europa.eu/delegations/kosovo/documents/press_corner/25012012_final_report_eu_eem_kosovo_2010.pdf (accessed 28 November 2013).

EU EOM (European Union Election Observation Mission) (2013) *Preliminary Statement: A Positive Step Forward for Democracy in Kosovo*, Press Release. Prishtina, 5 November. Available at: www.eueom.eu/files/pressreleases/english/preliminary-statement-in-kosovo-05112013_en.pdf.

European Commission (2012a) *Communication from the Commission to the European Parliament and the Council on a Feasibility Study for a Stabilisation and Association Agreement between the European Union and Kosovo** (COM(2012) 602 final). Brussels, 10 October. Available at: http://ec.europa.eu/enlargement/pdf/key_documents/2012/package/ks_feasibility_2012_en.pdf (accessed 28 November 2013).

European Commission (2012b) *Commission Delivers Visa Roadmap to Kosovo Government*, Press Release. Brussels, 14 June. Available at: http://europa.eu/rapid/press-release_IP-12-605_en.htm (accessed 28 November 2013).

European Commission (2013) *MEMO: EU Starts the Stabilisation and Association Agreement Negotiations with Kosovo*, Press Release. Brussels, 28 October. Available at: http://europa.eu/rapid/press-release_MEMO-13-938_en.htm (accessed 28 November 2013).

European Council (2013) *Conclusion*, 28 June. Available at: http://register.consilium.europa.eu/doc/srv?l=EN&f=ST%20104%202013%20REV%202 (accessed 28 November 2013).

Fagan, A. (2010) *Europe's Balkan Dilemma: Paths to Civil Society or State-Building?* London and New York: I. B. Tauris.

Hague, R. and Harrop, M. (2001) *Comparative Government and Politics: An Introduction*. 5th edn. New York: Palgrave.

ICG (International Crisis Group) (2010) *The Rule of Law in Independent Kosovo*, Europe Report No. 204. Prishtina and Brussels: ICG.

Ignatieff, M. (2003) *Empire Lite: Nation-Building in Bosnia, Kosovo and Afghanistan*. London: Vintage Random House.

Kaldor, M. and Vejvoda, I. (eds) (2002) *Democratization in Central and Eastern Europe*. London and New York: Pinter Publisher.

Ker-Lindsay, J. (2009) *Kosovo: The Path to Contested Statehood in the Balkans*. London and New York: I. B. Tauris.

Ker-Lindsay, J. and Economides, S. (2012) 'Standards before Status before Accession: Kosovo's EU Perspective', *Journal of Balkan and Near Eastern Studies*, 14 (1), pp. 77–92.

KIPRED (2013a) *A Comprehensive Analysis of EULEX: What Next?* Policy Paper No. 1/13. Prishtina: KIPRED.

KIPRED (2013b) *The Implementation of Agreements of Kosovo-Serbia Political Dialogue*. Policy Paper No. 4/13. Prishtina: KIPRED.

Knaus, G. and Cox, M. (2005) 'The "Helsinki Moment" in Southeastern Europe', *Journal of Democracy*, 16 (1), pp. 39–53.

Kostovicova, D. and Bojicic-Dzelilovic, V. (2006) 'Europeanizing the Balkans: Rethinking the Post-Communist and Post-Conflict Transition', *Ethnopolitics*, 5 (3), pp. 223–241.

Krasniqi, G. (2010) 'The International Community's Modus Operandi in Postwar Bosnia and Herzegovina and in Kosovo: A Critical Assessment', *Südosteuropa*, 58 (4), pp. 520–541.

Krasniqi, G. (2012) 'Overlapping Jurisdictions, Disputed Territory, Unsettled State: The Perplexing Case of Citizenship in Kosovo', *Citizenship Studies*, 16 (3–4), pp. 353–366.

Krasniqi, G. (2013) *Equal Citizens, Uneven 'Communities': Differentiated and Hierarchical Citizenship in Kosovo*. CITSEE Working Paper Series 2013/27. Edinburgh: CITSEE. Available at: www.citsee.ed.ac.uk/working_papers/files/CITSEE_WORKING_PAPER_2013-27.pdf (accessed 28 November 2013).

Lehne, S. (2012) *Kosovo and Serbia: Towards a Normal Relationship*. Carnegie Endowment for International Peace. Available at: www.carnegieendowmant.org/files/Kosovo_and_Serbia.pdf (accessed 28 November 2013).

Lemay-Hébert, N. (2013) 'Everyday Legitimacy and International Administration: Global Governance and Local Legitimacy in Kosovo', *Journal of Intervention and Statebuilding*, 7(1), pp. 87–104.

Lidén, K., Mac Ginty, R. and Richmond, O. P. (2009) 'Liberal Peacebuilding Reconstructed', *International Peacekeeping*, Special Issue, 16 (5), pp. 587–598.

Linz, J. J. and Stepan, A. (1996) *Problems of Democratic Transition and Consolidation: Southern Europe, South America and Post-Communist Europe*. Maryland: Johns Hopkins University Press.

Manners, I. (2002) 'Normative Power Europe: A Contradiction in Terms?', *JCMS: Journal of Common Market Studies*, 40 (2), pp. 235–258.

Montanaro, L. (2009) *The Kosovo Statebuilding Conundrum: Addressing Fragility in a Contested State*. FRIDE Working Paper 91. Madrid: FRIDE.

Palokaj, A. (2013) *Kosovo–EU Relations: The History of Unfulfilled Aspirations? Lost Opportunities in Kosovo's European Integration Process*. Prishtina: KFOS and Forumi 2015.

Papadimitriou, D. and Petrov, P. (2012) 'Whose Rule Whose Law? Contested Statehood, External Leverage and the European Union's Rule of Law Mission in Kosovo', *JCMS: Journal of Common Market Studies*, 50 (5), pp. 746–763.

Papadimitriou, D. and Petrov, P. (2013) 'State-Building without Recognition: A Critical Retrospective of the European Union's Strategy in Kosovo (1999–2010)', in Elbasani, A. (ed.) *European Integration and Transformation in Western Balkans: Europeanization or Business as Usual?* London and New York: Routledge, pp. 121–137.

Papadimitriou, D., Petrov, P. and Greiçevci, L. (2007) 'To Build a State: Europeanization, EU Actorness and State-Building in Kosovo', *European Foreign Affairs Review*, 12 (2), pp. 219–238.

Peci, E. (2013a) 'Kosovo Run-Off Polls Produce Dramatic Changes', *Balkan Insight*, 2 December. Available at: www.balkaninsight.com.

Peci, E. (2013b) 'EU Urges Kosovo to Pass Amnesty Law', *Balkan Insight*, 10 July. Available at: www.balkaninsight.com.

Pond, E. (2008) 'The EU Test in Kosovo', *The Washington Quarterly*, 31 (4), pp. 97–112.

Prelec, M. (2013) 'The Kosovo-Serbia Agreement: Why Less is More', ICG, 7 May. Available at: www.crisisgroupblogs.org.

Robinson, M. and Krstic, B. (2013) 'Voters Allege Coercion in Kosovo Ballot Central to EU Accord', *Reuters*, 17 November. Available at: www.reuters.com/article/2013/11/17/us-kosovo-election-serbs-idUSBRE9AG0B620131117.

Smolar, P. (2013) 'Europe and the Challenge of State-Building', *Press Europ*, 15 February. Available at: www.presseurop.eu.

Surroi, V. (2011) 'Regression of Three Albanian Societies', *Südosteuropa Mitteilungen*, 4, pp. 6–17.

Tansey, O. (2007) 'Democratization without a State: Democratic Regime-building in Kosovo', *Democratization*, 14 (1), pp. 129–150.

The Economist (2013) 'Kosovo's Election: Only a Minor Disturbance', 9 November. Available at: www.economist.com.

Weller, M. (2009) *Contested Statehood: Kosovo's Struggle for Independence*. Oxford: Oxford University Press.

Woodward, S. L. (2011) 'Varieties of State-Building in the Balkans: A Case for Shifting Focus', in Fischer, M., Austin, B. and Giessmann, H.J. (eds), *Advancing Conflict Transformation*. Farmington Hills: Opladen (The Berghof Handbook II).

Woelk, J. (2013) 'EU Member State-Building in the Western Balkans: (Prolonged) EU-Protectorates or New Model of Sustainable Enlargement? Conclusion', *Nationalities Papers: The Journal of Nationalism and Ethnicity*, 41 (3), pp. 469–482.

Zulfaj, J. (2013) 'Kosovo Symbol Dispute Shows Limit of EU Deal', *EU Observer*, 2 September. Available at: http://euobserver.com.

9 Not-so-great expectations

The EU and the constitutional politics of Bosnia and Herzegovina

Valery Perry[1]

Introduction

In 2005, the European Commission for Democracy through Law (the Venice Commission), the Council of Europe's (CoE) advisory body on constitutional matters, issued a report on Bosnia and Herzegovina's[2] Constitution that, among other damning statements, said that BiH's weak state structure was not able to 'effectively ensure compliance with the commitments of the country with respect to the Council of Europe.' It warned that 'with such a weak state BiH will not be able to make much progress on the way towards European integration' (Venice Commission, 2005: pt. 26). Over the course of the next eight years, BiH signed a Stabilisation and Association Agreement (SAA) with the European Union (EU) in 2008, and ratified it in 2010 (though it is still not in force due to unresolved constitutional issues). Between 2005 and 2012 BiH has received Instrument of Pre-Accession (IPA) funds aimed at preparing the country for its accession journey. EU officials have made regular trips to the country, as have countless CoE, Parliamentary Assembly of the Council of Europe (PACE), and bilateral delegations. Its neighbor Croatia entered the EU in July 2013, and Serbia began accession talks following compromises on Kosovo. While slow, halting, and non-linear, the region seems to be lurching its way towards an expanded Europe. BiH remains dead last in the EU 'regatta.'[3]

The 'pull' of Europe has been insufficient to provide BiH with the 'push' needed to reform its Constitution (Perry 2012). In fact, there is an increasing sense that policy makers think that constitutional reform is less needed than any forward motion of the country towards the EU – with *any* constitution, and by any means necessary. There is frustration among BiH and EU actors alike that the necessary Sejdić-Finci reform – the most well known constitutional challenge – was even included as a requirement for unfreezing the SAA and submitting a 'credible' candidacy application. (The other two are the adoption of a Law on Census and a Law on State Aid.) The extent to which Sejdić-Finci reform has increasingly been viewed through a lens of expediency rather than an opportunity to address the acknowledged flaws of Dayton suggests that constitutional reform, while potentially desirable to the EU, is not a non-negotiable requirement.

This chapter explores the extent to which BiH's constitutional reform journey has been influenced by its stated goal of EU membership, and whether the EU accession process itself is an incentivizing force for reform. Evidence suggests that the EU enlargement process is *not* a tool that will resolve BiH's core constitutional problems. While the Dayton Agreement did end the war, the Dayton Constitution has proved to be unworkable; in fact it has perhaps unwittingly left BiH as a sort of frozen conflict. Whether a new constitutional structure could help to 'unfreeze' BiH remains unknown. However, by virtue of being the single largest player in BiH, the EU will have an impact on the success or failure of constitutional reform, either through its promotion of and support for reform, or its willingness to accede to and prop up the very status quo the Venice Commission found to be unsuitable for an EU candidate.

Post-Dayton BiH constitutional reform – a short history

The problem

BiH's Constitution is a part of the General Framework Agreement for Peace (GFAP, or Dayton Agreement), embedded in Annex 4. The Constitution outlines the structure for a loose state, comprised of two entities (the Federation – itself a product of an earlier agreement between then-warring Bosniaks and Croats – and the Republika Srpska (RS)) and three constituent peoples (along with Others and citizens) (Constitution of Bosnia and Herzegovina). Some state-level competencies are defined (Article II(1)), while '(a)ll governmental functions and powers not expressly assigned in this Constitution to the institutions of Bosnia and Herzegovina shall be those of the Entities' (Article III(3)a). It provides for a Constitutional Court (Article VI), a Central Bank (Article VII), a means for amending the Constitution (Article X), and the possibility for the state to assume responsibility for additional matters as agreed by the Entities, or as 'are necessary to preserve the sovereignty, territorial integrity, political independence, and international personality of Bosnia and Herzegovina' (Article III(5)a). The Constitution commits the signatories and in turn the country to a raft of human rights agreements (Annex 1 to the constitution), references the primacy of the European Convention for the Protection of Human Rights and Fundamental Freedoms and its Protocols (Article II(2)), commits to the right of all persons in BiH not to suffer discrimination (Article II(4)), and the right of refugees and displaced persons to return to their pre-war homes (Article II(5)).

If the Constitution was implemented with any good will BiH could function. However, there is no shared vision of the country among the country's political leaders, and therefore there are different interpretations of the constitutional framework and role of the state. The various leading parties have alternately embraced devolution without ensuring anti-discriminatory practices (Serbs); sought greater centralization without securing sufficient checks and balances to ensure political confidence among the other main groups (Bosniaks); or sought to strengthen the rights of constituent peoples at the expense of the 'Others' (Croats). This difference in interpretation of the Constitution in letter and in spirit lies at the heart of the frozen conflict that continues to haunt the country.

Frozen or just cold?

The inability of the country's main ruling parties to come to any shared vision of BiH is both a result and a driver of the country's limbo status. The term 'frozen conflict' is most often used to refer to a number of conflicts in the former Soviet Union (Abkhazia, Nagorno-Karabakh, Ossetia, Transdniestria), though it is also used to describe Northern Cyprus (Crocker *et al.* 2004, 2005; Morar 2010; Wolff 2010; Zartman 2012). Until developments in 2013 vis à vis Serbia, Kosovo may have fit this description (Kennelly 2006).

While the term is not uniformly or universally defined, Licklider (2005: 33) provides useful framing: 'we use the term 'intractable conflict' to refer to a particular type of conflict, one that divides large groups of people and is either accompanied by large-scale violence now or will be in the foreseeable future ("frozen" conflicts).' He goes on to note that intractable conflicts resist settlement. In discussions of intractable conflicts, the concept is further explained: 'Still others are "frozen" in the sense that violence has ended, but no permanent settlement or resolution is in reach of the parties.' (Crocker *et al.* 2004: 7-8). Zartman (2012: 23) explains the non-linearity of the role of violence in conflict, writing:

> In a number of salient cases, identity-based violence has ended—in some cases for a long time—remaining frozen without any progress in reconciliation, as in Cyprus, Northern Ireland, Ethiopia-Eritrea, Nagorno-Karabakh, and Burundi. Such instances of conflict management inherently contain a promise for conflict resolution that must be implemented if the parties are to avoid falling back into conflict again; frozen conflicts do not naturally sublimate into the air, but can explode with deep violence, calling attention to their suspended state and the parties' unmet expectations.

Political conflict and lack of political reconciliation of any kind at the highest levels of power are characteristics of BiH. Hido Biscevic, former head of the Regional Cooperation Council, wrote that BiH appeared to be turning into a 'dormant frozen conflict' (Biscevic 2010). The EU has never used such language publicly. BiH is not generally considered to be in this category of intractable conflict as it could undermine the Dayton Agreement itself. Legally and formally, the GFAP provided a measure of 'closure' after the war. However, this agreement, differently interpreted by the formerly warring parties, and spottily implemented, may have provided only a veneer of stability and normalcy. The role of the international community – an element embedded into the GFAP just like the constitution[4] – in both seeking to end the war and building a role for itself in the peace may have the effect of glossing over the opposed visions of the country's leaders:

> One interesting aspect of post-Cold War international affairs is a mini-industry of peoples and organizations dedicated to encouraging combatants to stop killing one another and reach a settlement of some sort; they in turn make up part of the rather disparate group we call the "international community." Their work is frustrating because it is very difficult to tell whether progress has been made towards a settlement until the settlement itself is reached and has held for some time.
> (Licklider 2005: 34)

While success in stopping the bloodshed should not be underestimated, the consequent blueprint for peace has remained difficult to operationalize, as there are wide differences in the interpretation of the meaning of Dayton. Article III5(a) is perhaps the best example of the Dayton Rorschach test:

> Bosnia and Herzegovina shall assume responsibility for such other matters as are agreed by the Entities; are provided for in Annexes 5 through 8 to the General Framework Agreement; or are necessary to preserve the sovereignty, territorial integrity, political independence, and international personality of Bosnia and Herzegovina, in accordance with the division of responsibilities between the institutions of Bosnia and Herzegovina. Additional institutions may be established as necessary to carry out such responsibilities.

Where one pauses for breath when reading this makes the difference between the country having a state-level Ministry of Defense or a Supreme Court or not. Since 2006, the political environment has deteriorated to the point where these are not just abstract questions. RS rhetoric on secession is constant (Toal 2013). Croat interest in a third entity is a more subtle but still stubborn political undercurrent.

> Instead of a positive elite consensus for co-operation in order to establish mutual trust through power-sharing, the Bosnian party leaders from all of the three ethnic communities formed and still form an

ethnocratic power cartel based on a negative consensus to block each other in the decision making processes.

(Marko 2006: 209)

Cracks in the foundation

The inherent problems and contradictions in BiH's post-Dayton Constitution have been recognized for years (Venice Commission 2005; Marko 2006; Foreign Policy Initiative 2007). The first challenge to a core premise of the constitutional structure began with a lawsuit by Alija Izetbegović challenging the language in the entity constitutions. The RS Constitution noted the constituency of the Serbs, and others, while the Federation Constitution noted the constituency of the Bosniaks and Croats, and others (Case U 5/98). Izetbegović challenged this, arguing that the exclusion of some state-recognized constituent peoples from the entity constitutions violated the BiH Constitution. In 2000, the BiH Constitutional Court agreed, ruling that all three constituent peoples must be guaranteed equal status and rights, and that the entity constitutions must be revised to reflect this equality. It is important to note that the decision was made by the Bosniak judges together with the international judges on the Court, with the Croat and Serb judges noting reservations (Implementing), which Sebastian Aparicio (2009: 142) notes were 'mostly nationalistic and technical in nature.' Foreshadowing the bitter resistance to *any* constitutional reforms that might substantially affect the ethno-national power structure of the country, the entities were slow in implementing reforms, and the OHR brokered an agreement and ultimately imposed the amendments (Council of Europe 2002).

Another addition to the BiH constitutional debate came in 2005, when the Venice Commission issued 'The Opinion on the Constitutional Situation in Bosnia and Herzegovina and the Powers of the High Representative.' This assessed the compliance of the BiH Constitution with the European Convention for the Protection of Human Rights and Fundamental Freedoms (ECHR) and the European Charter of Local Self-Government, with a focus on 'the efficiency and rationality of the present constitutional and legal arrangements' in BiH (point 3). The opinion highlighted areas of concern in BiH's constitutional arrangements, including the country's weak federal arrangements; redundant and burdensome powersharing provisions that made 'effective government difficult, if not impossible' (point 29); the lack of a precise definition of vital national interests; the entity veto; and the exclusion of 'Others' from the Presidency and House of Peoples. In addition, the Opinion noted that the BiH Constitution 'was drafted and adopted without involving the citizens of BiH and without applying procedures which could have provided democratic legitimacy' (point 6).

A third development evolved as a part of a lawsuit on behalf of Dervo Sejdić (of BiH's Roma community) and Jakob Finci (of BiH's Jewish community), challenging the limitation of participation in the BiH Presidency and House of Peoples to the country's constituent peoples (Case of Sejdić and Finci 2009). In 2009, very much reflecting the Venice Commission opinion, the Court found that limiting participation in the Presidency and House of Peoples to just BiH's constituent peoples constituted unjustified discrimination.[5]

Seeking a solution

In a 2005 conference, Olli Rehn, then European Commissioner responsible for Enlargement, explicitly criticized the constitutional structure, calling for streamlining and efficiency:

> Ten years after we acknowledge the achievements of the Dayton Agreement, it is also time to recognize its limitations. It is time to reflect whether it provides Bosnia and Herzegovina with such an adequate constitutional and administrative framework that is needed to take the country forward in the process of European integration. With only a small dose of sarcasm, one may ask: How anyone can call a country ungovernable if it has as many as 13 governments for just over four million people? Which other country of the size of Bosnia and Herzegovina has over 700 members of several parliaments, over 180 Ministers, 13 Prime Ministers and three Presidents?
>
> (Rehn 2005)

The Venice Commission's opinion was a clear signal that reform was needed; as a body of the CoE, its non-binding opinion should have at minimum resonated strongly in the EU. Cooperation between the EU and the CoE is governed by a 2007 Memorandum of Understanding which confirms the CoE's role in establishing a benchmark for the rule of law and human rights, and which encourages close cooperative work (Council of Europe 2007). Further, as the *acquis communautaire* does not provide a framework for prospective member state constitutions, the EU must rely on the Venice Commission as the competent body for constitutional review.

However, in terms of practical political engagement on reform, Marko notes that ultimately 'it was left to the Americans to take the lead in a reform initiative,' which became known as the April Package (Marko 2006: 213; Batt 2009). The April Package unfolded as a series of consultations among American diplomats and advisors with the leadership of the ruling parties. From the beginning, both US and EU officials were careful to keep their distance from the initial 'unofficial' efforts, though as the process unfolded the US became more closely involved. A proposed package of amendments was agreed among participating parties (Hays and Crosby 2006), by design reflecting many of the issues noted by the

Venice Commission. It was a high-level political effort; there was little civic outreach or effort to explain the scope of reforms to citizens. In spite of agreement among the participating parties, the Package failed by two votes in the Parliamentary Assembly.

The Venice Commission reviewed the proposals, to confirm whether or not they would be compliant with CoE standards (Venice Commission 2006). However, European support was at best wavering. Sebastian notes that the European Delegation was the only institution showing some support, and then only in private. She goes on to note that while the EC Delegation in BiH recognized the need for functionality to move forward with accession, EU Foreign Policy Chief Javier Solana questioned the wisdom of a constitutional reform process (Sebastian 2007: 153). Individual EU members were involved in working with the US, meeting with party leaders and talking up reform. However, the EU as an *institution* remained concerned about constitutional reform processes stalling desired integration processes, and began to distance itself. Further, the urgency of the proposed reforms was minimized: 'EU actors assured domestic forces that constitutional changes were not a prerequisite for EU accession' (Sebastian 2007: 5). Sebastian argues that this had a negative impact on the negotiating environment, writing that 'domestic actors perceived the EU's ambivalence and aversion to risk; some felt that the EU was not fully committed, which undermined the final and more critical phase of the process' (Sebastian 2009: 243). Such differences in engagement, messages and optics among different elements of the EU family would continue to characterize reform efforts.

After this narrow failure, the political environment in BiH began to deteriorate, egged on by the escalating rhetoric of Haris Silajdžić and Milorad Dodik, the increasing readiness of the RS to block state level competencies and threaten secession, and the hands-off posture of the OHR (Democratization Policy Council 2008; McMahon and Western 2009; Bassuener and Weber 2010; Chivvis 2010; Toal 2013). The next reform effort would unfold in Prud from November 2008 to January 2009, with the main political parties (SDA, SNSD, and HDZ BiH) negotiating fundamental principles for constitutional reform as well as some key political matters, notably a census, state property, and Brčko. Different from the April Package, this effort was framed by the international community as 'home grown,' driven by BiH leaders (OHR 2009a). The parties were able to agree on their interest in transitioning the OHR to the EU Special Representative (EUSR) and the '5+2'[6] agenda often viewed as needed to signify the 'normalcy' required to move forward with EU accession (ICG 2009a). But constitutional reform remained stymied, reflecting conflicting visions. In January 2009, a joint statement announced a plan to reorganize the country into four territorial and administrative units. The Bosniak SDA's vision of the four units would (not surprisingly) be quite different than the Serb SNSD vision, which insisted on the RS remaining intact, and untouched. HDZ BiH's interests in the creation of new regions were clearly linked to Croat interest in a third entity or its equivalent (Bosnia's 'Dual Crisis'; Morrison 2011). Silajdžić responded to the deal as a plan to further divide up the Federation, while the SDP's Zlatko Lagumdzija called it a farce, criticizing it as too light on details to have any meaning, but then also detailing his objections to the census, Brčko and state property plans (BBC 2008). Dodik walked out in February saying that new talks would only be possible when others recognized the RS's right to secede. In the aftermath of the 'Prud Process,' heavy US pressure did at minimum result in the first amendment to the Constitution, related to the Brčko District (Council of Europe Parliamentary Assembly 2010).

The role of the EU in Prud was notable for two main reasons. First, dual-hatted High Representative/EU Special Representative Miroslav Lajčák was unable to move the process forward, demonstrating the weak 'pull' of the EU (Byrne 2009). Second, and revealing a theme that would continue, was the melding of talks about (ever weaker) constitutional reform together with the '5+2' reforms needed to close the OHR. In fact, press coverage in the aftermath actively decoupled constitutional reform from 5+2; Inzko noted the following in an interview:

> I also said that the change of the Constitution was not a condition for 5+2.... Although the change of the constitution at this point is not a condition for progress in the process of European integration, I am sure that it will have to be changed.
>
> (OHR 2009b)

Statements from the EU after Prud sought to frame it as a success, focused on the closure of the OHR (Rehn 2009). As it became evident that the 'process' was going nowhere, this initiative slipped from the radar screen.

A third effort, the 'Butmir Process,' consisted of two rounds of talks in October 2009. Carl Bildt, the Foreign Minister of Sweden (and BiH's first High Representative), attending on behalf of the EU Presidency, and US Deputy Secretary of State James Steinberg engaged directly with BiH's leading political parties. The talks got off to a bad start when Dodik failed to show up on time, travelling instead to Belgrade to meet Russian President Medvedev (Alic 2009). In addition, it became evident that there was not a unified international front. Bassuener and Weber (2010) explain the impact of this, and the results of sending the signal that constitutional reforms were in fact very much negotiable:

> OHR Closure – "transition" – was clearly Bildt's primary goal. The US State Department had been working quietly prior to Butmir to arrange some package of constitutional reforms prior to 2009. The Butmir process was from the outset a marriage of competing imperatives, with the US focused on a minimal package of constitutional changes and

meeting the 5+2 criteria, and the EU Presidency and institutions aimed at the bare minimum to transition – and it showed. Bildt gained the upper hand. But despite flailing international efforts to water down the package to a sufficient degree that Dodik might be willing to sign on, the effort failed. He repudiated the very concept of internationally convened constitutional discussions, but attended the second meeting at Butmir on October 20–21 regardless, at which he mooted the "peaceful dissolution" of the state. In so doing, he showed he had taken the measure of an international community desperate for a deliverable, and continued to manipulate it into further lowering the bar while giving nothing away. At the PIC [Peace Implementation Council] meeting a month later in Sarajevo, he claimed that Bildt had told him that any constitutional change, however minor, would suffice.

Aggressive comments from Dodik about hating BiH, demands from the Croats for reorganization according to four territorial units to get 'their own' entity, and poorly unified Bosniak positions created a negotiating environment in which mutually contradictory positions continued to dominate, painting parties into corners from which the only exit would be a loss of face or process termination. The proposal discussed was weaker than the April Package but still aimed at targeted strengthening and streamlining. The Butmir Process collapsed.

Bieber writes that the 'hasty and ill-prepared EU–US initiative' contributed to the sense of political crisis in the country, rather than helping to calm it down (Bieber 2010: 1). He further argues that the parties had little interest in engaging in the negotiations once it became clear that neither the US nor EU had substantive carrots or sticks, noting that the EU in particular had taken a 'contradictory line' on constitutional reform (ibid.: 1–2). Bassuener is similarly critical, noting Bildt's overriding interest in closing down the OHR as soon as possible (Bassuener 2009).[7]

In the wake of these 'top down' efforts, international support emerged for some 'bottom up' reform efforts, though it is interesting to note that the funding for these efforts did not come from the EU, but the US and the Swiss.[8] None managed to reach a sufficient number of citizens to catalyze a real movement and demand for constitutional reform. Further, none enjoyed sustained, high-level, visible support from the international community that might have helped to put wind in their sails against consistent domestic political opposition. And none were supported by the EU.

Constitutional reform and EU accession – the missing link?

When mired in the existential intransigence of constitutional politics in BiH, it is important to remember that many countries preparing for membership in the EU have needed to revise their constitutions. When EU enlargement among countries from Central and Eastern European (CEE) states began, the European Council agreed upon conditions and terms for enlargement at the Copenhagen Summit in 1993, affirming that any of the CEE states could join, once 'able to assume the obligations of membership by satisfying the economic and political conditions required' (European Council 1993: 12). The Criteria were affirmed at the Madrid Summit in 1995, where a condition was added to ensure countries could develop and strengthen the administrative and structural institutions needed to implement and harmonize their own domestic law with EU law (European Council 1995). While the accession cases of Malta, Poland, or the Czech Republic are certainly different than BiH, even seemingly well-functioning states have had to make reforms (Cremona 2001; Grabbe 2002; Kellermann 2002).

As a part of BiH's accession journey, the European Commission began issuing annual Progress Reports for BiH in 2005.[9] The 2005 report explains that '[p]rogress has been measured on the basis of decisions *actually* taken, legislation *actually* adopted and the degree of implementation' (European Commission 2005: 4, emphasis in the original). A review of the language of these reports on the specific issue of constitutional reform provides a rough barometer for considering the EU's non-negotiable requirements, thoughtful recommendations, and unmoored hopes.

The 2005 Report took place against the backdrop of the Venice Commission Opinion issued earlier that year. The Report's section on Democracy and the Rule of Law briefly explains the main features of BiH's Constitution, and notes that 'the adequacy of the Dayton constitutional system to the present circumstances is frequently questioned both within and outside the country' (European Commission 2005: 9). It further notes that '[f]rom a European integration perspective it is difficult to argue that the present constitutional order is optimal' (ibid.: 9), as swift decision making and reform implementation are hampered. Echoing the Venice Commission, the incompatibility of the election law's terms are noted as incompatible with Article 14 of the ECHR for the first of many times. A reader would recognize the dry 'neutral' tone, but would walk away certain that the EU was being clear that the constitutional set-up was unsatisfactory.

The 2006 Progress Report took place against a troubled backdrop – the April Package had failed, and political divisions intensified. The Report notes that:

> The evolution of the Bosnia and Herzegovina Constitution is necessary. Efforts need to be stepped up to create functional and affordable state structures which fully respect human rights and support the process of European integration. This constitutional reform cannot be imposed. It should be decided by consensus amongst the population of Bosnia and Herzegovina.
>
> (European Commission 2006: 6)

The 2007 Progress Report notes familiar refrains: 'Progress has been made under the current constitutional structure, but it prevents swift decision-making and therefore hinders reform and the capacity to make progress towards the EU' (European Commission 2007: 7). It references the failure of the April Package, noting that since that time no other attempts towards necessary reform had been made, and that '[w]ide disagreements between the political parties on the scope of the future constitutional reform continue' (European Commission 2007: 7). A new relevant issue was included, as the failure of the Entities to bring their constitutions in line with a March 2006 decision was explicitly mentioned:

> The Entities have failed to bring their constitutions into line with the March 2006 decision of the Constitutional Court of Bosnia and Herzegovina ruling that the Entity coat of arms, flag and anthem were not in line with the State-level Constitution of Bosnia and Herzegovina.
> (European Commission 2007: 7–8)[10]

The 2008 Progress Report, issued in a year in which Kosovo declared independence,[11] is similar to the 2007 report, noting no progress and the continued conduct of elections in violation of the ECHR (foreshadowing the Sejdić-Finci case). As in 2007, it notes that '[p]rogress has been made under the current constitutional structure, but it prevents swift decision-making and therefore hinders reform and the capacity to make progress towards the EU' (European Commission 2008: 7).

In 2009, the discussion on the Constitution was slightly different than in the previous two years, likely reflecting the Prud efforts. The EU comments reflect the reintroduction of constitutional reform onto the agenda. 'While progress has been made under the current constitutional structure, it still offers too many opportunities for political obstructionism,' going on to note, '[a]mong other things, the problem of blockages due to the entity voting rules needs to be addressed, and a structured definition of the vital national clause in the Constitution is necessary' (European Commission 2009: 7). The political section closed with the following assessment:

> Overall, there has been little progress in addressing the key European partnership priority of more functional and sustainable state structures and better respect for human rights and fundamental freedoms, including by agreeing and adopting the necessary constitutional changes. Constitutional reform has been limited to the amendment concerning the Brčko District.
> (European Commission 2009: 9)

Three developments shaped the environment in 2010: the Sejdić-Finci decision, the Butmir talks, and the coming elections. The 2010 Report reaffirms previous statements that the constitutional structure 'remains inefficient and is misused,' referencing in particular the lack of reforms aimed at preventing the blocking of needed EU relevant legislation (European Commission 2010: 8). For the first time the Federation is specifically noted: 'There are particular problems in the Federation, where competences of the Entity, Cantons and the municipalities overlap. Failure to harmonize legislation at the different levels, particularly in the smaller Cantons, adds to the arrangement's complexity' (European Commission 2010: 8). The constitutional overview in general was quite strong, referencing RS challenges to the country's territorial integrity and obstruction against state competencies, failure to meet the 5+2 criteria, and other failures of government. The section closes by noting that '[o]verall, there has been little progress on addressing the European Partnership priority, which requires measures to achieve many functional and sustainable institutional structures and better respect for human rights and fundamental freedoms, including by adopting changes to the constitution' (European Commission 2010: 9).

In autumn 2011, the Progress Report was issued in the shadow of two developments. First, the country had been unable to form a state-level government since the October 2010 elections. Second, following on threats from the RS to hold a referendum and to pull out of all state judicial bodies, EU Foreign Affairs Chief Catherine Ashton agreed to start a 'structured dialogue' on justice sector issues – in the view of some observers, rewarding RS threats (Hadzovic 2011; Jurisic 2011). As in 2010, the general lack of progress is noted, as is the particular problem of the Federation's 'complex and costly governance structures' (European Commission 2011: 7). It is interesting to note two new turns of phrase in the constitution review section. First, when referring to the country's complex institutional architecture, it is noted that it is 'subject to different interpretations' (European Commission 2011: 7). Further, following on the noted lack of Sejdić-Finci reform, it acknowledges that '[t]he lack of a shared vision by the political representatives on the direction of the country has hampered progress on this issue' (European Commission 2011: 7).

The 2012 Progress Report was issued in a year in which a government was finally established but was immediately beset with coalition battles, particularly among Federation parties. The specific weaknesses of the Federation are again noted as well as the observation that '[s]ome political representatives are questioning Bosnia and Herzegovina's capacity to function as a country and are calling for an Entity-level EU agenda separate from the Bosnia and Herzegovina State' (European Commission 2012: 8), a statement that clearly refers to the RS. The need for 'an effective coordination mechanism between various levels of government' for work related to EU laws *is* noted (European Commission 2012: 8): the word 'coordination' increasingly a buzzword for avoiding state-level competencies.

While the comments above relate to BiH's constitutional reform challenges, other issues included in the reports also shed light on both needed reforms and the flexibility of the EU to find extra-constitutional solutions to ease forward progress. Dick (2012: 2) reviewed five issues consistently covered in the Progress Reports, identifying an evolution in the way certain sectoral issues are assessed. For example, he argues that there was a significant drop in the use of imperative language recommending the establishment of a state-level Ministry of Agriculture (the recommendation being dropped entirely in 2011). In his analysis of language related to constitutional reform, he finds a shift away from framing the need for reform in terms of functionality and human rights, and towards fulfillment of PIC and European Partnership requirements. He finds minimal reference to the 2005 Venice Commission opinion, and little consistent guidance that might incentivize reform.

The state of play in 2012–2013: a commitment to stalemate

Four trends have become clear in the EU's role in the constitutional reform saga in BiH: public lip service to institutions, but practical primacy to the parties; a greatly lowered bar in terms of expectations for reform; a focus on Federation rather than state reform; and a focus on establishing a 'coordination mechanism' that would enable the country to 'coordinate' its way to the EU.

Sidelining the institutions

Bieber notes that EU engagement on constitutional reform should be pursued through the formal institutional process, not through party leaders (Bieber 2010: 4). This commitment to reform through BiH's elected institutions is often noted in statements, or through events aimed at sending an aspirational message to the country's leaders. In fact, approximately 1 million Euro of IPA funds were allocated in 2008 to support the development of parliamentary, institutional processes in support of constitutional reform; this money remained unspent for years and was then reallocated.[12] The reality suggests a certain amount of 'institutional theater'; decisions *are* ultimately being made by political leaders, representing the main parties.

In autumn 2011, a conference was held at the Parliament to encourage parliamentarians to take their responsibilities seriously, and engage in a shared quest for the Sejdić-Finci reform. Christian Schwartz-Schilling pointed to his own legislative experience, recalled the role of parliament in democratic processes, and implored the parliamentarians to develop a reform proposal and see this process as a chance to contribute to BiH's history. Another conference was held in autumn 2012, aimed at framing constitutional reform as a technical exercise, and one that other countries preparing for EU membership went through as well.[13] Representatives from Bulgaria, Slovenia, and other countries were brought in to share their experiences, as did speakers from the European Parliament, EUSR, and the Venice Commission. However, in the open discussion sessions there were no substantive comments or discussions on technical matters, no apparent interest in learning from other countries, rather poor participation, and no results; the notion that the parliamentarians are simply lacking the 'tools' to effectively 'do' reform was again proven false. Each of these efforts – and there have been countless others – is mere talk; EU representatives often participate, but there are no subsequent activities to keep any meaningful process afloat. Parliamentary officials attend the events to show professed commitment to the process while knowing full well the institution is hamstrung; outsiders fund the efforts as any activity is viewed as preferable to perceived disengagement; and it is understood the key decisions are being made by the party leaders.

The Sejdić-Finci saga illustrates the practical impotence of institutions in a system in which party discipline is paramount. A parliamentary committee was formed to work on the issue in 2010 and failed. In late 2011, a second Parliamentary Committee was appointed, meeting 14 times.[14] In March 2012 the Committee issued a report noting that they had failed to reach the level of political agreement needed to proposed amendments (Interim Joint Committee of Both Houses 2012). The Committee not only acknowledged their inability to reach an agreement, but then referred the process to the political parties.

Lowered expectations

The Committee *had* managed to agree on one thing: that their mandate for seeking a Sejdić-Finci remedy should be narrowly defined. Dodik's SNSD made it clear from the beginning that only minimal compliance was acceptable. Any hopes that Sejdić-Finci would address some of the core structural foundations of Dayton evaporated once a lowest common denominator approach prevailed. In fact, to unfreeze the SAA and move forward with accession, the EU noted its interest in just 'credible effort' on resolving Sejdić-Finci (Jukic 2012); even this has proven unattainable.

In 2012 and 2013 the entire exercise was boiled down to reverse engineering a remedy that would maintain a three-person Presidency while removing the ethnic markers from the Constitution.[15] This may seem simple; however, two main sticking points stubbornly remain. SNSD insists that *their* entity's representative continue to be *directly* elected by citizens in the RS, as under the current structure. This would mean that anyone in the RS *could* stand for a direct election. In the Federation, direct election of two presidents could require that they not be from the same 'people,' to prevent potential Bosniak domination. The direct election model, however, does not sit well with the Croat parties who, under the current system, feel that their representation has been improperly usurped by a Croat who, through a quirk in the election system, does not represent Croat interests as they see them. (For the past two mandates, Željko Komšić, a Croat and former member of SDP, won a seat on the Presidency, attracting a large number of non-Croat voters.) The Croats therefore have sought mechanisms to ensure that Croats vote for Croats, either through an indirectly elected Presidency; vote weighting schemes that would give higher vote value to Croats residing in Croat-majority districts; election district gerrymandering to create *de facto* Croat electoral units; or other schemes.[16] Some – including Dodik – have suggested an asymmetric approach, with the RS enjoying direct elections and the Federation indirect, though this has been opposed by the SDA, as well as others who suspect the potential for further litigation. While the EU has consistently noted that it would not engage in devising solutions for Sejdić-Finci, there have been ongoing exercises to determine other ways of creating a Croat electoral entity; for example, through introduction of some sort of 'electoral college.'

In its search to demonstrate sufficient 'credible effort' in seeking a remedy, the EUSR Peter Sørensen has even sought to press parties to move forward with the generally agreed-upon reform of the House of Peoples, leaving the Presidency reform outstanding but allowing for enough to at least unfreeze the SAA. Apparently, the Croat political leadership has rejected this possibility, recognizing their bargaining power.[17] The parties have more or less remained stuck in these positions. Accepting an indirectly elected Presidency would be the most simple and elegant solution. However, Dodik's resistance to this option has been consistent; he may recognize that he has little to lose by not budging, as he can claim to have offered a proposal, and that the lack of progress is related to a dysfunctional Federation.

In 2013, as the last of many 'deadlines' passed, the EU did become more visibly active, both through high-level press statements and assistance in looking for 'creative' solutions (Omeragic 2013). Enlargement Commissioner Štefan Füle and General Secretary of the CoE Thorbjørn Jagland expressed their concerns that the parties continued to fail. 'With the EU's help, several possibilities to implement the Sejdić-Finci judgment taking into account the political parties' proposals and concerns, have been thoroughly explored' (European Commission 2013; Klix 2013). Füle warned of consequences, noting that the next general elections in BiH would not be recognized (*Global Times* 2013). On 22 July, the Council of the European Union noted that the 2014 elections could be called into question if held under rules found incompatible with the ECHR (Jukic 2013). While in the press there is caution among EU officials not to assign blame, in private the pressure appears to be nearly solely focused on Federation parties. In early 2014, following on the February demonstrations and riots, the EU has more or less given up on this issue.

Shifting focus to the Federation

As the Sisyphean challenge of state-level reform has led many policy makers to question the wisdom of trying to pursue it at all, there has been a shift in focus to addressing the constitutional and structural problems of the Federation. In the wake of the 14-month inability to form a government – in large part related to Federation party dynamics – the US Embassy in BiH, with high-profile support from Ambassador Patrick Moon, began to focus attention on Federation reform. The US funded the Law Institute to work through a consultative process and offer proposals,[18] and from late 2012 through 2013 supported a five-member 'expert group' tasked with devising proposals. While ostensibly a grassroots effort, the US Embassy was strongly engaged, and set the parameters: reform should be aimed at improving functionality and ensuring the rights of the Croats, and should neither affect the state nor recommend a third entity.[19]

While few dispute that the Federation is dysfunctional, there are three main criticisms that can be drawn from this approach. First, it propagates the myth that the biggest problem in BiH is the Federation, while the RS is equally bankrupt, suffers a democratic deficit and wields and actively uses its treasured entity veto to block BiH legislation (Bahtic-Kunrath 2011). Second, the political energy and public statements on Federation reform detracts from the public discussion about the need for BiH reform. Third, the strict terms limiting the discussions (no third entity, no accompanying state reform) would fail to solve the central problem of the Dayton state and Constitution: the asymmetry caused by having three constituent peoples within two entities, which allows the RS to effectively drive the agenda while the other two peoples tussle for power like two kittens in a bag. Whether the Federation is reformed into three, six or eight cantons from the current ten, this core asymmetry would remain.

'Let's just focus on coordination'

Since the Venice Commission opinion, one of the factors noted as justifying constitutional reform is the need to prepare for effective EU candidate status, and the reforms required to work through the thousands of pages of requirements laid out in the *acquis*. A country unable to agree on reforms related to 'simple' issues could not be expected to manage such a task. As the pressure for constitutional reform has waned, there has been increasing talk of the need for a 'coordination mechanism' for BiH that would ensure a streamlined approach towards ticking the *acquis* boxes (Council of the European Union 2009; Jukic 2012). The RS has embraced this language, noting 'establishing a coordination mechanism would lead to a single voice in BiH on many different issues,' while 'respecting its constitutional order' (SRNA 2013). One could argue that this is practical; if such a mechanism *could* result in BiH's forward motion towards the EU, then perhaps that is indeed all that is needed. However, skeptics point out the failure of past coordination mechanisms (e.g., on policing, anti-corruption, education) or even note that BiH does in fact already have a Directorate for European Integration that should be able to serve this purpose. No coordination mechanism will function if there is no institutional independence and decisions continue to be made by leaders who lack the political will for compromise.

Concluding remarks

The issues stymying constitutional reform will not be resolved by conferences, workshops, or capacity building. In the current situation, constitutional reform is resisted because it makes sense for the parties to resist it. Even the Bosniaks, who would prefer a more centralized system, benefit from the dysfunctional politics that continue to allow for a political environment in which the politics of fear and patronage are paramount, minimizing political accountability and ensuring that parties can be voted in every two years without delivering results. The lack of political will, and this 'mutually beneficial stalemate,' leads one to question whether constitutional reform is possible in a frozen conflict, and whether the alleged EU magnet can *ever* incentivize meaningful reforms.

As described in other chapters in this volume, the ideology of the EU's enlargement effort is premised on the notion that EU membership is good, wanted, and a benefit for all involved. This worked splendidly in other countries in the post-Cold War period – Poland, the Baltics – that went through the accession process with gusto. None of these countries had 'stateness problems' when they began their accession process (Fukuyama 2005). However, the question for BiH remains: can a shared vision of EU membership replace or supplant the lack of a shared vision for BiH itself?

Many officials argue that it is critical to get BiH into the candidacy process as soon as possible, as only *then* will the real pressure of conditionality kick in (Füle 2013). While this sounds like a reasonable assumption, however, past experience seems to suggest that the sought after pressure could remain elusive. When BiH initialed the SAA in 2005 hopes were high that *that* would pave the way for reform; visa liberalization was another presumed incentive; the availability of various pre-accession funds has been viewed as yet another enticement. Yet none of these so-called milestones unclogged the core blockages, or changed the rules of the game sufficiently to promote a new culture of political will. This is because the fundamental nature of the state – as laid out in a Constitution open to many interpretations – affects and shapes the country's structure, function, and vision.

It is clear that while BiH's post-Dayton, post-war needs may overlap with its pre-Brussels, EU accession goals, the overlap is far from total. This is clear regarding constitutional reform. While the flaws of the Dayton Constitution may have deleterious effects on the health of the country in general, they may not be a deal breaker in terms of the EU accession process. This creates a schizophrenic environment, in which the political needs of the country can seemingly linger unaddressed, while technical accession efforts are attempted with vigor; the links between the failure of the technical with the dynamics of the political is often either not acknowledged, or papered over by lowering even technical expectations. Unfortunately, it is clear that there is no such thing as a 'technical challenge' in BiH; even the technical is political. The lack of support by the EU for meaningful constitutional reform lays bare this reality. While the CoE may continue to point to key and substantial constitutional shortcomings, and while PACE will visit and issue reports and call for structural changes, EU representatives in BiH and in Brussels no longer even reference the 2005 Venice Commission opinion as a baseline. The result of this divergence in apparent principles is that CoE or PACE opinions, reports, and statements are viewed as optional, peripheral, and, essentially, irrelevant by BiH decision makers. If only the technical terms of the *acquis* apply, why acknowledge other commitments, principles, standards, or obligations?

Some observers emphasize that the most important role the international community, including the EU, can play is to ensure that it is clear that 'drastic, unilateral alterations to Dayton are ruled out' (ICG 2009b: 20–21), presumably to reassure the RS (Batt 2009: 4). The challenge is how to balance the desire for security with the evident dysfunctionality of the status quo. The EU appears to be attempting to square this circle by emphasizing the technical, and seeking ways to shape the minimal technical needs to the BiH political environment, rather than to mold the BiH political environment to its own values, norms, and requirements.

The EU's aversion to playing a prescriptive role has proven to be an insufficient fit to the reality of BiH constitutional politics. As Govedarica[20] points out:

> It is true that the EU has had no clear stance towards Bosnia. For a long time the EU officials have believed that the mere process of European integration will solve the country's problems. However, when it was clear that it was not the case then the EU could not find adequate alternative instrument [sic].
>
> (Brljavac 2012: 27)

A consequence of the EU's attempts to engage on purely technical grounds and steer clear of constitutional debates is the further entrenchment of the status quo, and the tacit seal of approval on a limited interpretation approach to Dayton. 'Freezing' at a time of 'maximal' interpretations (as for example, under Ashdown's tenure), would likely have pleased some parties. 'Freezing' at a time in which state strengthening is being vigorously resisted and even past reforms are being questioned, would likely please the RS. The prospects for constitutional reform in such an environment seem dim.

If past experience with conditionality in BiH (police reform, visa liberalization, Sejdić-Finci) is any indication, it is likely that the EU will learn a counter-intuitive lesson: that *fewer* firm red lines should be set in BiH on constitutional or other potentially contentious political issues, and that reform conditionality and consequences are to be avoided. While some argue that such an approach is realistic, and focused on the long-term EU goal of enlargement, others suggest that less conditionality demonstrates that resistance to reform results in the successful lowering of expectations. It remains questionable whether such an approach will contribute to lasting conflict resolution. There are still feelings of grievance in BiH, a deeply felt lack of justice, and a sense that there are some who won and some who lost; these dynamics are played out in the constitutional interpretation debate.

The EU accession process is well-suited to accession; it is not demonstrably successful in conflict resolution. The EU's efforts to spend their way to reconciliation and peacemaking in Cyprus seem to have resulted in little real political or social progress in conflict resolution (Hazou 2012), and granting membership to Cyprus in spite of its continuing conflict and border issues incalculably skewed the balance of potential future negotiating parties. Is it possible that post-Dayton BiH is simply doomed to exist in this consociational constitutional agony (Oklopcic 2012)? This approach may be suitable for EU accession goals; however, the jury is out on whether it will be good for BiH's post-war democratic development and consolidation of a truly thawed, lasting peace.

Notes

1 All opinions are the author's alone.
2 Following the general use of term, the short forms 'Bosnia' and 'BiH' will be used.
3 BiH is possibly just ahead of Kosovo, which at the point of writing still had not signed any official agreements with the EU. See also Chapter 8 in this volume.
4 The Office of the High Representative (OHR) is established in Annex 10 of the GFAP.
5 Another relevant case concerns the denial of a political party's request to list a Bosniak (Ilijaz Pilav) from the RS as a candidate for the RS seat on the BiH Presidency (Appeal by Stranka za Bosnu i Hercegovinu 2006). Pilav alleged three violations of his rights under BiH law and the ECHR. The BiH Constitutional Court (in a 7–2 decision) dismissed his claims on the basis that the restrictions were reasonable. Pilav appealed to the European Court of Human Rights, where it is currently pending.
6 '5+2' became shorthand for the five objectives and two conditions required for the OHR to close. The five objectives were: an agreement on state property; an agreement of defense property; completion of the Brčko final award; fiscal sustainability; and entrenchment of the rule of law. The two conditions were a

signed SAA and the Peace Implementation Council's (PIC) sign-off on full compliance with the Dayton Agreement (PIC 2008).
7   An additional effort led by the Germans in late 2010 – referred to as the Heusgen or Merkel initiative – was again less about constitutional reform and more about creating conditions to close the OHR and facilitate BiH's EU accession process. Weber (2011) notes that Germany did not seek to coordinate with the EU in this effort, though its interests were focused on 'unblocking' BiH's political environment by sidetracking the 5+2 objectives and enabling the closure of the OHR.
8   For a review of civil society efforts, see Perry (2014).
9   In 2004, the Commission of the European Communities issued a Commission Staff Working Paper: *Bosnia and Herzegovina – Stabilisation and Association Report 2004*.
10 This was noted for a few years, but then, for all practical purposes, fell from the radar screen.
11 After the unilateral declaration of independence by Kosovo, the RS authorities said they would consider a referendum on the independence of the entity if a majority of EU and UN states recognized Kosovo as an independent state.
12 Interview with the European Union Delegation to Bosnia and Herzegovina (May 2011).
13 'The Role of Parliaments in the European Integration Process: Constitutional and Legal Challenges.' Sarajevo, October 29–30, 2012.
14 As a part of monitoring this process, the author inquired broadly about whether the Committee had ever actually worked through problems, laying out interests rather than positions, and seeking Venn-diagram like overlaps that could form the seeds of compromise. This did not happen. In fact, the Committee meetings were structured so that each party had the opportunity to present their mutually-incompatible positions, providing yet another opportunity for the reassertion of positions, and reducing the likelihood of future compromises that might be viewed as a retreat from originally stated principles.
15 Proposed reform of the House of Peoples has been less contentious.
16 The International Crisis Group suggested in a report in July 2012 that perhaps a system of colored ballots might serve to help to 'link' a voter's ethnicity with their vote, thereby ensuring that Bosniak voters could not vote for a Croat representative (ICG 2012). Efforts supported by the Konrad Adenauer Stiftung brainstormed options including mandatory citizen long-term registration on certain defined national community lists to prevent short term strategic voting.
17 Author discussions with experts in Sarajevo.
18 See www.boljafederacija.ba.
19 In the spring, the expert group offered 181 recommendations for reform. More information is available at: http://usembassysarajevo.blogspot.com/search/label/Federation%20reform.
20 Dobrila Govedarica, head of the Open Society Fund (OSF) in BiH.

Bibliography

Alic, A. (2009) 'Bosnian Impasse over "Dayton two",' *ISN Security Watch*, 6 November. Available at: www.isn.ethz.ch/Digital-Library/Articles/Detail/?lng=en&id=109294.

Appeal by Stranka za Bosnu i Hercegovinu [Party for Bosnia and Herzegovina] and Mr. Ilijaz Pilav, case No. AP-2678/06, para. 7 (2006). Available at www.ccbh.ba/eng/odluke/povuci_html.php?pid=67930.

Bahtic-Kunrath, B. (2011) 'Of Veto Players and Entity-Voting: Institutional Gridlock in the Bosnian Reform Process,' *Nationalities Papers*, 39(6), pp. 899–923.

Bassuener, K. (2009) 'What Next in Bosnia?' *Heinrich Böll Stiftung*, October 22. Available at: www.boell.de/en/navigation/europe-north-america-7682.html.

Bassuener, K. and Weber, B. (2010) *Are we There Yet?*, Democratization Policy Council Policy Brief. Available at: http://democratizationpolicy.org/images/policybriefs/policybrief1.pdf.

Batt, J. (2009) *Bosnia and Herzegovina: The International Mission at a Turning Point*. FRIDE Policy Brief. Available at: http://fride.org/descarga/PB5_Bosnia_Herzegovina_ENG_feb09.pdf.

BBC (2008) *Bosnian Social Democrats Leader Criticizes Prud Accord*. BBC Monitoring International Reports, December 12. Available at: www.accessmylibrary.com/article-1G1-190456761/bosnian-social-democrats-leader.html.

Bieber, F. (2010) *Constitutional Reform in Bosnia and Herzegovina: Preparing for EU Accession*. European Policy Center Policy Brief. Available at: www.kbs-frb.be/uploadedfiles/kbs-frb/files/verslag/epc-policy%20brief-04–2010.pdf.

Biscevic, H. (2010) 'Bosnia Stalemate Turning into "Frozen Conflict".' *Euractiv*. Available at: www.euractiv.com/enlargement/bosnia-stalemate-turning-frozen-conflict-news-343803.

Brljavac, B. (2012) 'Assessing the European Criteria in Bosnia and Herzegovina: A Litmus Test for the European Union', *Journal of Comparative Politics*, 5(1), pp. 4–23. Available at: www.jofcp.org/assets/jcp/JCP-January-2012.pdf.

Byrne, R. (2009) 'Dayton, Part II?' *The American Prospect*, April 2. Available at: http://prospect.org/article/dayton-part-ii.

Chivvis, C. (2010) 'Back to the Brink in Bosnia?' *Survival: Global Politics and Strategy*, 52(1), pp. 97–110.

Commission of the European Communities (2004) *Bosnia and Herzegovina – Stabilisation and Association Report*. Commission Staff Working Paper COM(2004)205.

Constitutional Court of Bosnia and Herzegovina (2000) *Case U 5/98 Partial Decision III*, July 1. Available at: www.venice.coe.int/docs/2000/CDL(2000)081-e.asp.

Constitutional Court of the Czech Republic (2012) *The Relations between the Constitutional Courts and the other National Courts, Including the Interference in the Area of the Action of the European Courts: Conference of European Constitutional Courts 12th Congress*, August 27. Available at: www.confcoconsteu.org/reports/rep-xii/Tsjechie-EN.pdf.

Council of Europe (2007) *Memorandum of Understanding between the Council of Europe and the European Union*. Strasbourg: Council of the European Union. Available at: www.coe.int/t/der/docs/MoU_EN.pdf.

Council of Europe Parliamentary Assembly (2010) *The Functioning of Democratic Institutions in Bosnia and Herzegovina*, 4, Doc. 12112, January 11.

Council of Europe Secretary General (2002) *First Quarterly Report, Bosnia and Herzegovina: Follow-up to Committee of Ministers Decisions Regarding Monitoring of Commitments and Implementation of Post-Accession Co-Operation Programme*. Available at: https://wcd.coe.int/ViewDoc.jsp?id=296231&Site=COE.

Council of the European Union (2009) *2933rd Council Meeting General Affairs and External Relations External Relations Brussels*, Press Release, March 16. Available at: http://europa.eu/rapid/press-release_PRES-09–63_en.htm?locale=en.

Cremona, M. (2001) 'Accession to the European Union: Membership Conditionality and Accession Criteria', *Polish Yearbook of International Law*, 25, pp. 219–240.

Crocker, C.A., Hampson, F.O., and Aall, P.R. (2004) *Taming Intractable Conflicts: Mediation in the Hardest Cases*. Washington DC: US Institute of Peace Press.

Crocker, C.A., Hampson, F.O., and Aall, P.R. (2005) *Grasping the Nettle: Analyzing Cases of Intractable Conflict*. Washington DC: US Institute of Peace Press.

Delegation of the European Union to Bosnia and Herzegovina (2013) 'EU Money for Economic and Tourism Capacity Building Projects Suspended.' Available at: www.europa.ba/News.aspx?newsid=5809&lang=EN.

DPC (Democratization Policy Council) (2008) 'Understanding and Breaking Bosnia and Herzegovina's Constitutional Deadlock: A New Approach for the European Union and United States.' Available at: http://democratizationpolicy.org/images/policybriefs/policybrief5.pdf.

Dick, P. (2012) *Requirements and Reforms, Cause and Effect: A Review of the European Union Progress Reports for Bosnia and Herzegovina for the Fulfillment of the Copenhagen Criteria*. Democratization Policy Council Policy Note, Washington DC.

European Commission (2005) *Bosnia and Herzegovina 2005 Progress Report*. Brussels: November 9.

European Commission (2006) *Bosnia and Herzegovina 2006 Progress Report*. Brussels: November 8.

European Commission (2007) *Bosnia and Herzegovina 2007 Progress Report*. Brussels: November 6.

European Commission (2008) *Bosnia and Herzegovina 2008 Progress Report*. Brussels: November 5.

European Commission (2009) *Bosnia and Herzegovina 2009 Progress Report*. Brussels: October 14.

European Commission (2010) *Bosnia and Herzegovina 2010 Progress Report*. Brussels: November 9.

European Commission (2011) *Bosnia and Herzegovina 2011 Progress Report*. Brussels: October 12.

European Commission (2012) *Bosnia and Herzegovina 2012 Progress Report*. Brussels: October 10.

European Commission (2013) *Bosnia and Herzegovina: Outstanding Issue on the EU Agenda*, Press Release, March 7. Available at: http://europa.eu/rapid/press-release_MEMO-13-186_en.htm.

European Commission (2013) *Commissioner Füle and Secretary General Jagland Regret the Lack of Progress in Implementing the Sejdić Finci Judgement*, Press Release, April 8. Available at: http://europa.eu/rapid/press-release_MEMO-13-316_en.htm.

European Council (1993) *Conclusions of the Presidency*, Madrid.

European Council (1995) *Conclusions of the Presidency*, Madrid. Available at: www.europarl.europa.eu/summits/mad1_en.htm.

European Court of Human Rights (2009) *Case of Sejdić and Finci v. Bosnia and Herzegovina*, Judgment 9, December 22. Available at: http://cmiskp.echr.coe.int/tkp197/view.asp?action=html&documentId=860268&portal=hbkm&source=externalbydocnumber&table=F69A27FD8FB86142BF01C1166DEA398649.

Foreign Policy Initiative BH (2007) *Governance Structures in BIH: Capacity, Ownership, EU Integration, Functioning State*. Available at: http://www.vpi.ba/upload/documents/eng/BiH_Governance_Structures.pdf.

Forum Gradana Tuzle. Available at: www.forumtz.com.

Forum of Tuzla Citizens (2010) Constitutional Reforms in Bosnia and Herzegovina

– Civil Initiative Project, Proposal of Amendments and Addenda to the Constitution of Bosnia and Herzegovina, Amendment 13.

Fukuyama, F. (2005) ' "Stateness" First,' *Journal of Democracy*, 16(1), pp. 84–88.

Füle, S. (2013) *Speech: Address to the Parliamentary Assembly of the Council of Europe*, Press Release, January 24. Available at: http://europa.eu/rapid/press-release_SPEECH-13-50_en.htm?locale=en.

Global Times (2013) 'EU commissioner warns BiH over implementation of 'Sejdić and Finci' ruling', April 12. Available at www.globaltimes.cn/content/774496.shtml#.UXz1JZXAKZYm (accessed 12 April 2013).

Grabbe, H. (2002) 'European Union Conditionality and the Acquis Communautaire', *International Political Science Review*, 23(3), pp. 249–268.

Hadzovic, E. (2011) 'Bosnia: Dodik Agrees to Drop Disputed Referendum,' *Balkan Insight*, May 13.

Hays, D. and Crosby, J. (2006) *From Dayton to Brussels: Constitutional Preparations for Bosnia's EU Accession*. Available at: www.usip.org/publications/dayton-brussels-constitutional-preparations-bosnias-eu-accession.

Hazou, E. (2012) 'Academics Question Point of EU Funding for Peace.' *Cyprus Mail*, October 28. Available at www.cyprus-mail.com/features/academics-question-point-eu-funding-peace/20121028.

ICG (International Crisis Group) (2002) *Implementing Equality: The 'Constituent Peoples' Decision in Bosnia and Herzegovina*. Balkans Report No. 128, April 16. Available at: http://reliefweb.int/sites/reliefweb.int/files/resources/6C1D3A9D91EC29EC85256B9D00640396-icg-bos-16apr.pdf.

ICG (International Crisis Group) (2009a) *Bosnia's Incomplete Transition: Between Dayton and Europe*. Europe Report No. 198, March 9. Available at: www.crisisgroup.org/~/media/Files/europe/198_bosnias_incomplete_transition___between_dayton_and_europe.pdf.

ICG (International Crisis Group) (2009b) *Bosnia's Dual Crisis*. Europe Report No. 57, November 12.

ICG (International Crisis Group) (2012) *Bosnia's Gordian Knot*. Europe Report No. 68, March 12.

Interim Joint Committee of Both Houses (2012) 'Submission of the Activity Report of the Interim Joint Committee of Both Houses to Implement the Decision of the European Court of Human Rights in Strasbourg in Relation to the Sejdić-Finci Case vs. Bosnia and Herzegovina'. *Interim Joint Committee of Both Houses to Implement the Decision of the European Court of Human Rights in Strasbourg in Relation to the Sejdić-Finci Case vs. Bosnia and Herzegovina*. No. 01,02-50-14-36-14/12, Sarajevo, March 13.

Jukic, E. (2012) 'Füle Downbeat on Bosnia's EU Integration', *Balkan Insight*, November 27. Available at: www.balkaninsight.com/en/article/fule-stated-no-progress-to-bosnia-eu-road-map.

Jukic, E. (2013) 'EU Ministers Chastise Bosnia over Reforms', *Balkan Insight*, July 23. Available at: www.balkaninsight.com/en/article/eu-ministers-urge-bosnia-s-reforms.

Jurisic, D. (2011) 'Izvinite, ministre, ali rusite drzavu,' *Dani*, December 23.

Katana, G. (2005) 'New Constitution Poses Challenges to Serbs and Croats,' *Balkan Investigative Reporting Network*, November 18.

Kellermann, A.E. (2002) *Preparation of National Constitutions of Candidate Countries for Accession*, 5th European Conference Organized by the European Institute of Public Administration, March 4–5.

Kennelly, K.G. (2006) *The Role of NATO and the EU in Resolving Frozen Conflict.* Master's Thesis. Naval Postgraduate School, Monterey, CA. Available at: www.dtic.mil/cgi-bin/GetTRDoc?AD=ada462609.

Klaric, S. (2013) 'A Wall of Bosnia's Own Making', *European Voice*, July 25.

Klix (2013) 'Füle: Nema više rokova, otkazuje se treća runda pregovora o pristupanju BiH EU', *Klix* (online), April 11. Available at: www.klix.ba/vijesti/bih/fule-nema-vise-rokova-otkazuje-se-treca-runda-pregovora-o-pristupanju-bih-eu/130411139.

Licklider, R. (2005) 'Comparative Studies of Long Wars', in Crocker, C.A., Osler Hampson, F., and Aall, P.R. (eds) *Grasping the Nettle: Analyzing Cases of Intractable Conflict*, US Institute of Peace Press, pp. 33–46.

Marko, J. (2006) 'Constitutional Reform in Bosnia and Herzegovina 2005–2006', *European Yearbook of Minority Issues*, 5, pp. 207–218.

McMahon, P.C. and Western, J. (2009) 'The Death of Dayton: How to Stop Bosnia from Falling Apart', *Foreign Affairs*, Autumn, pp. 69–83.

Morar, F. (2010) 'The Myths of Frozen Conflicts: Transcending Illusive Dilemmas', *Per Concordian: Journal of European Security and Defence Issues*, pp. 10–17. Available at: www.marshallcenter.org/mcpublicweb/MCDocs/files/College/F_Publications/perConcordium/perConcordamV1N2English.pdf.

Morrison, K. (2011) *Dayton, Divisions and Constitutional Revisions: Bosnia and Herzegovina at the Crossroads.* Available at: www.da.mod.uk/colleges/arag/document.../09(11)%20KM2.pdf.

OHR (Office of the High Representative) (2009a) *Prud Process Meeting Held in Sarajevo*, Press Release, June 25. Available at: www.ohr.int/ohr-dept/presso/pressr/default.asp?content_id=43649.

OHR (Office of the High Representative) (2009b) *Interview: Valentin Inzko, High Representative and EU Special Representative in BiH: 'Dialogue and compromise from Prud must be continued'*, Press Release, April 28. Available at: www.ohr.int/ohr-dept/presso/pressi/default.asp?content_id=43423.

Oklopcic, Z. (2012) 'The Territorial Challenge: From Constitutional Patriotism to Unencumbered Agonism in Bosnia and Herzegovina', *German Law Journal*, 13(1), pp. 23–50.

Omeragic, D. (2013) 'EU Je Ponudila Kreativno Razmisljanje', *Oslobodenje*, March 29, p. 5.

PIC (Peace Implementation Council) (2008) 'Declaration by the Steering Board of the Peace Implementation Council'. Available at: www.ohr.int/pic/default.asp?content_id=41352.

Perry, V. (2012) *Barriers to EU Conditionality in Bosnia and Herzegovina.* Woodrow Wilson Center for Scholars. Working Paper: The Working Group on the Western Balkans. Available at: www.wilsoncenter.org/sites/default/files/Perry%20Working%20Paper%20%237.pdf (accessed April 28, 2013).

Perry, V. (2014) 'Constitutional Reform Processes in Bosnia and Herzegovina: Top-down Failure, Bottom-up Potential, Continued Stalemate,' in Keil, S. and Perry, V. (eds), *Statebuilding and Democratization in Bosnia and Herzegovina*, Farnham: Ashgate (forthcoming).

Rehn, O. (2005) *From Peace-building to State-building*, at Conference 'Ten Years of Dayton and Beyond'. Geneva, October 20. Available at: https://inews.rferl.org/Neos/Budget/PressSurveyEng.nsf/04f4d804e5c9ab0fc1256b35003783e3/4ec120190dc57424c12570bb003a6a22?OpenDocument.

Rehn, O. (2009) *Consolidating stability and prosperity in the Western Balkans*, Press Release, April 24. Available at: http://europa.eu/rapid/press-release_SPEECH-09-190_en.htm?locale=en.

Sebastian, S. (2007) *Leaving Dayton behind: Constitutional Reform in Bosnia and Herzegovina*. FRIDE Working Paper 46. Available at: www.fride.org/download/WP46_Dayton_Bosnia_Herzegovina_EN_nov07.pdf.

Sebastian Aparicio, S. (2009) *State Building in Deeply Divided Societies: Beyond Dayton in Bosnia*. Unpublished Dissertation. London School of Economics.

SETimes (2009) 'BiH Main Parties Announce New Decentralization Agreement', *SE Times.com*, January 27. Available at: www.setimes.com/cocoon/setimes/xhtml/en_GB/features/setimes/features/2009/01/27/feature-01.

SRNA (2013) *Establish Coordination Mechanism SRNA*. Available at: www.srna.rs/novosti/121068/establish-coordination-mechanism.htm.

Swiss Cooperation Office in Bosnia and Herzegovina (2010) *Contribution to Constitutional Reform Project, Phase III: Final Report*.

Tanner, A. (2011) 'Bosnia Serb Leader a Threat to Stability: U.S. Cables', *Reuters*, April 6. Available at: www.reuters.com/article/2011/04/06/us-bosnia-dodik-usa-idUSTRE7353SS20110406.

Toal, G. (2013) ' "Republika Srpska will Have a Referendum": The Rhetorical Politics of Milorad Dodik', *Nationalities Papers*, 41(1), pp. 166–204.

Venice Commission (European Commission for Democracy through Law) (2005) *Opinion on the Constitutional Situation in Bosnia and Herzegovina and the Powers of the High Representative*, CDL-AD (2005) 004 2, March 11. Available at: www.venice.coe.int/docs/2005/CDL-AD(2005)004-e.pdf.

Venice Commission (European Commission for Democracy through Law) (2006) *Opinion on Draft Constitutional Amendments*, CDL(2006)027, April 6.

Weber, B. (2011) 'Germany's Shift on Bosnia Policy', *Democracy and Security in Southeastern Europe*, 2(6–7), pp. 13–18.

Wolff, S. (2010) *A Resolvable Frozen Conflict? The Domestic and International Politics of Self-Determination in Moldova and Transdniestria*. Available at: www.stefanwolff.com/files/A%20resolvable%20frozen%20conflict.pdf.

Zartman, W.I. (2012) *Preventing Identity Conflicts Leading to Genocide and Mass Killings*, New York: International Peace Institute.

Part III
Comparative perspectives

10 The European Union and the Western Balkans

Time to move away from retributive justice?

Olivera Simić

The EU, transitional justice and the Western Balkans

The field of transitional justice has been rapidly developing since the end of the Cold War. Initially, it had narrowly focused on justice and retribution, but over the years it has encompassed the study of how human rights abuses are confronted by societies emerging from violent conflicts or transitioning from authoritarian rule to democratic forms of government (Crossley-Frolick 2011). There are various definitions of transitional justice, but the most commonly cited by scholars is the one provided by the International Centre for Transitional Justice as 'a response to systematic or widespread violations of human rights that seeks recognition for victims and to promote possibilities for peace, reconciliation and democracy'.[1] In order to confront legacies of abuse, a variety of transitional justice mechanisms have been developed that fall within two broad categories: judicial and non-judicial. The former focuses on civil or criminal trials, either at local, national or international level, while the latter encompasses activities such as truth and reconciliation commissions, amnesty, vetting, lustration processes, reparation, memorialization, reconciliation, institutional reform, security sector reform, demobilization, disarmament and reintegration.

While much scholarly attention has focused on UN efforts to facilitate transitional justice in post-conflict societies, the EU is a largely ignored actor in this field (Crossley-Frolick 2011: 37). There is no precise definition of transitional justice within EU legal sources, nor do the founding treaties make any specific reference to it as an objective that needs to be achieved through various EU policies. Overall, there is no mention of transitional justice in the *acquis communautaire*. Davis criticizes the EU's lack of a coherent policy on transitional justice and argues that the EU should draw from its experience 'at home and abroad' in areas such as peace and institution building, in developing its own holistic approach in this field. As long as this is not the case, the EU will outsource its understanding of justice in crisis (Davis 2010: 7).

While the EU has no clear definition of transitional justice, conditionality seems to be a key concept adopted in its understanding of the field and offers a variety of justice mechanisms. The EU assumed that conditionality would help the countries in the Western Balkans to establish liberal democracies and functional states that are able to deal with the past. It prescribed a strategy while largely neglecting the local traditions, practices and existing civil society organizations that operate on the ground. The European solutions and strategies in the field of transitional justice are not part of the general EU practices, and consequently lack specific policies and operational guidelines for their implementation. As Boge argues, there is an assumption that all societies have to progress through '"Western" stages of state and social development' and that 'weak incomplete states have to be developed into "proper" Western-style states' (Boge 2006: 18). However, these 'Western' solutions could hardly work in a region that has experienced the erosion of the rule of law and has barely had any experiences with independent courts.

Despite the absence of clearly defined concepts, there are some instruments within the EU which allow for its implementation, both in the framework of the Development and Cooperation Policy and the Common Foreign and Security Policy (Avello 2008: 4). The EU establishes the framework of transitional justice through a variety of sources and policies, such as declarations, reports and consensus documents that promote human rights, development and democracy under what used to be known as the Community Pillar of the EU.

Although the Maastricht Treaty and the Lisbon Treaty did not make explicit references to transitional justice, several of their articles provided a legal framework in which the concept may be situated. Article 10A of the Lisbon Treaty establishes that EU action on the international scene shall be guided by the principles entrenched in democracy, the rule of law, respect for human rights and principles of the UN Charter and international law. Article 28B permits the EU to use civilian and military means, 'humanitarian and rescue tasks, peace-keeping tasks, tasks of combat forces in crisis management, including peace-making'. This aspect should be applicable to states in crisis or in the process of establishing peace. Article 130u(2) of the Maastricht Treaty clarifies that European policy in the sphere of development and co-operation should contribute to the general objective of development and the consolidation of democracy and the rule of law, as well as respect for human rights and fundamental liberties. In other words, the rule of law is one of the fundamental principles of the EU, and it is also highlighted in the Copenhagen Criteria, as one of the major conditions countries have to fulfil before they can join the Union. Furthermore, reconciliation, and dealing with the past more generally, is also of key importance, as the foundation of the EU goes back to the process of reconciliation between Germany and France after the Second World War. Overcoming historical legacies and dealing with the past in an appropriate framework to enable future cooperation is therefore of key importance for the normative framework of European integration more generally, and enlargement in particular.²

However, as Crossley-Frolick asserts, 'transitional justice is a relatively new area of concern of the European Union' that was 'until recently largely absent from EU polices promoting democracy, rule of law and human rights' (2011: 37). However, although it may have been *de iure* ignored, as Avello argues, it was 'de facto part of the programme and policy of the EU' (Avello 2008: 9). EU policies are increasingly tailored to complement broader security interests that primarily focus on the protection of human rights, the rule of law and the promotion of democracy, all key to human security as the 'new' strategic narrative for Europe (Crossley-Frolick 2011: 38; and Kaldor *et al.* 2007: 273). Following this direction, it comes as no surprise that the main strategy deployed in the Western Balkans has been based on conditionality.

This chapter critically analyses the EU's conditionality and its sole focus on international criminal justice. It examines some of the theoretical arguments in favour of the establishment of domestic judicial and non-judicial mechanisms of justice. It then turns to the origins, actors and motivations of regional efforts for the formation of RECOM, which seeks support from the citizens and governments in all successor states of the former Yugoslavia. Drawing on interviews with key funders of the RECOM initiative which the author conducted in December 2011, this chapter argues that the EU's recent support for RECOM, while welcomed, is not sufficient. The support needs to be reflected in EU policies that should move away from retributive justice as a principal strategy for reconciliation in the Western Balkans.

Conditionality as the EU transitional justice strategy

The countries in the former Yugoslavia are going through three simultaneous transitions: the transition from war to peace, from single party rule to pluralist democracy, and from communist planned economy to liberal market economy. Cooperation with the International Criminal Tribunal for the former Yugoslavia (ICTY) is the condition that these countries need to fulfil in order to become eligible for membership in the EU. The EU accession conditionality for the Western Balkans countries comprises two sets of criteria. The first are the political, economic and institutional criteria established by the Copenhagen European Council in 1993 for all candidate countries. The political criteria are defined as the 'stability of institutions guaranteeing democracy, the rule of law, human rights and the protection of minorities'.³ The second set of criteria is specific to the Stabilisation and Association Process for Southeastern Europe established by the Commission Communication in May 1999, and includes full cooperation with the ICTY, respect for human and minority rights, the creation of real opportunities for the return of refugees and internally displaced persons, and a visible commitment to regional cooperation.[4]

To demonstrate their human rights *bona fides*, the states in the former Yugoslavia must confront their responsibility for wartime atrocities by providing full cooperation with the ICTY, particularly focusing on the arrest and transfer of suspects for trial in The Hague (Peskin and Boduszyński 2011: 54). The first attempts to encourage transitional justice in Serbia through the use of conditionality came in early 2001 in a mandate set by the US State Department. After several years of non-compliance, conditionality was re-emphasized in 2005 when the EU focused again on Serbia's cooperation with the ICTY. The Tribunal has been perceived by the EU as a key factor in rebuilding the rule of law in the Western Balkans, which will end impunity for war crimes and facilitate reconciliation across the region. Cooperation with The Hague is also seen as 'essential' for 'further rapprochement with the European Union'.[5] The EU essentially adopted the view of many international lawyers that the truth about individual crimes and perpetrators, delivered in impartial proceedings at the international level, would challenge the region's collective ideologies, deter future conflict and facilitate reconciliation across ethnic divides (Alvarez 1999: 436).

Olli Rehn, the then EU Commissioner for Enlargement, also confirmed that the European leaders consider the ICTY as 'an essential element of reconciliation'.[6] The EU can also invoke 'programme conditionality', and has the right to close certain aid programmes if the country concerned fails to satisfy the external administrators with regard to 'specific reform targets or adoption of sectoral policies'.[7] According to the former ICTY Chief Prosecutor, Carla del Ponte, it was 'only thanks to the international pressure' that Croatia, Serbia and Montenegro cooperated with the ICTY' (Kanter 2006: 3; Wolfsteller 2005). Likewise, Florence Hartmann, a former ICTY spokeswoman, argues that 'EU conditionality and international pressure have proved to be the only effective means of overcoming their reluctance and eliciting the cooperation without which the tribunal would not have been able to fulfil [sic] its mandate' (Hartmann 2009a: 67). However, Spoerri and Joksić state that, while 'Serbia has succeeded in contributing to criminal justice, [it] has failed to partake in transitional justice' (2011: 4). The countries in the Western Balkans contributed to criminal but not to other forms of transitional justice due to the EU's conditionality which reduced transitional justice and war crimes to full cooperation with the ICTY. As such, the ICTY is the main actor of transitional justice, while other mechanisms have been marginalized and largely ignored (Armakolas and Vossou 2008).

While the strategy of conditionality brought the most wanted war criminals before the ICTY,[8] it failed to engage the governments of Serbia, Croatia and Bosnia and Herzegovina (BiH) in genuine remorse and concerns for the victims of war. As such, conditionality is largely perceived as a mechanical exercise of transferring war criminals as the result of international pressure, which has not lived up to its goal of fostering reconciliation in the region and individualizing guilt (Subotic 2009). On the contrary, none of the transfers have been followed up by the expression of explicit remorse and the acknowledgment that crimes were committed. As Meernik argues, there is little evidence to support the notion that the ICTY had a positive impact on societal peace in BiH since 'more often than not, ethnic groups responded with increased hostility toward one another after an arrest or judgement' (Meernik 2005: 273).

On 26 May 2011, the day of Ratko Mladić's arrest, the Serbian president Boris Tadić made reference to Serbia's 'moral responsibility', but did not mention any of the crimes for which Mladić was wanted (B92 2011). Similarly, the Croatian government still celebrate the operation 'Storm 95' as the national 'Day of Victory' in Croatia (Šarić 2011). However, Croatian officials fully disclosed information on General Ante Gotovina and this resulted in his arrest and consequent transfer to The Hague in December 2005. The officials in the Republic of Croatia publically celebrate and honour General Gotovina, although he has been held criminally responsible for the ethnic cleansing of 230,000 Serbs from the Kninska Krajina region.[9] On 15 April 2011, thousands of people gathered to watch the reading of the verdict on Gotovina live in the Zagreb main square. When the judge announced the guilty verdicts and sentenced Gotovina to 24 years in jail, the crowd booed and hissed, and some were in tears.[10] Only a few months later, on 20 November 2011, the director of an elementary school in Zagreb, Krešimir Mihajlović, put a poster with images of Gotovina and Markač on the school's entrance wall, followed by the words 'Croatian martyrs' and 'From victory and truth to justice'. Mihajlović reportedly stated that he believes this is a 'great educational method' for young children and that people who do not approve of his initiative should go to Serbia (Korljan 2011: 3). Although the ICTY focuses on the misdeeds of individuals, nationalists, such as Mihajlović, have argued that the tribunal is 'damning all their countrymen' (Peskin and Boduszyński 2003: 1117–1142).

Similarly, in BiH, a war criminal, Naser Orić, was also welcomed by the Bosnian presidency after his release from The Hague in July 2008. Biljana Plavšić too was welcomed after serving 11 years in prison for crimes against humanity. (For a detailed analysis of war criminals Orić and Plavšić and their reception in Bosnia, see Simic 2011: 1388–1407). Local politicians, such as Milorad Dodik in Republika Srpska, a close friend and ally of Plavšić, have expressed no will to work on reconciliation or sustainable state building in BiH. Dodik has recently reported that 'Bosnia and Herzegovina will fall apart. This state lives only on the infusion of the international community which has its own political interests for doing so and which forcibly keeps this country together.'[11]

One of the problems is that although the EU has made it a condition for progress in the accession process that the countries in the Western

Balkans cooperate with the ICTY, it has made no serious conditions for progress on domestic war crimes trials (Human Rights Watch 2004). This allowed Croatian elites 'to preserve [...] the Croatian national understanding of the character of the war and Croatia's role in it' (Subotic 2009: 121). On the other hand, almost 70 per cent of interviewees according to research done in Serbia in 2004, 2005 and 2006 believe that war criminals should be prosecuted in a local court and not abroad (Bjankini 2010: 93). At the beginning of 2003, the instrumentalization and localization of transitional justice mechanisms as a state building practice was seen in the establishment of the War Crimes Chambers (WCC) in Serbia, Croatia and BH, which have provided an avenue for legal redress for victims of war crimes. (For detailed analysis on the establishment and cases before the Chambers in Serbia, Croatia and BiH, see Dimitrijević 2009: 83).

The UN, EU and other members of the international community have influenced and encouraged the establishment of local courts that would prosecute cases involving low and intermediary level individuals accused of war crimes. As part of the exit strategy for the international community, the Office of the High Representative and the ICTY in 2005 initiated the establishment of a special WCC in Bosnia (UN Security Council 2003). The main principle guiding the establishment of the WCC was that 'accountability for war crimes is ultimately the responsibility of the Bosnian people' (Office of the High Representative 2004). Thus, the Chambers are seen as mechanisms that contribute directly to the foundation of the rule of law, national institutions and state building in the Yugoslav successor states (Security Council Press Release 2003). In this way, retribution through the domestic as well as the international legal system has become a key and exclusive transitional justice instrument through which the EU wants to build functional states with democratic governance.

While the efforts to transfer the most wanted war criminals to the ICTY have been praised by the international community, any moral and ethical national self-reflection on the crimes committed is lacking. It is obvious that conditionality alone is not sufficient to bring reconciliation to the region. As Rangelov argues, the ICTY proceedings are perceived locally not as punishment of individuals, but the whole nation (2006: 374). Likewise, the ICTY judgements or lack of them are not necessarily an indicator of who is a war criminal. Svetlana Broz observes that responsibility for the wars in Yugoslavia lies also with those people who are not prosecuted by the ICTY. She maintains that all three former leaders, Slobodan Milošević, Alija Izetbegović and Franjo Tuđman are responsible for war crimes. While only Milošević was prosecuted in The Hague,[12] indictments were prepared against Izetbegović and Tuđman, but they have never been brought to justice because they both died before being indicted.[13] However, Broz maintains that this fact 'does not release them from the accountability for the crimes they committed' (2011).

The EU needs to move away from its exclusive focus on retributive justice and embrace a more holistic approach to transitional justice suggested by the UN. The Secretary-General's 2004 Report emphasized a wide range of transitional justice mechanisms to be used in post-conflict societies by stating that while tribunals are important, truth commissions are a 'valuable complementary tool in the quest for justice and reconciliation'.[14] The Report defines transitional justice as processes that may include 'both judicial and non-judicial mechanisms, with differing levels of international involvement (or none at all) and individual prosecutions, reparations, truth-seeking, institutional reform, vetting and dismissals, or a combination thereof' (para 7). The concept of transitional justice has evolved and is no longer focused on the role of states, but has become more complex, while integrating various levels of analysis (international, national and local) and different actors, such as states, international organizations, non-governmental organizations, epistemic communities and global policy networks (Crossley-Frolick 2011: 33).

However, the EU adopted its very narrow understanding by putting its main emphasis on retributive justice and prosecutions of the war crimes committed in the countries of the former Yugoslavia. The human rights activist from Croatia, Vesna Teršelič, maintains that while the EU is open to policies such as the Hague conditionality policy, the policy of the EU falls short of being a transitional justice strategy, as a strategy of dealing with the past (Gorjanc Prelević 2012). Indeed, while transfers of war criminals to The Hague have dominated EU relations with the countries of the Western Balkans, domestic transitional justice mechanisms have largely been ignored by the international community (Rangelov 2006). Such political management and shaping of the Western Balkans by external forces, as Chandler argues, 'degrade the entire political process' by minimizing the opportunities for domestic debate and dialogue, while encouraging the collaboration of external administrators and political elites against the aspirations and wishes of local citizens (Chandler 2010: 80). In this context, the role of civil society becomes important to the EU which argues that it is more democratic than elected representatives (Gorjanc Prelević 2012). Led by this argument and only recently, the EU started to engage with the domestic, locally grown initiative, RECOM.

EU, civil society and RECOM: justice from below

Civil society groups are funded and encouraged to talk about the issues that the EU is keen to promote, such as crime, corruption, jobs and health care (Gorjanc Prelević 2012). With respect to the civil society in the Western Balkans, the European Commission has criticized aspiring Southeastern European members by claiming that:

> None of the countries can yet claim to have the level of vibrant and critical media and civil society that is necessary to safeguard democratic advances. For example, public and media access to information,

public participation in policy debate and accountability of government and its agencies are aspects of civil society that are still largely underdeveloped in all five of the countries.[15]

Civil society capacity building is seen as weak or problematic and as such in need of external support and assistance which will 'entrench a culture ... which makes forward momentum towards the EU irreversible' (European Commission 2002: 8). Despite the problems it encounters in all successor states, civil society has recognized that there is 'an overwhelming demand for a regional truth-seeking and truth-telling process led by a regional commission'.[16] As a result, the RECOM was initiated. It is a regional body of civil society organizations which represent and promote the initiative with the aim to establish the Commission.

Its power lies in a concerted regional approach, because the facts that have been established at the national level have been barely accepted throughout the whole region. Also, the previous attempts to establish truth and reconciliation commissions on a national level, in BiH and Serbia, failed.[17] Confronted with the challenge of integrating contested states across the region, and of facilitating institution building, the EU sees RECOM as a potential to overcome these difficulties (Rupnik 2011: 24).

RECOM strengthens the rule of law in the region by fulfilling the rights of victims to know what happened to them, their loved ones and the region they live in. It embodies regional cooperation, exchange of information and aims that are compatible with the normative state building goals of the EU in the Western Balkans, such as reconciliation, good neighborly relations and democratization. However, as its funders stated, RECOM has no ambition to be an alternative to the ICTY or local war crime tribunals. Still, they believe that the ICTY and local WCC's cannot find out the magnitude and facts about all war crimes committed nor can they bring all perpetrators to justice and return dignity to the victims and their families (RECOM 2012). Similarly, Marinko Jurčević, the Chief Prosecutor in the Prosecutor's Office of BiH, reported that:

> The Judiciary cannot work alone and in isolation. It should not bear exclusive responsibility and burden of our dark past and it cannot be expected that our courts and prosecutor's office in BiH alone can solve the trauma of post-conflict society in which we live.... Having in mind that only a handful of victims will take part in war crime trials, such a mechanism [RECOM] could represent the main forum for victims where they could talk about their suffering. The Commission for Truth [RECOM] and courts could complement each other.
> (2012)

Despite its focus on victims and establishing the circumstances and facts under which serious human rights violations and war crimes occurred,

RECOM is an extrajudicial body (Stojanovska 2011). As a truth-seeking and truth-establishing body, RECOM can contribute to state building and institutional reform by removing former abusers from government and improving institutional effectiveness and human rights standards. It is seen as a state building mechanism that will help local courts and contribute to the establishment of the rule of law. In order to define its potential for the rule of law, the funders have included not only members of civil society, but also of the judiciary and legal professionals in its consultation process across the region.

The representatives of the legal system and courts see RECOM as an important mechanism that will 'encourage victims and witnesses to participate in war crime trials' and assist in the 'collection of evidence' (Dolmagić 2010). RECOM should also deliver to the judiciary relevant information and reports, and in this way cooperate with the legal profession (Rodić 2010). As such, the initiative is important because it establishes democratic governance and the rule of law that will help to overcome the legacies of the past in the region. By doing so, it contributes to the process of state building in the Western Balkans. The combination of legal and civil society activity in the field of transitional justice is consequently of key importance for the establishment of legal systems that are seen as fair and just and for the implementation of reconciliation mechanisms that allow the societies in the former Yugoslavia to deal with the crimes committed during the violent break-up of the state. In terms of normative ideas, such as justice, reconciliation and democracy, this can be seen as an example of EU Member State building. However, it is important to point out that the EU supports RECOM, but did not initiate it.

In April 2011, civil society activists started collecting signatures for establishing RECOM, under the banner 'A Million Signatures for RECOM', across the region.[18] The aim of this campaign is to hand in the signatures to governments and parliaments in the region which are expected to support the initiative and make decisions on its establishment. The establishing of RECOM has so far been publically supported by the then Presidents of Serbia, Boris Tadić; Croatia, Ivo Josipović and Montenegro, Filip Vujanović, respectively. The President of the Federation of Bosnia and Herzegovina (one of two entities in Bosnia), Živko Budimir; the Prime Minister of Vojvodina, Bojan Pajtić; and the then Prime Minister of Montenegro, Igor Lukšić have also supported the initiative.[19]

The President of Croatia, Ivo Josipović, promised to promote the initiative as part of his regional activities. In a meeting with members of the RECOM Coalition, President Josipović stressed the importance of 'every attempt to clarify fates of the missing, mark each victim, and punish each crime, [which] is vital for victims, their families, and a society as a whole'.[20] Theorists and practitioners who deal with the transition of the successor states of the former Yugoslavia believe that RECOM can overcome the objective limitations of criminal trials such as their long duration and the insufficient capacities of the courts, as well as the old age, sickness or death of witnesses and victims (Kandić 2011). RECOM can provide a factual portrait of what happened in the former Yugoslavia in the period from 1991 to 2001, and why (Kandić 2011).

On 12 October 2011, the European Commission published a document titled 'The Enlargement Strategy and Main Challenges 2011–2012' along with the individual reports on the progress each country in the region has made. 'The Enlargement Strategy' sets the goals for the coming period and summarizes the candidates' progress in their integration into the EU. Progress reports represent an appendix to the 'Enlargement Strategy' in which the European Commission assesses the extent of progress made with regard to the process of European integration. These documents support RECOM as an important element of progress. This is in accordance with the European belief that its missions and Special Representatives are keen to listen to civil society organizations and people, while the leading political elites are not (Chandler 2010: 80).

Section 2.3 of 'The Enlargement Strategy', entitled 'Enhancing regional cooperation and reconciliation in the Western Balkans', specifies that the European Commission is closely monitoring these activities as they are essential for stability and membership in the EU. The document states that 'Initiatives by NGOs and civil society, such as [...] the Truth and Reconciliation Commission (RECOM) [...] play an important role in enhancing reconciliation beyond governments among the citizens of the region.'

Section 1.3 of the analytical report on Serbia, entitled 'Regional issues and international obligations', notes the importance of regional cooperation and good neighborly relations. The report makes a positive assessment of Serbia, stating that 'Serbia supports the RECOM initiative on reconciliation'. The official political support for the Initiative for RECOM is highlighted in section 2.3 of the report on the progress of BiH, Croatia, Macedonia, Montenegro and Kosovo, where it is emphasized that each of these countries 'continues to actively support [...] the RECOM Initiative'.

The EU is the principal financial and political supporter of RECOM. The European Instrument for Democracy and Human Rights (EIDHR) and the Dutch Embassy account for some 80 per cent of RECOM's current budget.[21] It is seen as a body that would directly promote the democratization goals of the EU and its Member States, by giving marginalized groups a voice in the process of transition.[22] This is in accordance with the Union's goals to achieve regional stability and security through the promotion of human rights, democracy and multilateralism (Juncos 2005: 100).

However, Mirsad Tokača, director of the Research and Documentation Centre based in Sarajevo, and one of the founders of RECOM, believes that the EU 'gave lots of money to the project although it does not have a clear strategy in this field [transitional justice] and has never had a dialogue with the Centre about RECOM'.[23] Tokača, who withdrew from the RECOM in December 2008, said that 'the project is doomed to fail since there is no political ambient in which it can flourish.' According to him, the idea of creating a regional commission is good, but of the governments from the former Yugoslavia none gave official endorsement to the project that went further than rhetorical support. However, according to Dragan Jerković, this is the next step that needs to be taken: advocacy towards governments with the aim that the RECOM statute becomes an international agreement within the legally adopted normative framework.[24]

Nataša Kandić, director of the Humanitarian Law Center in Belgrade, said that the EU and the European Commission have been a great financial and political supporter of RECOM so far.[25] There is overall support for RECOM from the European Parliament and the Council of Europe that have adopted resolutions which support the establishment of RECOM. According to Kandić, in this latest phase of RECOM, which is 'a transfer of RECOM activities from the civil society sector to the governmental executive power, we expect help from the EU'. Since not all EU countries recognized Kosovo, Kandić asserted that 'RECOM cannot expect from the European Commission to act on behalf of all EU members or to have an active role in the coordination of activities with respect to the institutionalisation of the RECOM initiative.' What is expected, however, is that the European Commission 'uses its influence on the governments in the region by regularly asking and encouraging the governments to cooperate in order to establish RECOM'. Such pressure is also expected from some EU Member States, namely those which recognized Kosovo.

Vesna Teršelič, director of Documenta from Croatia, likewise thinks that the fact that 'the RECOM initiative was mentioned in the Report of the European Commission about Croatia's progress in 2011 is a form of support that is more than welcome'.[26] However, Teršelič believes that any sort of direct pressure on governments, in the form of conditionality such as cooperation with the ICTY for example, would be counter-productive. Tokača has critiqued the EU for investing money in RECOM and similar projects which the EU 'has not properly assessed and understood' but has done so 'in order to say that it has done something in this field'.[27] He believes that the EU should 'invest money into the development of civil society', but 'listen to and have dialogues with it before it makes decisions about any investment'. Tokača trusts that investment should be made in educational projects focusing on young people, since 'we have a generation of young people indoctrinated with hatred'.

The fate of RECOM remains to be seen. Up until 5 July 2011 only 500,000 signatures had been collected across the former Yugoslavia.[28] According to Jerković, one of the challenges lies in the fact that the movement has a constant fluctuation of members and organisations. While some are joining, others are leaving the initiative. Individuals and organisations have different expectations and visions of this project and some do pull out from the initiative because their ideas or requests could not be supported.[29]

Another challenge is that RECOM, as a social movement and civil society initiative, has a very limited capacity for action (Markel and Lauth 1998: 6). RECOM needs state enforcement, support from the legal system and courts in order to see the light of day. Only then would it contribute to reconciliation and regional cooperation, and serve as a mechanism that could build civic trust between state institutions and communities.[30]

Conclusion

With the arrest of Mladić, cooperation with the ICTY and conditionality as a strategy with respect to the EU enlargement process has ceased. Yet, as Kandić asserts, the EU does not have a strategy on, or an answer to, for example, the demonstrations in Croatia after the verdict for General Gotovina was pronounced.[31] It also does not have a strategy of what should be done after the ICTY is closed and how to come to reconciliation and a stable peace. Although the EU supports RECOM, it still does not understand that only restorative initiatives, such as RECOM, have the potential to open a debate about the past, without which there is no reconciliation.[32]

Through the case study of RECOM, this chapter has demonstrated the clear and interventionist approach used by the EU to promote transitional justice processes, regional cooperation and reconciliation which affect the state building processes in the Western Balkans. The EU has shifted its focus from retributive to restorative justice only recently by focusing more on civil society and the reform of local courts that support the establishment of different reconciliation mechanisms, such as RECOM. The EU has demonstrated its support for this cross-border grassroots initiative, which aims at overcoming the legacy of the past through regional reconciliation. Together with its institutions, the EU has begun to engage in dialogues and support activities for civil society organizations in the region.

The challenge remains to engage the governments of the Western Balkans countries with the RECOM initiative in a way that would open up a three-way dialogue about the past: between victims, perpetrators and governments. As the largest civil society initiative to date, RECOM needs the EU's continuous rhetorical and financial support to become a major project of the countries in the region. Simultaneously, the EU needs to develop a clear restorative justice strategy in order to fully support the overcoming of the legacy of a recent violent past in the Western Balkans. Such a strategy should assist in the restoration of trust in state institutions

The European Union and the Western Balkans 203

and strengthen democracy by promoting accountability and revealing abuse.

By developing and enforcing such a strategy, the EU would demonstrate that it truly understands that only restorative initiatives are able to open up dialogues about the past and lead to reconciliation in the region. It would also respond to the major critique that EU Member State building faces: that it focuses too much on the Western concepts of liberal democracy without taking local traditions and practices into account. Finally, it would downplay the criticism that local governments and civil society have been neglected by the EU and other state builders. Although civil society has received considerable funding from the EU, it is still not sustainable and is unable to address major issues in the countries. RECOM might be the initiative to correct the EU's previous strategic framework that excluded civil society. Its full endorsement would demonstrate that the EU supports the idea that the strengthening of civil society organizations is crucial to state building and is one of the main building blocks of democracy.

Notes

1 ICTJ website, http://ictj.org/our-work/transitional-justice-issues, accessed 2 November 2013.
2 I would like to thank the editors of volume for their constructive and valuable comments on the previous drafts of this paper. My special thanks goes to Soeren Keil for sharing his perspectives with regards to the EU normative framework.
3 European Council in Copenhagen, Conclusions of the Presidency, *Bulletin of the European Union* 6–1993, Pt 1.13.
4 Commission Communication (1999) COM (1999) 235, *Bulletin of the European Union* 5–1999, Pt. 1.3.73; European Council Conclusions on Conditionality (1997) *Bulletin of the European Union* 4–1997, Pt.2.2.21.
5 Report from the Commission, 'The Stabilisation and Association process for South East Europe: Second Annual Report' (26 March 2003), 10.
6 European Union at the UN, 'Speech by Commissioner Olli Rehn: Commission Declaration on the Balkans 10 Years after Srebrenica' (6 July 2005), available at: www.eu-un.europa.eu/articles/en/article_ 4866_en.htm, accessed 26 December 2011.
7 European Commission, *Regional Strategy Paper 2002–2006*, 24. The 'external administrators' are international administrators who enforce and supervise the implementation of the EU regional strategic policies, programmes and projects.
8 Ante Gotovina, Radovan Karadžić and Ratko Mladić most recently.
9 *The Prosecutor of the Tribunal v. Ante Gotovina, Ivan Cermak and Mladen Markac*, Case No. IT-06-90-PT, 17 May 2007.
10 The Hague Justice Portal, 'Verdict in Gotovina *et al.* delivered by the ICTY', 15 April 2011, available at: www.haguejusticeportal.net/eCache/DEF/12/550.html, accessed 28 November 2011. Likewise, Bosnian Croat general Tihomir Blaškić, whom the ICTY Appeals Chamber sentenced to nine years imprisonment for abusing detainees, upon his arrival at Zagreb airport in November 2005 was greeted by crowds of people and received with honours by the Croatian government. See also, Drago Hedl, 'Disquiet at Hero's Homecoming',

Institute for War and Peace Reporting, 9 November 2005, available at: http://iwpr.net/report-news/disquiet-%E2%80%9Chero%E2%80%99s-homecoming%E2%80%9D, accessed 12 February 2013.
11 Milorad Dodik, the Prime Minister in Republika Srpska, stated for the *Alternative TV News*, 16 December 2011.
12 However, Milošević escaped a verdict due to his death in a Hague prison in March 2006.
13 The ICTY investigation of Izetbegović started, but all legal proceedings against him were dropped when he died. The ICTY indictment of Croatian General Ante Gotovina lists Tuðman as a key participant in a 'joint criminal enterprise'. Judge Jean-Claude Antonetti stated that 'Mr. Tudjman was not charged because he is dead, but alive, he would have been on the accused bench.' See *Radio Free Europe*, 'Tudjman would have been charged by war crimes tribunal', 10 November 2000; *ICTY Weekly Press Briefing*, 22 October 2003, statement of Florence Hartmann, spokeswoman for the Office of Prosecutor, available at: http://web.archive.org/web/20090409114136/www.un.org/icty/briefing/2003/PB221003.htm, accessed 20 January 2012; Lajco Klajn, *The Past in Present Times: The Yugoslav Saga* (Lanham, MD: University Press of America, 2007), 282.
14 UN Security Council, *Report of the Secretary-General*, 'The Rule of Law and Transitional Justice in Post-Conflict Societies' (2004) UN Doc S/2004/616. The new UN Secretary-General's Report was submitted to the Security Council which reaffirms transitional justice as a crucial component of the UN's broader work on the rule of law. See UN Security Council, Report of the Secretary-General, 'The Rule of Law and Transitional Justice in Post-Conflict Societies' (2011) UN Doc S/2011/634.
15 European Commission, *Regional Strategy Paper 2002–2006*, 10–11.
16 Report on the Seminar, 2009, 'European Integration and Transitional Justice: Prospects and Policy Options for Restorative Justice in the Western Balkans' (Brussels, 1 December 2009), 1.
17 The Truth and Reconciliation Commission for Serbia and Montenegro was established in 2001, abolished in 2003 and failed to produce any results. The members could not agree on the Commission's mandate and composition. It lacked political will, and more importantly, it was not recognized as an impartial body within Serbia and across the region. Dejan Ilic, 'The Yugoslav Truth and Reconciliation Commission: Overcoming Cognitive Blocks', *Eurozine*, 23 April 2004, available at: www.eurozine.com/pdf/2004-04-23-ilic-en.pdf, accessed 1 February 2013; Nenad Dimitrijević, 'Serbia after the Criminal Past: What Went Wrong and What Should Be Done', *International Journal of Transitional Justice* 1(2) (2008): pp. 157–169. In BiH, in 2000 a national coordinating body was formed by members of different civil society organizations, with the goal to establish the truth and reconciliation commission. However, the commission has never seen the light because of the socio-political environment which was hostile to its creation. Sanela Basic, 'Bosnian Society on the Path to Justice, Truth and Reconciliation', in Martina Fischer (ed.), *Peace-Building and Civil Society in Bosnia-Herzegovina. Ten Years after Dayton* (Munster, Lit Verlag, 2006), 373; Alan Heil, 'A Truth and Reconciliation Commission for Bosnia and Herzegovina?', *Washington Report on Middle East Affairs*, June 2000, available at: www.wrmea.com/component/content/article/213/3295-a-truth-and-reconciliation-commission-for-bosnia-and-herzegovina.html, accessed 15 January 2013.
18 Coalition for RECOM, available at: http://zarekom.org/press/Signature-Campaign/index.en.html, accessed 13 January 2014.
19 Institutions' Support, available at: http://zarekom.org/press/Institutions-Support/index.en.html, accessed 7 January 2014.

20 RECOM Initiative's Public Advocacy, Report, 7 July 2011, available at: www. zarekom.org/uploads/documents/2011/07/i_1535/f_2/f_2101_en.pdf,accessed 14 December 2013.
21 RECOM, 'Process RECOM Financial Report for Period December 15, 2008–August 31, 2011', available at: www.zarekom.org/documents/Financial-Report.en.html, accessed 24 November 2011.
22 Report on the Seminar, 'European Integration and Transitional Justice'.
23 Interview with Mirsad Tokača, 9 December 2011.
24 Interview with Dragan Jerković, the director of *The Center for Democracy and Transitional Justice* based in Banjaluka, 28 Nov 2011.
25 Interview with Nataša Kandić, 9 December 2011.
26 Interview with Vesna Teršalić, 20 December 2011.
27 Interview with Mirsad Tokača, 9 December 2011.
28 *Bilten RECOM*, November 2011.
29 Interview with Dragan Jerković, 28 Nov 2011.
30 Report on the Seminar, 'European Integration and Transitional Justice'.
31 Interview with Nataša Kandić, 9 December 2011.
32 Ibid.

Bibliography

Armakolas, I. and Vossou, E. (2008) *Transitional Justice in Practice: The International Criminal Tribunal for the Former Yugoslavia and Beyond*, UNISCI Discussion Papers No. 18.

Alvarez, J. (1999) 'Crimes of State/Crimes of Hate: Lessons from Rwanda', *Yale Journal of International Law*, 24, pp. 365–483.

Avello, M. (2008) *European Efforts in Transitional Justice*, FRIDE Working Paper No. 58.

B92 (2011) 'Uhapsen-Ratko-Mladić', 26 May. Available at: www.b92.net/info/vesti/index.php?yyyy=2011&mm=05&dd=26&nav_category=64&nav_id=5146044 (accessed 15 November 2011).

Basic, S. (2006) 'Bosnian Society on the Path to Justice, Truth and Reconciliation', in Fischer, M. (ed.) *Peace-building and Civil society in Bosnia-Herzegovina: Ten Years after Dayton*, Münster: Lit Verlag.

Bjankini, S. (2010) 'EU Values and Expectations in Serbia: Challenges, Possibilities and Confrontation', in Listhaug, O., Ramet, S.P. and Dulic, D. (eds) *Civic and Uncivic Values in Serbia: After the Fall of Milosevic*, Belgrade: Women in Black.

Boge, V. (2006) *Traditional Approaches to Conflict Transformation: Potential and Limits*, Berlin: Berghof Research Center for Constructive Conflict Management.

Broz, S. (2011) *Nekad Bilo*, Radio Television of Republic of Serbia, 27 November.

Chandler, D. (2010) 'The EU and Southeastern Europe: The Rise of Post-liberal Governance', *Third World Quarterly*, 31(1), pp. 69–85.

Crossley-Frolick, K. (2011) 'The European Union and Transitional Justice: Human Rights and Post-Conflict Reconciliation in Europe and Beyond', *Contemporary Readings in Law and Social Justice*, 31(1), pp. 33–57.

Davis, L. (2010) *The European Union and Transitional Justice: Initiative for Peacebuilding*, New York: International Center for Transitional Justice.

Dimitrijević, N. (2008) 'Serbia after the Criminal Past: What Went Wrong and What should be Done', *International Journal of Transitional Justice*, 1(2), pp. 5–22.

Dimitrijević, V. (2009) 'Domestic War Crimes Trials in Serbia, Bosnia-Herzegovina and Croatia', in Batt, J. and Obradovic-Wochnik, J. (eds) *War Crimes, Conditionality and EU Integration in the Western Balkans*, EU-ISS Chaillot Paper No. 116, Institute for Security Studies.

Dolmagić, J. (2010) 'Nacionalne konzultacije sa pravosudjem', Zagreb, 26 February.

European Commission (2002) *The Stabilisation and Association Process for South East Europe: First Annual Report*, COM (2002) 163 final, Brussels, 4 April.

European Union at the UN (2005) *Speech by Commissioner Olli Rehn: Commission Declaration on the Balkans 10 Years after Srebrenica*. Available at: www.eu-un.europa.eu/articles/en/article_ 4866_en.htm.

Gorjanc Prelević, T. (2007) 'Why RECOM matters?', *Balkan Insight*. Available at: http://old.balkaninsight.com/en/main/info/2405777.

Hartmann, F. (2009a) 'The ICTY and EU Conditionality', in Batt, J. and Obradovic-Wochnik, J. (eds) *War Crimes, Conditionality and EU Integration in the Western Balkans*, EU-ISS Chaillot Paper No. 116, Institute for Security Studies.

Hartmann, F. (2009b) 'Europe and the Necessity of Adopting a Transitional Approach to Restorative Justice in the States of the Former Yugoslavia', in Kostovicova, D. (ed.) *The European Union and Transitional Justice: From Retributive to Restorative Justice in the Western Balkans*, Belgrade: Humanitarian Law Center.

Heil, A. (2000) *A Truth and Reconciliation Commission for Bosnia and Herzegovina?* Washington Report on Middle East Affairs, June.

Hedl, D. (2005) 'Disquiet at Hero's Homecoming', *Institute for War and Peace Reporting*, 9 November. Available at: http://iwpr.net/report-news/disquiet-%E2%80%9Chero%E2%80%99s-homecoming%E2%80%9DD.

Human Rights Watch (2004) 'Croatia: EU Must Address Domestic War Crimes Trials', 19 December.

ICTY (International Criminal Tribunal for the former Yugoslavia) (2003) *ICTY Weekly Press Briefing*, 22 October. Available at: http://web.archive.org/web/20090409114136/www.un.org/icty/briefing/2003/PB221003.htm (accessed 20 January 2012).

Ilić, D. (2012) 'The Yugoslav Truth and Reconciliation Commission: Overcoming Cognitive Blocks', *Eurozine*, 23 April. Available at: www.eurozine.com/pdf/2004-04-23-ilic-en.pdf (accessed 1 February 2012).

Juncos, A. (2005) 'The EU's Post-Conflict Intervention in Bosnia and Herzegovina: (Re)integrating the Balkans and/or (Re)inventing the EU?', *Southeast European Politics*, 2, pp. 88-108.

Jurčević, M. (2006) 'Prvi regionalni forum za tranzicijsku pravdu: Incijative i perspective na zapadnom Balkanu', Sarajevo, 5–6 May 2006, in *Koalicija za REKOM, 'Konsultativni process o utvrdjivanju cinjenica o ratnim zlocinima I drugim teskim krsenjima ljudskih prava pocinjenim na podrucju nekadasnje SFRJ'*. Available at: www.zarekom.org/uploads/documents/2011/07/i_1575/f_1/f_2871_sr.pdf. (accessed 18 January 2012).

Kaldor, M., Mary E. Martin, M. E. and Selchow, S. (2007) 'Human Security: A New Strategic Narrative for Europe', *International Affairs*, 83(2), pp. 273–288.

Kanter, J. (2006) 'EU Threatens to Freeze Talks with Serbia', *International Herald Tribune*, 28 February.

Korljan, Z. (2011) 'Ravnatelj Mihajlovic: Stavio sam u skolu Gotovinu i Markaca ... kome smeta nek' ide u Srbiju', *Jutarnji List*, 20 November.

Lajco, K. (2007) *The Past in Present Times: The Yugoslav Saga*, Lanham, MD: University Press of America.

Markel, W. and Lauth, H.-J. (1998) 'Systemwechsel und Zivilgesellschaft. Welche Zivilgesellschaft braucht die Demokratie?', *Aus Politik und Zeitgeschichte*, B6–7/98, 30 January.
Meernik, J. (2005) 'Justice and Peace? How the International Criminal Tribunal Affects Societal Peace in Bosnia', *Journal of Peace Research*, 42(3), pp. 271–289.
Office of the High Representative (2004) *War Crimes Chamber Project: Project Implementation Plan*, Registry Progress Report, Sarajevo, 20 October.
Peskin, V. and Boduszyński, M. P. (2003) 'International Justice and Domestic Politics: Post-Tudjman Croatia and the International Criminal Tribunal for the Former Yugoslavia', *Europe-Asia Studies*, 55(7), pp. 1117–1142.
Peskin, V. and Boduszyński, M. P. (2011) 'Balancing International Justice in the Balkans: Surrogate Enforces, Uncertain Transitions and the Road to Europe', *International Journal of Transitional Justice*, 5, pp. 52–74.
Prosecutor of the Tribunal v. Ante Gotovina, Ivan Cermak and Mladen Markac (2007) Case No. IT-06–90-PT, 17 May.
Rangelov, I. (2006) 'EU Conditionality and Transitional Justice in the Former Yugoslavia', *Croatian Yearbook of European Law and Policy*, 2, pp. 365–375.
RECOM (2011) *Process RECOM Financial Report for Period December 15, 2008–August 31, 2011*.
REKOM (2011) *Vreme istine u bivsoj Jugoslaviji*, 8 April. Available at: www.zarekom.org/vesti/Vreme-istine-u-bivsoj-Jugoslaviji.sr.html (accessed 8 January 2012).
Report from the Commission (2003) *The Stabilisation and Association Process for South East Europe: Second Annual Report*, 26 March.
Report on Seminar (2009) 'European Integration and Transitional Justice: Prospects and Policy Options for Restorative Justice in the Western Balkans', 1 December, Brussels.
Rodić, G. (2010) 'Regionalne konsultacije sa visenacionalnim zajednicama o Inicijativi za osnivanje REKOM', 28 August, Mostar.
Rupnik, J. (2011) 'The Balkans as a European Question', in Rupnik, J. (ed.) *The Western Balkans and the EU: 'The Hour of Europe'*, EU-ISS Chaillot Paper No. 126, Institute for Security Studies.
Šarić, F. (2011) 'J. Kosor s kninskog stadiona pozdravila Gotovinu i Markača', *Vecernji list*, 5 August. Available at: www.vecernji.hr/vijesti/j-kosor-kninskog-stadiona-pozdravila-gotovinu-markaca-clanak-316361 (accessed 23 November 2011).
Simic, O. (2011) 'Bringing "Justice" Home: Bosnians, War Criminals and the Interaction between the Cosmopolitan and the Local', *German Law Journal*, 12, pp. 1388–1407.
Spoerri, M. and Joksić, M. (2011) *The Ethics of a Justice Imposed: Ratko Mladić's Arrest and the Cost of Conditionality*, Carnegie Council.
Stojanovska, M. (2011) 'RECOM Initiative Aims at Confronting Region's Past', *SETimes*, 16 May. Available at: www.setimes.com/cocoon/setimes/xhtml/en_GB/features/setimes/articles/2011/05/16/reportage-01.
Subotic, J. (2009) *Hijacked Justice: Dealing with the Past in the Balkans*, Ithaca: Cornell University Press.
The Hague Justice Portal (2011) 'Verdict in Gotovina *et al.* delivered by the ICTY', 15 April. Available at: www.haguejusticeportal.net/eCache/DEF/12/550.html.
Radio Free Europe (2000) 'Tudjman would have been charged by war crimes tribunal', 10 November.

UN Security Council (2003) *Security Council Briefed on Establishment of War Crimes Chamber within State Court of Bosnia and Herzegovina*, Press Release, SC/7888, 8 October.
UN Security Council (2004) *Report of the Secretary-General. The Rule of Law and Transitional Justice in Post-Conflict Societies*, UN Doc S/2004/616.
UN Security Council (2011) *Report of the Secretary-General 'The Rule of Law and Transitional Justice in Post-Conflict Societies*, UN Doc S/2011/634.
Wolfsteller, P. (2005) '"EU Must Push Serbia, Croatia on Suspects": Del Ponte', *Reuters*, 1 September.

11 The political economy of accession

Forming economically viable Member States

Will Bartlett

Introduction

The Western Balkan states have been in a process of transition for over 20 years; in the case of the successor states of former Yugoslavia since well before the breakup of the country, and in the case of Albania since the collapse of the communist regime in 1991. The EU has had a strong influence on the transition path since the end of the Kosovo war in 1999, and the subsequent start of the accession process for the post-communist states of the region. The Thessaloniki Declaration of 2003, which stated that all the countries of the region had a prospect of becoming member states, was the first clear statement of intent by the EU to launch an enlargement process for the whole region. Since then, all Western Balkan countries have signed Stabilisation and Association Agreements (SAAs);[1] Macedonia was the first to sign an SAA in 2001, followed soon after by Croatia, and several have become candidate states (Macedonia, Montenegro, Serbia); Croatia, joined the EU in July 2013.

This chapter considers the economic dimension of the enlargement process. The Copenhagen criteria require that before a country becomes a member of the EU it must have a 'functioning market economy'. However, the European Commission's 2013 'enlargement package' assessed that none of the current Western Balkan countries have a functioning market economy, presenting a stumbling block to their accession. In this chapter, I show that this assessment is at odds with the real situation and that by any reasonable assessment all the countries do in fact have functioning and viable market economies, but that they fall down on the institutional aspects of the economic conditions for EU membership. The problem is that they have 'too much' market and 'too little' (or too weak) state institutions that could ameliorate the adverse social effects of an unregulated market system, and insufficient state intervention that would stabilize their economies in the face of external shocks such as the recent economic crisis. The EU has lately recognized that the state sector needs to be strengthened through improvements in the quality of governance. However, the emphasis is on institutional reforms of the state, not on a greater role for state intervention in the economy. The challenge facing these countries is extrication from the current economic crisis, which has largely spilled over from the Eurozone. Reliance on market forces alone is unlikely to achieve this outcome. A greater focus on a coordinated regional development strategy with the support of the European development banks could hold out some hope of extrication from the crisis.

In supporting this argument, the chapter begins with an overview of the economic transition in the Western Balkans before moving in the third section to an account of the political economy of the enlargement process. The following sections analyze the different dimensions of the concept of a 'functioning market economy' as seen in the development of capitalism in the Western Balkans, including macroeconomic stabilization, microeconomic liberalization, financial sector development, institutions and the role of the state, international trade liberalization and competitiveness issues. The penultimate section analyzes the outcomes of the transition process and the final section concludes.

Economic transition in the Western Balkans

Economic transition is a process of institutional reform that replaces a centrally planned state-owned economic system with a system of private ownership and market economy (Roland 2000). The ideas that spurred the transition process in the early 1990s following the collapse of the communist systems in the region were the dominant ideologies of neo-liberalism that held sway at the time. The former Yugoslavia was one of the first countries in the socialist world to engage in such a process of economic transition at the end of the 1980s (Coricelli and Rocha 1991; Bartlett 2008). The Yugoslav economist Branko Horvat even argued that the transition began as far back as 1965 when central planning was abandoned and the state granted autonomy to public enterprise managers to run socially-owned 'self-managed' enterprises, effectively introducing a liberal form of market socialism.

In socialist Yugoslavia, economic growth in the 1960s and 1970s had been rapid and the economy grew at or near its full potential rate of growth of around 4 per cent per annum. In the 1980s, this growth episode came to a shuddering halt as the international debt that had been accumulated within the decentralized "Dinar-zone" weighed down on the economy (Bartlett 1987). As more recently in the Eurozone, the solution to economic crisis in a monetary union without a strong central fiscal authority (the model that had been developed in Yugoslavia) required the imposition of fiscal consolidation within the republics, which undercut domestic growth. The World Bank and the IMF backed a series of stringent structural adjustment programmes, leading to a profound economic crisis (Lydall 1989). As part of the structural adjustment, at the end of the 1980s the Yugoslavs began a process of market reforms that were designed to replace the social ownership of the major firms in the economy by a system of private ownership based on sales of shares to workers. The Marković plan, named after the Prime Minister of the time, was partially successful but was interrupted by the wars of Yugoslav succession.

Two of the new independent states, Croatia and Macedonia, followed the Marković plan with even more radical moves towards privatization and market liberalization in the early 1990s (Adamovic 1995), as did Albania (Hashi and Xhillari 1999), while the other newly formed states adopted their own privatization and market reform programmes in the late 1990s and early 2000s (Bartlett 2008). Economic transition was led by new political elites that were strongly influenced by neoliberal ideas that were current at the time, and by the influence of some important international donor organizations such as USAID, while the EU was not really involved in the process of economic reform until the 2000s.

Yet other voices were also present. The German development bank KfW was active in Croatia in the 1990s, and helped to establish a domestic development bank, the Croatian Bank for Reconstruction and Development (HBOR), along continental state interventionist lines. The drive to privatize was therefore only partially implemented, although where it was successful it caused enormous damage as a new elite of brash tycoon capitalists engaged in a ruthless process of asset stripping the former socially owned enterprises, causing unemployment to rise and deepening a recession that was linked to the break-up of the country.[2] Albania was also at the forefront of economic reform, though in a far more dramatic fashion as the collapse of central authority destroyed the planned economy (Vaughan-Whitehead 1999). In Macedonia, privatization was carried out on a case-by-case basis, mostly involving sales to existing enterprise managers, and was mostly completed by 2000; privatization based on a voucher system was carried out in Bosnia and Herzegovina in 1999–2001 (Donais 2002).

Privatization began later in Serbia, Montenegro and Kosovo with very mixed effects, mostly negative (Vujačić and Petrović Vujačić 2011). In Serbia, outright sale of enterprises was the model chosen in the early 2000s, with no attempt at involving workers in the process. The best firms were sold to foreign investors, including some UK hedge funds. Here the neoliberal ideology was dominant, led by USAID and other donors that followed a similar ideology. As part of the privatization process, the banking sectors throughout the region were privatized to foreign banks mainly from EU countries. The sale of the domestic banking sectors took place in the aftermath of the banking crises of the late 1990s, linked to the financial crisis in Russia and other emerging market economies, and to the damaging effects on the domestic banks of bad loans made during the tycoon privatization of the large industrial companies in the early stages of transition.

Political economy of enlargement policy

The accession process that came on the agenda in the period following the democratic transitions in Croatia and Serbia in 2000 was therefore superimposed upon the neoliberal transition that was already underway. The accession process has not in itself been fundamentally market-oriented, as it focuses on transposing the EU *acquis* onto the countries of the region, and governing the pace at which the countries make progress towards eventual membership. Conditions are set down and evaluated in a rather non-transparent way in order to enable the EU to slow down or speed up the process depending upon the internal political interests within the EU, rather than being a fully objective process of rules and procedures. While the accession criteria set out the importance of a 'functioning market economy', the variability of the meaning of 'market economy' within the EU mean that these criteria are couched in very general terms and do not give the same centrality to the market as a self-equilibrating mechanism that had been promoted by the supporters of neoliberal capitalism in the early years of transition.

The 'Copenhagen criteria' that must be met by a candidate for membership of the EU had been established in the context of the earlier round of enlargement of the countries of Central and Eastern Europe. In relation to the Western Balkans they have been further developed and refined. The economic aspects of the Copenhagen criteria are to establish 'a functioning market economy as well as the capacity to cope with competitive pressures and market forces within the Union'.[3] The EU norm of a 'functioning market economy' is further defined by a number of sub-criteria including: (1) macroeconomic stability, including price stability, sustainable public finances and external accounts; (2) microeconomic liberalization and pro-market reforms defined as the 'free interplay of market forces', including liberalized prices and trade and 'free market entry and exit' of firms; (3) a 'sufficiently developed' financial sector; (4) the development of institutions supportive of a market economy defined as an adequate legal system and enforceable property rights. Set out in this rather general way, the concept of a 'functioning market economy' could be considered as the norm for the EU, and as the way in which the EU tries to extend the economic dimension of its normative power in the region. However, the norm is rather fuzzy, and not clearly defined, in large part due to the different forms of market economy that exist within the EU, a point which the literature on the 'varieties of capitalism' has elegantly explained (Hall and Soskice 2001).

Once a functioning market economy has been established, the additional 'competitiveness' criteria require that countries have sufficient human and physical capital, adequate sectoral and enterprise structures, limited state influence on competitiveness and 'sufficient' trade and investment integration with the EU. It is also expected that there should be a 'broad consensus about essentials of economic policy', meaning in effect that the ideology of a free market economy is accepted and there will be no backsliding to former arrangements of central economic planning or workers' self-management.

The EU monitors progress towards the economic conditions through a set of progress reports and adopts the annual Enlargement Strategy. The 2013 progress reports gave specific opinions on economic preparedness of the candidate and potential candidate countries as shown in Table 11.1.

The assessments highlighted in the 2013 progress reports emphasize the need for further reform of the institutional framework of the market economy. Of course, this is a never-ending process, just as the EU Member

Table 11.1 Extracts from 2013 progress reports

Albania	Albania has made further progress towards becoming a functioning market economy. It should ... [implement] ... structural reforms, including ... reinforcing the rule of law and property rights, fighting corruption, addressing payment arrears, as well as developing infrastructure and enhancing human capital.
Bosnia and Herzegovina	Bosnia and Herzegovina has made little further progress towards a functioning market economy. Considerable further reform efforts need to be pursued to enable the country to cope with competitive pressure and market forces within the Union over the long-term.
Kosovo	Kosovo has moved towards establishing a functioning market economy ... [but] ... considerable reforms and investments are needed to enable Kosovo to cope over the long term with competitive pressure and market forces.
Macedonia	The country remains well advanced and, in some areas, has made further progress towards becoming a functioning market economy and should be able to cope with competitive pressures and market forces within the Union in the medium term, provided that it vigorously implements its reform programme in order to reduce significant structural weaknesses.
Montenegro	Some progress has been made towards a functioning market economy. However, Montenegro needs to strengthen competitiveness, by improving productivity and attracting further Foreign Direct Investments into other sectors in addition to tourism and real estate.
Serbia	State presence in the economy is significant and state-owned companies continue to accumulate big losses. The functioning of market mechanisms is hampered by legal uncertainty and corruption.

Source: Memos on key findings of the 2013 Progress Reports, European Commission, 16 October 2013.

States themselves are encouraged to pursue vigorous reform programmes. The emphasis on institutional reform provides a conveniently elastic measure of compliance with the Copenhagen criteria for a functioning market economy, and gives the impression of an assessment process that has a strong political element rather than being based on fully transparent and objective measurement. The following sections assess the different aspects of the various criteria against available data.

Macroeconomic stability

By the mid-2000s at least, it appeared that the macroeconomic stability criteria had been fulfilled. All the Western Balkan countries had eliminated inflation with the partial exception of Serbia, which never quite managed to achieve price stability following the hyperinflation of the mid-1990s.[4] Inflation in Serbia has consistently been above the other Western Balkan countries and only fell to single-digit levels in 2009 (see Figure 11.1).

In 2001, a regular procedure for economic and fiscal surveillance was established for the candidate countries to prepare them for participation in multilateral surveillance and economic policy coordination procedures within the Economic and Monetary Union. "Pre-Accession Economic Programmes" (PEPs) were introduced to ensure appropriate economic, fiscal and structural policies, consistent with their EU membership applications (DG ECFIN 2007). A similar, but smaller, programme was launched with the potential candidate countries, which were required to submit "Economic and Fiscal Programmes" (EFPs) to the Commission for assessment. The EFPs outline the medium-term policy framework, including public

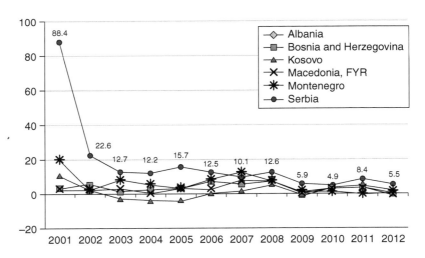

Figure 11.1 Annual inflation rates, 2001–2012 (%) (source: World Bank Development Indicators, online data).

finance objectives and structural reform priorities needed for EU accession. Albania, Bosnia and Herzegovina, Montenegro and Serbia submitted their first EFPs in December 2006. The Commission has published its assessment of these programmes on an annual basis ever since.[5] These assessments complement the policy messages given by the Commission in its annual 'enlargement package', as well as the European Partnership documents, and the bilateral economic dialogues with the countries. While the economic chapters of the Progress Reports of the annual enlargement package assess past developments, the EFP assessments are forward looking, taking into account governments' medium-term plans.

Overall the assessments have been rather gloomy. For example, the 2011 EFP assessment stated that 'for Albania and Bosnia and Herzegovina the quality of the programmes has in some instances deteriorated and not all the authorities appear fully committed to the exercise' (DG ECFIN 2011: 5). In 2013, the assessments commented that 'Bosnia and Herzegovina's economy is characterized by a large government sector with limited efficiency, while Albania needs to substantially improve the functioning of its energy sector' (DG ECFIN 2013: 7), and that 'even after several years of fiscal consolidation there remains ... ample room for streamlining Bosnia and Herzegovina's public sector' (DG ECFIN 2013: 23).

Although there seem to be many reasons to criticize the fiscal programmes and practices in the Western Balkan countries, in practice, the data do not reveal that there have been excessive budget deficits over time. Figure 11.2 shows the average budget deficits for the period 2005–2011. It can be seen that only Albania and Croatia exceeded the standard 3 per cent threshold that is often used to gauge whether a deficit

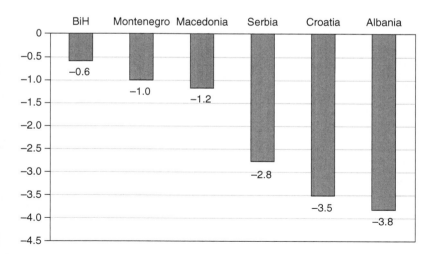

Figure 11.2 Average annual general government budget deficits, 2005–2011 (% GDP) (source: Eurostat online data).

is too high and should be reined back. The fact that Croatia's average deficit was above this threshold did not prevent her from achieving EU membership in 2013. Other countries in the region performed better on this criterion than Croatia, although it should not be a surprise that the position of most countries deteriorated during the economic crisis after 2008. In 2013 the fiscal position in several countries deteriorated dramatically, especially in Serbia in the run up to the March 2014 election. Serbia's budget deficit in early 2014 had reached around 7 per cent of GDP, requiring urgent corrective actions by the new government. Albania also ran into a similar fiscal crisis at the same time, following several years of high growth forced by over-investment in infrastructure projects of dubious economic value.

Overall, the EU policy towards the Western Balkans has been one of surveillance and monitoring and providing advice; setting strict rules for fiscal consolidation has been left to the IMF, and only in those countries that have IMF programmes such as Bosnia and Herzegovina. EU conditionality has been more flexible and ambiguous, leaving room for significant manoeuvring in the assessment of performance.

Microeconomic liberalization

The microeconomic criteria for accession emphasize the 'free interplay of market forces' (including liberalized prices and trade) and 'free market entry and exit' of firms. These microeconomic criteria have been fulfilled, in so far as a fairly liberal market system has been established in most countries. Most state-owned and socially owned enterprises were privatized by the end of the 1990s, with the exception of 'late reformers' Serbia and Kosovo where privatization dragged on through the 2000s. Therefore, by the time the EU began to influence economic policy, the countries were all well on the way to privatization.

As can be seen from Table 11.2, by 2012, all the Western Balkan economies had achieved a high degree of price liberalization as measured by the European Bank for Reconstruction and Development (EBRD) Transition Indicator scores. In fact, Macedonia and Albania had reached complete price

Table 11.2 Extent of price liberalization in the Western Balkans, 2012 (EBRD transition indicator scores)

Macedonia	4.33
Albania	4.33
Croatia	4.00
Montenegro	4.00
Serbia	4.00
Bosnia and Herzegovina	4.00

Source: European Bank for Reconstruction online data. Note: the EBRD transition indicator scores range from 1 = no liberalization to 4.33 = complete liberalization.

Table 11.3 Ease of starting a business, 2013 (rank order)

Top group		Bottom group	
Macedonia	7	Albania	76
United Kingdom	28	Croatia	80
Portugal	32	Italy	90
Greece	36	Kosovo	100
Slovenia	38	Slovak Republic	108
Denmark	40	Germany	111
France	41	Poland	116
Serbia	45	Austria	138
Hungary	59	Spain	142
Romania	60	Czech Republic	146
Bulgaria	65	Bosnia and Herzegovina	174
Montenegro	69		

Source: World Bank Ease of Doing Business database.

liberalization defined as a score of 4.33, with Croatia and the other Western Balkan countries at only a slightly lower level of price liberalization.

One of the criteria to evaluate whether a country has a functioning market economy is that it enables 'free market entry and exit of firms'. The World Bank measures the ease of starting up a business in 189 countries around the world. The rank position of a number of European countries is shown in Table 11.3. These include the Western Balkan countries and a number of other comparator countries in Europe at different levels of development. It can be seen that the Western Balkan countries are distributed throughout this spectrum, with both good performers (Macedonia) and poor performers (Bosnia and Herzegovina) and with most other Western Balkan countries somewhere in the middle of the range. What is striking about this data is the relatively poor performance of Germany and Austria, which appear in 111th and 138th place, behind all the Western Balkan countries apart from Bosnia and Herzegovina, which in 174th place is near the bottom of the list. This evidence again makes it hard to understand that the Western Balkan countries are not yet considered to be 'functioning market economies'.

Financial sector development

In relation to the financial sector, the criteria defining a functioning market economy are that a country should have a 'sufficiently developed' financial sector. In the late 1990s, several of the banking systems in many Balkan countries experienced a financial crisis, which underlined the weakness of the domestic financial systems following the collapse of socialism, the onset of the transition and the breakup of Yugoslavia. Pyramid savings banks collapsed in 1997 in Albania,[6] Macedonia and Serbia; in

Croatia the banking crisis of 1998–1999 was led by the collapse of the Dubrovačka banka, which had made a series of unwise investments in the tourism industry. Following these failures of the domestic banking sector, foreign banks began to enter the region buying up local banks and transforming the financial sector into one that was largely owned by banks from EU Member States such as Austria, Italy and Greece (see Figure 11.3). Starting from a position in which foreign ownership of bank assets was less than 20 per cent in each country in 1998, the share rose rapidly over the next decade so that by 2005 around 90 per cent of bank assets were in foreign ownership in each country except Serbia, where foreign ownership has remained at around 75 per cent.

Foreign ownership of the banking sector has led to a deep economic integration of the Western Balkan countries into EU capital markets, a process that fuelled a credit boom throughout the early and mid-2000s in the years up to the start of the economic crisis of the Eurozone. The penetration of foreign banks into the region led to the rapid financialization of the economies and to a modern and effective retail-banking sector. The downside was a build-up of consumer and corporate debt, which caused severe problems when the flow of credit came to an end. The sudden stop in credit growth in turn led to a pronounced increase in non-performing loans held by the banks.

Starting in 2009, the inflow of foreign credits dried up and the region experienced a severe credit crunch. A continuing process of deleveraging by the foreign banks sucked the oxygen out of these economies, and led to a rapid increase in non-performing loans (NPLs), as many companies ran into difficulties during the recession and were unable to finance their

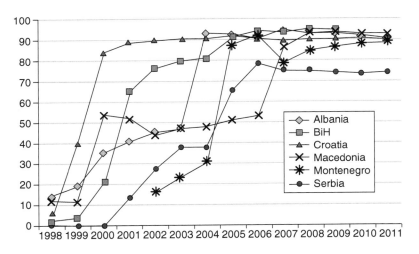

Figure 11.3 Share of banks assets in foreign ownership, 1998–2011 (%) (source: EBRD online data).

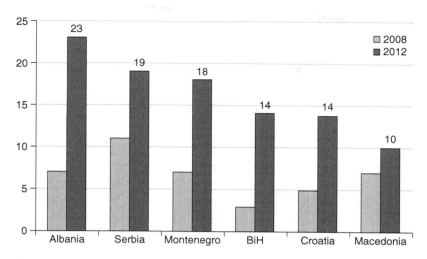

Figure 11.4 Increasing share of non-performing loans in total bank loans to the private sector, 2008 and 2012 (%) (source: World Bank Development Indicators online data).

loans (see Figure 11.4). In some cases, as in Albania and Macedonia, the rise in NPLs was exacerbated by the irresponsible behaviour of governments, which sought to meet fiscal consolidation targets by delaying payments to private sector suppliers, thereby further intensifying the squeeze on companies. Not surprisingly, many small businesses that supply the state have fallen into debt and are unable to repay their loans to the banks. The consequence has been that the rate of NPLs, which was at fairly modest levels of less than 10 per cent of total loans in 2008, reached 23 per cent in Albania, 19 per cent in Montenegro and 18 per cent in Serbia in 2012.

Institutions and the role of the state

Despite the move towards a market economy, the public sector in most Western Balkan countries has remained a prime source of employment because privatization destroyed more jobs than were created by the new private sector, while the entry of new small firms was insufficient to take up the surplus labour force. This circumstance was fertile breeding ground for patronage, nepotism and clientelism of all types. The public sector became a playground for political opponents to reward their supporters with economic benefits in the form of a secure public sector job and the prospect of a relatively good pension. Access to these jobs required educational qualifications, but these were often easily bought in the increasingly corrupt public education system where low paid teaching staff were often in a position to ensure that favoured students achieved good grades even if not justified by academic results. A large private university sector also emerged in which quality was questionable but an academic degree was virtually ensured to fee-paying students. All of this gave an impetus for the issues of institutional capacity building, the rule of law and public sector reform to rise to the top of the EU accession agenda. This has been reflected in the priorities of the IPA programme, which has given prime place to projects that address these issues. The increased focus on institutional reform and the concept of 'good governance' provides a new twist to the EU's normative agenda for the creation of 'functioning market economies'. However, as with the basic concept of the functioning market economy, the institutional framework implied by the norm of good governance is rather flexible, reflecting the diverse governance frameworks and political cultures in the EU, and therefore provides a rather loose guide to the reforms that are required under the banner of conditionality, and one that can be manipulated by both sides. The EU manipulates the good governance norm according to the waxing and waning of the eagerness for EU enlargement, while the accession countries manipulate by creating fake institutions that tick boxes but often have little real impact (Noutcheva 2009).

The new 'post-Washington consensus' recognizes the need for a strong role for the state to support the market and the important role of institutions in economic development.[7] Policy makers increasingly recognize the importance of reliable state institutions, courts, judiciary, public administration and effective public financial management (Cohen and Lampe 2011).[8] Concern about corruption in the public sector has also risen up the policy agenda, due to the perception that corruption reduces the efficiency of the private sector by favouring specific sections of the political and economic elite.

Table 11.4 shows the rank position of the Western Balkan countries on a set of measures of government effectiveness. The governance indicators are based on research carried out annually in 215 countries. The data show the percentile rank, or the proportion of countries that had lower scores for the indicator. The table demonstrates that the Western Balkan countries were in the top half of the ranking for regulatory quality, but had lower ranks for the rule of law and political stability. Taking each country separately, Croatia and Montenegro were consistently in the top half of the distribution of scores across countries on all dimensions. On the other hand, Bosnia and Herzegovina and Kosovo were in the bottom half in five of the dimensions of governance quality. The control of corruption appears as particularly weak in Albania and Kosovo. The potential candidate countries (Albania, Bosnia and Herzegovina, and Kosovo) scored significantly worse than the candidate countries across all dimensions, suggesting that the quality of governance is a key driver of candidate status.[9]

Table 11.4 Governance indicators, percentile rank, 2012

	Albania	BiH	Croatia	Montenegro	Macedonia	Serbia	Kosovo
Regulatory quality	56	51	67	53	61	51	53
Voice and accountability	50	**45**	64	56	50	56	**42**
Government effectiveness	**45**	**39**	72	60	52	51	**42**
Control of corruption	**27**	**49**	57	55	59	**48**	**30**
Rule of law	**35**	**48**	60	55	**48**	**44**	**36**
Political stability	**40**	**29**	64	64	**33**	**39**	**15**
No. dimensions below 50th percentile rank	4	5	0	0	2	3	5

Source: Worldwide Governance Indicators database.

This conclusion is born out by an examination of the relevant documents of the European Commission that assess the preparedness of countries to achieve candidate status. For example, in commenting on Albania's Economic and Fiscal Programme for 2013, DG ECFIN concluded that 'efforts need to be stepped up to reinforce the legal system, strengthen the rule of law, fight corruption and enhance human capital' (DG ECFIN 2013: 11). In relation to Bosnia and Herzegovina, the 2013 Progress Report (EC 2012: 27) observes that:

> [t]he rule of law is weak and the judicial system often does not function efficiently, is subject to obstruction by the parties and does not cover commercial activities adequately. Enforcement of commercial contracts remains a lengthy process, which involves 37 procedures and takes an average of 595 days.

International trade liberalization

In 2000, the EU began to cut the tariff barriers facing the Western Balkan countries through autonomous trade measures, and subsequently formalized this through the introduction of SAAs. The initial elements of the SAAs (the 'Interim Agreements') concerned international trade, over which the Commission has competence and does not require ratification by the EU Member States. The interim agreements pulled down trade barriers between the EU and the accession countries, initially by removing barriers to Western Balkan exports to the EU, but gradually also eliminating import tariffs on goods imported from the EU to the Western Balkan states. For example, the SAA with Bosnia and Herzegovina, which entered into force in 2008, entailed an immediate reduction in Bosnian duties on industrial goods originating in the EU followed by the complete elimination over the next one to five years of all remaining import duties.[10] Not surprisingly, this opened the doors to a flood of imports from the EU to the Western Balkan countries.

By 2011, all the Western Balkan states were importing goods and services from the EU equivalent to more than half of their GDP (see Figure 11.5). Macedonia and Montenegro were the most open economies with imports equivalent to 74 per cent and 66 per cent of their GDP respectively. For all countries, a significant share of their imports originated from the EU, ranging from 40 per cent in Montenegro to 64 per cent in Albania. Each country imported goods and services from the EU equivalent to more than one quarter of their GDP, with Macedonia importing goods and services equivalent to 40 per cent of her GDP from the EU. Considering the data relating to imports, it is hard to avoid the conclusion that by 2011, the Western Balkan countries had become highly open economies.

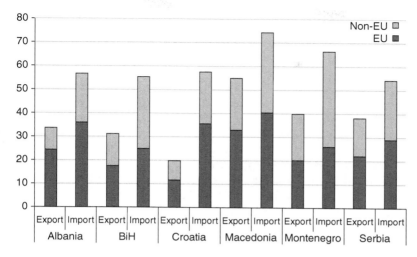

Figure 11.5 Exports and imports of goods and services, 2011 (% GDP) (source: World Bank Development Indicators online database).

However, the situation was very different in relation to exports. The share of exports of goods and services in GDP was, on the whole, far below the share of imports, resulting in large deficits in the balance of trade in goods and services. The trade deficit was especially pronounced in Croatia, which did not however prevent Croatia from becoming an EU member in July 2013. The trade deficits of all the countries reflect their low levels of competitiveness, and the relative failure of the neoliberal transition process after a period of 20 years.[11]

Competitiveness

The weak export competitiveness of the Western Balkan countries reflects the failures of the neoliberal transition and growth policies. As accepted by numerous EU assessments, a major failure has been the lack of attention to the institutional framework within which transition and growth take place. Too much reliance was placed on macroeconomic stability and microeconomic liberalization, on the basis that markets in the Western Balkans would be self-equilibrating, and in the absence of government intervention would lead to sustainable growth. In practice, as suggested above, the economic growth that took place in the 2000s was mainly driven by large inflows of external capital that fuelled a consumer boom, rather than investment in productive assets and infrastructure. Labour productivity growth has been relatively low in most countries except Albania[12] and the quality of public services such as education and health care has deteriorated. All this has undermined the competitiveness of the economies.

Macroeconomic polices have also tended to undermine competitiveness by maintaining fixed exchange rates designed to anchor inflationary expectations. These have undercut exports by creating non-competitive conditions for export industries and have underpinned the chronic balance of trade deficits.

The weakest aspects of the institutional framework at the microeconomic level has been the lack of competition in many important sectors due to quasi-monopolization by powerful tycoon interests that had benefited from privatization processes adopted with little concern for social justice. The SME sector has been held back by unfriendly regulations, which were kept in place by ruling elites who had no interest in allowing competition to threaten their interests. The anti-market consequences of passing state and social property over to narrow economic elites with strong political connections to incumbent ruling parties have not been sufficiently addressed and remain a stumbling block to EU membership.

Through its SAAs, the EU encourages countries to establish competition regimes, and consequently Competition Agencies have been established in each of the enlargement countries. However, these have been mainly toothless institutions, and the economies have remained hamstrung by powerful monopolies under the ownership of the tycoon capitalists. Where the tycoons did not simply engage in asset stripping of the privatized firms, they kept tight control over the markets, raising prices and reducing growth through low investment and a lack of interest in workforce training and skills. Even though Competition Agencies have been established, in most countries, they have had little impact on market structure.

In addition, the EU has discouraged subsidies in the form of state aid to large domestic strategic companies. In the case of Bosnia and Herzegovina, for example, the SAA explicitly ruled out state aid to the steel industry, with the aim of eliminating state aid over a number of years. Only Croatia managed to resist this conditionality with continuing support to the shipyards on the Adriatic coast. But even these had to be abandoned as a final condition of EU membership.

Outcomes of the transition and accession processes

At the end of the 2000s, political events had created new conditions for economic growth, and for a while substantial growth was achieved at around the full capacities of the economies. Between 2003 and 2008 growth rates of 4 per cent per annum or more were typical in the region. However, as explained above, this growth was largely driven by external inflows of credit as a product of unconstrained financialization. Since 2008, the economic crisis of the Eurozone has hit the countries of the Western Balkans as a severe shock and revealed that the apparent macroeconomic stability of the 2000s was built on thin foundations (Bartlett and

Prica 2013). Public budget deficits soared and austerity measures were put in place to ensure a fierce reduction in public expenditure. The issue of macroeconomic stability rose to prominence and a new set of measures were introduced to bring the macroeconomic policies of the accession countries into line with the broad EU policy of austerity and deflation as the main response to the economic crisis.

The region has experienced a double-dip recession, with an initial recession in 2009 followed by a further downturn in 2012 (see Figure 11.6). Croatia was hardest hit and never quite managed to return to growth; her economy has been in recession for four years. Soon after joining the EU the Croatian economy was placed within the EU's Excessive Deficit procedure, effectively placing macroeconomic management directly in the hands of the European Commission. The double-dip put all the Western Balkan countries into recession in 2012 with the sole exception of Albania. Although seemingly immune to the recessionary effects in the early years of the crisis, even Albania eventually succumbed to the crisis effects as the impact of the recession in Greece adversely impacted remittances from Albanian workers employed there. By the third quarter of 2013, the Albanian economy was also experiencing recession.

The crisis has also had a severe social impact with soaring rates of unemployment especially among young people. Figure 11.7 shows unemployment in the region compared to two countries of the European

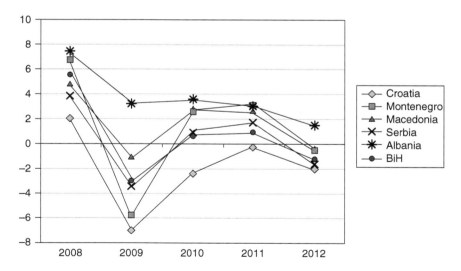

Figure 11.6 Growth of real GDP, 2008–2012 (% per annum) (source: Eurostat online data for candidate and potential candidate countries, variable code [cpc_ecnagdp] except Croatia for the years 2008–2012 where the data are variable code [nama_gdp_k] from the main Eurostat database).

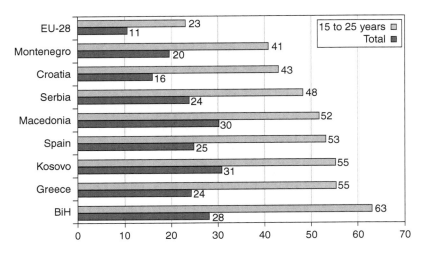

Figure 11.7 Unemployment and youth unemployment rates, 2012 (%) (source: Eurostat online data; for BiH, Macedonia, Serbia: National Statistical Bureaux).

periphery (Greece and Spain). It can be seen that the unemployment rate in several countries of the Western Balkans is close to that of the crisis-hit Eurozone periphery, and is even higher in Bosnia and Herzegovina, Kosovo and Macedonia, while unemployment in Serbia is similar to the levels in Greece and Spain. Similarly, youth unemployment has reached spectacular levels; the rate of youth unemployment in Bosnia and Herzegovina is the highest in Europe followed closely by Kosovo, which equates to the Greek situation. Youth unemployment in Macedonia is at a similar level to Spain.

The response of the national and international policy makers has been to call for fiscal consolidation and a speeding up of structural reforms. For example, the Serbian Progressive Party, which achieved an absolute majority in the Serbian elections of March 2014, has prioritized labour market reforms to remove employment rights for established employees, and pension reforms to introduce a compulsory private pension system. The IMF also emphasizes structural reforms in its advice to the region (Kovtun *et al.* 2014).

The sudden collapse of private foreign capital inflows of private credit and Foreign Direct Investment (FDI) has, to some extent, been compensated by increased inflows of public capital, although non-concessional inflows of public finance have also fallen in some cases. The European Investment Bank (EIB) and the EBRD have been instrumental in keeping investment flows alive and have introduced numerous projects to finance infrastructure and private sector development, coordinated through the

Table 11.5 Aid dependency: international assistance flows and FDI, 2010–2012 (%)

	ODA/FDI	OOF/FDI	TOF/FDI
Albania	28	13	40
BiH	135	15	150
Kosovo	139	−2	137
Macedonia	49	23	72
Montenegro	16	12	28
Serbia	71	37	108

Source: Table 11.1; UNCTAD online data.

Notes
FDI = Foreign Direct Investment; ODA = Official Development Assistance; OOF = Other Official Flows; TOF = Total Official Flows = ODA + OOF.

Western Balkans Investment Framework. However the real developmental effect of these loans is not known. The main sectors of investment have been energy and transport, while private sector credit lines have also been opened. The social sector has been largely ignored.

As the growth model based upon the market premise has failed to underpin sustainable growth and job creation in the region, the publicly owned European and international development banks have been mobilized to fill the investment gap and provide a much needed boost to growth. Over the period 2010–2012, the total flows of both official development assistance and other public sector financial flows exceeded the inflows of FDI in Bosnia and Herzegovina, Kosovo and Serbia, signifying a high degree of aid dependency in these countries (see Table 11.5).[13] In the case of Bosnia and Herzegovina and Kosovo, the inflows of concessional loans and grant aid predominate. The balance of flows of non-concessional public loans to Kosovo became negative as repayments exceeded new inflows of this type of assistance. Non-concessional loans from the international development banks and other sources were relatively large in Serbia. It is somewhat ironic that the international development banks have come to pay such a large role in several of the Western Balkan countries, especially considering that the main objective of both the transition reforms and the accession process has been to establish functioning market economies with minimal involvement of domestic development banks or state aid to industry.

Conclusion

The above analysis demonstrates that the neoliberal path of transition combined with credit-fuelled growth, rapid trade opening, combined with the adverse effects of the Eurozone crisis have been disastrous for the Western Balkan region, which has become a super-periphery of the EU (Bartlett 2009; Bartlett and Prica 2013). Unemployment has risen to levels as high or more so than the worst in the peripheral states of the EU. The region has been systematically starved of credit as foreign banks have withdrawn their capital to reinforce their domestic capital base through a process of widespread deleveraging.[14] The levels of skills provided by underperforming education systems are insufficient to build a knowledge-based economy. Inequality is rising and poverty is deepening, while governments in the region are riven by corruption and inefficient practices. Several of the Western Balkan economies have become dependent on inflows of international assistance for their survival.

The current debate about the need for a new growth model lacks any reference to the EU social market economy of the continental style. A tremendous experiment in neoliberal market economics has been tried, albeit in contradictory ways and with many attempts at resistance. It has led, despite EU assessments to the contrary, to fully functioning market economies, accompanied by underperforming states. The EU has recognized that the state sector needs to be strengthened through improvements in the quality of governance. However, the emphasis is on institutional reforms of the state, not on a greater role for state intervention in the economy, despite the fact that the European development banks are playing an increasingly interventionist role in supporting a coordinated programme of infrastructure investment in the region. Moreover, international actors such as the World Bank have emphasized the need for a further reduction in the size and role of the state, and have argued for reductions in the size of the social protection systems in the region through the mechanism of targeting support on the poorest sections of society through extensive means testing of benefits. The EU has very little influence in the social policy dimension where policy has been mainly influenced by the neoliberal ideology of the international financial institutions.

The Western Balkan candidate and potential candidate countries do seem to have functioning market economies – but markets that function in a sense 'too well', without any countervailing powers or automatic stabilizers that would be provided by an effective system of social protection. Trade unions are weak, and the state apparatus is unable to guide economic development in a coordinated way. The countries of the Western Balkans lack real development strategies and their economies are in several cases dependent on inflows of international assistance. Economic policy therefore often depends on the vagaries of foreign policy advisors who often provide contradictory advice. The enlargement process seeks to ensure the creation of functioning market economies. But in this chapter it is argued that there are substantial grounds to believe that the Western Balkan countries do already, in effect, have rather well functioning market economies. The challenge facing these countries is extrication from the current economic crisis, which has largely spilled over from the Eurozone. Reliance on market forces alone is unlikely to achieve this outcome. A greater focus on a coordinated regional development strategy with the support of the European development banks could hold out some hope of extrication from the crisis. The alternative must be to expect more years of stagnation and a limited prospect of reaching the mirage of conditionality for eventual membership in the privileged club of EU Member States.

Notes

1 The exception is Kosovo, which is currently (May 2014) in the process of preparing an SAA with the EU.
2 As an authoritative study of privatization in Croatia concluded:

> Unfortunately, privatization in Croatia achieved the opposite effect to that which had been expected. Instead of increased efficiency of enterprises, greater market competition, and the growth of employment, the achieved results were diametrically opposed: an increase in unemployment, a reduction of output, falling national wealth and the appearance of criminals in the economy who could be neither controlled nor effectively prevented.
>
> (Petričić 2000: 8)

3 See http://ec.europa.eu/economy_finance/international/enlargement/criteria/index_en.htm.
4 For an account of the mechanics of price stabilization in the newly independent states in the early 1990s, see Kraft (1995), and of hyperinflation in FYR Yugoslavia (Serbia and Montenegro), see Lyon (1996).
5 According to the 2007 assessment (DG ECFIN 2007: 4) these showed 'the determination of the governments to advance further stabilization, structural reforms and productivity gains in order to allow sufficiently high growth in order to catch up to their neighbours and to raise social standards in the countries'.
6 On the pyramid schemes in Albania, see Jarvis (1998).
7 In 2000, the originator of the Washington consensus wrote: 'It is appropriate to go beyond the Washington Consensus by emphasizing the importance of the institutional dimension' (Williamson 2000: 262).
8 Cohen and Lampe point out that 'political elites in the Western Balkans ... found themselves shifting their focus from the previous imperative of reducing the role of the state to redefining the quality of state institutions and making them more supportive of the market economy' (Cohen and Lampe 2011: 118).
9 For a similar conclusion on the competitiveness gap between candidate and potential candidate countries, see Sanfey and Zeh (2012).
10 The reductions in import duties were by an initial 50 per cent with total elimination of duties one year later for one list of goods such as raw materials and primary industrial products, by an initial 25 per cent with total elimination over three years for a second list of goods such as textile products, and by an initial 10 per cent with subsequent elimination over a period of five years for a third list of goods such as clothing. See SAA Annexe I: 'Tariff concessions of Bosnia and Herzegovina for Community industrial products'.
11 Cohen and Lampe (2011: 473) conclude that the major challenges facing the Western Balkan countries are 'how to raise the competitive level of exports from their already-functioning market economies so that they will ... reduce the large trade deficits [and] attract foreign investors to their enterprises'.
12 Between 2003 and 2012, the rate of growth of GDP per employed person was 5.4 per cent per annum in Albania, whereas in Bosnia and Herzegovina it was

2.4 per cent, in Croatia 1.5 per cent and in Macedonia just 1.3 per cent (calculated from data from World Bank Development Indicators database).
13 On aid dependency in the Western Balkans, see Kekić (2001).
14 On the deleveraging behaviour of foreign banks, see the regular *CESEE Deleveraging and Credit Monitor*, a publication of the Vienna initiative established by the major international financial institutions and the European Commission.

References

Adamovic, L.S. (1995) 'Economic Transformation in Former Yugoslavia, with Special Regard to Privatisation', in Ramet, S.P. and Adamovic, L.S. (eds) *Beyond Yugoslavia: Politics, Economics and Culture in a Shattered Community*, Boulder, CO: Westview Press.

Bartlett, W. (1987) 'The Problem of Indebtedness in Yugoslavia: Causes and Consequences', *Rivista Internazionale di Scienze Economiche e Commerciali*, 34(11/12), pp. 1179–1195.

Bartlett, W. (2008) *Europe's Troubled Region: Economic Development, Institutional Reform and Social Welfare in the Western Balkans*, London: Routledge.

Bartlett, W. (2009) 'Economic Development in the European Super-Periphery: Evidence from the Western Balkans', *Economic Annals*, LIV(181), pp. 21–44.

Bartlett, W. and Prica, I. (2013) 'The Deepening Crisis in the European Super-Periphery', *Journal of Balkan and Near Eastern Studies*, 15(4), pp. 367–382.

Cohen, L.J. and Lampe, J.R. (2011) *Embracing Democracy in the Western Balkans: From Post-Conflict Struggles to European Integration*, Baltimore, MD: Johns Hopkins University Press.

Coricelli, F. and Rocha, R. (1991) *Stabilization Programs in Eastern Europe: A Comparative Analysis of the Polish and Yugoslav Programs of 1990*, Working Paper WPS 732, Washington, DC: World Bank.

DG ECFIN (2007) *2007 Economic and Fiscal Programmes of Potential Candidate Countries: EU Commission's Assessments*, European Economy Occasional Papers 38, Brussels: Directorate-General for Economic and Financial Affairs.

DG ECFIN (2011) *2011 Economic and Fiscal Programmes of Potential Candidate Countries: EU Commission's Assessments*, European Economy Occasional Papers 81, December, Brussels: Directorate-General for Economic and Financial Affairs.

DG ECFIN (2013) *2013 Economic and Fiscal Programmes of Albania and Bosnia and Herzegovina: EU Commission's Overview and Country Assessments*, European Economy Occasional Papers 158, December, Brussels: Directorate-General for Economic and Financial Affairs.

Donais, T. (2002) 'The politics of privatisation in post-Dayton Bosnia', *Southeast European Politics*, 3(1), pp. 3–19.

European Commission (2012) *Commission Staff Working Document: Bosnia and Herzegovina 2012 Progress Report*, 10.10.2012, SWD(2012) 335 Final, Brussels.

Hall, P.A. and Soskice, D. (2001) 'An Introduction to Varieties of Capitalism', in Hall, P.A. and Soskice, D. (eds) *Varieties of Capitalism: The Institutional Foundations of Comparative Advantage*, Oxford: Oxford University Press, pp. 1–70.

Hashi, I. and Xhillari, L. (1999) 'Privatisation and Transition in Albania', *Post-Communist Economies*, 11(1), pp. 99–125.

Jarvis, C. (1998) *The Rise and Fall of the Pyramid Schemes in Albania*, IMF Working Paper WP/98/101, Washington, DC: International Monetary Fund.

Kekić, L. (2001) 'Aid the Balkans: The Addicts and the Pushers', *Journal of Southeast European and Black Sea Studies*, 1(1), pp. 20–40.

Kovtun, D., Meyer, A., Murgusova, Z., Smith, D. and Tambunlertchai, S. (2014) *Boosting Job Growth in the Western Balkans*, IMF Working Paper WP/14/16, Washington, DC: International Monetary Fund.

Kraft, E. (1995) 'Stabilizing Inflation in Slovenia, Croatia and Macedonia: How Independence has Affected Macroeconomic Policy Outcomes', *Europe-Asia Studies*, 47(3), pp. 469–492.

Lydall, H. (1989) *Yugoslavia in Crisis*, Oxford: Clarendon Press.

Lyon, J. (1996) 'Yugoslavia's Hyperinflation, 1993–1994: A Social History', *East European Politics and Society*, 10(2), pp. 293–327.

Noutcheva, G. (2009) 'Fake, Partial and Imposed Compliance: The Limits of the EU's Normative Power in the Western Balkans', *Journal of European Public Policy*, 16(7), pp. 1065–1084.

Petričić, D. (2000) *Kriminal u hrvatskoj pretvorbi: tko, kako, zasto*, Zagreb: Abakus.

Roland, G. (2000) *Transition and Economics: Politics, Markets and Firms*, Cambridge, MA: MIT Press.

Sanfey, P. and Zeh, S. (2012) *Making Sense of Competitiveness Indicators in South-Eastern Europe*, EBRD Working Paper No. 145, London: European Bank for Reconstruction and Development.

Vaughan-Whitehead, D. (1999) *Albania in Crisis: The Predictable Fall of the Shining Star*, Cheltenham: Edward Elgar.

Vujačić, I. and Petrović Vujačić, J. (2011) 'Privatization in Serbia: Results and Institutional Failures', *Economic Annals*, LVI(191), pp. 89–105.

Williamson, J. (2000) 'What should the World Bank Think about the Washington Consensus?', *World Bank Research Observer*, 1592, pp. 251–264.

Part IV
Conclusion

12 Theory and practice of EU Member State building in the Western Balkans

Soeren Keil and Zeynep Arkan

The last two decades witnessed important shifts in the EU's relations with the wider world, in line with the transformations taking place in the international system, the EU's neighborhood and its changing composition. These changes have impacted on the role attributed to and performed by the EU in international affairs, as well its capacity and actorness as a regional and world power. As a key component of the EU's overall foreign policy, enlargement policy was also affected by these changes. Enlargement, in the early days of the process of integration, was based solely on a geographic criteria – the candidate being a 'European state'. Over the years, the enlargement policy of the EU evolved into a comprehensive and detailed process that included a number of EU institutions and a set of criteria to be fulfilled by the applicant states on the path to membership. The increasingly comprehensive nature of the policy required more active EU involvement in guiding the states and assessing their progress in terms of the membership requirements. However, taking into consideration the experiences of the previous enlargement rounds, it can be concluded that the EU has never been involved in candidate countries as much as it currently is in the Western Balkan states. Through its direct and indirect involvement, the EU is attempting not only to prepare these states for EU membership, but also to shape them through instruments such as conditionality, incentives and direct intervention. In terms of the standards that these states are expected to fulfill, the EU no longer solely focuses on the Copenhagen criteria, political and economic adaptation and legislative alignment with the Union's *acquis communautaire*, 'but also on the consolidation of statehood in the region, both external (state borders) and internal (autonomous governance)' (Noutcheva 2012: 2). In this respect, the EU is involved in a complex Member State building process, which affects not only the relationship between the EU and (potential) candidate countries, but the nature of the enlargement process as a whole. With each round, the enlargement policy of the EU is becoming more multidimensional and multilayered, involving a variety of actors both within the EU and the (potential) candidate states.

From a broader foreign policy perspective, the case of Western Balkans presents an important and existential challenge to the EU. What was usually perceived as the collective failure of the European states to respond to the conflicts in the region and its dependence on the United States even in its own backyard led to a reconsideration of the Union's fledgling foreign policy and saw the beginnings of security and defence policy in action (Edwards 2011). The gradual strengthening of the EU's military and civilian muscle through its various missions and its continued presence in the region were further enhanced through diplomatic channels and the EU's special envoys (Noutcheva 2012). The more active and direct involvement of the EU in the region during the reconstruction stage soon led to the development of a complicated and often interventionist relationship between the Union, its envoys and the Western Balkan states as the focus of the EU shifted from security to accession. The EU not only wanted to extend the borders of the 'European zone of peace', whose foundations were laid in the aftermath of the Second World War, to its immediate neighborhood, it also aimed to reform and restructure the Western Balkan states in line with its own image of how a proper 'European' state should look. This is exactly the point where the EU's 'normative power' is stretched to its limits. The idea that the values and norms that the EU is founded upon in the form of peace, liberty, democracy, the rule of law, respect for human rights and fundamental freedoms, also serve as the basis of its relations with the wider world does not sit well with the by and large interventionist and coercive means through which the EU sought to transform the Western Balkan countries. The experimental means employed by the EU in the region helped reproduce not only the already highly asymmetrical relationship between the EU and the countries in the region, but also the EU's de facto empire, based on the assumption that what is good for (Western) Europe is necessarily good for the rest of the world.

As the case study contributions to this volume demonstrate, the reform and restructuring practices and accession guidance of the EU has attempted to build Member States which were modeled on a standardized understanding of a 'normal' EU Member State. The flaw of the EU's approach, however, stemmed from the lack of 'normal' or standard Member States within the Union; there was no specific model to base the reforms and transformations on. Too different were the current members, and even the countries that joined in 2004, 2007 and 2013. In comparison, the candidate and potential candidate countries of the Western Balkans were fundamentally singular in terms of the key elements of their state organization and governance capacity. Over time, the extension of the EU's conditionality to policy areas which are not part of the *acquis* has resulted in ambiguous messages and incoherent policies on the part of the EU. More importantly, it has allowed local elites to use and abuse the EU integration card for their own purposes, as Valery Perry demonstrated clearly in the case of Bosnia. Even in instances where the reform efforts of the Union have shown some success, such as in the case of Croatia that joined the Union in 2013, or Montenegro, the current frontrunner in the region, there remain doubts over the extent of deep-rooted reforms and their local ownership, as well as genuine value transformation.

Yet it has to be noted that the picture is not completely bleak. There are limited but positive examples of the EU's 'transformative power' in various different policies of the Western Balkan states. From the rights of national minorities to the improvement of the rule of law, there are a number of success stories to recount. But these remain restricted to those policy areas in which the EU has a clear portfolio and that are part of the Union's legal framework, the *acquis communautaire*. Furthermore, these pockets of success are often limited in the extent to which deep-rooted reforms have taken place, instead of a narrow adoption of EU law without any practical changes. As Sanja Badanjak argued in her chapter on Croatia, even in the country that became an EU Member State in July 2013, there remain a number of concerns regarding the application of EU law and the adoption of European norms and values. The situation is worse in countries which are internally and externally contested, as Simonida Kacarska demonstrated in her discussion on Macedonia. The EU perspective has not been able to bring Macedonians and Albanians closer together for a joint European future, and the EU has been unable to influence the name dispute of the country with Greece. Macedonia is also a key example that illustrates how indecisiveness and divisions within the EU can negatively affect the enlargement process. The fact that Greece has been able to veto the start of negotiations for years questions the whole process driven by the European Commission and undermined by the behaviour of Member States. A similar situation can be found in Kosovo, as Mehmet Musaj and Gëzim Krasniqi noted. In a situation where five EU Member States have still not even recognized the independence of Kosovo from Serbia, it has become very difficult for the EU to be an active player on the ground and motivate long-term changes. While the EU has more recently announced the beginning of the Stabilisation and Association Process (SAP) for Kosovo, it remains to be seen how the five Member States that have not recognized the country's independence will act, once the EU launches negotiations on a Stabilisation and Association Agreement with Kosovo.

As an approach, EU Member State building was designed to address the fundamental weaknesses of the Western Balkan states. These include weak governments, contested statehood, strained neighborly relations and the existence of a large network of patronage and mafia-style networks that link official politics with organized crime. So far, there has been little success in addressing these issues. The reasons for this are many and lie equally in the divisions within the EU and the incoherent policies implemented, and resistance from local elites to more long-term changes. It is therefore time for the EU to think about a Plan B. This does not have to be a fundamental diversion from the SAP as such. Instead, the framework of the SAP remains useful in addressing the challenges in the region. What is needed is a clearer European agenda for the region, which focuses on comprehensive criteria for the countries, including a clear roadmap with fixed dates for when these countries will join if they fulfil the EU's requirements. Furthermore, the EU needs to ensure that it speaks with one voice regarding the accession processes of the Western Balkan states. In a process where different European actors promote different standards, it should not be surprising if local elites seek to undermine the process and manipulate it to their advantage. The quarrel between the Commission and Greece (and Bulgaria) over the start of membership negotiations with Macedonia is a good example of this.

Moreover, it is important that the EU identifies the core issues in each of the Western Balkan states and addresses them within the enlargement process. A clear case of such an entrenched core issue is Serbian nationalism. Without engaging with deep-rooted Serbian nationalist sentiments, which still promote the idea of a 'Greater Serbia', it is hard to see how Serbia will ever be able to converge its internal and external policies with European norms and values. By ignoring this, the EU continues to allow Serbian elites to use nationalist and hostile rhetoric towards its neighbors (most notably Kosovo, but also Bosnia). Yet the message from Brussels is that Serbia is a European country and will be a member of the European family soon. Therefore, for Union policies to succeed in truly reforming these states, it is important that the EU shifts its focus away from political elites. As the chapters in this volume have demonstrated, political elites are often part of the problem, not the solution, in the Western Balkans. Yet the EU's enlargement process remains elite-focused with little engagement of civil society and other alternative actors. While they are not the solution to all problems, these other actors often voice alternatives, critique their own governments and provide a critical perspective. Including them in the enlargement process would also allow the Union to be closer to the people of the region, who after all still strongly support the EU integration of their countries.

Finally, not all of the EU's policies for the region have been well designed and successfully implemented. Therefore it is important for the EU to re-evaluate its own criteria and reform efforts, and objectively analyse what works and what does not. As Will Bartlett argued in his chapter, many in Brussels still believe that the region needs more free market reform. It is only recently that a shift has taken place which focuses more on strong state institutions, which can moderate and even intervene in the market if it fails to serve the interests and welfare of a country's citizens. Olivera Simić made a similar argument regarding the issue of transitional justice in her chapter. She stated that the EU's focus on retributive justice was important for the region, but not enough, as it has not encouraged processes of reconciliation and long-term regional cooperation. Sometimes, admitting that a policy might not work or might not be the best, and changing it, is also a sign of strength for the EU.

The EU's endeavours to stabilize the region through a European perspective and integration into European structures have so far faced a number of difficulties in the Western Balkan states, which led to the questioning of the EU's 'pull' or attraction in the region and its 'transformative power'. Yet what the contributions in this volume have demonstrated is that the vast majority of the citizens and political elites in the region support their countries' integration into the EU. It is also argued that many Western Balkan countries share the same problems and challenges, from corruption to the integration of minorities, from economic disparities to weak administrations. Hence, while each country should be assessed according to its own merit, an enlargement process which would take these regional connections and historical legacies into account might also open the door for new synergies. The current approach according to which each country would join the Union individually when it is ready, could be succeeded by an approach which focuses on the integration of the region as a whole. In Eastern Europe, this has resulted in distinctive synergies and cooperation projects between different countries to ensure they would all be able to join the EU together. For the Western Balkans, it is certainly worth thinking about a shift towards a 'big bang enlargement' approach (Keil 2009).

The accession of the Western Balkan states into the Union remains a key challenge for the EU, its various institutions and Member States. It also remains a key challenge for the citizens and political elites of the region. Yet a new approach, which would refocus the EU's attention on the common concerns, problems and challenges of the region, and on the welfare of its people might just be what is needed to address some of the weaknesses of the current approach, and breathe life into the current enlargement fatigue within the EU. After all, the EU made a promise towards the countries in the region. Their future lies in Europe. A new enlargement approach would be the way forward for Europe to keep its promise and demonstrate that it can act as a coherent and potent foreign policy actor, in its immediate neighborhood and the wider world.

References

Edwards, G. (2011) 'The Pattern of the EU's Global Activity', in Hill, C. and Smith, S. (eds) *International Relations and the European Union*, New York: Oxford University Press, pp. 40–63.

Keil, S. (2009) 'Von Dayton über Sarajewo nach Brüssel', in Kurth, H. (ed.) *Bosnien und Herzegowina 2014 – wo wollen wir hin?*, Friedrich-Ebert-Stiftung: Sarajevo, pp. 296–320.

Noutcheva, G. (2012) *European Foreign Policy and the Challenges of Balkan Accession*, Routledge: New York.

Index

Page numbers in *italics* denote tables, those in **bold** denote figures.

Afghanistan 23
Ahtisaari, Martti 132–3
Ahtisaari Plan 146, 147, 151
Albania: banks **218**, 219, **219**; economic transition 211, *213*, **214**, 215, **215**, 216, *216*, *217*; foreign aid *227*; governance quality 220, *221*, 222; membership application 32, 45; potential candidate status 6; recession 225, **225**; trade **223**
Albanian communities: Kosovo 131, 132, 134; Macedonia 109
amnesty law, Kosovo 155
Anastasakis, O. 103
anti-corruption policies *see* corruption
April Agreement *see* Brussels Agreement
April Package 168–9, 171, 172, 173
Ashton, Catherine 133, 174
Association of the Serb Municipalities 153, 154, 155, 156
Austria 47, 217, 218
Avello, M. 193
Aydin-Düzgit, S. 59

banks 211, 217–19, **218**, **219**
Barroso, José Manuel 48, 49, 50n3
Bassuener, K. 170–1
Belgium 57, 130
Belgrade Agreement 88–9
Belloni, Roberto 24
benchmarks 37–8, 39, 41, 45
Biarritz Summit 124
Bieber, Florian 22–3, 150, 151, 171
Bildt, Carl 170–1
Biscevic, Hido 165
border disputes 37

Börzel, T. A. 21
Bosnia and Herzegovina 9, 22; banks **218**, **219**; constitutional reform 23, 163–81; Croatian involvement in 60; economic transition 211, *213*, **214**, 215, **215**, 216, *216*, *217*, 224; and EU accession process 171–9; fake compliance 23; foreign aid 227, *227*; governance quality 220, *221*, 222; potential candidate status 6; recession **225**; sidelining of institutions 175–6; Stabilisation and Association Agreement 41, 163, 176, 179, 224; trade **223**; unemployment 226, **226**; visa liberalization 179; war criminals 195
Bosniaks 164, 165, 167, 169, 171, 177; *see also* Federation of Bosnia and Herzegovina
Bosnian Serbs 164, 165, 166, 167, 169, 174, 176, 177, 178
Broz, Svetlana 196
Brussels Agreement 127, 152–6
Brussels European Council (2003) 35
budget deficits 215–16, **215**, 225
Bulatović, Momir 84
Bulgaria 20, 24, 29, 39, 42, 104, 176
Bunce, V. J. 63, 69
business startup 217, *217*
Butmir Process 170–1, 173
Buzek, Jerzy 113

Čaldarović, O. 74
candidate status 39; and governance quality 220, 222; Macedonia 6, 108; Montenegro 6, 85, 93; potential 6, 34–5; Serbia 6, 124, 127, 130, 134

Caplan, Richard 19
CARDS (Community Assistance for Reconstruction, Development and Stabilisation) programme 41, 68
Central and Eastern Europe (CEE) 5, 34, 39, 40, 41, 63, 104, 172
Central European Free Trade Agreement (CEFTA) 61, 66
CFSP *see* Common Foreign and Security Policy (CFSP), EU
Chandler, David 6, 23–4, 93, 94, 106, 197
civil service modernisation, Croatia 59, 70–1
civil society 192, 203; Croatia 68; and European Commission 197–8; Kosovo 155; Montenegro 87, 89, 91, 92, 95; RECOM 197–202; Serbia 130
Cologne European Council (1999) 34
Common Foreign and Security Policy (CFSP), EU 4, 88, 144, 157, 192
competitiveness 212, 223–4
compliance thresholds 36–8
Concordia mission 107
conditionality 36–40, 191–2; Macedonia 108–15; political 102–6, 108–15; Serbia 124–34; as transitional justice 193–7
conservative-Catholic movement, Croatia 72, 73
Constitutional Charter of Serbia and Montenegro 89
Constitutional Court, Bosnia and Herzegovina 167, 168
Constitutional Court, Croatia 73
constitutional reform: Bosnia and Herzegovina 23, 163–81; Croatia 64; Serbia 131–2
contested statehood 21–5
Cooperation and Verification Mechanism (CVM) 42
Copenhagen Criteria 16, 19, 20, 37, 172, 193; Croatia 69; economic 16, 212; political 16, 104, 110, 193
Copenhagen European Council (1993) 16, 34, 172
corruption 42, 104, 219–20; Croatia 39, 59, 62, 71, 74–5, 76; Kosovo 149
Council of Europe: Bosnia and Herzegovina 163, 168, 169; Croatia 61, 66; Montenegro 95; and RECOM 201
Croatia 9, 57–76; accession 6, 49; accession negotiations 39, 46–7, 67, 68; banks 211, 212, **218**, **219**; civil service modernization 59, 70–1; corruption 39, 59, 62, 71, 74–5, 76; economic problems 62–3; economic transition 211, 215–16, **215**, *216*, *217*, 224; governance quality 220, *221*; judiciary and fundamental rights 39, 42; minority rights 59, 60, 62, 72–4; path toward EU 58–69; recession 225, **225**; Stabilisation and Association Agreement 41, 60–1, 64–5, 66; trade 223, **223**; unemployment 63, **226**; war criminals 65, 68, 195, 196
Croatian Communist Party 60
Croatian Serbs 62, 67, 72, 74
Croats (Bosnia and Herzegovina) 164, 165, 166, 167, 170, 171, 176–7
currency, Montenegro 87
CVM *see* Cooperation and Verification Mechanism (CVM)
Cyprus 24, 29, 32, 43, 146, 180
Czech Republic 172

Dačić, Ivica 127, 152
Dayton Accords 60, 164, 166
de Maizière, Thomas 148
del Ponte, Carla 194
democratic consolidation 10, 104, 105, 141, 155
democratic deficit 145
Democratic Opposition of Serbia (DOS) 125
Democratic Party (DS), Serbia 125, 126, 127, 132
Democratic Party of Serbia (DSS) 125, 126, 131
Democratic Party of Socialists (DPS), Montenegro 84, 85, 86, 89
Democratic Party of the Albanians (DPA), Macedonia 109, 112
Democratic Union for Integration (DUI), Macedonia 109
democratisation 9, 19, 20, 192, 193; and conditionality 103, 105; Croatia 59–60, 62, 63, 69; Kosovo 9, 10, 141–2; Montenegro 85, 93, 95; Serbia 125
Development and Cooperation Policy, EU 192
Diez, T. 26
differentiated integration 44
Dimovski, Ilija 113
Djelić, Bozidar 126
Djindjić, Zoran 125, 128

Dodik, Milorad 169, 170, 171, 177, 195
DOS *see* Democratic Opposition of Serbia (DOS)
DPA *see* Democratic Party of the Albanians (DPA), Macedonia
DPS *see* Democratic Party of Socialists (DPS), Montenegro
DS *see* Democratic Party (DS), Serbia
DSS *see* Democratic Party of Serbia (DSS)
DUI *see* Democratic Union for Integration (DUI), Macedonia
Đukanović, Milo 84, 88
Džihić, V. 144

East Timor 143
Eastern enlargement 5, 34, 39, 40, 41, 63, 104, 172
Economic and Fiscal Programmes (EFPs) 214–15
economic crisis 5, 42–3, 44, 46, 218–19, **219**, 224–7, **225**, **226**, 227
economic growth 210, 223, 224, **225**
economic reconstruction, Kosovo 144–6
economic transition 210–11, *213*; *see also* political economy of enlargement policy
Eide, Kai 131
Election Code of Montenegro 95
elections: Bosnia and Herzegovina 173, 177; Croatia 60, 63, 64, 65, 66; Kosovo 154, 155; Macedonia 109, 112, 113; Serbia 124, 125, 126, 127
employment 219; *see also* unemployment
enlargement fatigue 43, 48–9
enlargement policy 4–5, 15–17, 19–21, 32–3; commitment 34–6; conditionality 36–40; engagement 40–1; and internal integration 44–5; legacies of past enlargements 42–3; national rules 45, 46; shifts in member states preferences 45–7; shifts in position of Commission 48–9; shifts in public opinion 47–8; *see also* political economy of enlargement policy
Epstein, R. A. 76
equilibrium clause 39–40
ethnic cleansing 131, 196
ethnic minorities: in Croatian government 67; *see also* minority rights

EULEX mission 22, 132, 134, 146–51
European Agency of Reconstruction (EAR) 144
European Bank for Reconstruction and Development (EBRD) 226
European Charter of Local Self-Government 167
European Commission 17, 39, 50n1; Bosnia and Herzegovina 172–4; and civil society 197–8; Croatia 39, 67, 74; and enlargement policy 43, 46, 48–9; 'Enlargement Strategy' 200; Kosovo 144, 157–8; Macedonia 108, 112, 113, 114–15; Montenegro 89–90, 93, 94, 95; political conditionality 102, 104, 105, 111; and RECOM 201; Serbia 122
European Convention for the Protection of Human Rights and Fundamental Freedoms 164, 167, 172, 177
European Council 17, 34–6, 50n2; Croatia 67–8; Kosovo 157; Macedonia 108, 114; Montenegro 93, 94; Serbia 124
European Court of Auditors 148
European Court of Human Rights 23
European Instrument for Democracy and Human Rights (EIDHR) 200
European Investment Bank (EIB) 226
European Movement 57
European Parliament 17, 176, 201
European Partnerships 41; Macedonia 110; Montenegro 92
European Union Monitoring Mission (EUMM) 144
European Union Special Representatives (EUSRs) 22, 110, 157, 169, 170, 176
Europeanisation 92, 103, 122–3; Kosovo 146–7
Eurozone crisis 43, 44, 46, 51n11

Fagan, Adam 125, 126, 130
fake compliance 23, 116, 220
Federal Republic of Yugoslavia (FRY) 84–5, 86–90, 122, 123–4
Federation of Bosnia and Herzegovina 164, 167, 170, 174, 176–7, 178
Feira European Council (2000) 34
Feith, Pieter 132
financial assistance 41, 194; Bosnia and Herzegovina 163, 175, 179; Croatia 68, 71–2; Kosovo 144; Montenegro 84, 93; *see also* foreign aid

financial crisis 5, 42–3, 44, 46, 218–19, 219, 224–7, 225, 226, 227
financial sector development 212, 217–19, 218, 219
Finci, Jakob 167–8
Finland 47
First Agreement of Principles Governing the Normalisation of Relations see Brussels Agreement
foreign aid 125, 129, 226–7, 227; see also financial assistance
Fouéré, E. 45
France 17, 42, 46, 47, 132
Freyburg, T. 68
frozen conflicts 165–7
FRY see Federal Republic of Yugoslavia (FRY)
Füle, Štefan 48–9, 112, 113, 157, 177

G17+ party, Serbia 129
Gallagher, T. 76
Gay Pride events, Croatia 73
General Framework Agreement for Peace (GFAP) see Dayton Accords
Germany 17, 45, 46, 47, 134, 217
'good neighbourly relations' requirement 37, 124, 135
Gotovina, Ante 68, 196
Govedarica, Dobrila 180
governance quality 219–22, 221
Grabbe, H. 44, 105, 110
Greece 29, 46, 146, 218; and Macedonia 39, 47, 106–7, 108; unemployment 226, 226

Hadžić, Goran 130
Hague see International Criminal Tribunal for the Former Yugoslavia (ICTY)
Hartmann, Florence 194
Haughton, T. 76
HDZ (Croatian Democratic Union) 60, 61–2, 63, 64, 65–7
Helsinki Committee for Human Rights 125
Helsinki European Council (1999) 34, 90, 98n4
High Level Accession Dialogue (HLAD) 112
Hillion, C. 45
homosexual communities, Croatia 72, 73
Horvat, Branko 210
Howitt, Richard 113

Hughes, J. 104, 105
human rights 130, 168, 192, 193, 194; Bosnia and Herzegovina 164; Montenegro 95; Serbia 125
human security 193
Hungary 29

ICJ see International Court of Justice (ICJ)
ICO see International Civilian Office (ICO)
ICTY see International Criminal Tribunal for the Former Yugoslavia (ICTY)
IMF 210, 216, 226
independence declarations: Croatia 60; Kosovo 126, 133, 141, 144, 145, 152
inflation 214, 214
Innes, A. 105–6
institution building, Kosovo 143, 144–6
institutional reform 212, 214, 219–22, 221
Instrument Pre-Accession Assistance (IPA) 41, 93, 163, 175
interim benchmarks 38, 39, 51n6
internal integration 44–5
International Centre for Transitional Justice 191
International Civilian Office (ICO) 146, 149
International Civilian Representative (ICR) 149
International Court of Justice (ICJ) 37, 133, 152
International Criminal Tribunal for the Former Yugoslavia (ICTY) 19, 37, 193, 194–6, 198; Croatia 61, 65, 66, 67, 68; and Serbia 38, 47, 90, 124, 128–30, 194
international isolation, Croatia 61–3
international recognition, Croatia 60
intractable conflicts 165–7
IPA see Instrument Pre-Accession Assistance (IPA)
Iraq 23
Italy 46, 47, 218
Izetbegović, Alija 167, 196

Jagland, Thorbjørn 177
Jerković, Dragan 201–2
Joksić, M. 194
Josipović, Ivo 199
Jović, D. 65, 66
Judah, T. 135

judicial reforms 104
judiciary and fundamental rights 38, 39, 42
Jurčević, Marinko 198

Kandić, Nataša 201, 202
Karadžić, Radovan 127, 130
KFOR 131, 134
KLA *see* Kosovo Liberation Army (KLA)
Knaus, Gerald 143
Koska, V. 72, 73
Kosovo 140–59; and Belgrade Agreement 88; democratisation 9, 10, 141–2; economic transition 211, *213*, **214**, *216*, *217*; EULEX mission 22, 132, 134, 146–51; fake compliance 23; foreign aid 227, *227*; governance quality 220, *221*; international administration 142–7; path toward EU 156–8; potential candidate status 6; and Serbia 124, 125, 129, 130–4, 148, 150, 151–6; sovereignty 140, 141–2, 146, 150–1, 156, 157; state building 134, 140, 142–7; unemployment 226, **226**; visa liberalization 157
Kosovo-Albanians 131, 132, 134
Kosovo Liberation Army (KLA) 131
Kosovo Serbs 131, 134, 141, 153, 154, 155
Koštunica, Vojslav 123–4, 125, 126, 128, 129, 131, 132, 133
Kramer, H. 144

Lagumdzija, Zlatko 170
Lajčák, Miroslav 170
Law on Amnesty, Kosovo 155
Lazarević, Vladimir 129
Lehne, S. 152
Lemay-Hebert, N. 143
LGBT (lesbian, gay, bisexual, and transgender) communities, Croatia 72, 73
liberal peacebuilding 143
Licklider, R. 165, 166
limited statehood 21–5
Linz, J. 104, 141, 142
Lisbon Treaty 20–1, 157, 192
long-distance state building 23
Luxembourg European Council (1997) 34

Maastricht Treaty 192
Macedonia 9, 10, 102, 106–16; banks 218, 219, **219**; candidate status 6, 108; economic transition 211, *213*, **214**, **215**, *216*, *217*; foreign aid *227*; governance quality *221*; name dispute 47, 106–7, 108; negotiations blocked 39, 47; political conditionality 108–15; recession **225**; Stabilisation and Association Agreement 41, 108; trade 222, **223**; unemployment 226, **226**; visa liberalization 111
macroeconomic stability 212, 214–16, **214**, **215**, 225
Madrid European Council (1995) 172
Magen, A. 105
Malta 32, 172
Manners, Ian 25, 26, 58, 68, 85, 106, 124
market integration 19
market liberalisation 211, 216–17, *216*, *217*
Marko, J. 166–7, 168
Marković plan 211
May Agreement, Macedonia 109–10
Meernik, J. 195
membership applications 45–6; Albania 32, 45; Croatia 66, 67; Montenegro 85, 93; Serbia 45, 124
Merkel, Angela 46
microeconomic liberalization 212, 216–17, *216*, *217*
migration 46
Mihajlović, Krešimir 196
Milošević, Slobodan 84–5, 86, 125, 128, 129, 131, 196
minimalist states 22–3, 150–1
minority rights 135, 193; Croatia 59, 60, 62, 72–4; Serbia 125
Mladić, Ratko 130, 195
Montenegro 83–98; banks **218**, **219**; candidate status 6, 85, 93; economic transition 211, *213*, **214**, 215, **215**, *216*, *217*; foreign aid *227*; governance quality 220, *221*; impact of EU 92–5; interim benchmarks 38, 39; recession **225**; and Serbia 23, 84–5, 86–90, 125–6; state building 86–92; trade 222, **223**; unemployment **226**; visa liberalization 94–5
Moon, Patrick 178
Morlino, L. 105
multi-level EU membership 44

NATO 19, 23, 66, 153
Netherlands 42, 46, 47, 130

Nice European Council (2000) 35
Nikolić, Tomislav 127
non-governmental organisations (NGOs): Montenegro 87; Serbia 130
non-performing loans (NPLs) 218–19, **219**
Noutcheva, G. 23, 59

O'Brennan, J. 106
OFA *see* Ohrid Framework Agreement (OFA)
Office of the High Representative (OHR) 167, 169, 170
official development assistance 226–7, *227*
Ohrid Framework Agreement (OFA) 9, 107, 109, 114
'open-ended' negotiations 43, 51n10
opening benchmarks 38, 41
Orentlicher, D. 128
organised crime: Bulgaria 42; Kosovo 134, 148, 149
Orić, Naser 196
OSCE (Organisation for Security and Co-operation in Europe) 95, 125, 142, 153

Papadimitriou, D. 147
Petrov, P. 147
Plavšić, Biljana 196
plebiscites *see* referenda
Poland 172
police: Bosnia and Herzegovina 6, 7, 22; EU missions 107; Kosovo 153; Montenegro 86
political conditionality 102–6; Macedonia 108–15
political criteria 16, 104, 110, 193
political dialogue condition 102–3, 108–15
political economy of enlargement policy 209–10, 212–29, *213*; competitiveness 212, 223–4; economic crisis 224–7, **225**, **226**, *227*; financial sector development 212, 217–19, **218**, **219**; institutional reform 212, 214, 219–22, *221*; macroeconomic stability 212, 214–16, **214**, **215**, 225; microeconomic liberalization 212, 216–17, *216*, *217*; trade liberalization 222–3, **223**
Portugal 20
post-conflict management 19
potential candidate status 6, 34–5

power-sharing 22–3
Pravda, A. 105
Pre-Accession Economic Programmes (PEPs) 214
Prelec, Marko 155
Presidency, Bosnia and Herzegovina 167–8, 176–7
price liberalization 216–17, *216*
Pridham, G. 105
privatization 65, 144, 211, 216, 224
Prodi, Romano 48, 49
programme conditionality 194
prosecutions, war crimes: domestic 196; *see also* International Criminal Tribunal for the Former Yugoslavia (ICTY)
protests, Croatia 65
Provisional Institutions of Self-Government (PISG), Kosovo 142
Proxima mission 107
Prud Process 169–70
public opinion: Croatia 59, 62–3, 64, 65, 68; and enlargement policy 47–8; Serbia 130
public sector 219–20

Raan, Iviča 66
Rangelov, I. 196
recession 225, **225**; *see also* economic crisis
RECOM 197–202
reconciliation 19, 192–3, 194–5, 196; Cyprus 180; RECOM 197–202
referenda: Bosnia and Herzegovina 174; Croatia 59, 72, 73–4, 76; Montenegro 84, 85, 90–2; Serbia 132
reform fatigue 48–9
refugees 37, 194; from Bosnia and Herzegovina 164; from Croatia 62, 72
regional cooperation 19, 37, 124, 135, 194
Regional Cooperation Council 19
Rehn, Olli 48, 49, 168, 194
Republika Srpska (RS) 164, 166, 167, 169, 174, 176, 177, 178
retributive justice 193–7
Richter, S. 68
Roma communities, Croatia 72–3
Romania 20, 24, 29, 42, 104, 146
RS *see* Republika Srpska (RS)
rule of law 130, 168, 192, 193; Croatia 39, 59; Kosovo 144; Montenegro 95
Rule of Law Mission, Kosovo 22, 132, 134, 146–51

246 *Index*

Russia 132, 141

SAAs *see* Stabilisation and Association Agreements (SAAs)
Samardžija, V. 68
Sanader, Ivo 25, 66, 74, 76
SATM *see* Stabilisation and Association Process Tracking Mechanism (SATM)
Schedler, A. 104
Schwartz-Schilling, Christian 175
SDSM *see* Social Democratic Union of Macedonia (SDSM)
Sebastian Aparicio, S. 167
Sedelmeier, U. 76
Sejdić, Dervo 167–8
Sejdić-Finci judgment 23, 163–4, 173, 174, 175, 176, 177
Serb communities: Bosnia and Herzegovina 164, 165, 166, 167, 169, 174, 176, 177, 178; Croatia 62, 67, 72, 74; Kosovo 131, 134, 141, 153, 154, 155
Serbia 122–35; accession negotiations 39; banks **218**, **219**; candidate status 6, 124, 127, 130, 134; conditions on 124–34; cooperation with ICTY 38, 47, 90, 124, 128–30, 194; economic transition 211, *213*, 214, **214**, 215, **215**, 216, *216*, *217*; foreign aid 125, 129, 227, *227*; governance quality *221*; impact of EU on political system 124–7; and Kosovo 124, 125, 129, 130–4, 148, 150, 151–6; membership application 45, 124; and Montenegro 23, 84–5, 86–90, 125–6; recession **225**, 226; Stabilisation and Association Agreement 38, 41, 47, 124, 126, 127, 129, 130, 131, 132, 133; trade 152, **223**; unemployment 226, **226**; visa liberalization 124, 126; war criminals 127, 128–30, 195, 196
Serbian People's Party (SNS) 91
Serbian Progressive Party (SPS) 127, 226
Serbian Radical Party (SRS) 126, 127, 131
Šešelj, Vojislav 129, 131, 136n7
Silajdžić, Haris 169, 170
Slovakia 146
Slovenia 46–7, 176
Smith, K.E. 110
smuggling, Kosovo 134
SNP *see* Socialist People's Party (SNP), Montenegro

SNS *see* Serbian People's Party (SNS); Serbian Progressive Party (SPS)
Social Democratic Union of Macedonia (SDSM) 111–13
Socialist Party of Serbia (SPS) 126, 127, 131
Socialist People's Party (SNP), Montenegro 84, 85
Solana, Javier 88, 89, 107, 126, 133
Sørensen, Peter 177
Sošić, M. 67
sovereignty, Kosovo 140, 141–2, 146, 150–1, 156, 157
Spain 20, 141, 146, 226, **226**
Special Representative of the Secretary General (SRSG) 142
Split protest, Croatia 65, 66
Spoerri, M. 194
SPS *see* Socialist Party of Serbia (SPS)
SRS *see* Serbian Radical Party (SRS)
SRSG *see* Special Representative of the Secretary General (SRSG)
Stabilisation and Association Agreements (SAAs) 17, 19, 38, 222, 224; Bosnia and Herzegovina 41, 163, 176, 179, 224; Croatia 41, 60–1, 64–5, 66; Kosovo 157; Macedonia 41, 108; Montenegro 92–3; Serbia 38, 41, 47, 124, 126, 127, 129, 130, 131, 132, 133
Stabilisation and Association Process (SAP) 5–6, 18, 19, 21, 37, 123, 193; Federal Republic of Yugoslavia (FRY) 124; Kosovo 145; Montenegro 89
Stabilisation and Association Process Tracking Mechanism (SATM) 145
Stabilisation and Association Reports 41, 122
Stability Pact for Southeastern Europe 19, 65, 145
'standards before status' principle 131
Staničić, M. 68
state building 6–7, 8–10, 16–17, 19, 20, 27–9; and contested statehood 21–5; Kosovo 134, 140, 142–7; long-distance 23; Montenegro 86–92; and RECOM 199
status-neutral approach 132, 134, 146, 149, 154
Steinberg, James 170
Steiner, Michael 131
Stepan, A. 104, 141, 142
structural adjustment programmes 210–11, 226
Subotić, J. 122, 123

Surroi, V. 151

Tadić, Boris 126, 127, 129, 131, 195, 199
Tansey, O. 142, 145
Teršelič, Vesna 197, 201
Thaçi, Hashim 152
Thessaloniki Agenda 67–8, 90, 145
Thessaloniki European Council (2003) 6, 35, 37, 124
thresholds, compliance 36–8
Tokača, Mirsad 200–1
trade: Kosovo boycott 152; liberalization 222–3, **223**; sanctions 125
Transparency International 74
Treaty of Rome 4
Tuđman, Franjo 61, 63, 196
Turkey 17, 18, 32, 43, 45, 46, 47
Twinning projects 41

unemployment 7, 63, 225–6, **226**
United Kingdom 44, 46, 132, 134
United Nations: Charter 192; General Assembly 133, 152; Security Council 128, 132, 142, 146, 147; and Serbia 125; UNOSEK 132–3
United Nations Interim Administration Mission in Kosovo (UNMIK) 131, 142–4, 146
United States 19, 23, 125, 129, 132, 170, 178
Uzelac, G. 59

Vachudova, M. A. 42, 62, 67, 72
Vasilev, G. 114
Venice Commission 163, 167, 168–9, 172, 176
Verheugen, Günter 48, 49
veto of accession process 39, 40, 45, 46–7, 130, 237
visa liberalization: Bosnia and Herzegovina 179; Kosovo 157; Macedonia 111; Montenegro 94–5; Serbia 124, 126
VMRO-DPMNE, Macedonia 109, 112, 113

war crime trials: domestic 196; *see also* International Criminal Tribunal for the Former Yugoslavia (ICTY)
War Crimes Chambers (WCC) 196, 198
war criminals 194–6; Bosnia and Herzegovina 195; Croatia 65, 68, 195, 196; Serbia 127, 128–30, 195, 196
Weber, B. 170–1
Western embassies, attacks on 133
Woelk, J. 145, 159
Wolchik, S. L. 63, 69
Woodward, S. L. 28, 143
World Bank 210, 217, 228

youth unemployment 226, **226**
Yugoslavia, economic transition 210–11

Zagreb Summit 35, 64, 65
Zartman, W.I. 165

eBooks from Taylor & Francis

Helping you to choose the right eBooks for your Library

Add to your library's digital collection today with Taylor & Francis eBooks. We have over 50,000 eBooks in the Humanities, Social Sciences, Behavioural Sciences, Built Environment and Law, from leading imprints, including Routledge, Focal Press and Psychology Press.

Choose from a range of subject packages or create your own!

Benefits for you
- Free MARC records
- COUNTER-compliant usage statistics
- Flexible purchase and pricing options
- 70% approx of our eBooks are now DRM-free.

Benefits for your user
- Off-site, anytime access via Athens or referring URL
- Print or copy pages or chapters
- Full content search
- Bookmark, highlight and annotate text
- Access to thousands of pages of quality research at the click of a button.

Free Trials Available

We offer free trials to qualifying academic, corporate and government customers.

eCollections

Choose from 20 different subject eCollections, including:

- Asian Studies
- Economics
- Health Studies
- Law
- Middle East Studies

eFocus

We have 16 cutting-edge interdisciplinary collections, including:

- Development Studies
- The Environment
- Islam
- Korea
- Urban Studies

For more information, pricing enquiries or to order a free trial, please contact your local sales team:

UK/Rest of World: **online.sales@tandf.co.uk**
USA/Canada/Latin America: **e-reference@taylorandfrancis.com**
East/Southeast Asia: **martin.jack@tandf.com.sg**
India: **journalsales@tandfindia.com**

www.tandfebooks.com

Printed by PGSTL